THE AVRO VULCAN

David W. Fildes

Hephaestus, the god of fire, especially the blacksmith's fire, was the patron of all craftsmen, principally those working with metals. He was worshiped predominantly in Athens, but also in other manufacturing centres. He was the god of volcanoes. Later, the fire within them represented the smith's furnace.

The Romans took Hephaestus as one of their own gods attaching the myth and cult to their god of fire and calling him Vulcan (Volcanus).

Dramatic view of the first prototype Vulcan VX770.

THE AVRO
VULCAN

THE SECRETS BEHIND ITS DESIGN AND DEVELOPMENT

David W. Fildes

First published in 2012 and reprinted in this format in 2017 by
Pen & Sword AVIATION
An imprint of
Pen & Sword Books Ltd
47 Church Street, Barnsley
South Yorkshire
S70 2AS

ISBN 978 1 47388 667 4

A CIP catalogue record for this book is
available from the British Library

Printed and bound by CPI Group (UK) Ltd, Croydon, CR0 4YY

Pen & Sword Books Ltd incorporates the Imprints of Pen & Sword Aviation,
Pen & Sword Family History, Pen & Sword Maritime, Pen & Sword Military,
Pen & Sword Discovery, Pen & Sword Politics, Pen & Sword Atlas,
Pen & Sword Archaeology, Wharncliffe Local History, Leo Cooper,
Wharncliffe True Crime, Wharncliffe Transport, Pen & Sword Select,
Pen & Sword Military Classics, The Praetorian Press, Claymore Press,
Remember When, Seaforth Publishing and Frontline Publishing

For a complete list of Pen & Sword titles please contact
PEN & SWORD BOOKS LIMITED
47 Church Street, Barnsley, South Yorkshire, S70 2AS, England
E-mail: enquiries@pen-and-sword.co.uk
Website: www.pen-and-sword.co.uk

Foreword

Looking back over many years of flying I am still amazed and impressed by the imagination, energy, scale, and diversity of the British aviation industry in the post war period. Famous names of people and companies, most now sadly no longer with us, fill the corridors of my memory and even now stir my imagination. My mind sees graceful creations such as the Hunter, Lightning, Gnat, and Comet sweep elegantly past, while others perhaps less graceful but equally important lumber by in the shape of the Argosy, Hastings, Twin Pioneer, and the mighty Beverley. Then, in tight formation, come the mighty trio, which formed the V Force, the Valiant. Victor, and Vulcan; the last named being the subject of this impressively researched book.

My first sighting of the mighty delta was, as a student pilot with the RAF, in the mid sixties. At that time the various Commands came to the flying training stations to exhibit their wares and to tempt the youthful and unwary in their direction. Most fellows wanted Fighters but not all could go there, while others, for no reason I could understand, wished to go on to Transports; perhaps a civil career was their aim. For my part, I fell under the spell of the Vulcan; her shape and power held me in thrall.

Since those days I have had the privilege and pleasure, as squadron pilot, test pilot and display pilot, of flying nearly one hundred types of aircraft ranging through fighters, bombers, transports, and helicopters; scary at times, thrilling at others, but nearly always enjoyable. It is now wryly amusing to me to reflect that my early hesitant flying days were almost as close in time to the date of the first flight, by A.V.Roe, of a powered aeroplane in the United Kingdom in 1908, as they are to the present time.

Whenever asked which aircraft was my favourite I find it difficult to select one over another but in any reply the Vulcan, for me, is and always will be in that special list. She had her faults and like any lady could be demanding but these minor blemishes were more than outweighed by her good points; that one fine example remains flying today is worthy testimony to the affection the Delta lady has won in the heart of the British public.

This impressively researched book addresses an area of the life of the Vulcan not previously covered in such detail. Here we can trace the design, development, and production of the aircraft, not solely through the facts and figures exhaustively collected and collated from technical manuals, but also through the human stories of those involved at the time. For me these accounts give life to the narrative and create a fascinating insight to a great period of our aviation heritage.

Al McDicken
Test Pilot

I was delighted when David asked me to write a short postscript to Al McDicken's Foreword to this publication. I have known the author for over 30 years and his resolve and dedication in producing this work has filled me with admiration. Every Vulcan and associated advanced project documents held in the Avro Heritage Centre at Woodford has been thoroughly investigated and a great deal of unknown material made available to the reader for the first time.

I have no hesitation in commending this book as the definitive work on what has become an icon of aviation, the Avro Vulcan.

Harry Holmes
Chairman
Avro Heritage Centre, Woodford

Acknowledgements

To my friend and colleague, Harry Holmes, for his support and encouragement over the years. Also to Tony Blackman, Reg Boor, George Lee, George Jenks, Chris Gibson and Ray Williams who gave some useful advice. I would also like to thank J. F. Henderson for his line drawing of the Vulcan and Al McDicken for the foreword.

From an idea by Charles (later Sir Charles) Masefield, under the directorship of Dr. Peter Summerfied, Harry Holmes and myself were tasked to establish an Avro Heritage Centre at the BAE Systems site at Woodford.

With the closure of the BAE Systems Woodford facility it was decided to keep the Heritage Centre. It is now run as a Charitable Trust and known as the Avro Heritage Museum. It has proven a great source for the information in this book.

The photographic department had a picture contact filing system which provided the date when the photograph was taken.

One of a series of pictures taken by Avro photographer Paul Cullerne. It shows XM575 of No.44 (Rhodesia) Squadron flying over its base at R.A.F. Waddington on 10th August, 1982.

Dedication

Roy Chadwick in the drawing office at Chadderton, pictured with Jimmy Turner Chief Draughtsman (centre) and a young draughtsman Geoff Taylor (Left).

Roy Chadwick in his office at Chadderton.

The Two Roy's pictured together in 1945, commemorating the completion of the Lancaster Production Group.

I would like to dedicate this book to members of the XM603 Club who were retired members who had worked on the Avro Vulcan XM603 at Woodford since 1985. In 2007 the club members were stood down when their numbers started to deplete and others became too old to support the aircraft. Their legacy still continues today in the Avro Heritage Centre at Woodford.

Not to be forgotten are the two Roy's. Roy Chadwick was Technical Director and was instrumental in the early design of the Type 698 in 1947, which was eventually to become the Vulcan. Chadwick died at Woodford on 23rd August, 1947, whilst on a test flight of a Tudor II airliner and never saw the design reach fruition. Proud of being a Lancastrian and Mancunian he will be long remembered as a pioneer in the annals of aviation.

At the time of Roy Chadwick's death Sir Roy Dobson was General Manager at Avro and carried on Roy Chadwick's legacy. Sir Roy helped establish Avro Canada and later became Chairman of the Hawker Siddeley Group of Companies.

Both Roy Chadwick and Sir Roy Dobson are interred in the Woodford Parish Church grave yard which over looks the Woodford airfield.

I would also like to recognise the contributions made by the workforce at both Chadderton and Woodford and their dedication in producing one of the worlds most iconic aircraft and to the pilots and crews who flew the mighty Vulcan.

David William Fildes

Bibliography

Bob Lindley letter — Avro Heritage

Memo from J.A.R. Kay — Avro Heritage Ref No.698/D04872

Avro Vulcan Development Potential October 1952 — Avro Heritage Ref No.698/D04767

Avro: *History of an Aircraft Company* — Harry Holmes ISBN 1 85310 531 7

Handley Page Victor, Roger R. Brooks Part 1 — Pen & Sword publication ISBN 1 84415 411 4

Type 698 brochure April 1948 — Avro Heritage Ref No.698/D04731

Type 698 brochure September 1948 — Avro Heritage Ref No.698/D1153

Comparison with Olympus Mk2 & Mk3 engines Nov 1950 — Avro Heritage Ref No.698/D04802

Comparison with OR/230 Requirement — Avro Heritage Ref No.698/D04727

Rolls-Royce Avon IPB 29 issued 1949 — Avro Heritage Ref No.698/D1408

Rolls-Royce Conway IPB 30 issued December1949 — Avro Heritage Ref No.698/D04733

Type 698 brochure January 1950 — Avro Heritage Ref No.698/D04729

707B progress reports Sept 1950 - April 1952 — Avro Heritage Ref No.707/D0901

707B & 707A progress reports 1952 — Avro Heritage Ref No.707/D0900

British Secret Projects — Chris Gibson & Tony Butler ISBN 978 1 85780 280 0

Type 698 Specification I.P.B.32 January 1951 — Avro Heritage Ref No. 698/D04735

Armstrong Siddeley 698 Component Type Record. December 1951. — Avro Heritage Ref No.698/D3702

Armstrong Siddeley Sapphire, June 1953 for VX770 — Avro Heritage Ref No.698/D1077

In Flight Refuelling and Tanker January 1954 — Avro Heritage Ref No.698/D1144

Avro Vulcan Development December 1954 — David Fildes collection

Vulcan Test Pilot, Tony Blackman — ISBN 13: 9781906502300

The 'Secret' world of Vickers Guided Weapons (Blue Boar project) — John Fobat ISBN 10 7524 3769 0

Alert Readiness and Rapid Take-Off — Avro Heritage Ref No.698/D1037

In Flight Refuelling & Tanker — Avro Heritage Ref No.698/D07815

B.Mk2 A.&.A.E.E. Preview Trials — Avro Heritage Ref No.698/D0950

Armstrong Whitworth Sapphire Pilot & Servicing — Avro Heritage Ref No.698/D1077

Vulcan B.Mk1 Type Record Rolls-Royce Conway — Avro Heritage Ref No.698/D1627

In-flight refuelling January 1954 brochure — Avro Heritage Ref No.698/D07815

B.Mk2 survey of flight development, 1959 — Avro Heritage Ref No.698/D0950

Avro 707B VTOL to ER.143T IPB53 issued 1954 — Avro Heritage Ref No.707/D0201

Avro Vulcan Development December 1954 — David Fildes collection

Accident Report (VX777) July 1954 — Avro Heritage Ref No.698/D1381

Avro Vulcan B.Mk2 Brochure March 1956 — Avro Heritage Ref No.698/D2478

Avro Vulcan Phase 5 Development November 1956 — Avro Heritage Ref No.698/D07477

Avro Vulcan Phase 6 Development 1960 — Avro Heritage Ref No.698/D1776

Avro Vulcan Phase 6 Revised Crew Layout 1960 — Avro Heritage Ref No.698/D04762

Avro Vulcan Phase 6 Development 1962 — Avro Heritage Ref No.698/D1036

Skybolt notes — Avro Heritage Ref No.698/D07123

Vulcan B.Mk1 Carriage of Blue Steel — Avro Heritage Ref No.698/D1079

Vulcan B.Mk1 Installation of Blue Steel XA903 — Avro Heritage Ref No.698/D10207

Vulcan B.Mk2 Preview Trials — Avro Heritage Ref No.698/D0950

Olympus Series 10101 Engine Lecture Notes — David Fildes collection

Olympus Series 30101 Engine Change Unit AP — David Fildes collection

Chapters

Introduction

The mission of the Vulcan was initially to provide a credible nuclear deterrent capability for the United Kingdom during the Cold War.

This was the vision of politicians and Government authorities during the Post War period and helped to maintain the values and freedoms of Western Democracy that we have today.

The service life of the Avro Vulcan is well documented, less so is the design and development. I have included projects which were proposed and never came to fruition. Rather than give an authors' view of the reports, where possible I have given extracts of these reports to give a less biased view, along with articles, memos and letters. Most of the book is in chronological order to give an impression of progress during the time period of the Vulcan development.

From recently discovered photographs the book contains previously unpublished and rare pictures along with the more familiar ones for completion. The majority of the pictures were taken by the Avro photographic department and in particular Paul Cullerne who was Avro's chief photographer.

I have not included metric measurements and weights as these were not given in the original documents. It is interesting to note that United States still use the Imperial measurements system.

When the first prototype made its first flight it was known as the Avro Type 698.

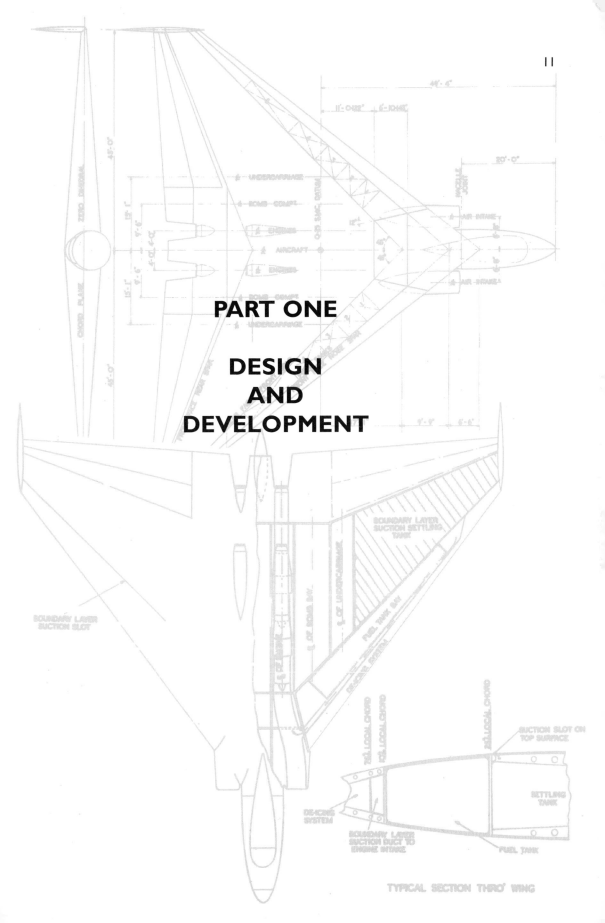

PART ONE

DESIGN
AND
DEVELOPMENT

TYPICAL SECTION THRO' WING

About the Company

The Avro Company can trace back its origins to1908 when Alliott Verdon Roe built his first biplane and later the more famous Triplane; he formed the company A.V. Roe & Co. based at Brownsfield Mill, in Manchester, along with his brother Humphrey. It was registered on New Year's Day 1910 as an aeroplane manufacturer and became a Limited Company on 11th January 1913.

The Company was to become popularly known as AVRO and in the First World War it produced the Type 504, which was to become the first Avro aircraft to be used on a bombing raid, when three specially converted aircraft famously attacked the Zeppelin sheds at Friedrichshafen on 21st November 1914. Large orders were received for the 504 and this meant finding new premises. These were based at Clifton Street, Manchester and a site acquired from the nearby engineering firm Mather and Platt Limited. Later a design and experimental department was also established at Hamble, Southampton.

Avro also had a facility at Alexandra Park aerodrome in Manchester which they had to vacate. In 1925 the company moved these facilities to New Hall Farm at Woodford, Cheshire, and this meant dismantling one of the hangars at Alexandra Park for relocation to Woodford and which is still there today. These premises were further expanded in the 1930's and in 1939 a new assembly facility and runway were built.

The new premises at Newton Heath was to remain the head office for more than twenty years, before a government aircraft expansion programme developed in the late 1930's and the company was charged with setting up a new factory at Chadderton. These premises were to become the headquarters and manufacturing unit and during the Second World War were the heart of Avro's wartime work.

Avro also operated a large underground factory at Yeadon, Yorkshire and for several years the company's experimental flight was based at Ringway Airport, Manchester.

As the Avro Lancaster came into service a service repair depot was established at Bracebridge Heath, Lincoln. The repair organisation expanded rapidly and Langar, Nottinghamshire was opened in 1942 to cope with the re-building and assembly of damaged aircraft.

In 1954, a new Weapons Division was formed and based at Woodford, responsible for the design and development of a stand-off bomb, which was to be carried by the Vulcan bomber. The Weapons Division rate of expansion was considerable. During 1956 a new weapons branch was set up at Salisbury, South Australia and technicians from Woodford were transferred to Salisbury.

Later acquisitions included a design group at Harrow and a research and development group at Chertsey, Surrey.

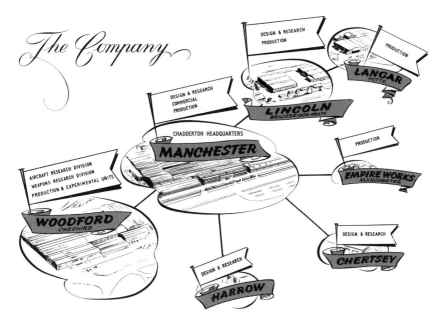

The Company

Avro sites associated with the design and manufacture of the Avro Vulcan in the late 1950's.

Woodford new assembly, pictured in 1945, the building was commissioned in 1939 along with the Chadderton factory as part of a Government aircraft expansion programme.

Avro pioneering achievements

Avro developed a considerable reputation in designing and manufacturing aircraft led by the two "Roy's". Roy Dobson joined Avro's in August 1914 under Roy Chadwick and later became General Manager at Avro. Roy Chadwick who had joined the company in 1911, was to become Chief Designer. Of his notable achievements were the Avro Baby the world's first true light aeroplane, the Bison, a fleet gunnery spotter; the Tutor, a replacement for the 504, the standard trainer for the Royal Air Force and the majority of the world's airforces; the record breaking Avian and Cadet, popular light aircraft for club and private flying; and the versatile Anson, used initially for Coastal Reconnaissance, the Anson became the backbone of the Empire Air Training Plan. Later it continued in service in a variety of training roles, on communications and transport. Later the Anson continued in service with both Military and Civil operator's world-wide with over 11000 being manufactured.

Roy Chadwick was to gain world wide recognition when he designed the Avro Lancaster Bomber which was a development of the Avro Manchester. The Manchester was Avro's first all metal aircraft and marked a turning point in Avro design. It also led to a successful lineage of aircraft which was to end with the Avro Shackleton, a Maritime reconnaissance aircraft manufactured throughout the 1950's. The knowledge gained on the Lancaster was also to find its way into the design of the Vulcan.

The Lancaster Bomber was nearly never built, Roy Dobson received a letter from Air Chief Marshall Sir Wilfrid Freeman dated 29th July 1940, which stated that Avro were to drop plans for the Manchester III (Lancaster) as they were to build the Handley Page Halifax, it was only with the intervention of Roy Dobson and Roy Chadwick, who less than a day later went to the Ministry of Aircraft Production and successfully put their case forward for production of the Manchester III, which eventually became the Lancaster. This rivalry was to continue between Handley Page and Avro, and even extended to Vulcan and Handley Page Victor aircraft.

Roy Chadwick (left) and Roy Dobson discuss the merits of the Avro York transport aircraft, a derivative of the Avro Lancaster design.

Roy Chadwick pictured with a model of his most famous design, the Avro Lancaster. Above is a picture of the Avro Lincoln prototype bomber at Ringway, Avro's Experimental Department which was only a few miles from Woodford. The Lincoln's Lancaster linage can clearly be seen in this photograph. The Lincoln was replaced by the "V" bombers when the latter entered service in the mid 1950's.

Avro first venture into designing an all jet aircraft was the Tudor 8 pictured here on the 6th September, 1948.

Delta pioneers

Dr Alexander Lippisch

It is generally acknowledged that Dr Alexandra Lippisch made important contributions to the understanding of delta and flying wings. Lippisch's most famous design being the Messerschmitt Me163 rocket-powered interceptor. His first tailless glider flew in 1927. Experience on a series of Storch tailless gliders led Lippisch to concentrate increasingly on delta-winged designs. This interest resulted in five aircraft, numbered Delta I - Delta V, which were built between 1931 and 1939. In 1933, the reorganised Deutsche Forschungsanstalt für Segelflug (DFS - "German Institute for Sailplane Flight") led to the Delta IV and Delta V being designated as the DFS 39 and DFS 40 respectively.

Wind tunnel research in 1939 had suggested that the delta wing was a good choice for supersonic flight, and Lippisch set to work designing a supersonic, ramjet-powered fighter, the Lippisch P.13a, however, the project had only advanced as far as a development glider, the DM-1 when World War Two ended. After the War Lippisch left Germany to continue his research in the U.S.A.

Early tailless design research

When the first tender brochure was produced by Avro for the Type 698 it was a delta aircraft of tailless design. Sir W. G. Armstrong Whitworth Aircraft Ltd which was part of the Hawker Siddeley Group of company's was involved in laminar flow wing, boundary layer suction and general drag reduction research. This led to them designing a tailless flying wing aircraft as far back as early 1942. In March 1945, the AW 52g glider was flown in this configuration. A larger jet powered version of the flying wing shown below first flew on 13th November 1947, designed by John Lloyd, the AW 52 started life in 1944 under specification E.9/44, as a proposed flying wing bomber/airliner with a span of 120ft, and the aircraft was to prove useful in understanding the effects of laminar flow and aerodynamic control. They also entered a proposal for the B35/46 specification with the type AW 56 flying wing which was considered the third best contender to meet this specification at the Tender Design Conference held on 28th July, 1947. With this experience Armstrong Siddeley were to become involved in various ways in the design and production of the Avro Vulcan.

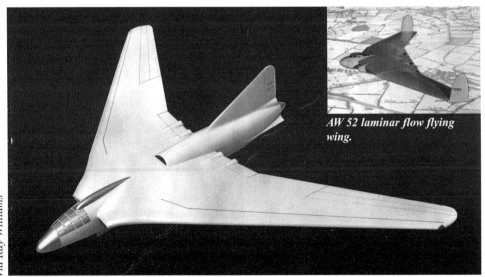

AW 52 laminar flow flying wing.

Via Ray Williams

Sir W. G. Armstrong Whitworth Aircraft Ltd., proposal to meet the B35/46 specification.

"The Avro Babes"

Avro Headquarters at Chadderton July 1947.

In early January 1947, a small group of talented individuals, Chief Projects Engineer Bob Lindley (27), Donald Wood Aerodynamics (31), Peter Martin (24), Ronald Wilson (21), and Edward Jones (23), were tasked to design an advanced bomber to meet specification B.35/46. The specification and operational requirements together with an invitation to tender were received by A. V. Roe Co Ltd (Avro) in December 1946, with a closing date being the end of February later extended to the end of May. It called for a medium range bomber to cruise at a Mach number of 0.875 for a still air range of 3,350 nm at a height of 50,000ft with a recommendation that the gross weight should not exceed 100,000lb.

The group were based in a tiny room at the front of A. V. Roe Co Ltd (Avro) factory at Chadderton, there they had to endure Mr Shinwells fuel crisis in the freezing conditions of an empty factory. Roy Chadwick CBE had recently been promoted to Technical Director was away ill with shingles at the time and on returning was surprised at some the ideas the group had come up with.

This led to Chadwick enthusiastically taking on board a delta wing design, unfortunately Roy Chadwick was killed along with Chief Test pilot Bill Thorn in the crash of an Avro Tudor during a test flight, shortly after the first tender was issued in May 1947. The project was then led by Stuart Duncan "Cock" Davies who survived the Tudor crash. He had taken over as Chief Designer when Roy Chadwick was promoted to Technical Director in 1946. General Manager, Sir Roy Dobson was also due to go on the test flight but had to take a telephone call at the last minute and decided not to delay the flight.

Roy Chadwick had been a passionate advocate of the Delta project and his tragic death on 23rd August, 1947 was a serious blow to the Company. However, shortly afterwards, Mr William S. Farren

Sir William S. Farren pictured in his office at Chadderton 5th April, 1948.

later (Sir William), a well respected expert within Government and aviation circles and a former Director at the Royal Aircraft Establishment (RAE) at Farnborough, joined the Avro Company as Technical Director after a short stay at Blackburn aircraft in 1946. His experience and expertise gave added confidence within the Ministry of Supply that Avro could proceed with the project and by January 1948 two prototypes were ordered.

Bob Lindley recollections

A letter donated to the Avro Heritage Centre at Woodford, brought to light the origins of the Avro Vulcan. The letter was sent to Sir Roy Dobson, Managing Director of Avro in 1952, from Robert (Bob) N. Lindley, on the proposal for a book on the Delta project. His recollections on the project were based entirely on memory due to Bob not having any documentary evidence. The following is the main content of this letter, with comments from the author.

The Operational Requirement (O.R.) for the aircraft was put to the company in December 1946 together with an invitation to tender with the closing date being February 1947, which was amended to a later date. The Project Office received their copy in January 1947 but before they were able to get very far the great fuel shortage hit the plant which was closed down. Bob Lindley, Head of Special Projects team and Donald Wood, were able to get hold of an office, which had belonged to the Resident Technical Officer (R.T.O.) to carry on their study. Another upheaval was taking place at that time as Roy Chadwick was at home suffering from shingles.

The performance requirements of the Operational Requirement (O.R.) were rather startling to people nurtured on Lancaster and Tudor aircraft, and the only jet investigations made up to that time were for the Tudor 8 and the Brabazon 3 projects, with the latter designed for a number around Mach ·7.

The original conception of the Delta was not a result of spontaneous inspiration, but was arrived at by what seemed at the time to be an honest design study encompassing a whole series of aircraft, some with tails, some tailless, each type checked for a range of aspect ratios and weights. In retrospect Lindley shuddered to think how much reliance was placed on the wing weight formula used, but the end product seemed to justify the means.

The first preliminary study was made for aircraft of aspect ratios not less than four, and the results clearly showed that the aircraft required would be tailless and would have a much lower aspect ratio - probably about two. A second investigation covering the lower aspect ratios gave a solution at 2·4, which was inevitably a delta wing. Bob knew that Lippisch had been working on a delta fighter and was able to see some reports on his coal burning ram jet delta in Frankfurt during a trip to Germany in 1945 and the possibility of making use of this configuration for a bomber was most intriguing. More elaborate checks were made, but only served to confirm the Delta configuration.

The design study in the first part of the original issue of the brochure was an elaboration of that used to arrive at the configuration. The basic method of this study was the same as used originally.

The original arrangement of the aircraft was, of course, somewhat more advanced than that which was finally proposed in the brochure, as it would look advanced even today. It had boundary layer suction combined with a movable cockpit, so that the pilot could have good vision even when the aircraft was at 30° incidence, and it had a very advanced arrangement of combined elevator, air brakes and variable area jet pipe nozzle.

Just about the time these first drawings were finished Roy Chadwick recovered from his illness. Chadwick was considerably shaken to see the proposal - he had left the project as a sort of jet propelled Lincoln and returned to find something apparently from a Buck Rogers comic strip in its place. He expressed his doubts very forcibly - Lindley remembers going home and sulking all weekend as he was very much in love with his project and couldn't stand the criticism. However, by Monday, Roy Chadwick had decided that it had its good points, and from there on he waded in with great enthusiasm and did much to make it a practical aeroplane.

During this period of early development the aircraft underwent a number of changes. One proposal had five Avon or Sapphire jet engines. Both engines were in fact to power the first prototype Vulcan. In the interests of simplicity it was decided to go for a twin engine version and for this it required an engine of around 20,000 lb. static thrust. Chadwick had written around the aircraft engine industry for proposals for such an engine and the replies were very interesting, ranging from supreme optimism from Armstrong Siddeley to complete pessimism from Metropolitan Vickers. Bob recall's Chadwick taking an l/48th scale model of this twin-engine version up to London. The model was left with Air Marshal Sir John Boothman - Chadwick described how Boothman had "flown" it round the office presumably making appropriate noises.

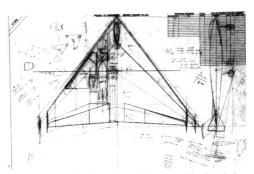

Well known sketch proposed by Roy Chadwick for a twin engine delta wing aircraft.

At this stage the project department heard of the Bristol T.E.1/46 jet engine, which was being designed for the Aircraft Division of Bristol Aeroplane Company, it was to be used in a long range, high flying bomber designated Type 172. The general specification of the Type 172 was similar to the Ministry of Supply specification that was later responsible for the Vulcan and Victor. The project office at Bristol's prepared a brochure that was submitted to the Ministry of Supply in March 1946 and in July of that year the T.E.1/46 engine specification was issued.

Later to be named 'Olympus' it was investigated by the Initial Projects Department at Chadderton and a four engine aircraft was designed using this engine and was adopted for the tender brochure on the Avro Type 698 which was submitted to the MoS in May 1947 just six months from the initial MoS B35/46 requirement.

The other feature that was kicked around considerably was the crew accommodation. The first proposal had the crew compartment inside the wing, with the pilots under two fighter type hoods. Then the requirement for a jettisonable crew compartment was emphasised, and much effort was devoted to getting the crew into the minimum nacelle, demountable just aft of the pressure bulkhead, and with a multiple parachute packed into the fairing aft of the canopy this design was put forward in the brochure. Unfortunately this requirement was later dropped due to the considerable research time required to solve the technical problems of having this type of system. In those days the radar scanner was also installed inside the wing.

The first issue of the brochure was finished, in April 1947. After completing this drawings were produced for a 1/24th scale plastic model. Some work on a civil version of the aircraft, employing a slightly higher wing loading and operating at a lower height than the bomber project and would have made attractive trans-Atlantic aircraft - headwinds didn't seem to worry it too much.

In 1944, Roy Dobson put Stuart Davies in charge of a Special Projects Group to look at new aircraft designs for the future of the Company. Davies employed Jim Floyd as Chief Project Engineer and a youthful apprentice Bob Lindley.

In 1945, Avro had taken over the Victory Aircraft facilities at Malton Ontario, Canada and a new Company was set up known as Avro Canada. In 1946, Stuart Davies asked Jim

Floyd to join the new company to work on a new jetliner; this led to Lindley being promoted to Chief Project Engineer. Lindley left Avro in 1949 to join Canadair and then went to work for Avro Canada, where he joined his colleague Jim Floyd. Lindley had a reputation for solving engineering problems and went on to be Chief Engineer on another delta project the Avro Arrow. After cancellation of the Avro Arrow, he then went to the Space industry in the USA and later joined NASA on the Shuttle program becoming Director of Engineering and Operations for manned space flight.

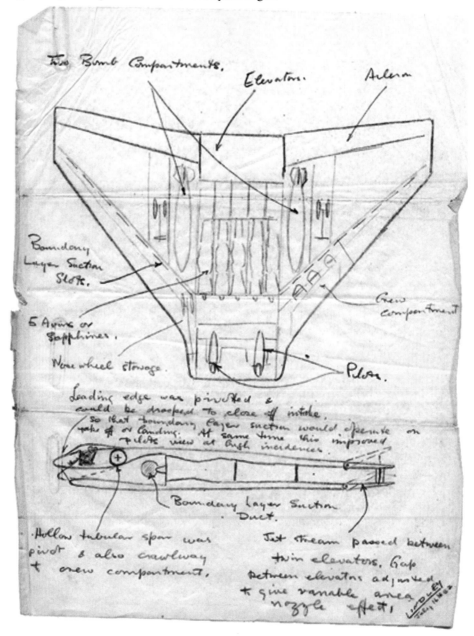

Bob Lindley sketch of early thoughts on meeting the B35/46 specification

Specification B35/46

SECRET
MINISTRY OF SUPPLY
PRINCIPLE DIRECTORATE OF TECHNICAL DEVELOPMENT
This document is the property of H.M. Government
SPECIFICATION No B35/46

MEDIUM RANGE BOMBER
This specification is to be regarded for contract purpose as forming part of the Contract
Agreement and being subject to the same conditions.
Approved by: H Grinsted Director of Aircraft Research and Development
Date: 24.1.47

1 - GENERAL

1.01   This specification is issued to cover the design and construction of a medium range bomber for worldwide use by the Royal Air Force.

1.02   The operational requirements are stated in Appendix B to this specification.

1.03   This specification gives only the particular requirements for the type in amplification of the current general design requirements stated in:

(i)   AP970 with Amendments up to and including AL 38.

(ii)   Aircraft Design Memoranda. Standardisation Design Memoranda, and Standard instruction Sheets current to the 1st November 1946.

(iii)   Specification No. DTD. 1208 (Issue IV) and amendments 1-5 inclusive thereto. And these requirements shall be completely fulfilled except where varied by this specification, or where the prior written consent of P/DTD (A) has been obtained.

1.04   It is essential that the design of the aircraft be suitable for economic production of at least 500 aircraft at a maximum rate of not less than 10 per month.

1.05   Subsequent chapter references in this specification are to AP 970 (as amended by AL 38) in all cases.

II - DESIGN REQUIREMENTS

Engines

2.01   Precautions shall be taken to prevent the entry of debris into the air intake.

Engine Failure on Take-Off

2.02   In the event of a single engine failure at any stage of the take off the pilot shall either be able to pull up safely without damage, or be able to continue the take-off. In either event the operation must be completed within 150% of the take-off distance specified in Appendix 'B'. In the event of the take-off being continued it shall not be necessary for the pilot to operate trimmer, flap, and undercarriage or throttle controls until he has reached a height of 100ft.

Emergency Escape

2.03   The provisions for emergency escape by the crew shall be in accordance with JAC Paper 339.

Protection of Landing Flaps

2.04   The design shall be such as to minimise damage to any part of the aircraft by water, mud, or stones thrown up by the wheels.

Twin Contact Tyres

2.05   Provision shall be made to allow for the correct operation of the nose wheel unit with a twin contact tyre of suitable pressure so should shimmy occur, a twin contact tyre can be fitted without any modification other than a wheel change being necessary.

Cockpit Colour

2.06   The pilots and bomb aimer's stations shall be finished internally in matt black. The only variation permitted is the use of red for marking emergency controls and exits.

Fire Prevention

2.07   Installation of any combustion heaters or auxiliary power plants shall be in accordance with JAC Paper 336.

Pressure Cabin

2.08   A pressure cabin shall be installed in accordance with Chapter 718 for which p = 9.0 lbs. per square inch.

2.09   With the aircraft on the ground the pressure of the air in the cabin shall be raised to 9lbs.per square inch. With the pressure supply cut off the time taken for the pressure to fall from 9.0 to 4.5 lbs. per square inch shall be noted and shall be not less than one minute.

III - EQUIPMENT
General

3.01   Equipment shall be fitted or provided for in accordance with the Appendix 'A' to this specification.

IV - STRENGTH AND STIFFNESS
Stressing Weight

4.01   Strength calculations for the take-off and flight cases (W2 of Chapter 305) shall be based upon the maximum all up weight of the aircraft when carrying the following.

   (i)   The tare weight items shown in column 10 of the Appendix A and such removable non standard parts as will be necessary for the contractor to supply and fit in order that the military load may be carried.

   (ii)   The removable military load defined in Appendix 'A' and approximate to the duties of paragraph of the Appendix 'B'.

   (iii) The fuel and oil appropriate to the range of paragraph 12 of the Appendix 'B'.

4.02   Strength calculations for landing (WI of Chapter 305) shall be based upon the take-off weight less the weight of bombs and half of the total fuel.

Main Flight Cases

4.03   The requirements of Chapter 201 shall be satisfied at the weight W2, with the basic flight envelope of that chapter having the following values: n1 = 2.7 VD speeds corresponding to Mach numbers up to and including 0.95 but need not exceed 435 knots EAS VB = 0.8VD or the maximum speed in level flight which ever is the greater.

4.04   The design shall be such that following take-off the above value of n1 will increase to at least 3.0 by the time one quarter of the still air range specified in paragraph 12 has been has been achieved, and will not subsequently fall below this value.

Parking and Picketing

4.05   The design shall be in accordance with JAC Paper 325, except that the factor will be 1.5 and the wind speed 65 knots (75mph).

V - TESTS
Contractor's Flight Trials

5.01   Prior to the delivery of the first aircraft, it shall be certified to the P/DTD that:

(a)   The aircraft has been subjected to a schedule of flight tests agreed at a meeting to be held by AD/RDL2 approximately one month before the first flight. This schedule will in general be based upon Parts 9 and 10 of AP970 current at that time.

(b)   The above-mentioned tests have shown the aircraft as safe to be flown by authorised Service Pilots.

APPENDIX 'B' TO SPECIFICATION B35/46

1.   The Air Staff require a medium range bomber land plane capable of carrying one 10,000lb bomb to a target 1,500 nautical miles from a base which may be anywhere in the world. The aircraft will be required to attack targets at great distance inside the enemy territory and it must be assumed that it will be plotted by radar and other methods for a large part of its flight. It must, therefore be capable of avoiding destruction by making the inevitable attack from ground and air launched weapons difficult. To this end it must have:

(a)   A high cruising speed the cruising speed shall be such that attacking fighters will have to fly at a speed at which they will tend to become un-manoeuvrable.

(b)   Manoeuvrability at high speed and high altitude - the design must be such that the aircraft can turn rapidly without loss of height or much loss of speed when at maximum cruising height.

(c)   A high cruising height - The cruising height must be such that ground launched weapons can only be guided at long range and such that the design of the intercepting enemy aircraft will be difficult.

(d)   Capacity for carrying adequate warning devices - these will be needed to detect the approach of ground launched weapons and the proximity of opposing aircraft to be effective the warning device must have long range and may therefore be large. Adequate provision must be made for mounting such a warning system so that it can scan the required field.

(e)   Capacity for carrying defensive apparatus - Such as proximity fuses exploders and homing or guided missile jamming devices.

2.   The size of the pressure cabin must be as small as possible.

3.   Visual and electronic bomb aiming positions are required.

4.   Maximum performance is the ultimate aim and must not be sacrificed unduly for ease of maintenance.

5.   It must be possible to operate this aircraft from existing H. B. type airfields and the maximum weight when fully loaded ought, therefore, not to exceed 100,000lbs. The Air Staff is to be informed if the weight will be exceeded.

6.   The aircraft must be suitable for large-scale production in war.

PERFORMANCE

7.   The performance requirements apply to operation in all parts of the world.

8.   The aircraft must be capable of cruising at maximum continuous cruising power at heights from 35,000ft to 50,000ft. at a speed of 500 knots.

9.   The maximum speed in level flight should be as high as possible but it is not essential that it should exceed the cruising speed.

10. The Flying characteristics must not become dangerous when the speed temporarily rises above the top level speed in the course of combat or other manoeuvres and the Mach No increases to a maximum of 0.90 but a speed restriction is acceptable below 25,000 ft.

11. The aircraft will be required to fly under all weather conditions. For this reason it must be capable of comfortable slow speed during the landing approach. The final approach speed should not exceed 120 knots and good manoeuvrability must be maintained at this speed.

12. The Maximum operational radius of action with a 10,000lb bomb load must be 1500 miles. To attain this still air range of 3,350 nautical miles at a height of 50,000 ft with a 10,000 lb bomb carried on the outward and return flight is required.

Climb

13. The aircraft must be capable of reaching 45,000ft with the full load less two and a half hours fuel. The ability to climb above this height is desirable but not essential.

Ceiling

14. The aircraft must cruise at 50,000 ft with full load less two and a half hours fuel. The ability to climb above this height is desirable but not essential.

Take-Off

15. At sea level under tropical, conditions, the aircraft must clear a 50ft screen within 1500 yards from rest in still air with a cross wind of up to 20 knots at right angles to the take-off path. To achieve this rocket take-off equipment would be acceptable. (The development of the RATOG was required to cover this requirement).

Landing

16. The aircraft must be capable under tropical conditions of landing in cross winds of up to 20 knots and coming to rest within 1,400 yards after crossing a 50 ft screen in still air with half the permanent fuel load and no bombs or within 1,700 yards with full fuel/bomb load. When landing with the full fuel bomb load a slight reduction in the normal safety factors would be acceptable. The Air Staff will accept fuel jettisoning to enable the landing requirements to be met subject to the operation not talking more than 5 minutes.

Flight with one or more engines stopped

17. The aircraft must meet current Air Staff requirements regarding engine failure on take off. It must be capable of maintaining 45,000ft with one engine stopped and 30,000ft with two engines stopped when carrying full load less one hour's fuel. The stopping one engine must not reduce the range by more than 20%.

ARMAMENT

18. The aircraft will rely upon speed, height, and evasive manoeuvre for protection. It will not carry orthodox defensive armament but will be equipped with early warning devices, radar counter measurers to deflect a beam on which a ground or air launched weapon may be launched.

19. A new range of bombs will be carried designed for stable flight from maximum operational height and speed of this aircraft.

20. The aircraft is required to bomb at its operational ceiling in all weather conditions and therefore the majority of bombing will be with the target hidden by cloud or darkness. It is necessary therefore to carry the new radar bombing equipment under development, which makes use of all radar and D.R navigational data to feed the

bombing computer. When the target can be seen, however, a visual bombsight fed from the same bombing computer will be used and must be fitted in a position to afford the maximum clear view.

Bombs

21.   Capacity is to be provided for a total bomb load of 20,000 lb composed of bombs of the following dimensions.

Type	Max Diam.	Overall Length	Distance C.G from nose
10,000lb H.C.	40 inch	290 inch	80 inch
6,000lb H.C.	32 inch	225 inch	63 inch
1,000lb H.C.	16.5 inch	110 inch	30 inch
Special Bomb	60 inch	290 inch*	80 inch*

*First estimate only

22.   As an alternative, capacity must be provided for carrying a bomb of the dimensions as shown under 21 (Special Bomb) and additional fuel which may be carried in detachable tanks in the bomb cells to meet range requirement stated in paragraph 12 above provided these tanks can be installed or removed in not more than 5 hours.

23.   The opening of the bomb doors or other method of release of bombs must not appreciably alter the speed or trim of the aircraft so that it would affect bombing accuracy.

24.   It must be possible to release bombs at any speed at which the aircraft is capable of flying. Clearance is required to enable bombs to be released when diving or climbing at an angle of 15 degrees or with up to 10 degrees of side slip.

Bomb Sights

25.   This aircraft will be required to bomb from all heights up to 50,000ft using either visual or electronic bomb sights.
Provision is to be made for fitting N.B.C. with visual sighting head.

26.   The bomb selecting and fusing are to be at the navigation /blind bombing station.

27.   Bomb release and jettisoning switches are to be fitted at the pilot's station, the visual bombing position and at the navigation /blind bombing position.
Space is to be made available for bomb guiding equipment.

Bomb Loading

28.   Performance must not be prejudiced by designing to use existing bomb handling gear.

29.   Provision must be made for carrying a vertical camera and illuminating apparatus for night photography in order to record the fall of bombs and release points.
Photographic recording of the readings of electronic bomb sights will be required.

CREW STATIONS

30.   The crew will consist of five:
First Pilot, Second Pilot (under training), two Navigator/bomb aimer/radar operators, one Wireless /Warning and Protective Device Operator.

Pressure Cabin

31.   The crew are to be accommodated in one pressure cabin. The cabin is to be large enough to allow each member of the crew to move from his seat during flight. The

cabin pressure should not be below the equivalent of 8,000ft on the flight to and from the target but may be reduced to the equivalent of 25,000ft in the combat area. Particular importance is attached to keeping the size and hence the weight and vulnerability of the pressure cabin as small as possible. No equipment that can be remotely controlled is to be carried in the cabin. Cabin pressure, humidity and temperature are to automatically control. To reduce fatigue, the maximum crew comfort must be provided.

Pilots Station

32. The pilot must have the best possible view as specified by AP970 and in particular he must have a good view downwards over the nose of not less than 15 degrees from the horizontal in level flight. His seat is to be as comfortable as possible. It is too be adjusted for height and in a fore and aft direction. The slope of the back is to be adjustable and it is to have folding armrests.

33. The engine instruments are to be visible to the pilot. These are to be kept to the absolute minimum and no instrument is to be provided which is not essential for the correct operation of the aircraft. Instruments required for maintenance check or to indicate something about which the pilot can do nothing in flight are to be excluded. If instruments not required during flight are necessary for pre flight running up and ground test, they are to be provided on a separate and preferably detachable panel outside the pressure cabin. All fuel cocks are to be in reach of the pilot. Engine starting must be from the pilot's seat. Fuel contents and gallons gone meters are to be visible to the first pilot and navigator.

Navigators Stations

34. The two Navigator/bomb aimer/radar operators should be accommodated at a combined station. This station should be as comfortable and quiet as possible and will be required to contain all the navigation instruments, radar navigation controls and indicators, electronic bomb aiming presentation and other radio equipment as detailed in para 62.

Visual Bombing Station

35. A visual bombing station readily accessible from the navigation station is to be provided. The clear field of vision must be 10 degrees aft of vertical to horizontal forward and as wide as lateral, view as possible.

Wireless Operators Station

36. The Wireless Operators Station will contain all attack warning devices and controls for counter measure devices such as proximity fuse exploders. It must be as comfortable as possible.

PROTECTION
Warning Devices

37. Radar warning devices to detect the launching and approach of ground or air launched weapons or opposing aircraft must be provided to cover at least the whole lower and rear hemispheres.

Crew

38. An appreciation is required of the loss of performance entailed by providing armour against attack by weapons capable of producing fragments equivalent to

0.5 inch A.P. Ammunition and also to provide protection from 0.5 inch gun attack within a 60 degrees including angle from a stern is required. A decision on the requirement for this armour will be made after appreciation for each design submitted has been studied by the Air Staff.

Fuel Tanks and Pipelines

39.   (a)   Self-sealing is not required but tanks not easily damaged in a crash are to be provided. Neither the tanks nor tank compartments must contain anything capable of acting as a wick for the fuel. Self-sealing pipelines are not required.

(b)   Tank purging by inert gas is required for all tanks.

(c)   Tanks must be so arranged or compartmented that one whole does not cause the loss of more than 10% of the remaining fuel.

Fire Protection

40.   An approved type of fire extinguisher system is required for the engine and tank compartments.

NAVIGATION

41.   In order that continuous accurate navigation may be possible over the great distances involved it is essential that this aircraft should be equipped with:

(a)   A long range automatic D.R. System and

(b)   A long range fixing system.

42.   Since radio systems based on transmission from the ground are liable to jamming, and are unlikely to provide a sufficient degree of accuracy it is highly desirable that except for homing, the navigation of this aircraft should be independent from the ground.

43.   The automatic D.R. system will comprise a type of navigational and bombing computer to which navigational information is supplied by an H2S set of long range and moderate definition, the bombing information being supplied by separate high definition equipment which may operate on a different frequency. In addition at a later date a system of measuring track and ground speed utilising the Doppler principle may be coupled to the n.b.c.

44.   For fixing positions there are two requirements:-

(a)   **H.2.S.** - To pinpoint and identify over or near land.

(b)   **Astro** - A completely automatic astro system will be developed during the life of the aircraft and an optically correct glass panel in the roof of the aircraft above the navigator's station will be required.

Short Range Navigation

45.   Equipment is required for completely automatic homing, orbiting, approach and landing. The system will also provide a short range fixing aid.

46.   An automatic radio compass for use in emergency will also be wanted. This will work in conjunction with the main W/T communication set, which will incorporate automatic coding and teleprinter facilities as soon as they are developed.

OTHER FEATURES
Engine Installation

47.   It is preferred that the aircraft has no less than four and no more than six engines.

48.   The engines need not be installed as power plants if this will in anyway prejudice the performance. Within reason performance must take precedence over ease of access and maintenance.

49.   Attention is given to flame damping.

Ground Handling

50.   Catapult or trolley launching is not acceptable. Arrester gear for landing is not acceptable.

Icing and Misting

51.   A means must be provided to prevent all windows required for flying or for search from becoming obscure by ice, snow rain or internal misting. The system must be effective through out the speed and height range of the aircraft.

52.   The aircraft must be capable of flying through all normal icing conditions.

Emergency Exits

53.   The complete pressure cabin must be jettisonable. Such a cabin must be provided with parachutes to reduce the falling speed to a value at which the occupants will be unhurt when hitting the ground while still strapped in their seats. If such a jettisonable unit cannot be provided the seats must be jettisonable.

Ditching and Flotation

54.   A good ditching and flotation characteristics are desirable but must not prejudice the performance.

Dual Control

55.   The 2nd pilot's seat must be suitable for giving and receiving dual instructions and must be sufficiently comfortable to be occupied for the full endurance of the aircraft. Complete duplication of all instruments is not required but the blind flying panel must be provided for each pilot. A design in which the 2nd pilot must leave his seat to allow access to the nose is acceptable.

Fuel and Oil

56.   Controls for fuel cocks and pumps must be as simple as possible.

Undercarriages

57.   The undercarriages must be such that the aircraft can use airfields built to the present H. B. Standard.

Controllability

58.   The aircraft will be required to land in very bad weather conditions by day and night. It must therefore, be easy to fly with good response to the controls when making the final approach to land. it must also be as manoeuvrable as possible at maximum height and speed as violent manoeuvres will be the only defence against aircraft, and guided or homing weapons. Air brakes are to be fitted.

EQUIPMENT
Flying Equipment

61.   (a)   Night Flying: - Full night flying equipment is to be provided including U/V cockpit lighting.

       (b)   Automatic Pilot: - An automatic pilot is required. This is to be suitable for coupling to the bomb aiming equipment.

(c)   Automatic Blind Flying Equipment:- Automatic blind flying equipment is required and will be coupled with the automatic pilot.

Navigation

62.   The navigational equipment that will be required may be summarised as follows.

   (a)   Non Radio.
      (i). Remote indicating gyro compass with the necessary repeaters.
      (ii). Stand by magnetic compass.

(iii).   Navigation and bombing computer.

   (b)   Radio (including Radar).
      (i).   Long range navigation system, consisting of H2S with NBC.
      (ii).   Rebecca/BABS or SCS51 in conjunction with autopilot.
      (iii).   High Altitude radio altimeter, preferably incorporated with NBC.
      (iv).   Automatic radio compass for use with main W/T set.
      (v).   Main W/T Equipment.
      (vi).   Multi Channel VHF equipment.
      (vii).   Intercommunication equipment.
      (viii).   Radio-teleprinter with automatic coding facilities to operate main W/T equipment.
      (ix).   Cloud and collision warning system.
      (x).   IFF.

Defensive Equipment

63.   An early warning system capable of detecting intercepting aircraft attacking from a cone of 45 degrees from the rear.

64.   Equipment for detonating fuses will be required.

Window Launching

65.   'Window' or the equivalent counter measure launching equipment is to be provided outside the pressure cabin.

Oxygen

66.   Oxygen is required for the full endurance at 20,000 ft. An emergency oxygen system is to be provided in case the cabin is perforated. This must provide sufficient oxygen for all members of the crew for up to four hours at 30,000 ft.

Dinghies

67.   Each member of the crew is to be provided with a Type 'K' dinghy. A type 'H' is to be provided in a blow out storage.

Parachutes

68.   Back type parachutes will be worn by all members of the crew.

Pyrotechnics

69.   A 6-cartridge signal discharger is required.

Air Ministry D.O.R. (A)
December 1946
DB 57990/3/632 60 1/47

Tender memo - April 1947

Below is a memo from J. A. R. Kay to "Teddy" Fielding works manager, asking for the manufacturing cost of the Type 698 built to specification B.35/46.

A. V. ROE & CO. LIMITED, MANCHESTER
MEMORANDUM

11th. April, 1947.

From: J.A.R. Kay.　　　　　　　　　　　　To: Mr. Fielding.

TENDER FOR B.35/46 BOMBER

This is just a note to remind you that our tender for this aircraft is due at the beginning of the last week of this month. To all intents and purposes therefore I must have my figures finished by April 25th and as I shall be in London all next week this will therefore only leave me five days in which to complete the job.

For your information the machine is, as you know, of Delta wing design with a structure weight of 24,000lbs, an equipped airframe weight of 33,000lbs. and an all-up-weight of 100,000lbs. Lindley in the Projects Office has drawings which give a good line as to what is required.

The following are a few points which I have noticed whilst talking to him today and I wonder if you would be so good during my absence as to start up some preliminary thought on what we are going to put in respect of man hours, jig and tools costs and so on.

1. The aeroplane has a span of approximately 90 feet and I believe excluding the jettisonable fuselage it has a chord of something like 60 feet; the depth of the wing section is approximately 8 feet. You will see therefore that this is a very big structure and I know that Mr. Chadwick wants it building all in one piece. This would of course mean that it would have to be built at Woodford and the assembly jig would be a most enormous contraption.

2. The aeroplane has a small fin and rudder tacked on to the outboard tips of the wing. Fuselage is of fairly orthodox construction.

3. There will be combined elevators and ailerons which as far as I know will be of orthodox construction.

4. There are no flaps.

5. There will be two pairs of bomb doors which as far as Projects people know at the moment are of orthodox construction.

6. The fuselage itself is a very small one perched right out in the nose but has to be jettisonable with all the complications involved.

7. As far as the wing construction is concerned the whole of the leading edge must be of lamina flow construction, that is the whole leading edge to the front face of the spar. Of this leading edge the forward part consists of the various Thermal De-Icing tanks and the rear half consists of integral tanks. These integral tanks will have a top and bottom skin which in itself forms the skin of the leading edge and must therefore be lamina flow.

8. The spars are likely to be of orthodox boom and web construction both front and rear with orthodox ribs between the two.

The above will give you a rough idea of the main points which I have noticed.

Initial brochure - May 1947

Text from the initial brochure dated May 1947 by Avro to meet B.35/46 specification.

INTRODUCTION
SPECIFICATION NO. B.35/46
MEDIUM RANGE BOMBER

A perusal of the above Specification shows that the aeroplane in its present form is no longer, a sound basis for planning the new types of military aircraft and that the high speeds called for will require the employment of all known aerodynamic improvements and considerable new research work in aerodynamics, as well as the development of much more powerful Jet engines that are at present available.

Our study of the problems produced by the Specification has resulted in the conclusion that a Delta Wing design is the only one which will meet the speed, range, load and gross weight limitations laid down.

We have used in our design study all the available information of which we are aware from British and German Reports.

We submit that the Delta Wing design provides a neat solution to the requirements of the Specification and whilst admitting that the Delta Wing is at present largely an unknown quantity, we feel confident that it will be less difficult both aerodynamically and structurally to develop the Delta Wing than either a swept wing aeroplane with tail, or the V type tailless aeroplane.

It appears to us that the control and stability problems of the Delta wing are no more difficult than those of the other types, and structurally the Delta Wing has an enormous advantage over any other form of aeroplane.

The Delta Wing is simple in form and is inherently adapted to take care of both flexural and torsional loadings due to the great depth of wing section, even with a low thickness chord ratio.

The Delta wing also automatically provides such a great mount of internal space that even in a comparatively small size it can house the power plant and all the loads inside the wing if necessary.

In the particular design we are submitting we have used an extension to the nose of the wing to form a crew nacelle, in order to comply with the requirement that the crew should be able to be parachuted down in the section of the aircraft which they normally occupy. This with the air intakes and jet pipe tails are the only excrescences on the clean aeroplane form.

It may be possible to delete the wing tip fins when research work has been done. These are fitted to take care of the small out of balance thrust moment which would occur in the event of an engine failure.

We give below a brief statement of the way in which we arrived at the Delta Wing solution to the B.35/46 Specification:-

1. The speed requirement of 500 knots at heights between 36,000ft. and 50,000ft. when the speed of sound is 574 knots implies that the critical Mach. No. (Mach. No. for start of rapid increase in drag with speed) must be greater than 0.872.

2. This critical Mach. No. implies the necessity for a thin wing of high speed section with a large sweep back. We should investigate wings of 10% and 12% thickness chord ratio with the Squire high speed aerofoil and the NACA 0012-0,55-40 and with a sweep back up to 45° on the wing quarter chord line.

3.   The critical Mach No. is a function of the lift coefficient (C_L) (decreasing with increase of C_L) as well as wing section and sweep back and it will be necessary to use a low value of C_L in order to achieve a high Mach number.

A mean value of C_L of about 0.2 is indicated, vide FORSCHUNGSBERICHT NO.1910.

4.   Taking the above as a basis of investigation we should consider layout designs for:-

      a.   A swept back wing aeroplane with fuselage and tailplane.

      b.   A "VEE" tailless swept back wing.
             and

      c.   A Delta Wing.

5.   These investigations should also consider aspect ratios 2, 4 and 6.

6.   We will assume that the R.D.T. wing weight formula will apply.

7.   We will assume that Jet engines of suitable size will be developed, with characteristics at least as good as the "Avon".

The following is the result of the preliminary investigations which indicate that both (a) and (b) designs are unacceptable as they exceed the permissible A.U.W. by a considerable amount, whilst the Delta Wing design can just comply with the A.U.W. requirement and achieve the required speed, range and bomb load.

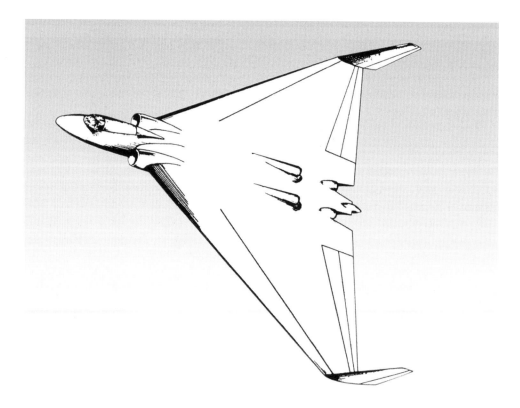

Drawing from the first tender brochure, it clearly shows the delta wing to best advantage and the tailless design.

Brief description

The aircraft is an all-metal Monoplane of Delta Wing form designed to comply with all the requirements of specification No. B.35/46.

It is propelled by four Jet engines, each of approximately 9,000lbs. static thrust capacity. The engines are completely buried in the wing.

The fuel is carried in the leading edge of the wing in ten separate tank compartments, each holding one-tenth of the total fuel capacity. These compartments are fitted with flexible tanks which are removable through access doors in the main spar web.

The crew are housed in a nacelle which forms a continuation of the nose of the aerofoil. This nacelle has been kept as small as possible compatible with adequate room for the crew to perform their duties.

It is pressurised by means of centrifugal blowers driven off the auxiliary gear boxes.

A fairing behind the pilot's canopy contains the parachutes for supporting the nacelle after it is released from the aircraft, and the doors of this canopy are opened by means of a static line attached to the main aircraft structure and the door release, with a secondary manually operated release inside the nacelle.

The engines have been kept very close to the centre line of the aircraft so that the offset thrust in the case of an engine failure in very small and should be easily controlled -

(a) By the fact that a steerable nose wheel is fitted to the tricycle undercarriage and (b) by the wing tip rudders.

Owing to the low wing loading no landing flaps are proposed. Later results may show that suitable means of increasing the lift can be provided on a Delta Wing design.

The normal tricycle undercarriage arrangement is used and tyre pressures have been limited to 90 lbs/sq.in. If necessary, larger wheels and tyres can be fitted, and there is ample space within the wing to stow the undercarriage.

Twin wheels are used on all undercarriage legs and long travel shock absorbers are provided so that there is ample shock absorption capacity to take care of severe landing conditions.

The bombs are housed inside the wing, two bomb compartments being provided, each capable of taking the special bomb. All other specified bomb loads can be conveniently accommodated inside the bomb bays.

All equipment which can be remotely controlled is housed in the wing, the radio equipment being carried immediately aft of the crew's nacelle so as to reduce to the minimum the length of all conductors.

It is proposed to suppress all external aerials and the H2S scanner is mounted inside the wing with a suitable area of the bottom plating made in timber construction. A drawing showing the proposed aerial system is given in the brochure.

The longitudinal control of the aeroplane is by means of elevons mounted on a trimmer portion at the trailing edge of the wing and by fins and rudders on the wing tip to provide directional control.

The trimming portion of the longitudinal control is operated through irreversible screw jacks and the elevons are aerodynamically balanced and statically balanced.

Dual controls are provided in the cockpit.

The aeroplane meets all the performance requirements of the Specification except that the altitude at the target would be 49,000ft instead of 50,000ft. and the Gross Weight will be 104,000 lbs. instead of 100,000 lbs.

Thermal Anti-Icing is fitted on the lines developed on the "Lancaster"; heat is taken from the jet pipe.

The aircraft is suitable for large scale production in war-time and is, in fact, simpler to manufacture than existing types, with the exception that the leading edge of the wing up to 25% of the chord will have to be of laminar flow construction, which will require considerably more care in manufacture than has been customary in the past, but this will, of course, apply to all future high speed aeroplanes.

The geometry of the Delta Wing is particularly suited to take both flexural and torsional loads and the achievement of a very low structure weight. The great depth of the wing in the centre, namely, 7.8 ft. for a span of 90 ft. illustrates this point.

An examination of Drawing IPD3, which show the distribution of the main loads and in particular the heavy fuel load, brings out in a marked way the distribution of weights across the span. This in conjunction, with the shear and bending moment, further illustrate the ease with which a low structure weight can be attained.

We consider that the Delta Wing form will give the lowest possible percentage structure weight of any form of aeroplane.

The pilot's view will be particularly good and it is anticipated that the crew's nacelle will be exceptionally quiet owing to the use of the Jet engines which are well behind the nacelle, and the heavy lagging which will be provided in the nacelle, both as sound and heat insulation.

The special features of this design are as follows:-

a. Delta Wing design. This can be considered as a special feature, as up-to-date aero planes of this type have not been flown.

b. The bomb compartments are capable of carrying two of the large "special" bombs.

c. A very large central compartment is provided on the centre line of the aircraft, with an overall length of 30', a maximum height of 7.8' and a width of 3.5', for the accommodation of all remotely controlled equipment, engine driven accessory gearboxes, batteries, pressurisation equipment, etc.,
    This large compartment is entered through a door at the rear end on the under surface of the wing. The large volume available enables all the equipment to be easily stowed, inspected and maintained.
    Doors in the walls of this compartment give easy access to the power plants, and smaller doors in the bomb compartment walls give access to the other side of the power plants.

d. The radio and radar equipment which can be remotely controlled, is mounted in the nose wheel compartment as close as possible to the nacelle so as, to give short electrical leads, and, this equipment is very accessible when the aircraft is on the ground and the nose wheel doors open.

e. All aerials will be enclosed as shown on the relative Drawing. This includes the H2S Scanner which is mounted in the outer portion of the wing, which has a non-metallic wing, covering over a suitable area to give the necessary visual angles.

f. The engines are mounted very close to the centre line of the aircraft so that in the event of an engine failure at take-off or in flight, there is very little offset thrust moment.

g. Boundary layer suction control is provided over the span covered by the elevons. This suction is obtained by means of a large valve in the air intake just ahead of the point where it bifurcates. The valve will be operated by an electrical actuator and is only in operation during take-off and landing.

h. Thermal anti-icing of the wing leading edge, the engine air intake leading edges and the fins is provided, the general construction being on the lines of that developed on the "Lancaster" by Flight Refuelling Ltd and A.V., Roe & Co. The necessary heat is obtained by tapping from the four jet pipes.

i. 25% of the wing chord is of laminar flow construction on the lines developed by Sir W. G. Armstrong Whitworth Aircraft Ltd.

j. Longitudinal control and trimming is effected by means of trimmer surfaces which are controlled, by means of irreversible screw jacks with electric actuation, and by differentially operated elevons which are both aerodynamically and, statically balanced. The elevon aerodynamic balance is of the vented type and is shown in the drawings included in this Brochure.

k. A droppable nacelle is provided at the nose of the wing for the accommodation of the crew. The parachutes are housed in a fairing behind the pilot's canopy and the parachute housing is opened by means of a static line attached to the main aircraft structure. The separation will be very rapid, as the main aircraft will loop when the crew's nacelle is detached. All control piping and electrical connections will be arranged to separate easily when the nacelle is parachuted.

l. An exceptionally low percentage structure weight can be attained in the Delta Wing owing to the combination of very low aspect ratio and very high taper ratio.
For comparison we can compare the B.35/46 with a "Lincoln" The B.35/46 has a span of 90' and a wing depth of almost 8' at the centre line, whilst the "Lincoln" with a span of 120' has a wing depth of 2.88' at the centre line.

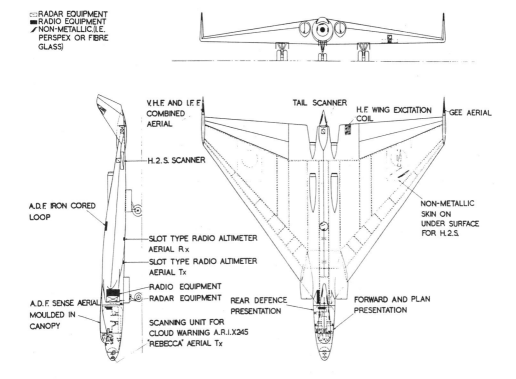

Tender drawings

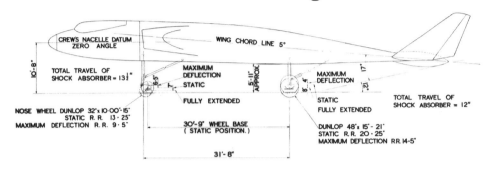

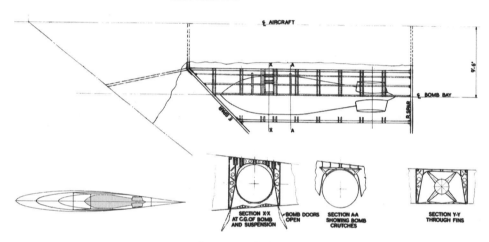

"SPECIAL BOMB" INSTALLATION

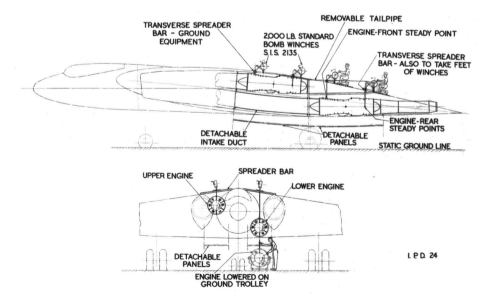

METHOD OF ENGINE REMOVAL

AVRO TYPE 698   SPECIFICATION B35/46

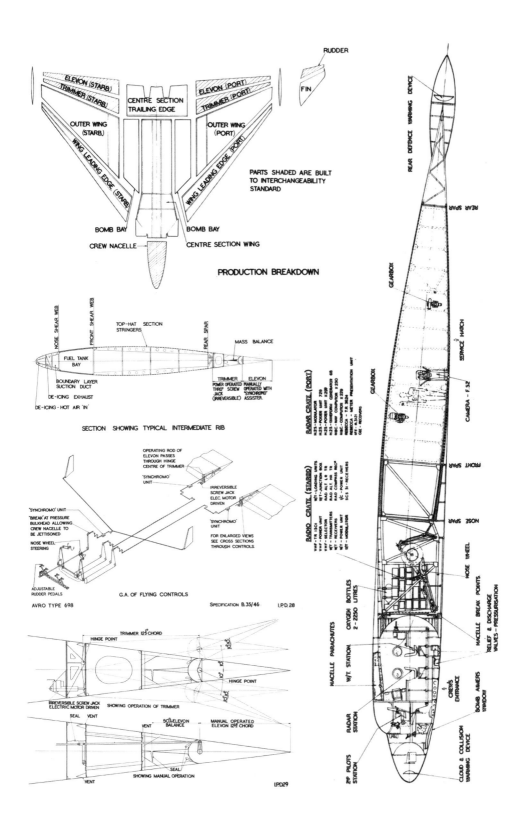

PARTS SHADED ARE BUILT
TO INTERCHANGEABILITY
STANDARD

PRODUCTION BREAKDOWN

SECTION SHOWING TYPICAL INTERMEDIATE RIB

G.A. OF FLYING CONTROLS

AVRO TYPE 698

SPECIFICATION B.35/46

I.P.D. 28

Nacelle arrangements

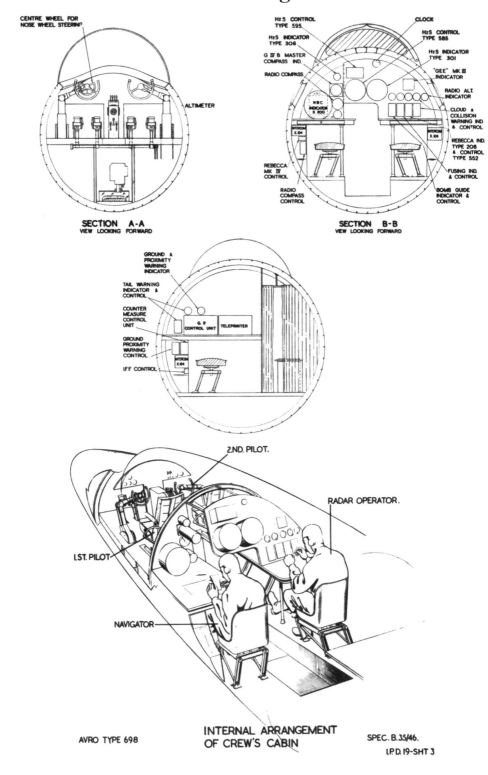

SECTION A-A
VIEW LOOKING FORWARD

SECTION B-B
VIEW LOOKING FORWARD

INTERNAL ARRANGEMENT
OF CREW'S CABIN

AVRO TYPE 698

SPEC. B.35/46.

I.P.D.19-SHT 3

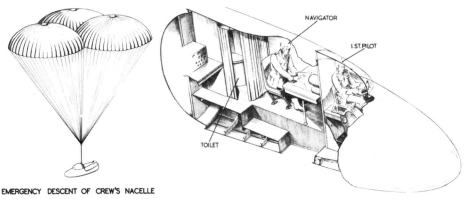

EMERGENCY DESCENT OF CREW'S NACELLE

AVRO TYPE 698   SPECIFICATION B 35/46
                  I.P.D. 21

AVRO TYPE 698   INTERNAL ARRANGEMENT OF
                  CREW'S CABIN.... PORT SIDE

                  SPEC. B.35/46
                  I.P.D. 19-SHT 1

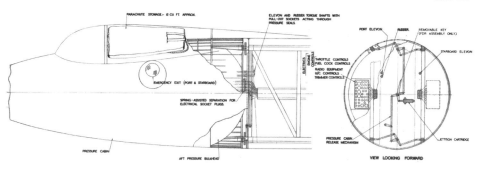

ARR^{GT.} FOR PRESSURE CABIN JETTISON

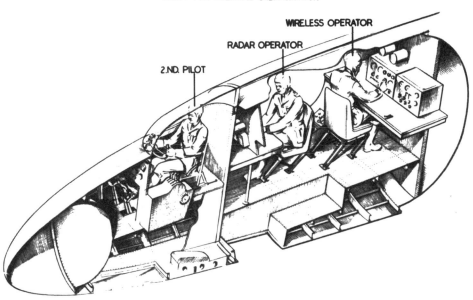

AVRO TYPE 698   INTERNAL ARRANGEMENT OF
                  CREW'S CABIN, STARBOARD SIDE.

                  SPEC. B.35/46.
                  I.P.D. 19-SHT 2

General Arrangement

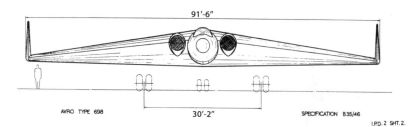

AVRO TYPE 698

91'-6"

30'-2"

SPECIFICATION B.35/46

I.P.D. 2 SHT. 2.

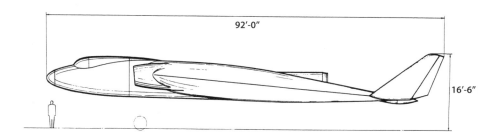

92'-0"

16'-6"

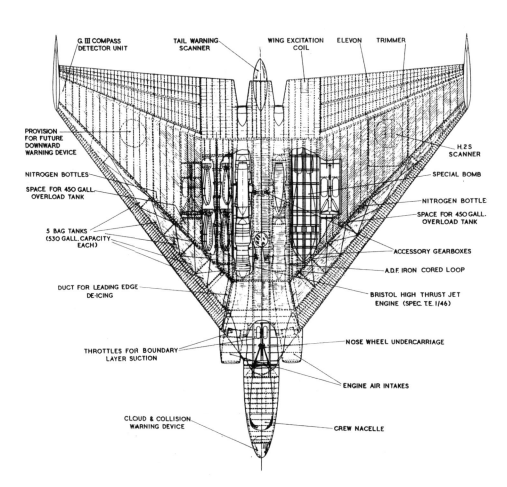

G. III COMPASS DETECTOR UNIT

TAIL WARNING SCANNER

WING EXCITATION COIL

ELEVON

TRIMMER

PROVISION FOR FUTURE DOWNWARD WARNING DEVICE

NITROGEN BOTTLES

SPACE FOR 450 GALL. OVERLOAD TANK

5 BAG TANKS (530 GALL. CAPACITY EACH)

DUCT FOR LEADING EDGE DE-ICING

THROTTLES FOR BOUNDARY LAYER SUCTION

CLOUD & COLLISION WARNING DEVICE

H.2 S SCANNER

SPECIAL BOMB

NITROGEN BOTTLE

SPACE FOR 450 GALL. OVERLOAD TANK

ACCESSORY GEARBOXES

A.D.F. IRON CORED LOOP

BRISTOL HIGH THRUST JET ENGINE (SPEC. T.E. 1/46)

NOSE WHEEL UNDERCARRIAGE

ENGINE AIR INTAKES

CREW NACELLE

Early model

This view shows the staggered arangement of the engines to advantage. The model was destroyed in a fire at Chadderton in October 1959.

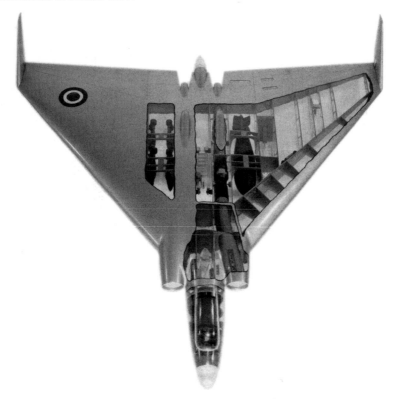

The flying controls were based on those developed for the Armstrong Siddeley AW52 and consisted of an unusual arrangement of double elevons along the wing trailing edge.

Tender competitors

By June 1945 Handley Page had stolen a march on Avro and had started to design a bomber with an "all up weight" (AUW) of 100,000 lb that had four jet engines. As part of a MAP fact finding visit to Germany's research establishments, Handley Page analysed the Horten Brothers tailless aircraft designs and began to study the concept of producing an aircraft combining a swept wing with jet engines.

A brochure was produced by Handley Page in February 25th, 1946 for an aircraft of 122ft span to carry a 10,000 lb bomb at 520 knots over a still air range of 5000 miles. The aircraft was later to be given the type number HP80, which became known as the Handley Page Victor.

In June 1946, a third draft of Air Staff requirements was issued. The chief of staff submitted their first request for an atomic bomb to the Ministry of Supply (MoS) in August 1946. By November 7th, 1946, the final draft of operating requirement OR229 was circulated.

On the 25th January, 1947 the B35/46 tender document was issued. Seven aircraft company's responded, these included Armstrong Whitworth (AW56), Avro (Type 698), Bristol Aircraft Ltd., (Type 172), English Electric, Handley Page (HP80), Shorts (PD1) and Vickers.

Later studies showed the HP80 as lead contender due to its innovative, high aspect ratio, crescent wing which was most likely to achieve the required altitude, speed and range. Seen here is the first prototype WB771 at the S.B.A.C. Show at Farnborough in 1953, its first flight was on 24th December, 1952. It was to crash on 14th July, 1954 during a low level high speed fly past at Cranfield.

Sir Fredrick Handley Page on 25th July, 1947 wrote a letter to Stewart Scott-Hall, Principle Director of Technical Development (Air) headed 'Crescent and Delta Wings' giving reasons why his company turned down the Delta wing.

A tender design conference was held on 28th July, 1947 to discuss the merits of the submitted tenders. These had been studied by a special projects group under the Aerodynamic Flight Section at the R.A.E. at Farnborough. Of the seven aircraft companies that submitted formal tenders it was concluded that the most advanced was the Avro submission and that Handley Page and Armstrong Whitworth were declared runners up. It was agreed that the Armstrong Whitworth, Avro and Handley Page submissions should continue with wind tunnel research. Many of these preliminary studies were based on research at R.A.E. which had the only large scale high speed wind tunnel research facility in the UK.

A meeting held at the Ministry of Supply on 27th November, 1947 approved the Avro Type 698 project in principle. At the same meeting the firm stated their views on the need for flying models to supplement normal wind tunnel research.

Bristol's continued research into a high speed long range bomber with swept back wings with the Type 174 and 176 to Spec E8/47 but work was not proceeded with after a mock-up conference in October 1948. Fairy's had also undertaken a project to this specification.

Further additions and amendments were made to the B35/46 specification first of these being issue two dated 1st June, 1948 which was distributed on 15th June, 1948 to Avro and Handley Page. It was the practice of the day to order two prototypes before a decision was made to proceed with a production contract. Avro received an order for two prototype Type 698 bombers, VX770 and VX777 to contract 6/ACFT/1942/CB.6(a) dated 22nd June, 1948. Handley Page received contract 6/ACFT/1875/CB.6(a) for two prototypes WB771 and WB775 dated 11th March, 1949.

Because of the advanced nature of the B35/46 specification, Short Brothers and Harland Ltd., of Belfast (Shorts) submitted a tender to a lower specification as a fallback option. It was built to operating requirement OR239 and tender B14/46 dated 11th August, 1947. A decision was taken to order the Vickers Type 660 instead of the SA4 later named Sperrin and the project was cancelled. The Short SA4 Sperrin, of which only two prototypes were built, was relegated to experimental and test duties in support of the V-bomber programme.

Photo From the George Jenks collection.

The Short Sperrin VX158 first flew 10th August, 1951 over two months after the first prototype Vickers Valiant had flown. It had an AUW of 115,000lb; with a maximum speed of 564 mph and a range of 3,860 n.m., powered originally by four Rolls-Royce Avon jet engines. The Sperrin was of more conventional design apart from the engine layout.

Vickers were issued with tender B9/48 to OR229 on 3rd August, 1948 which was ostensibly written around the Vickers Type 660, which later became known as the Vickers Valiant. The Type 660 had a lower performance than the Avro 698 and Handley Page HP80 but offered the advantage of being available at an earlier date. The Valiant was to be first of the "V" bombers and the first to enter RAF service.

The Vickers Valiant was powered by four Rolls-Royce Avon jet engines. The prototype WB210 first flew on 18th May, 1951 and officially named Valiant the following month. The first prototype crashed in January 1952 due to an in flight fire. The Valiant wing had a "compound sweep" configuration and had a 45° angle of sweepback in the inner third of the wing, reducing to an angle of about 24° at the tips.

Development brochure - April 1948

Since the issue of the original tender brochure for the delta bomber, many problems had arisen. A considerable number of these were solved by alterations to the layout of the aircraft; these changes were given in a development brochure dated 6th April 1948.

Recent Design Developments

(a) **All-moving wing tips for aerodynamic control for Mach Numbers exceeding 0.9.** Development work in the R.A.E. high-speed wind tunnel has shown a general need for special means to retain adequate control at air speeds somewhat above the critical Mach number. The solution indicated by R.A.E. was the addition of all-moving pointed wing tips and these have been applied to the Delta bomber. This addition to the plan form caused a considerable aft movement of the required C.G. necessitating a complete re-disposition of the equipment. An extra advantage associated with the addition of these pointed wing tips was an increase in aspect ratio from 2.5 to 3.0 which was in line with R.A.E. advice for obtaining a greater height over the target.

(b) **Revised wing section to give an improved critical Mach number.** High speed wind tunnel tests at R.A.E. showed that two changes in the original wing section were desirable to increase the critical Mach number and to reduce the low-speed profile drag. The first was to reduce the thickness chord ratio from 12% to 10% and the second was to move forward the chord wise position for maximum thickness from 40% to 30%. With these two alterations we feel confident that the critical Mach number of the aircraft will attain the value 0.88 which we have chosen for normal cruise.

(c) **Revised bomb load accommodation.** Following the re-arrangement of the engines in line abreast and the thinning of the wing, it was found preferable to use a single bomb bay on the centre line of the aircraft instead of the two bomb bays shown in the tender brochure. With the single bomb bay, space is available for a cylindrical special bomb; this represents the most difficult shape of special bomb that the aircraft specification can include.

(d) **Radar installation.** Following a meeting with T.R.E. representatives, the H2S scanner was removed from its original location in the outer wing and positioned in the nose of the crew's nacelle with the object of providing it with full forward vision. As agreed by D. O. R. the cloud and collision warning device has been deleted to make way for it.

(e) **Undercarriage installation.** Advantage has been taken of the rearward movement of the required C.G. as referred to in (a), to retract the main undercarriage units forward instead of aft. This enables the wheels to be housed in the thickest part of the wing section so that no bumps are caused on the wing surface even with the t/c ratio reduced to 10%.

(f) **Structure weight.** An increase of 2000 lbs. in wing structure weight has been found unavoidable, most of this increase being due to the new R.A.E. torsional stiffness criterion to prevent wing flutter.

(g) **Operating height.** In spite of the above weight increase there has been a net gain of 2,300 feet in mean cruising height for the redesigned aircraft, resulting from the reduced wing thickness and increased aspect ratio. The actual mean cruising height for the revised aircraft is now 51,400 feet based on the requirement range of 5,350 nautical miles.

Future Design Problems

Whilst the changes made in section (1) have solved many of the design problems which have been met up to the present, it is clear that a large number of outstanding points will require much more research and development before satisfactory solutions are reached. Facilities are necessary for this work to proceed on high priority since, unless this is arranged, serious delay to the satisfactory completion of the full scale Delta bomber may result. A summary is given below of the chief of these problems and some indication is given of how we propose to investigate them.

(a) 1/3 Scale Flying Model

In order to investigate the problems involving control, stability and response at comparatively low speed and low altitude conditions, it is proposed to construct a 1/3rd scale aircraft which will be easy to produce, involving, as it does, wooden construction for the most part, together with the adoption of existing standard items such as main undercarriage units, nose wheel, controls, seat, sliding hood installation, etc. In general the performance of the 1/3rd scale aircraft with its Derwent V engine will be 400 m.p.h. E.A.S. up to 10,000 feet. This will enable all preliminary aerodynamic investigation in flight to be undertaken. In particular it is desired to investigate the problems concerning the landing of the Delta aircraft. It is intended that an automatic camera box will record the necessary instrumentation.

(b) 1/2 Scale Flying Model

In order to investigate the problems surrounding the operation of the Delta aircraft at the Mach numbers and operating altitude used by the Delta bomber, it is proposed to construct a 1/2 scale flying model. Unlike the 1/3rd scale model, this aircraft will simulate the full scale aircraft much more closely and it will enable a check on performance, control, and stability to be made. Even using maximum continuous cruise power from its two Avon engines, the 1/2 scale model is expected will be capable of cruising at the specification speed of 500 knots at altitude up to 60,000ft if required.

It is intended that the aircraft should be constructed of metal to the order of smoothness required on the full size aircraft and it will provide the works with valuable experience, in the technique to be adopted in this type of construction.

(c) Torsional Stiffness Requirements.

The latest tentative requirements suggested by the R.A.E. are showing a high weight penalty. Much thicker skins have had to be fitted to the wing in order to meet these requirements and while this will help the problem of aerodynamic smoothness, it is felt that the question of the weight penalty is so important that further research on stiffness requirements should be urged in order that a more precise stiffness criterion can be provided.

(d) Rib design.

Whilst this is not difficult in itself, considerable doubt exists as to the intensity and distribution of chord wise air loading on an aircraft of the Delta type. If these conditions are severe the rib weight may be increased.

(e) All-moving wing tip control.

As indicated in (a), section 1, we have provided in our basic layout and design for the development of the tip control. It must be apparent however, that there will be considerable structural difficulties, with perhaps excessive weight penalties in order to bring this form of control to a satisfactory and flutter free state of development. It is felt, therefore, that further investigation should be undertaken on alternative methods of control.

(f) Layout of the crew's nacelle

Now that in response to Telecommunications Radar Establishment (T.R.E.) requirements, the scanner has been mounted in the nose of the crew's nacelle, it is apparent that the conflicting requirements of view for the pilot, the H2S scanner and the visual bomb aimer will require a very careful investigation to arrive at an optimum arrangement.

A considerable alleviation of the problem, both from the standpoint of structural design, as well as general arrangement, would result if a scanner of 4 feet diameter could be used instead of the present model.

(g) Jettisoning of crew nacelle

Difficulty has been experienced in the design of a nacelle attachment strong and rigid enough to withstand normally imposed loads yet capable of being readily and positively broken in an emergency. This item will probably require considerable research.

Airbrakes and/or dive brakes

(h) Wind tunnel investigation on this subject is required

Airbrakes are necessary to prevent float on landing and also to enable engine r.p.m. to be kept up during the approach, in case of a baulked landing. Built-in thrust spoilers may also be required for the latter reason.

Dive brakes will be necessary to prevent the aircraft from exceeding a Mach number beyond which the aerodynamic control is not satisfactory. No information is yet available either on the form which these dive brakes should take or on their location on the aircraft.

(i) Landing technique

It is desired to draw special attention to the need for adequate research work to enable the best technique for landing a Delta aircraft to be arrived at before the design of the full-scale bomber has proceeded too far.

The choice is whether the aircraft should be landed in the normal manner, or whether it should be flown straight on to the ground from a carefully controlled powered approach. In the latter case, special long travel undercarriage units will have to be developed to limit the load factors on impact.

It is felt that this problem should be investigated on the 1/3rd scale model, flight trials being preceded by adequate low-speed wind-tunnel investigation involving ground effect, backed by suitable response calculations.

(j) Air intakes

The present location of the engines just ahead of the rear spar has involved air intakes of 34 feet length so long as leading edge entries are used.

Consequently, an analysis of alternative air intake layouts will be undertaken to ascertain a design which will give optimum performance, taking into account installed weight as well as ram efficiency.

A test in the high-speed tunnel will be necessary to check the high Mach number suitability of any intake proposed as a result of this work.

(k) Control surfaces

As shown in the general arrangement drawing of the 1/3rd scale model our proposals to begin this development involve the use of a control surface hinge at 85% of the chord, as much as possible of the span being used.

The outer portions are intended to operate as ailerons and the remainder as elevators. As much control surface area as possible has been provided with the intention that, as experience is gained, part of the inner portion of the elevators can be fixed, so as to simulate the area occupied by the jet pipes on the full-scale aircraft.

Before the flight stage is reached, it is proposed that the control surface arrangement should be tested in the wind-tunnel at a suitably high Reynold's number.

(l) **Wind tunnel models**

To assist in the research into the above problems, two wind tunnel models will be constructed.

    (a)   A low speed model 1/15th scale to investigate control and air intake problems.

    (b)   A high speed model 1/36th scale to check drag and critical Mach number.

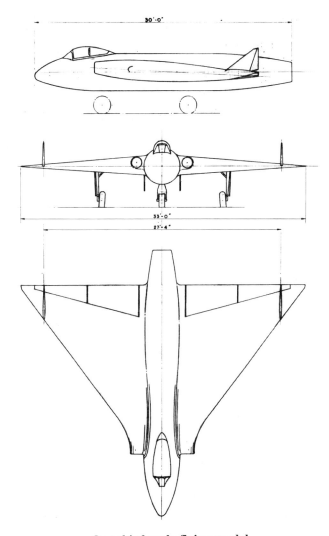

One third scale flying model
Wing Span 33ft. Length 30ft. Total structure weight 2,911 lb. Gross weight 7,972 lb.

Amended design - April 1948

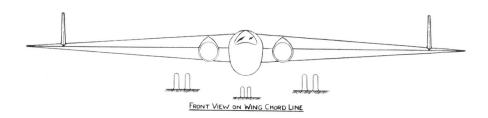

FRONT VIEW ON WING CHORD LINE

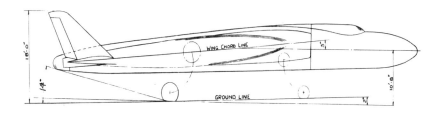

WING CHORD LINE

GROUND LINE

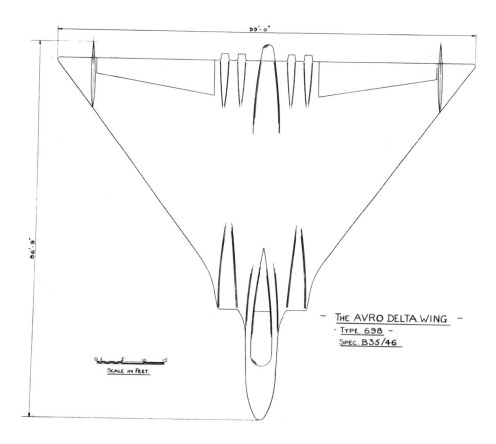

39'-0"

86'-9"

THE AVRO DELTA.WING
- TYPE. 698 -
SPEC. B35/46

SCALE IN FEET.

Inside view

Proposed one third scale model

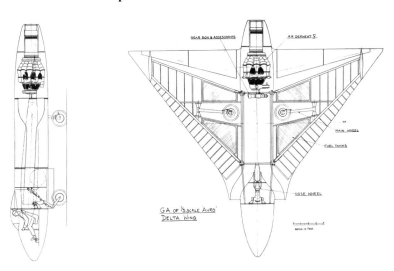

GA of 1/3 SCALE AVRO DELTA WING

Full scale version

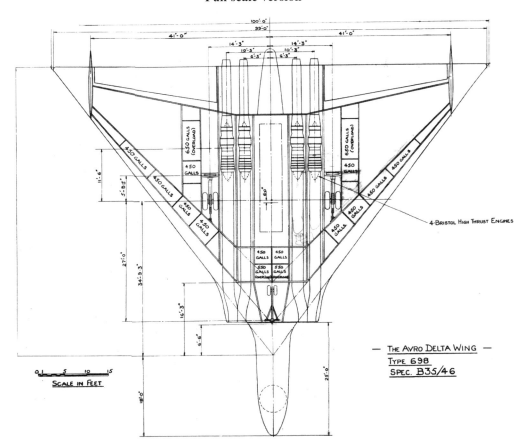

THE AVRO DELTA WING —
TYPE 698
SPEC. B35/46

SCALE IN FEET

Avro Type 710
Half scale flying model

Both the half scale and one third scale models were given an Instruction to Proceed (ITP) on the 8th June, 1948. Serial numbers VX799 and VX808 were allocated to the 710 and VX784, VX790 to the Avro 707 small delta aircraft.

On 30th September William Farren had a meeting with the MoS at Thames House, Chaired by H. M. Garner, the Ministry of Supplies Principle Director of Scientific Research (Air), which involved J. E. Serby, Director of Military Aircraft Research and Development (DMARD), J. G. Willis, Avro project designer, Morien Morgan, who later became Chairman of the Supersonic Transport Aircraft Committee (STAC) in 1956, which led to Concorde and Handel Davies from the Farnborough aero department and the Ministry's H. F. Vessey and H. G. Jones.

It was decided that Avro could drop the 710 half scale flying model, however it was not officially cancelled until the 15th February, 1949.

710 Weight Data

	lbs.	lbs.
Total Structural Weight	6,203	
Total Power Plants x 2 Avon's + accessory items	4,540	
Total Fuel Tanks and System	504	
Other Weights	1400	
Aircraft Equipped Weight		**12,647**
Fuel + Pilot 200lb	7004	
Total Aircraft for take-off		**19,651**

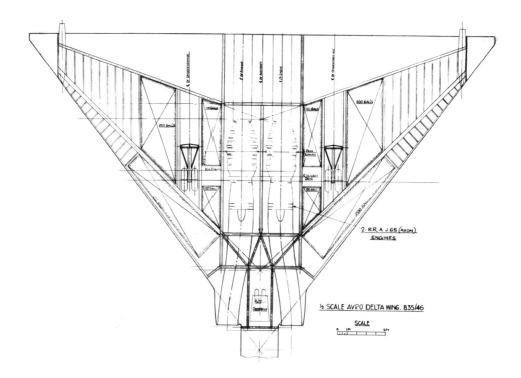

½ SCALE AVRO DELTA WING. B35/46

2- R.R. A.J.65 (AVON) ENGINES

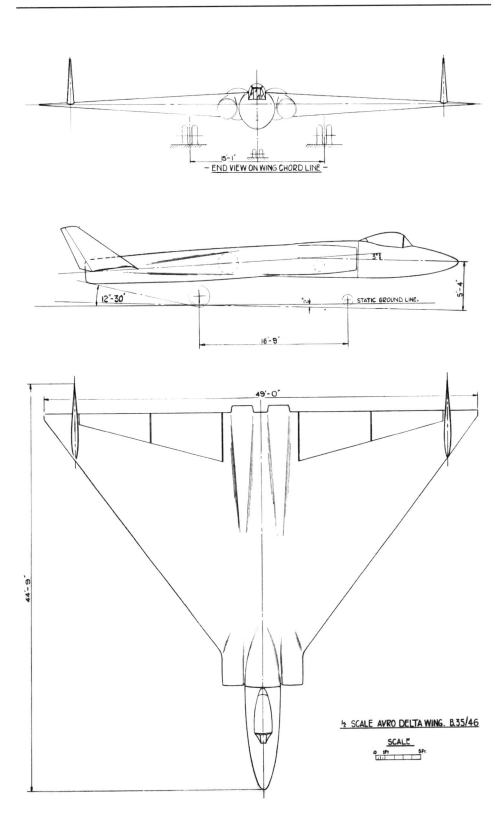

— END VIEW ON WING CHORD LINE —

15'-1"

STATIC GROUND LINE.

12°-30'

5'-4"

3"L

16'-9"

49'-0"

44'-9"

½ SCALE AVRO DELTA WING. B.35/46

SCALE

Design and flight programme - April 1948

The following statement covers the period of time required to design, build and deliver for initial flight test the 1/3rd and 1/2 scale flying models. These periods use the Instruction to Proceed (I.T.P.) for both aircraft as a time datum.

(1) 1/3rd scale model

To completion of design	8 months.
To initial flight test	12 months

Over the design period of eight months, the design man-hours are made up as follows:-

8 draughtsmen in Project Development Office	9600 man-hours.
6 loft men in Full Scale Layout Office	7200 man-hours.
TOTAL.	**16800 man-hours**.

(2) 1/2 scale model

To completion of design	17 months.
To initial flight test	21 months

Over the design period of seventeen months, the design man-hours are made up as follows:-

(a)   First eight months.

4 draughtsmen in Project Development Office	4820 man-hours
10 draughtsmen in Main Design Office	12000 man-hours
2 loft men in Full Scale Layout Office	2400 man-hours

(b)   Last nine months.

12 draughtsmen in Project Development Office	16320 man-hours
10 draughtsmen in Main Design Office	13600 man-hours
6 loft men in Full Scale Layout Office	8160 man-hours
TOTAL	**57,280 man-hours**

Thus, allowing three months for flight trials on the 1/2 scale model it is intended that all necessary design data from the two models should be available in two years from the Instruction to Proceed (I. T. P.).

Strength test specimen

In the interest of safety and structural development, it is proposed to carry out comprehensive strength tests on a complete specimen of the B.35/46 airframe.

We have carefully, considered this matter paying full attention to the various scale specimens the results of our investigations are as follows:-

1. Full Scale Specimen

This is by far the most desirable specimen and would no doubt be most acceptable to the Royal Aircraft Establishment (R.A.E.). The time factor would, however, mean that most of the design work would have to be carried out before the test results were known.

2. Half Scale Specimen
(Built as the full scale aircraft)

This is the next most desirable specimen and it could be expected to give valuable results within a reasonable time. It would, however, require considerable design work additional to that already required for the 1/2 scale flying model. With the existing man-power position this cannot be considered.

3. Half Scale Specimen
(Replica of 1/2 scale flying model)

This is the easiest and quickest solution but it is not acceptable as a representative test. The specimen would be different from that of the full scale aircraft both in main structure and detail and for this reason the results would not be representative, so being of little value in the design of the full-scale machine.

4. Half Scale Specimen
(Compromise)

This alternative would require modification of the proposed design of the flying model, so that both flying model and test specimen were reasonably representative. This would involve complication in design over existing schemes, although the manufacture of the two machines would be identical.

The test results would be of value although not authoritative. Interference with the design programme is, however, again the main objection to this proposal.

From the above investigation we have come to the conclusion that the most desirable specimen and the only one which will be authoritative is the full scale.

We are, therefore, proposing to carry out ourselves a series of tests, as dictated by requirements, on a full scale specimen of the B35/46 airframe. This will, of course, require the design, construction and erection of a suitable test rig, and it is our suggestion that this should consist of a straight forward steel framework designed to support the specimen and loading gear in such a way that the unit is self-contained.

We are at present considering the possibilities of various arrangements, and it is our belief that with the equipment envisaged we would be able to carry out static and repeated loading tests which would be of great value in the development of the B.35/46.

Comparison of wing planforms

Shown are the preliminary investigations into the comparison of different wing planforms produced by Avro to show the advantages of the Delta wing.

The B35/46 specification required a still air range 3,350 nautical miles at 500 knots T.A.S. at 50,000ft mean height, carrying 10,000lb bombs on the out and return journeys.

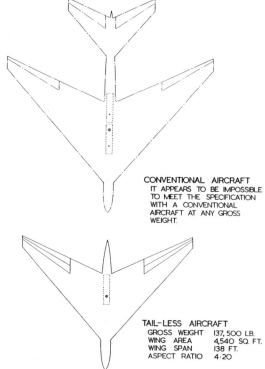

CONVENTIONAL AIRCRAFT
IT APPEARS TO BE IMPOSSIBLE TO MEET THE SPECIFICATION WITH A CONVENTIONAL AIRCRAFT AT ANY GROSS WEIGHT.

DELTA WING AIRCRAFT
GROSS WEIGHT	101,000 LB.
WING AREA	3,340 SQ. FT.
WING SPAN	89 FT.
ASPECT RATIO	2·38

TAIL-LESS AIRCRAFT
GROSS WEIGHT	137,500 LB.
WING AREA	4,540 SQ. FT.
WING SPAN	138 FT.
ASPECT RATIO	4·20

Comparison with OR.230

A more demanding operating requirement OR.230 was issued (further to OR.229 which led to the B35/46 specification). Avro issued a study by the Projects Office in July 1947 on a comparison of the Type 698 with the OR.230 operating requirement, shown below is an extract from that report.

"On finding that the B.35/46 delta wing design could achieve the range called for in OR.230 although at a lower altitude over the target but at the speed of 500 knots, it appeared of interest to know what size delta wing aircraft would be required to meet OR.230 requirements in full, that is to say, to raise the operating altitude from 46,500 ft to 50,000 ft at the target to have full load factors.

The answer was somewhat startling, as it brought the gross weight up to 190,000 lb. This appeared to be a heavy price to pay for an increase in altitude of 3,500 ft at the target. The OR.230 would require four jet engines of 15,000 lb static thrust each compared with the B35/46 four 9,410 lb static thrust engines.

One advantage of the OR.230 would be its ability to carry 30,000 lb of bombs as against 20,000 lb of bombs for B35/46 shorter ranges."

It is interesting to note that when the final version of the Vulcan was produced it had a wing span of 111 ft 0 in, had more powerful engines, the Rolls-Royce Olympus 301 which could develop 20,000 lb static thrust and a maximum take-off weight of 204,000 lb.

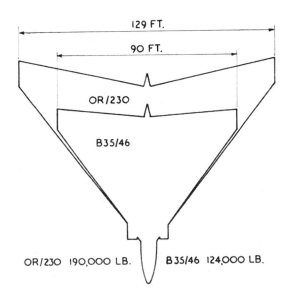

129 FT.

90 FT.

OR/230

B35/46

OR/230 190,000 LB.   B 35/46 124,000 LB.

	OR/230	B35/46
PERFORMANCE SUMMARY		
RANGE-NO ALLOWANCES-N.MLS.	4350	4,350
CRUISING SPEED-KNOTS	500	500
CRUISING MACH NUMBER	0·88	0·88
HEIGHT OVER TARGET-FT.	50,000	46,500
C_L OVER TARGET	0·192	0·184
BOMBS-OUT&RETURN-LB.	10,000	10,000
TAKE OFF GROSS WEIGHT·LB.	190,000	124,000
OVERLOAD LB.	NIL	20,000
FUEL REQUIRED GALLONS	10,550	7,350

GENERAL DATA	OR/230	B35/46
DESIGN GROSS WEIGHT-LB.	190,000	104,000
GROSS WING AREA SQ.FT.	5940	3,364
TAKE OFF WING LOADING-LB./SQ.FT. :—		
A) AT DESIGN GROSS WT.	32·0	31·0
B) AT OVERLOAD GROSS.WT.	–	37·0
C_{Do} (500 KNOTS 50,000 FT.)	0·00705	0·00738
ASPECT RATIO	2·80	2·40
WING SPAN - FT.	129·00	90·00
ROOT CHORD -FT.	79·80	65·00
TIP CHORD · FT.	12·85	9·75
LENGTH O.A.-FT.	120·00	92·00
TOTAL ENGINE STATIC THRUST- LB.	60,000	36,560
NUMBER OF BOMB COMPARTM'TS	3	2
CAPACITY OF EACH BOMB COMPARTMENT :-		
1) SPECIAL BOMB	1	1
2) 10,000 LB.H.C.	1	1
3) 6000 LB.H.C.	2	2
4) 1000 LB.M.C.	10	10

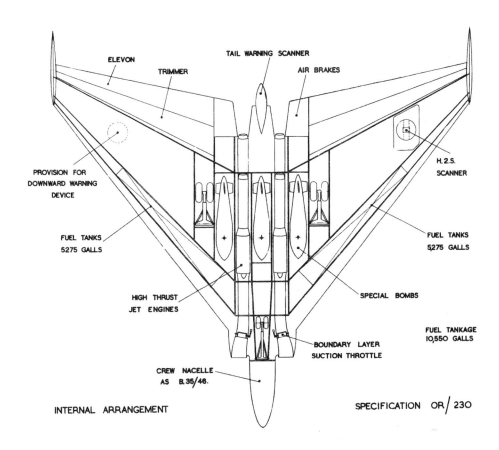

ELEVON

TRIMMER

TAIL WARNING SCANNER

AIR BRAKES

PROVISION FOR
DOWNWARD WARNING
DEVICE

H.2.S.
SCANNER

FUEL TANKS
5275 GALLS

FUEL TANKS
5,275 GALLS

HIGH THRUST
JET ENGINES

SPECIAL BOMBS

FUEL TANKAGE
10,550 GALLS

BOUNDARY LAYER
SUCTION THROTTLE

CREW NACELLE
AS B.35/46.

INTERNAL ARRANGEMENT

SPECIFICATION OR/230

Britain's nuclear bomb

At this stage it worth noting that Avro made reference to a "special bomb" which was in fact a nuclear bomb as envisaged at that time built to Operating Requirement OR1001. It was eventually to be known as Blue Danube and was even larger than Barnes Wallis Tallboy bomb which had a length of 21 ft and a diameter of 38 inches.

The British Government had been aware of the properties of a "super-bomb" as outlined in the 1941, Otto Frisch and Rudolf Peierls memorandum on the effects of a uranium super bomb. Interestingly as both were Germans they were officially classified as "enemy aliens" In fact, the 1941 Maud report was largely based on this memorandum and influenced both American and British thinking on the production of a nuclear bomb.

The first plutonium bomb was built in America and first tested on the 16th July, 1945 in the desert of New Mexico. The U.S.A. had started on the atomic bomb in 1942, with considerable assistance from the British government and physicists. It was scheduled to be dropped on Germany and specific targets had been selected, but with the ending of the war in Europe, it was politically deemed that the war with Japan should come to an early closure. Thus America became the first country to use such a device in anger, on 6th August, 1945, when they dropped a uranium-based weapon on the Japanese City of Hiroshima.

The British venture into building an atomic weapon was for national security, political and diplomatic purposes. A report was prepared by William Penny in October 1946 on the validity of a nuclear weapon, as a result Labour Prime Minister, Clement Attlee and a select group of cabinet ministers decided to proceed with the project on the 8th January, 1947.

The first test of the weapon, known as Operation Hurricane, was detonated on one of the Montebello Islands, Western Australia on 3rd October, 1952. This led to the first deployed weapon, the Blue Danube in November 1953. The warhead was in a ballistic shaped casing with four flip-out fins to ensure a stable ballistic trajectory. Blue Danube started to be replaced in 1958 when production was diverted to the smaller Red Beard, Plutonium nuclear weapon, which became operational in 1961. Blue Danube was retired in 1962.

Shown below is the opening paragraph of the 1941 Otto Frisch and Rudolf Peierls report.

Memorandum on the properties of the
Radioactive "super-bomb"

The attached detailed report concerns the possibility of constructing a "super-bomb" which utilises the energy stored in atomic nuclei as a source of energy. The energy liberated in the explosion of such a super-bomb is about the same as that produced by the explosion of 1,000 tons of dynamite. This energy is liberated in a small volume, in which it will, for an instant, produce a temperature comparable to that in the interior of the sun. The blast from such an explosion would destroy life in a wide area. The size of this area is difficult to estimate, but it will probably cover the centre of a big city.

In addition, some part of the energy set free by the bomb goes to produce radioactive substances, and these will emit very powerful and dangerous radiations. The effect of these radiations is greatest immediately after the explosion, but it decays only gradually and even for days after the explosion any person entering the affected area will be killed.

Some of this radioactivity will be carried along with the wind and will spread the contamination; several miles downwind this may kill people.

Jet engine development

Britain led the way with the rapid development of the jet engine after the Second World War which was the major driving force in the development of high performance aeroplanes. Avro aeroplanes were used to test a wide variety of these engines.

Avro Lancaster with the Manchester based company Metropolitan-Vickers F.2/4 jet engine, Britains early axial flow engine.

Rolls-Royce Nene powered Tudor VIII pictured July 1948. The Derwent V was a scaled down version of the Nene.

ROLLS - ROYCE DERWENT

This engine was to power the Avro Type 707 series of Delta aircraft. The Derwent used a centrifugal compressor and was an improved development of the Rolls-Royce Welland, a renamed version of Frank Whittle's Power Jets W.2B.

Rolls-Royce had inherited the design from Rover when they took over their jet engine development in 1943 and was substantially redesigned over the original Power Jets W.2B/23. It was the second Rolls-Royce jet engine to enter production and was the chosen engine for many post World War Two British jet aircraft.

ROLLS - ROYCE AVON

When the first prototype 698 flew it was powered by four Rolls-Royce Avon jet engines, due to the Bristol Olympus engine not being available. The Avon was the first axial flow engine designed and produced by Rolls-Royce. The engine entered production in 1950, with the original RA.3/Mk101 providing 6,500 lb of thrust. It was also to power the Vickers Valiant bomber.

ARMSTRONG SIDDELEY SAPPHIRE

The Armstrong Siddeley Sapphire started life as the Metropolitan-Vickers F.9 Sapphire which was a larger version of Metrovicks Beryl jet engine. The Beryl was Britain's early attempt at an axial flow engine, from research at the R.A.E. at Farnborough under the guidance of Alan Arnold Griffith who joined Rolls-Royce in 1939 and Hayne Constant. The Sapphire replaced the Rolls-Royce Avon's on the first prototype Vulcan VX770.

BRISTOL OLYMPUS

The Bristol Olympus was to power Service versions of the Vulcan. It provided the development potential required for the Vulcan. It started with a thrust rating for the Vulcan of 9,500 lb which later increased to 20,000 lb thrust. Bristol Siddeley Engines merged with Armstrong Siddeley in 1959 and formed the Bristol Siddeley Company. Rolls-Royce purchased Bristol Siddeley in 1966 and continued the development of the Olympus.

ROLLS - ROYCE CONWAY

The Conway was the main competitor to the Olympus jet engine and was developed within same time period. A development programme was started with Vulcan VX770 in 1957 but tragically halted when VX770 crashed at the Syerston Air Display in 1958. The development programme continued with Vulcan XA902 in 1959. The Conway later went on to power the Handley Page Victor B2.

Major landmarks

By June 1948, two prototypes were ordered to contract 6/acft/1942/CB6(a) dated 22nd June, 1948 and in September 1948, a new major design landmark was reached, the moveable wing tips had disappeared to make way for a central fin and rudder the central fin would also provide for an attachment of a tail plane should this have to prove necessary.

The elevon had been split into elevators and ailerons. Another major change was in the air intake configuration from the large circular "pitot entry" to a rectangular nose entry. The design was pretty much frozen by then with work by the RAE enabling final dimensions to be completed this included the engine intakes and wing leading edge.

The general outline had been hardened to allow design to begin, it was felt however that concern on possible aerodynamic troubles with the configuration it did not justify such an immediate commitment. In view of the fact that the first scale model 707 was scheduled to fly in September 1949, it was felt that final decisions which particularly influenced control layout and design could be deferred for about a year. This programme fitted well within the actual design office commitments at that time. In fact it was not until May 1950, that the first detail drawings were issued.

The air intake configuration changed from the large circular "pitot entry" to a rectangular nose entry.

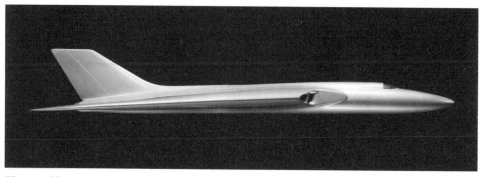

The movable wing tips and wing tip fins had given way to a central fin and rudder.

Brochure description - September 1948

Specification B.35/46 called for a Medium Range Bomber to cruise at a Mach number of 0.875 for a still air range of 3,500 nautical miles at a height of 50.000 feet, with a recommendation that the gross weight should not exceed 100,000 lb.

In order to delay compressibility effect and ensure approaching this high value of M, we have had to adopt a high degree of sweep back, using N.A.C.A. 0010 for the wing section, and to use a small value of cruising C_L which also provides for manoeuvrability margin.

The operational height necessitates a jettisonable cabin for the crew.

The Radar H2S requirements and limitations necessitate that it should be in the nose of the aircraft.

The dimensions of the special bomb require a large compartment free from structural obstructions.

A tail warning scanner is also a necessity.

These requirements dictated the minimum frontal area and size of the fuselage.

By virtue of the considerable sweepback and comparatively low wing loading, together with certain structural limitations in housing the bomb and engines, the C.G. was required at about 0.33 of mean chord.

The foregoing requirements and restrictions were conveniently met by the Delta layout shown in the brochure.

DEVELOPMENT PROGRAMME

In view of the fact that full scale aerodynamic data on Delta aircraft is practically non-existent, it is deemed necessary to build a Third Scale flying model. Primarily we want to be assured of satisfactory flying and control qualities at comparatively low speed research. In order to simplify our design problems and to accelerate the completion of the aircraft, therefore, the first model will be designed for speeds up to the order of 300 knots E.A.S. Additionally, a considerable number of existing component parts are being built into the aircraft.

Depending on the result we get from this model, we may decide to build a slightly modified version capable of attaining higher speeds.

The next stage in the development would be to make a full scale flying model which would be considerably simplified from the final prototype to the extent of deleting the complicated Service fuel system and bomb bays, Service equipment etc., as well as making no provision for the jettisonable nacelle. Advantage will be taken in building this model to incorporate the final design of wing. This would also accelerate the structural test programme.

Our estimate for first flying dates for these aircraft is approx. As follows:-
Third Scale Mid 1949.
Special simplified full scale 1950.
First complete prototype 1951.

STRUCTURE

The airframe, which is, of course, mostly wing structure, has been designed to meet a maximum factored acceleration of 4.5g. The wing will be constructed to provide laminar flow over about 20% of the chord.

It consists basically of a box beam in the forward part of the wing, together with a rear spar at 80% of the chord. Between these two spars, ribs are mounted to support the numerous stringers which, in turn, support the large area of wing skin. Forward of the box beam is a stiff leading edge covered with 12 S.W.G. skin in which is installed the structure for the thermal de-icing system. Where heavy concentrated big loads occur such as at the undercarriage, engines etc., stiffened plate web ribs are used. In the engine bays the support ribs are made of steel where necessary to meet the fire prevention requirements, and adjacent light alloy structure, is protected by the addition of steel shields.

The box beam consists of two main spars, at 10% and 25% chord with upper and lower surfaces of 12 S.W.G. skin stiffened with Zed type extruded stringer. Beam or girder type channel section ribs are mounted between the spars to support the stringers. Cells for the flexible fuel tanks are put into the box beam, inner skins being added as necessary, while between the tank cells bulkhead ribs are fitted serving the double purpose of dividing the cells and providing rigidity of the box.

Aft of the box beam braced ribs are used, supported at the beam and at the rear spar. Rolled section top hat stringers are fitted span wise to support the skin between the spars, the ribs themselves not being attached to the skin but supporting only the stringers. Most of the wing skin between the spars is of 16 S.W.G., which together with the 12 S.W.G. skin of the nose and box beam, combine to give adequate torsion stiffness on the basis of stiffness criteria for conventional wings.

The crew's nacelle, which is basically of semi-monocoque construction, is secured to the airframe proper by four pick-up points, all of which can be instantaneously broken, together with controls etc., to enable the nacelle to be jettisoned.

CREW NACELLE

The problem here is to provide stability to the nacelle after jettisoning. We may accomplish this by a combination of drogues with ejection from the body of the aircraft. Investigations are in hand to determine the best way of doing this. Notice the sliding doors for the bomb site in the drawing shown.

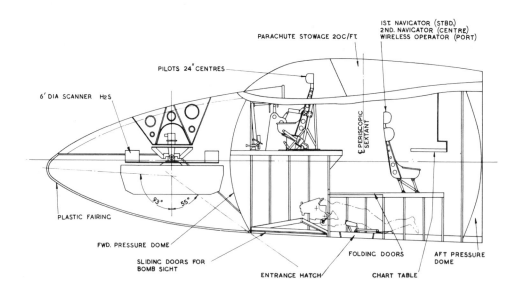

CONTROLS

These will be provided by the inner half of the trailing edge acting as elevator, and the outer half as ailerons.

A conventional central fin and rudder is provided of approximately the same sweepback as the wing.

We anticipate that the aircraft will be controllable up to probably a little more than M=0.9 with this arrangement. Although this satisfies the specification requirements, we are providing air brakes to prevent excessive speed in certain manoeuvres.

At the high speeds envisaged, control forces will be large. To attempt to operate conventional aerodynamically balanced surfaces directly would require prohibitively large power controls. We propose to provide a power servo tab system. The servo tab may be partially spring controlled in order to provide some adjustable coupling with the main surface over small angles, which should facilitate power adjustment.

Additionally, the design of the swept central fin is such that a tailplane could be fitted, should we encounter trouble during the course of flight tests.

POWER PLANTS

The final bomber will be equipped with four Bristol high-thrust jet engines which give a maximum sea level static thrust of 9140 lb.

Engine accessories are mounted on the engine itself, but the aircraft accessories would be duplicated on two auxiliary gearbox. We are endeavouring to arrange these gearbox in such a manner that each is driven by two engines through freewheel drives. Should we find this too difficult, the alternative is to drive a gearbox from each outboard engine, the accessories being arranged in order to provide suitable duplication.

The air intake design is being investigated. The first proposal is shown on the general arrangement drawing and is a leading edge ram entry at the wing root. This arrangement is well tried and should give good results, both as regards intake efficiency and profile drag.

The second proposal is for an under wing flush air intake just aft of the main spar. This type of entry is new in conception, and research into its characteristics will be necessary before its properties can be assessed. One of the advantages of this arrangement is that space becomes available to increase the tankage by probably another 3,000 gallons if required.

FUEL SYSTEM

The fuel system has not yet been developed in detail, but certain principles are established. Flexible crash proof tanks will be fitted, with provision for pressure refuelling. Each tank will have an electric booster pump. In view of the considerable fore and aft distance over which the fuel tanks are placed, an automatic system will be required for feeding fuel to the engines without appreciable C.G. movement.

AIR CONDITIONING

Independent two-stage blower systems will be fitted, one to either auxiliary gearbox. The cabin will be pressurised to a maximum differential pressure of 9 lb. /sq. in which is sufficient to give 8,000 feet cabin conditions at an altitude of 47,000 feet, which is the commencement of the cruise. At the end of the cruise, with bombs gone, the height has risen to 58,800 feet, and the cabin height will have increased to 10,000 feet by virtue of the 9 lb./sq. in. in maximum differential pressure.

At a cruising altitude of 50,000 ft, about half the heat required in the cabin under Sub-Arctic winter conditions is supplied by the blowers. The output of the 40,000 B.T.U. /hr combustion heater is decided by the requirement for deflation to 25,000 feet cabin conditions over the target.

Refrigeration equipment is needed to provide cabin cooling to the extent of 17,500 B.T.U. /hr. This will enable the cabin temperature to be kept down to 90° while, operating on the ground under Tropical Summer conditions (106°F ambient).

UNDERCARRIAGE

A tricycle undercarriage has been provided which retracts completely within the basic outline of the wing and nacelle.

The nose wheel is of simple design and is housed in the nacelle immediately aft of the jettisonable cabin. Nose wheel steering is provided to facilitate manoeuvring on the ground.

The main undercarriage is of unusual design in that each leg is fitted with two wheels, each wheel, having twin tyres mounted side by side. This arrangement gives an adequately small tyre diameter, so that the wheel retraction does not cause bumps on the lower wing surface. A tyre pressure of 85 lb. /sq. in. will be used for the normal gross weight of 110,000 lbs. It is considered that this will permit satisfactory operation from standard heavy bomber runways. The tyre pressure will be 95 lb. /sq. in. for the overload gross weight of 125,000 lbs.

DRAG

The component drag analysis was made using the RAeS. Aerodynamic Data Sheets. Laminar flow was assumed up to a transition point of 20% chord on wing and fin. Transition taken at the nose of the fuselage. Reynolds numbers were taken for V=500 knots at 50,000ft. Drag on the wing by integration of drag at 20 chord wise positions. Wing t/c = 10% at 0.3c.

Parasitic drag breakdown at 100ft per sec is a follows:-

	Plan Area. (sq.ft.)	Surface Area. (sq. ft.)	Reynolds No.	C_{Do}	Do at 100ft/sec.
Wing.	2738		$10.29 \times 10^5 xc$	.00466	180 lb.
Fuselage.	-	1275	90.5×10^6	0.00231	35 lb.
Canopy (2).	-	74.4	13×10^6	0.00340	3 lb.
Fin	228	-	16×10^6	0.00590	16 lb.
				TOTAL.	**234 lb.**
Air Intakes					14 lb.
Exhaust Pipe Bulges					2 lb.
Interference, leaks etc.. (7%).					17.5 lb.
				TOTAL PARASITIC DRAG.	**267.5 lb.**

Based on gross wing area of 3250 sq. ft.

$C_{Do} = 0.00692$

Induced drag is based on the equation:-

$$C_{Cdi} = \frac{1.24C_L^2}{\pi A} = 0.1309C_L^2$$

(Note, the Greek letter "pi" in the denominator and A for Aspect ratio)
We consider the span factor of 1.24 to be reasonable in the light of past experience and comparable calculations for Delta aircraft. By 1951 the factor of 1.24 was changed to 1.1 following wind tunnel tests and flights with the Avro 707B.

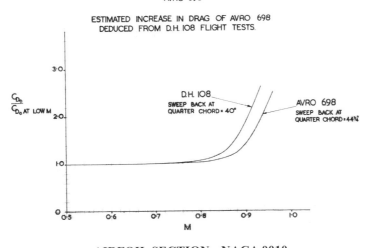

AVRO 698

ESTIMATED INCREASE IN DRAG OF AVRO 698
DEDUCED FROM D.H. 108 FLIGHT TESTS.

AIRFOIL SECTION - NACA 0010

The NACA airfoils are airfoil shapes for aircraft wings developed by the National Advisory Committee for Aeronautics (NACA). The shape of the NACA airfoils is described using a series of digits following the word "NACA." The parameters in the numerical code can be entered into equations to precisely generate the cross-section of the airfoil and calculate its properties. Note: Sir George Caley did a cross section of a trout which was similar in cross section to that used on the Vulcan.

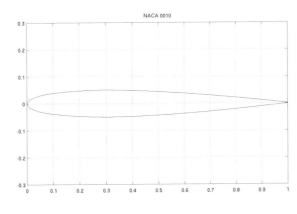

NACA 0010

Wind tunnel testing

Type 698 model at the R.A.E. 11ft high speed wind tunnel, autumn 1951.

The wing tunnel programme was divided into low-speed and high-speed portions, the former being carried out jointly by Avro, the R.A.E. and the National Physical Laboratory, and the high-speed part being undertaken solely by the R.A.E., whose 11 ft wind tunnel was at that time the only one in the country capable of handling such work.

Avro had investigated the effect of planform and section modifications on the characteristics of the aircraft at high subsonic speeds up to and above the design cruising lift coefficients. These tests indicated that substantial improvements in both the drag-rise critical Mach number and the drag rise with increase in lift coefficient could be realised by modifying the wing sections across the span.

The reasoning behind these improvements was that the characteristics of a wing at high Mach numbers were closely related to the sweepback of the maximum-suction line, and this is adversely affected by root and tip effects. At the root the peak-suction line tends to become normal to the centre-line to attain continuity, and this causes a reduction in sweep over the inner part of the wing. At the tip the high induced incidences move the peak-suction line forward, again reducing its sweep. The R.A.E. therefore evolved a wing in which the maximum thickness of the wing sections was progressively moved forward from tip to root and the sweepback of the peak-suction line maintained over a much greater proportion of the span than on a wing of similar planform but with constant section throughout.

So advantageous were the effects of this modification that early in 1950 the 698 wing was redesigned to incorporate the R.A.E. recommendations. Although unchanged in planform, the new wing had a section which was progressively modified to bring the point of maximum thickness very near to the leading edge at the root; the flow in this area was in any case appreciably influenced by the fact that the inboard portions of the wing were occupied by the power plants and their ducting.

To some extent the modified surface can be described as a crescent wing (chosen by Handley Page for the H.P.80) contained within a delta planform, the latter giving increased area and easing the structural problems.

Summarised, the following were the other wind tunnel programmes in the initial stages: R.A.E. high-speed tunnel, fully representative model of the 698 and half-wing pressure-plotting model; R.A.E. low-speed tunnel, complete model with intakes; Avro low-speed wind tunnel, complete model without intakes, in addition to load and pressure measurements on canopies, bomb doors, undercarriage, airbrakes and similar components; and N.P.L. compressed-air tunnel, various tests over a wider range of Reynolds numbers than could be obtained in the other tunnels.

Long before the wing was finally settled Avro had embarked on a massive programme of basic aerodynamic research. Broadly speaking, the following were the principal questions posed by the new configuration: what was the maximum usable lift coefficient likely to be achieved by the full-scale wing; would the combination of low wing loading and low aspect ratio require exaggerated angles of attack at take-off and landing; would the stalling behaviour of the wing have serious effects on longitudinal stability; would the aircraft be unduly sensitive to c.g. travel, and what useful c.g. range would be achieved without a tailplane; and how would the aircraft fly when it was subjected to compressibility.

Most of the high-subsonic stability and control problems were quite capable of being settled by wind tunnel testing, but Avro felt that the crucial problem of unpredictable behaviour at take-off and landing could be properly resolved only by building a manned research aeroplane representing a scale model of the eventual 698.

At this point it is worth noting the work of Osborne Reynolds at Manchester University. During his 37 years at the University he devoted himself to classical mechanics, in 1873 he studied fluid mechanics and introduced the concept of "Reynolds Number" in 1883, for which he was to become best known.

This parameter is used to characterise different flow instabilities, such as laminar or turbulent flow: laminar flow occurs at low Reynolds numbers, where viscous forces are dominant, and is characterised by smooth, constant fluid motion, while turbulent flow occurs at high Reynolds numbers and is dominated by inertial forces, which tend to produce random eddies, vortices and other flow instabilities.

An ideal situation would be to test the wind tunnel model at the same Reynolds Number that the aeroplane experiences in flight, in order to achieve "dynamic similarity". In an atmospheric tunnel this requires a quarter scale model to be subject to four times the flight velocity, which is rarely possible in practice in such a tunnel. The National Physical Laboratory (NPL) compressed-air tunnel goes some way to overcoming this difficulty.

Reynolds number is important in the calculation of a body's drag characteristics. This is important when calculating the optimal cruise speeds for low drag (and therefore long range) profiles for aeroplanes.

As stated Avro was using the RAE wind tunnels at Farnborough for drag analysis. This was to prove particularly useful in the design of the engine intakes as shown in the September 1948 brochure; these intakes had led to unacceptable drag rise and the R.A.E. suggesting that Avro were due for a set back.

Avro decided to redesign the engine intakes at the root and this led to a three month delay to the issue of detailed drawings to the works.

Wind tunnel models showing the final intake design, the picture also shows the one quarter scale wooden model taken, December 1954.

Proposed twin cockpit design - August 1948

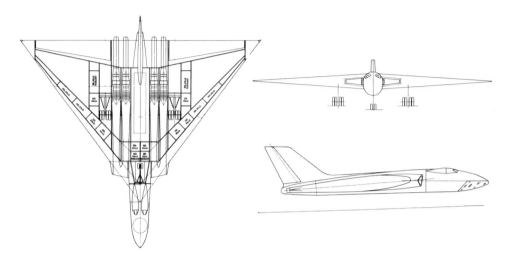

Amended Type 698 design - September 1948

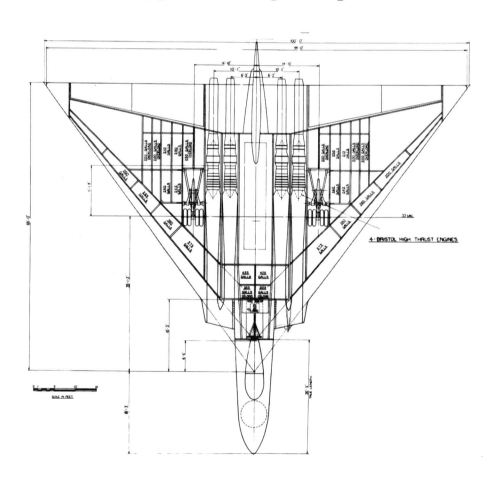

Lightened version prototype

Four Rolls-Royce AJ 65 (Avon) power plants

Weight data

	Weight lbs.	% Take-off weight
Structures	27,210	41.862
Power	12,312	18.957
Fuel & Oil Supply	750	1.153
Fixed Services	3,000	4.616
Fixed Equipment	2,640	4.062
Contingency	684	1.052
Tare Weight	**46,600**	**71.692**
Removable load crew two at 200 lb each	400	.615
Basic Operationally Equipped Weight	**47,000**	**72.307**
Bomb, Payload, Freight, Fuel and Oil	18,000	27.693
Take-off weight	**65,000**	**100.000**

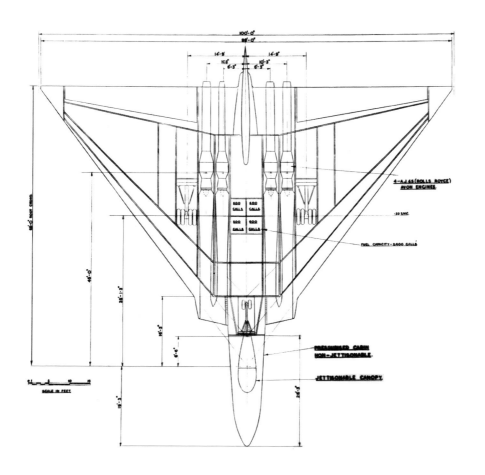

Effects of typical failures on performance

In the event of failure of two engines it is not possible to fly at 500 knots at any height or weight. For example if one or two engines fails over target as the bomb is dropped and pressure cabin failure, height reduced to 38,000 ft.

Flight plan low level

Effect on range and weight of descending to 2000ft over the target

So far we have only considered the capabilities of the aeroplane in a straight forward flight plan. Technical requirements may necessitate using this aircraft for marker technique, which may mean descending to about 2,000 feet in the vicinity of the target for a short period of time we have, therefore, prepared a curve to show the effect on gross weight and range of such a flight plan, flying at 500 knots over the target for 15 minutes.

The higher speed at 2,000 feet increases the structure weight by 1,500 lb. Since a marker bomb of maybe 2,000 lb. would be used instead of the special bomb, the 8,000 lb. difference in weight could contribute towards the additional fuel required to complete the specification range.

For this operation, therefore, the gross weight might be in the region of about 113,000 lb. at take-off.

This flight plan is, of course, only permissible providing the structure is stiffened up as required.

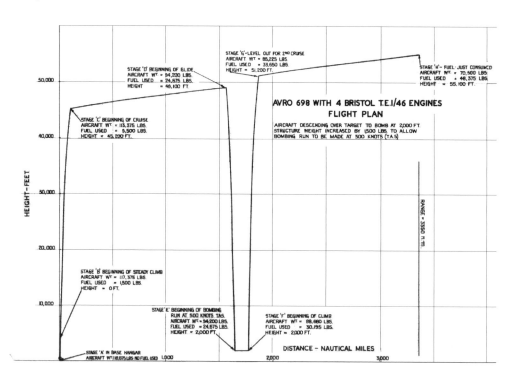

Test rig proposal - September 1948

The B35/46 contract called for a full size structural test specimen, shown is an extract from that report dated 22nd September, 1948.

Requirements

To test a complete aircraft reproducing the conditions appropriate to the worst stressing case or cases in a manner which will put loading on the specimen approaching as nearly as possible to that which actually occurs during the particular manoeuvre being considered.

General Description

The aircraft is constrained in the vertical, and fore and aft planes but is free to rotate laterally. A stabilising system is used to prevent any appreciable amount of unbalance in roll, but this has at present not been considered in detail.

The most important part of the rig is a reinforced concrete floor in which there are strong points at 8' 0" pitch patterned in squares. Each of these points will have a load carrying capacity of 15 tons tension on which the normal factor of 4 is required, making the failing load 60 tons. A compression load of at least equal magnitude to the tensile one is necessary.

The strong points themselves when not in use will be flush with the surface of the floor, which in turn will be flush with the surrounding hangar floor. When a point is to be picked up it would be screwed out from the floor until there was sufficient clearance to fit the attachments.

Load Application

Load would be applied through hydraulic tension jacks, all of which are coupled to a common hydraulic reservoir so that the pressure in each jack is the same. The reservoir is fed by three "Dowty Live Line Mk.5." pumps driven by 1.25 h.p. electric motors at 1420 r.p.m. which we have already. - This arrangement will facilitate loading the specimen to 100% factored load in $5^{1}/_{2}$ minutes.

Counterpoising

The specimen is fully counterpoised. Only in the case of the nose is a special structure necessary to carry counterpoise weight. In other cases the loading gantries will serve as counterpoise weight supports. The general method is to balance each portion of the structure and the linkage, probably separately, by hanging weighted pans from the overhead structure with wire ropes and pulleys. Approximately 17 tons of lead is required for this.

Location

The rig is to be either in a new building, or in No.5 Hangar at the Flight Sheds, Woodford. Hangar No.5 has ample room for the rig.

Size of rig for future aircraft

On the general arrangement drawing RD.14.31/1 an outline of a larger rig is shown. This, it is felt, would cater for any type of aircraft - Delta Wing or conventional up to 150,000 lb. A.U.W. The strong points would still only require to be of 15 tons load carrying capacity as the intensity of loading would not increase. However, the larger floor would not accommodate the nose of a conventional aircraft, but 20 ft. of ordinary reinforced concrete hangar floor, aft of the rear of the special floor would allow this, and we know that ordinary floor would deal with these nose loads. There is sufficient space in the hangar to accommodate this 20 ft.

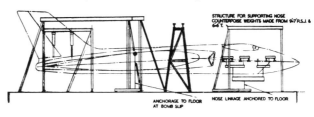

Third scale flying model - September 1948

DESCRIPTION

As mentioned under the Development Programme, this aircraft is primarily intended to provide data covering low speed flying and control qualities of Delta aircraft. To this end, the first aircraft will be limited to the maximum speed of 300 knots E.A.S, in order to simplify design problems and accelerate its completion. As will be seen from the general arrangement drawing, this aircraft is considerably out of scale as regards the wing body combination. The aircraft is provided with one Derwent engine mounted in the rear of the fuselage aft of the rear spar. Provision is made in the forward section for a single pilot and aft of the pilot for automatic observers recording of essential flight data. This aircraft utilised many existing components such as Athena controls and undercarriage, also Meteor nose wheel and pilot's canopy. A single fuel tank of approximately 210 gallons is mounted on the c.g. of the aircraft, this provides for about 30 minutes cruising at height.

It was thought desirable to provide conventional aerodynamically balanced controls, these occupied the whole of the trailing edge, the inner half was used for elevator, the outer half for aileron. Calculations and wind tunnel tests have showed that a central fin was necessary in order to provide desirable l_v and n_v qualities.

The general performance figures showed the capabilities of this aircraft into the high speed range. It was seen that with reasonable allowance for compressibility effects, the aircraft should be capable of reaching a Mach number of .9 in normal flight between 35,000 and 40,000 feet.

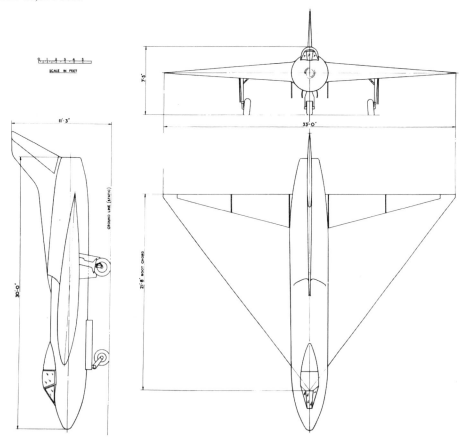

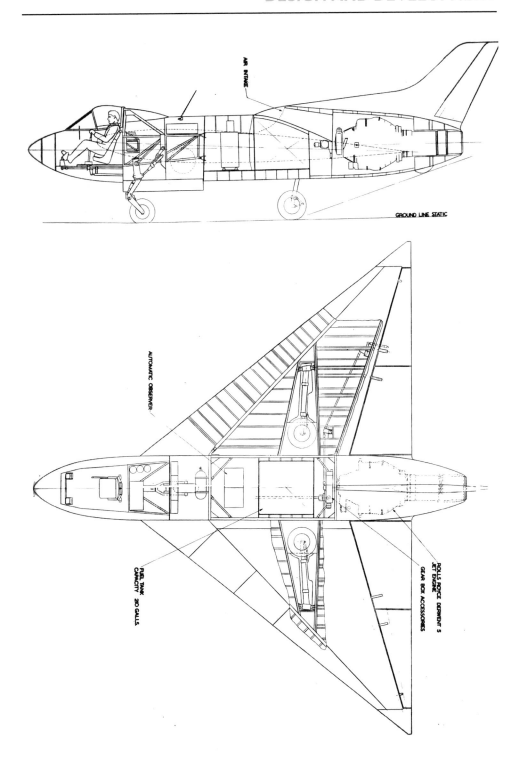

In May 1948, detail of the first Type 707 third scale delta commenced in the Chadderton Drawing Office and by June 1948, the first general Type 707 arrangement and line drawings were issued to the shops for tooling and planning purposes.

Type 707 - Ministry of Supply specification

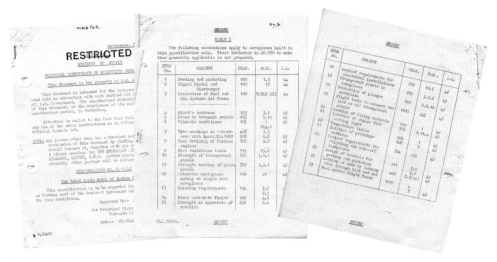

On 22nd October, 1948 a document was issued for the manufacture of a one third scale model of medium bomber to specification no. E.15/48. It was issued by the Ministry of Supply, Principle Directorate of Scientific Research (Air), to A. V. Roe. It was amended when the first 707 tragically crashed.

I. GENERAL

1.01   This specification is issued to cover the design and construction of a one third scale model of the A.V. Roe medium range bomber design to Specification B.35/46 (Issue II).

1.02   This specification states only the particular requirements for the type in amplification of the current general design requirements stated in:

(i)   A.P.970 (Restricted Edition) with amendments up to and including AL48.

(ii)   Aircraft Design Memoranda and Standard Instruction Sheets current on 1st April, 1948 and these requirements, shall be completely fulfilled except where

(a)   varied by this specification or

(b)   where the prior written concurrence of the P.D.S.R.(A) has been obtained or

(c)   where, due to the unconventional nature of the design, departures are necessary and cannot readily be anticipated, in which case the concurrence of the P.D.S.R.(A) shall be obtained at the earliest possible opportunity.

1.0.3   Subsequent chapter references in this specification are to A.P.970 (Restricted Edition as amended by AL.48 AL.2 in all cases.

II. OPERATING REQUIREMENTS

General

2.01   The aircraft is required to reproduce and investigate the low speed control and stability characteristics of the full scale aircraft.

Performance

2.02   All performance requirements relate to the ICAN standard atmosphere.

2.03   The maximum level speed should be at least 350 knots E.A.S. altitude up to 10,000 ft.

2.04   Sufficient fuel shall be provided for the following:- engine starting, take-off and climb to 30,000 feet, 15 minutes at full throttle followed by 30 minutes cruising at that height.

2.05   The take-off distance to 50 feet shall not exceed 1,200 yards at the all-up weight defined by paragraph 5.01.

2.06   The landing distance from 50 feet shall not exceed 1,200 yards a with half fuel remaining.

Crew accommodation

2.07   Provision is required for a pilot. An ejection seat need not be fitted provided that the maximum permissible flying speed does not exceed 300 knots E.A.S.

Amendment.

2.08   *(i) An ejector seat shall be fitted and shall satisfy the requirements of Chapter 735 issued with A.L. No.45 to A.P.970. (ii) Consequential changes to the design shall include such provisions as are necessary to enable the stability requirements of Chapter 601 paragraphs 8 and 9 to be met.*

III. DESIGN REQUIREMENTS

3.01   The aircraft shall be fitted with one Derwent 5 engine.

3.02   In interpreting the requirements of Chapter 703, paragraph 2, the aircraft shall be suitable for aerobatics including inverted flying for 15 seconds.

Controls

3.03   The inner portion of the trailing edge controls shall operate as elevators and the outer portions as ailerons. Rudders shall be provided for directional control. *(Wing)* Air brakes shall be fitted to allow the speed of the aircraft to be limited.

Tyre Pressures

3.04   The limits of Chapter 301; paragraph 3, need not be observed.

Brakes Emergency System.

3.05.   An emergency system capable of operating the air brakes should the normal system fail shall be provided.

IV. EQUIPMENT

General

4.01   Equipment shall be fitted or provided for in accordance with the Appendix 'A' to this Specification (No.1824).

Radio

4.02   Duplicated VHF. equipment is required.

Anti-spin Parachute

4.03   An anti-spin parachute shall be installed in accordance with Chapter 716 of A.P.970.

V. STRENGTH STIFFNESS

Stressing Weight

5.01   Strength calculations for tale-off, flight and landing shall be based on the maximum all up weight of the aircraft when carrying full fuel and equipment.

Main Flight Cases

5.02   In the basic flight envelope of Chapter 201 the following shall be assumed:- $n_1 = 6.7$

$V_D = 400$ knots E.A.S. or a speed equivalent to a Mach No.of 0.8, whichever is less.

Alighting and Take-off

5.03   The requirements of Chapter 304 with amendments up to and including AL.43 shall be met on the weight defined by para 5.01. AL.2.

Avro Type 707 (VX784)

The issue drawings commenced in June 1948, with the complete aircraft assembled at Woodford in August 1949. After preliminary taxiing trials it was dismantled and transferred by road to the Aeroplane and Armament Experimental Establishment at Boscombe Down on August 26th, 1949.

The aircraft was ready to fly on 4th September, 1949 Eric Esler took off at 7.50 pm and after a twenty minute flight, landed in half light. Short flights continued on the following two days and on the 6th September Esler flew to Farnborough where it was a static exhibit during the rest of the SBAC Show. During this period there were five flights totalling two hours thirty minutes and the general results were extremely favourable. Unfortunately on 30th September the aircraft crashed near Blackbushe airfield, Hampshire, killing Eric Esler at the early age of 31, a verdict of accidental death was returned at the inquest.

Early model from the September 1948 tender brochure.

The Type 707 contract E15/48 was issued in June 1948.

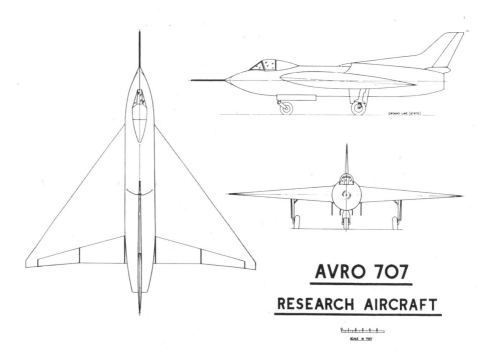

AVRO 707

RESEARCH AIRCRAFT

Final general arrangement drawing of the first 707, flown by Avro test pilot Eric Esler.

Design history

With the instruction to design and build the first 707 in January, 1948 it was agreed between the Ministry and the Company right from the start that as the primary object was to provide design data for the 698 and not to act as a research aircraft on delta in general, the details of the design would be settled by Avro.

Furthermore, as the main object was to explore low speed flying characteristics there was no need to complicate the design by specifying an unduly high performance. The maximum E.A.S. was fixed at 400 knots and the limiting Mach No. at 0.85. The ministry staff confined their efforts to specifying and agreeing the design speeds, overall strength factors and most importantly agreeing to the derogations from Ministry Air Publication (AP.970), which was necessary to ensure that the first prototype was built at speed.

No power controls were fitted; all controls were fitted with elliptic type nose balances and geared tabs.

It was recognised that some form of air brake would be required, but ideas in this respect were far from fixed. The 707 design provided for flap type brake at the rear end of the fuselage and under wing flaps at the centre section in the vicinity of the front spar. Wind tunnel test before flight showed that the fuselage brakes were liable to produce considerable disturbances on the rudder and these were locked out of action.

The aircraft was built to specification E.15/48 reference number 7/Acft/3715/RDT2 dated 22nd October, 1948 which was issued to Avro on 31st November, 1948. The issue of drawings for the first Avro Type707 commenced in June 1948 and progress was rapid with the complete aircraft assembled in August 1948.

Description

The first 707 was designed primarily for research into the control and stability characteristics of the swept back wing aerofoil at low speeds. Power was supplied by a single Rolls-Royce Derwent V turbo jet engine, housed in the rear section fuselage, giving a static nominal thrust or 3,600 lb at sea level conditions. A tricycle undercarriage was fitted; with the nose wheel retracting rearwards into the fuselage structure and the two main wheel units retracting inwards into the wing.

The fuselage is constructed of three jig-built sections comprising a nose and a rear section, the latter being divided into two separate assemblies designated as front and rear portions. The nose accommodated the pilot's cockpit and the nose wheel undercarriage; the front portion of the rear section housed the automatic observer panels, fuel tank and engine air intake, incorporating also the wing spar attachment joints; the rear portion formed the engine installation structure and the jet pipe outlet and carried the rear-wards sloping fin and rudder. A tail skid was fitted on the undersurface of the fuselage below the jet pipe and housing for a G.Q. anti-spin parachute was located below the rudder and incorporated a detachable end cap. Two fuselage air brakes were fitted and located one on each side of the fuselage below the rudder unit. These were deleted on later versions of 707 aircraft.

Each wing was of the two spar, stressed skin type, having a leading edge sweepback of 52 degrees 27 minutes. Both ailerons and elevators were hinged on brackets attached to the rear spar with the elevators inboard, the two components forming the wing trailing edge. The Lockheed main wheel undercarriage units were supported by front and rear beams located between the spars. Each beam was attached to the front portion of the rear section fuselage at the inboard end and to the inner face of the front spar at the outboard end. An air brake was also fitted forward of each undercarriage bay in the wing undersurface, this was deleted on later versions of 707 test aircraft.

AVRO TYPE 707

DESCRIPTIVE
AND
MAINTENANCE NOTES

Close up view of the unique engine air intake.

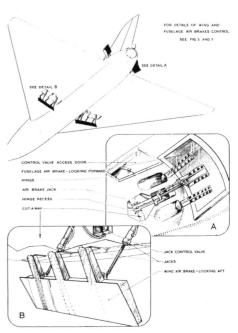

FOR DETAILS OF WING AND
FUSELAGE AIR BRAKES CONTROL
SEE FIG.5 AND 7.

SEE DETAIL A

SEE DETAIL B

CONTROL VALVE ACCESS DOOR

FUSELAGE AIR BRAKE – LOOKING FORWARD

HINGE

AIR BRAKE JACK

HINGE RECESS

CUT AWAY

A

JACK CONTROL VALVE

JACKS

WING AIR BRAKE – LOOKING AFT

B

FIG.6 WING AND FUSELAGE AIR BRAKES

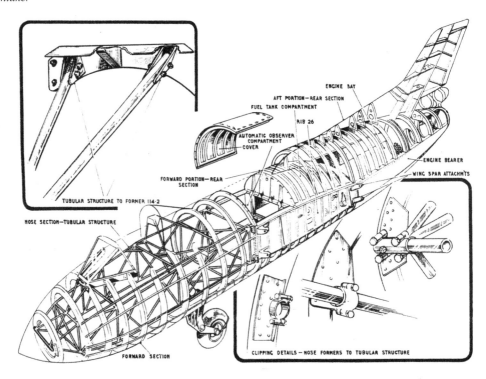

TUBULAR STRUCTURE TO FORMER 114·2

NOSE SECTION – TUBULAR STRUCTURE

ENGINE BAY

AFT PORTION – REAR SECTION

FUEL TANK COMPARTMENT

RIB 26

AUTOMATIC OBSERVER
COMPARTMENT
COVER

FORWARD PORTION – REAR
SECTION

ENGINE BEARER

WING SPAR ATTACHMNTS

FORWARD SECTION

CLIPPING DETAILS – NOSE FORMERS TO TUBULAR STRUCTURE

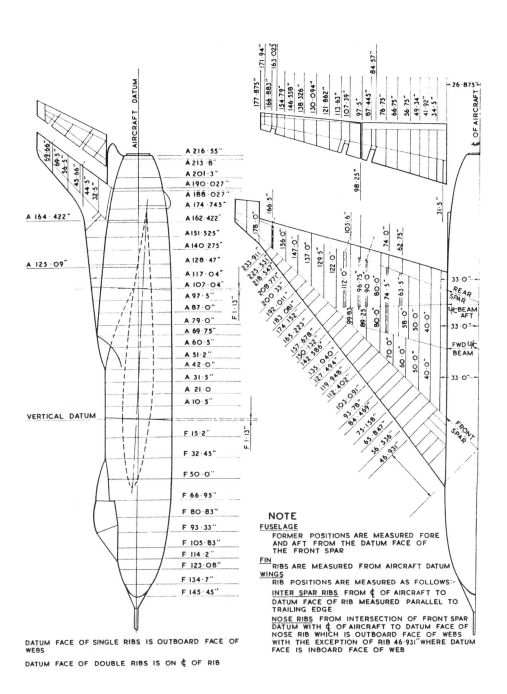

FIG. 2 FORMER & RIB POSITIONS

NOTE

FUSELAGE
FORMER POSITIONS ARE MEASURED FORE
AND AFT FROM THE DATUM FACE OF
THE FRONT SPAR

FIN
RIBS ARE MEASURED FROM AIRCRAFT DATUM

WINGS
RIB POSITIONS ARE MEASURED AS FOLLOWS:-

INTER SPAR RIBS FROM ₵ OF AIRCRAFT TO
DATUM FACE OF RIB MEASURED PARALLEL TO
TRAILING EDGE

NOSE RIBS FROM INTERSECTION OF FRONT SPAR
DATUM WITH ₵ OF AIRCRAFT TO DATUM FACE OF
NOSE RIB WHICH IS OUTBOARD FACE OF WEBS
WITH THE EXCEPTION OF RIB 46·931" WHERE DATUM
FACE IS INBOARD FACE OF WEB

DATUM FACE OF SINGLE RIBS IS OUTBOARD FACE OF
WEBS

DATUM FACE OF DOUBLE RIBS IS ON ₵ OF RIB

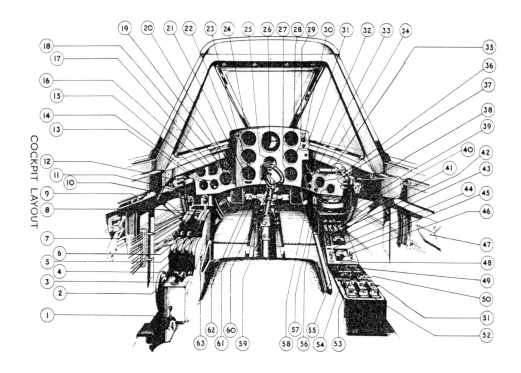

COCKPIT LAYOUT

KEY TO FIG. 3

(1) Anti-spin parachute control lever
(2) Elevator trimmer tab control handwheel
(3) Emergency air release lever
(4) H.P. fuel cock control lever
(5) L.P. fuel cock control lever
(6) Parking brake control lever
(7) Emergency air reserve supply
     release lever
(8) Undercarriage control push-button
(9) Silica-jel cartridge
(10) Throttle lock
(11) Throttle control lever
(12) Air brakes control levers
(13) Vacuum gauge
(14) Hydraulic pressure gauge
(15) Emergency air pressure gauge
(16) Undercarriage test push-button
(17) Accelerometer
(18) Undercarriage door warning lamp
(19) Brakes pressure gauge
(20) Undercarriage position indicator
(21) Altimeter
(22) Generator failure warning lamp
(23) Machmeter
(24) Air speed indicator
(25) Direction indicator
(26) Artificial horizon
(27) Engine speed indicator
(28) Rate-of-climb meter
(29) Turn-and-bank indicator
(30) Low fuel level warning lamp
(31) Turn-and-bank indicator switch

(32) Jet pipe temperature gauge
(33) Fuel contents gauge
(34) Burner pressure gauge
(35) Hood manual control handle
(36) Oil pressure gauge
(37) Hood jettison release handle
(38) Compass, Type 6A/1672
(39) Auto-observer contact-breaker
(40) Fuel pump contact-breakers
(41) V.H.F. push-button
(42) Generator cut-out and re-set push-buttons
(43) Voltmeter
(44) Ground/Flight switch
(45) Ammeter
(46) Pressure head switch
(47) Electric controller. Type 12 for V.H.F.
(48) Fuel pump test push-buttons
(49) Pressure head test push-button
(50) Re-light and boost test switch
(51) Fuse boxes
(52) Starboard console
(53) Master switch
(54) Engine starter push-button
(55) Seat adjusting lever
(56) Fuel pressure gauge
(57) Engine fire extinguisher push-button
(58) Engine fire extinguisher warning lamp
(59) Control column
(60) Brakes control lever
(61) Camera control switch
(62) Rudder pedals
(63) Engine control box

Interesting view showing fuselage airbrakes, these were never used as wind tunnel test showed that they would cause disturbances round the rudder area and were locked. Also shown is the housing for a anti-spin parachute.

Eric "Red" Esler, test pilot

Squadron Leader, Samuel Eric "Red" Esler, DFC was a former RAF Coastal Command pilot and joined Avro in June 1948 from the Miles Aircraft Company. Eric was Avro's deputy chief test pilot flying the Tudor 8 experimental aircraft to a height of 40,000ft in 47 minutes on 29th August, 1948. This was the first pressurised flight by a four jet research airliner. His nick name was due to his crop of ginger hair.

With the absence of chief test pilot Jimmy Orrell, who was in Canada to fly the Avro C-102 Jetliner, Esler was given the task of all test flying of the Type 707. In fact Esler was on the same Empire Test Flying School Course No.2 in 1945 with Jimmy Orrell.

Red as he was known by his pilot friends pictured in his office at Woodford.

Proving the way

Pictured at Woodford VX784 in August 1949. It was built to test the low speed envelope of the delta planform. The aircraft was dismantled and delivered to Boscombe Down, where it made its first flight on the 4th September, 1949.

VX784 pictured at Woodford August 1949.

On static display at the SBAC Show in 1949.

VX784 made its first public appearance at the 10th annual exhibition of the S.B.A.C Show at Farnborough in September 1949. Eric "Red" Esler was the only pilot to fly the first protoype 707.

Type 707 - VX784 Pilot's Report

Taxiing and Flight Trials at A. &A.E.E., Boscombe Down,
2nd - 6th September, 1949.

2nd September, 1949

High speed taxi trials (100 m.p.h.) to assess undercarriage and brakes. Undercarriage satisfactory, nose wheel not too strongly self-centring. Brakes improved with use and considered satisfactory, the wide track undercarriage and small differential on brakes cause slight instability when braking heavily.

3rd September, 1949

High speed runs to assess controls. With trim in neutral position, elevators much too heavy to raise nose wheel up to 120 m.p.h., though some feel could be felt in controls at approximately 70 m.p.h, the rudder becoming effective at 60 m.p.h. Aircraft into hangars to reduce anti-balance tab ratio of elevator.

4th September, 1949 (A.M.)

High speed runs; elevators much too heavy. Further run with elevator trim set 4 divisions nose up, with elevator held hard back nose wheel lifted sharply off ground at 100 m.p.h., aircraft became airborne at about 103 m.p.h. I. A. S., approximately, necessary to push elevator forward to replace aircraft on ground. A further high speed run to check elevator for over balance in the fully forward position no sign of over balance. As a result of heavy braking it was necessary to change wheels and brakes.

4th September, 1949

Further run to bed in new brakes and wheels. Aircraft was then hopped with elevator trim 2 divisions tail heavy the stick was held hard back (both hands) the nose wheel lifted off just under 100 m.p.h., and the aircraft became airborne at approximately 102 m.p.h., to the extent of some 3 or 4 feet. At the same time the port wing started to drop and aileron was very slow in lifting it, also ailerons were heavy. Aircraft was immediately throttled back and put on ground.

It was then decided to take the aircraft off on its initial flight as handling seemed satisfactory above 110 m.p.h.

4th September, 1949
Take-off 19.50 for twenty minutes.

First flight (Elevator trim 2 division's tail heavy).

The stick was held hard back throughout the take-off run, for the nose wheel lifted sharply at approximately 100 m.p.h., the aircraft lifted off at approximately 105 - 110 m.p.h., (this almost as soon as the nose lifts to a reasonable angle estimated 10°) the lift off is sudden to a height at 3 to 5 feet from the ground where the aircraft stays until a speed of approximately 130 m.p.h, is indicated. The acceleration from here is quite fast and on crossing the boundary the speed is 180 - 200 m.p.h. climbing at 180 - 200 m.p.h., the Rate of Climb is in the order of 4 - 5,000 ft/minute.

Controls:

The aileron and elevator are extremely heavy at speeds of 120 m.p.h., and above, the rudder is light over the small angles used, the rate of roll with yaw is high.

The aircraft was climbed to 8,000 feet and speed reduced to 140 m.p.h., when it appeared to be quite stable in all axis. Speed was then increased to approximately 170 m.p.h., and bottom wing air brakes were extended slowly, the force to hold the change of trim with under wing air brakes is high and they need to be extended a little at a time and re-trimmed at each stage. As the air brakes get out to an angle of 30° a slight high frequency buffet is felt on the elevator. Undercarriage was lowered at approximately 170 m.p.h.; there is no noticeable change of trim fore and aft, though there was a considerable yaw and resultant roll to the right due to the fact that Starboard undercarriage leg comes down first.

Owing to poor light and difficulty in seeing the runway, the aerodrome lights were requested, the aircraft was approached in a low flat approach at 150 m.p.h, with a fair amount of power, coming over the boundary about 145 - 150 m.p.h. the engine was cut, When about three feet from the ground the aircraft has a natural and momentary hold-off but quickly sank onto the ground at approximately 120 m.p.h. No excessive braking was required to bring the aircraft to rest in approximately 1800/2000 yards.

Four further flights were carried out during which the aircraft has been flown from speeds of 130 m.p.h., to 280 m.p.h. no oscillations about any axis were noticed the aircraft at all times being quite stable.

The approach and landing speeds have been maintained to 140 - 150 m.p.h., owing to the extreme heaviness of the ailerons and the roll with yaw in bumpy air.

It is felt that once the ailerons are lightened off the approach speed will in all probability be reduced to approximately 120 m.p.h. It is recommended that this speed be got down to before flying the aircraft into Woodford.

Diary of Flights:			T.O.Time.	Time in air
1st	Flight	4. 9. 49.	19.50	20 mins.
2nd	Flight	5. 9. 49.	18.05	40 mins.
3rd	Flight	6. 9. 49.	10.30	40 mins.
4th	Flight	6. 9. 49.	12.00	30 mins.
5th	Flight	6. 9. 49.	(To Farnborough 18.15 for S.B.A.C. Show)	20 mins.

Signed. ....
Test Pilot.

Circulation List:

Sir Roy Dobson,	Mr. W. S. Farren	Mr. S. D. Davies,
Mr. R. Reynolds,	Mr. J. G. Willis. Flight Test Section.	Pilots (2).

Type 707 Recollections

By Albert D. (Derry) Chapman, Aerodynamics

Derry joined Avro in 1948, working in Aerodynamics at Chadderton. There were just six people handling Tudor, Athena and Anson flight test work along with Shackleton, 698 and 707 design work, fortunately from the work load viewpoint there was no high speed wind tunnel in those days at Woodford.

The go-ahead had been given to build a one third scale delta the half scale (Avro 710) being shelved, the Avro 707 was given the ministry specification No. E15/48. When the design was frozen, the planform represented the 698 except for the absence of the leading edge intakes.

With the urgency of the day the requirement was to design and fly the aircraft within twelve months. Steps were taken to use components from P1052 (nose undercarriage), Athena (main under carriage) and Meteor (cockpit canopy). The wing leading edge had 52.43° sweepback; the leading edge was kinked with sweepback over the aileron span.

With the crash of the first 707 (VX784) it was found that there was a huge loss of elevator power when the airbrakes were extended. These were only fitted to the wing undersurface. This was determined by model tests carried out in the Blackburn & English Electric wind tunnels at Brough and Warton respectively after the accident. The technical Director at the time Sir William Farren witnessed the crash on his way back from Farnborough and gave his observations to the chief aerodynamicist, Eric Priestly.

Design work had been going along on the high speed derivative (the 707A) whilst construction of the low speed 707 (VX784) had been proceeding. A temporary halt to this work took place as design of a replacement low speed aircraft was commenced on the Type 707B.

As a result of wind tunnel testing, the airbrake design was changed and a larger fin and rudder designed; the fuselage was lengthened forward of the wing and detail changes made to the elevator, the airbrakes were now on both upper and lower wing surfaces.

After difficulties experienced on take-off the nose wheel leg was lengthened to put a bit of incidence on the wing on the initial take-off run and much later (after flight 199), the air intake was enlarged on Rolls-Royce recommendation; a spring tab added to the elevator and a yaw damper tab fitted to the rudder, this was to be the final form.

One fact that intrigued Derry was that after the major grounding (after flight 199) the rigging was checked and it was found that the wing had developed more anhedral from 0.18° to 0.85°. Whether this had occurred prior to the grounding or during it was never ascertained. Incidentally, it was supposed to be zero!

One feature regarding the first 707A was that one of the wings (he could not remember which one) was fitted with hundreds of pressure tapping holes for measurement of surface pressure in flight. The 707A first flew with manual controls but was later adapted to powered ailerons and elevators - these gave some clues to what jack size would be needed for Type 698.

Getting to the root of the problem

In December 1949 a brochure was issued by the Initial Projects Department for the design of the 698 with four Rolls-Royce Avon (R.A.3 Rating) engines to meet specification B.35/46. In fact when the first prototype flew it was powered by four Avon's due to the Bristol Olympus engines not being available.

Note the angle of sweep at wing root intakes, which changed when it became apparent to the R.A.E. that a compressibility drag rise would take place at a lower Mach number, resulting in a degradation in performance to unacceptable levels, unless the sweepback at the centre section could be increased over the then design value.

This led to the redesign of the wing root by displacing the line of maximum thickness of the centre part of the wing near the air intake forward some 15% of the root chord. This led to scrapping of the complete lines of the wing and all structure detail that had been schemed.

This decision was made at the end of 1949, the first issue of the basic dimensions went to the works in February, 1950 and detail drawings were produced in May, 1950. This was to lead to a three month delay in issuing new drawings.

Wing root design December, 1949, note the faired cockpit.

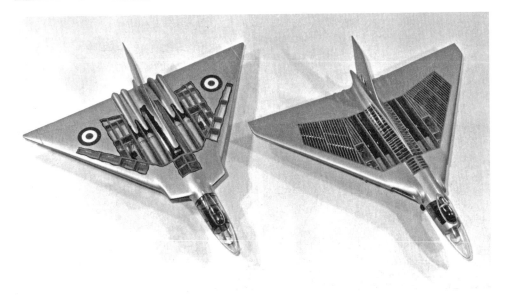

Avon power - December 1949

December 1949 drawing for an Avon powered Type 698. This was one of the first drawings showing the modified layout of the fuel tanks, engine air intake and redesigned wing tips following wind tunnel testing at the R.A.E.

Leading particulars

Span	97.0 ft
Overall length	93.88 ft
Maximum height	27.33 ft
Hangar weight	135,400 lbs
Target distance	2,110 n.m.
Maximum range	4,220 n.m.
Cruise at 400 knots true airspeed	
Four Avon power plants	5,600 lb at sea level March/1949
Height over target	40,350 ft
Sweep-back of 1/4 chord	42.2 degrees
Aerofoil section	N.A.C.A. 0010

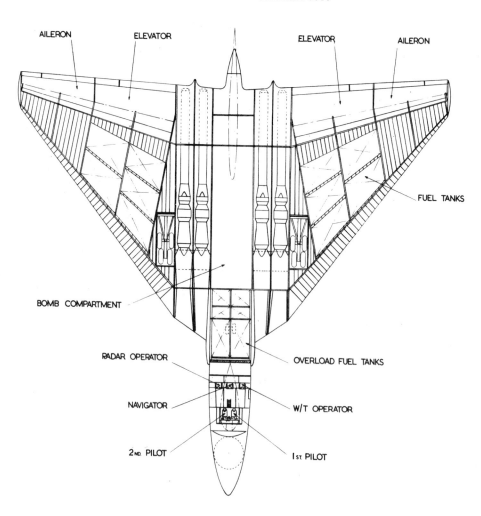

Major developments January 1950

Initial Projects Brochure

This brochure incorporated the developments and improvements found necessary as a result of considerable detail design work to the layout presented in the previous brochure dated September, 1948. Shown below is the text from that brochure.

The dimensions of the special bomb require a large compartment free from structural obstructions, and if we aim at the minimum frontal area we are forced to a planform involving a root chord of about 63 feet. Combining this with the sweepback required, together with a low cruising C_L value which necessitates a moderate wing loading, we arrive at a near Delta planform. This also has the advantage of a clean aerodynamic shape with the minimum of excrescences.

The alternative would be a much larger body with a moderate wing root chord, such that the wing structure could pass through the body and over the large bomb bay. This inevitably leads one to a much higher aspect ratio swept back wing with considerable excrescences, and presenting problems on control etc., which would lead one to incorporate a normal type tail unit. We believe such a design would have a much higher gross weight and probably a higher drag and more severe aero elastic problems, apart from the difficulty of stowage of fuel, with consequent restriction on range.

Wing pressure distribution tests on swept back wing models have shown that the sweep effect at the wing root is considerably reduced, due to the backward movement of the peak suction isobars, and that this effect can be alleviated by bringing the maximum wing thickness location progressively forward towards the wing root.

Early model showing the internal structure. Models played an important part in the development of the Type 698.

The 698 wing sections, therefore, are now arranged as follows:

The root section is of 13% thickness chord ratio with maximum thickness at 15% of the chord. This section progressively changes to NACA 0010 at the wing transport joint. From the transport joint the section changes linearly to an 8% thick Squire "B" section at the tip.

The Squire "B" section at the tip reduces the bad suction effects that would occur if the tip section were N.A.C.A. 0010.

The present brochure incorporates most of the recommendations brought to light from R.A.E. wind tunnel tests. Nevertheless, there is a great need for flight evidence on the behaviour of this type of aircraft. Accordingly three 1/3 scale flying models are to be built, the first two covering the low speed flying qualities. The first of these aircraft has been built and flew at Boscombe Down on 4th September, 1949. This aircraft made five successful flights, and in the words of the pilot "it behaves like an ordinary aeroplane". These results exceeded our expectations with regard to take-off, landing and general flight handling, and it is regretted that the flight trials terminated in a fatal accident. The cause of this is not yet known, but the evidence suggests that there was nothing wrong with the fundamental aerodynamics and flying qualities of the Delta aircraft.

The second 1/3 scale aircraft should be flying in the spring of 1950.

The third of these models should be available for flight tests towards the end of 1950. This model will have several aerodynamic improvements to enable it to attain similar Mach number conditions to that of the bomber, and will investigate high speed control problems and the pressure distribution over the wing.

The Specification calls for two prototypes and a full scale test specimen, together with secondary test specimens. We propose to build the first prototype in a considerably simplified form, i.e. without full detail provision for military equipment and possibly with a simplified fuel system. Additionally we propose to fit Rolls-Royce Avon engines, since the reliability of the engines on a novel aeroplane of this type must be beyond question. This would accelerate initial flight tests and enable us to obtain much needed full scale data. Preliminary test specimens, together with a reduced gross weight on this prototype would give us confidence in proceeding with flight tests from a strength point of view.

STRUCTURE

As explained under the general notes the dimensions of the special bomb, together with the necessity for small frontal area involves a two spar design, at least in the centre section. The structure is designed to meet a maximum factored acceleration of 4g. The leading edge of the wing is being designed with a view to obtaining as near a laminar flow finish as possible, at least up to the front spar.

The basic construction follows normal practice with front and rear spar connected together with conventional ribs. The leading edge will be constructed of 14 SWG skin and will house the ducting and detail provisions for the Thermal de-icing system. The fuel tanks are supported in elliptical containers built into the ribs between spars. The wing skinning between span will be 16 SWG. Calculations have shown this to be necessary in order to meet the torsional stiffness criterion as applied to conventional wings. The between spar skinning will be in the form of span wise narrow strips with stringers attached by the Redux process. These panels will then be attached direct to the top of the ribs. The crew's nacelle follows standard Avro construction, both in detail design and in order to meet pressurisation requirements.

CONTROLS

The Delta layout with its near straight trailing edge enables us to adopt conventional elevators and ailerons. We regard this as a distinct advantage compared to the elevon arrangement normally adopted on a swept back trailing edge. A conventional single fin and rudder will be provided with approximately the same sweep back as the wing.

We anticipate that the aircraft will be controllable up to above M = 0.9 with this arrangement. In order to prevent the aircraft attaining excessively high diving speeds with the possibility of control difficulties, we are providing air brakes. At the present time our proposals are to fit these in the top and bottom surfaces of the wing immediately forward of the engines.

There are two methods of control operation available to us on this high speed design, either a full power system which simplifies the aerodynamics of the problem, although considerably complicates the mechanical installation, or by a servo control system which involves us in difficult aerodynamics but simpler mechanical problems. For either system we propose to adopt a sealed Irving type balance arrangement.

Both schemes are being developed and our final decision will depend on the results of the high speed 1/3 scale flying model, which will be equipped with similar sealed balance spring tab controls,

We are aware of the possibility of a servo tab type of control losing its effectiveness at the high speed end of the scale, also because of the large area involved it may be that the pilots stick forces will be excessively large. An additional complication of the servo system would be a loss of stability stick free which may prove embarrassing under certain conditions. With either system, however, we may fit trimming tabs, since they would obviously be of great use over a considerable part of the speed range.

With the servo control system the ailerons would be mechanically interconnected, but it may be possible to avoid such mechanical interconnection with the elevators. We had suggested earlier that in the event of the servo system stick forces proving excessively large at high speed, that some form of power assistance should also be provided. We now regard this as being probably unreliable, particularly from the point of view of the non-linear control characteristics when working with the automatic pilot.

In the event that we decide to use full power controls, these would consist of completely duplicated power units at each surface on each side of the aeroplane. This would mean that the loss of one unit would result in a 25% loss in control power, and basically represents a quadrupled form of power supply.

CREW NACELLE

The original Specification called for a jettisonable crew's nacelle. We believe we could provide for this satisfactorily from a mechanical point of view, but in view of the difficulties and doubts with regard to the stability of the nacelle after jettisoning, we are proposing to avoid this design feature for the time being until the aerodynamic problems of this procedure have been overcome.

POWER PLANTS

At the moment there are two alternative engines envisaged which will cope with the performance requirements of this aircraft. These are the Bristol Olympus jet engine with a maximum sea level ICAN static thrust of 9,000 lbs. and the Rolls Royce Conway engine with a thrust of 9,700 lbs.

The engine compartments in the wing would be basically capable of taking either of the above two engines, and in the case of the prototype, the Rolls Royce Avon engine also.

The air intakes will take the form of a normal wing root leading edge entry. This arrangement is well tried and should give good results, both as regards intake efficiency and drag.

The centre of gravity of this aircraft must, of necessity, be held to close limits, and during the various stages of design would be controlled by adjusting the location of the engines fore and aft in the engine compartments. In the event that their location finally comes fairly well aft, we propose to try the underwing flush type of intake on one of the prototypes.

The only accessory we envisage driven from the engine will be a single 30 kilowatt starter generator operating at 115 volts D.C. All other secondary forms of power units and accessories will, therefore, be driven electrically. In the event of starter generators not being developed in time the alternative would be to fit separate starter and generator systems.

We are making a careful detailed analysis of the pros. and cons. of hydraulics, electrics and pneumatics. The weight analysis shows that there is very little to choose between the various systems. The emphasis will, therefore, be on servicing and reliability in operation through the extreme temperature conditions envisaged. We believe that these conditions will be most satisfactorily with a hydraulic system.

FUEL SYSTEM

The 8,300 gallons of fuel will be carried in fourteen flexible crash proof tanks. The tanks will be grouped for each engine but cross feeds will enable any engine to receive fuel from any tank.

Due to the necessarily wide distribution of tanks throughout the aircraft, fuel will have to be consumed in the correct order to avoid changes in flight trim. The crew will be relieved of this task by an automatic sequencing of tanks through a simple selector switch driven by a gallons gone transmitter on each engine. The selector switch will cut down all fuel pumps except one to half working speed, this ensuring consumption of fuel from the full speed pump yet maintaining reserve feeds from remaining tanks in case of a pump failure. Manual override will be provided under the control of the second pilot for all pumps. A further emergency precaution will be available to the 1st pilot, a 3-way position switch on the pilots panel will enable fuel to be transferred from a forward tank to an aft tank or visa versa for ballast purposes. The tanks will be pressurised to $1\frac{1}{2}$ lbs. per square inch. differential by means of the nitrogen purging system to assist in preventing fuel boiling. Pressure refuelling and defuelling will be provided.

The controls of the fuel system will be on the starboard console at the second pilots' position and presented in the form of a label representing the layout of the aircraft with each switch positioned geographically relative to the unit it controls.

Total contents of fuel available will be shown on the pilots panel, the fuel available to each engine (without operation of cross feeds) will be indicated on the fuel control panel. Individual tank contents will be available by the depression of a switch.

AIR CONDITIONING AND ANTI-ICING

Between 8,000 feet and 7,000 feet the cabin altitude will be 8,000 feet, and above 47,000 feet a differential pressure of 9 lbs. per square inch will be maintained. There will be provision for decreasing the cabin altitude to 25,000 feet in combat conditions.

The source of air will be tapping on the inboard engine compressors which will provide a normal delivery of 10 lbs./min. to the cabin. In the event of failure of an inboard engine a minimum supply of 5 lbs./min. will be available. Provision will be made for an automatic increase of the flow to 50 lbs./min. from each inboard engine in the event of the cabin being punctured. Automatic Temperature Control equipment will maintain the cabin temperature at any figure set by the crew between -5°C and +20°C. Sufficient heat will be available in the normal flow to maintain a cabin temperature of +20°C in ambient temperatures down to -80°C. An air cycle refrigerator will ensure that a cabin temperature below +20°C will be maintained in Tropical Summer Conditions.

AIRFRAME ANTI-ICING

A hot air thermal anti-icing system will provide protection against ice accretion for all leading edges, for an ambient temperature of -25°C a water concentration of 0.5 grams/cubic metre, a drop diameter of 20 microns and an altitude range of 0-30,000 feet. The source of heat will be tapped at the high pressure end of the engine compressors. In the event of failure of up to one engine on each side, provision will be made for the whole supply to be obtained from the remaining engines.

UNDERCARRIAGE

A tricycle undercarriage will be fitted which retracts completely into the normal contour of the aircraft. The nose wheel is of simple design and retracts into the underside of the fuselage just aft of the pressure cabin. It is fitted with steering gear to facilitate manoeuvring on the ground.

The main undercarriage is rather less orthodox, being of a twin tandem arrangement on each side of the aircraft. This arrangement permits the use of smaller wheels (with consequent improved stowage in the wing) and yet enables low runway loading figures to be used. For the range of 3350 nautical miles using Conway engines giving an A.U.W. of 112,750 lbs. the tyre pressures would be 79 lbs. per square inch and the Runway Loading Number 20. For the range of 4.902 nautical miles using Olympus engines giving A.U.W. 141,550 lbs. tyre pressures would be 101 lbs. per square inch and the Runway Loading number 29.

The maximum possible range of this aircraft appears to be in the region of 5,000 nautical miles, although obviously at the take-off weights involved the take-off run would be considerably increased and the height over the target would be reduced. The strength factors would, of course, be also reduced by approximately 20%.

It should be a matter of considerable interest to note that the Bristol Olympus engine is capable of development.

(i) To permit obtaining 12,000 lbs. take-off thrust. By way of comparison, with the same take-off weight and fuel as required for the normal specification range of 3350 nautical miles with the 9,000 lbs. thrust engine, the 12,000 lb. engine would increase the height over the target by 6,000 ft. and reduce the take-off run by about 20%. The range however, is reduced by approximately 400 miles.

(ii) By derating the engine to 8250 lb. static thrust and over speeding for take-off and climb to give comparable thrust to that of the 9000 lb. engine, but cruising at 100 r.p.m. This would increase the height over target by 2,000 ft. for the 3350 nautical mile range and increase the maximum range by 100 nautical miles,

As an alternative development, if we consider taking off with the maximum fuel capacity of 8,300 gallons, the height over the target would be 51,500 feet and the maximum range 4,600 nautical miles which makes an interesting comparison with the normal Olympus long range performance set out.

We need hardly add that rocket assistance could be provided to improve take-off if necessary.

A natural progression

Original tender design May, 1947.

Stuart D. Davies pictured here in his office at Chadderton. Davies joined Avro in January 1938 as assistant designer to Roy Chadwick. He was appointed experimental shop manager in April 1940 and Chief Designer in 1946 when Chadwick was made Technical Director. Due to his Cockney background Stuart was known as "Cock" Davies.

Amended design submitted September, 1948.

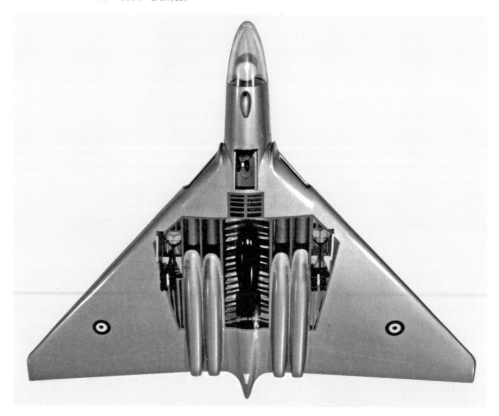

Final design to prototype standard in 1950, showing bomb bay and special bomb.

Covering all the bases

An Initials Project Department (I.P.D.) report dated 9th November, 1950 compared the effects of being fitted with Olympus Mark 3 engines of 12,000 lb. static thrust. The Mk3 engines offered an increase in altitude and range at increased operating weight. The report also looked at the effects of fitting a tail plane and increased wing span and lengthened fuselage with four Olympus B.OL.2 engines.

Tailplane

Model test and flight experience on two tailless aircraft had shown that under certain conditions the longitudinal damping of such aircraft may reduce or become non-existent at high Mach number. There was no evidence that this phenomenon would occur on the 698, but was desirable to consider the action to be taken to remove the difficulty, should it arise. In the first place, if there is found to be an undamped oscillation at Mach number well above normal flight conditions, it will be reasonable to damp it by the use of an automatic control on lines which have already proved successful. If such an oscillation occurs within the speed range below to slightly above the critical Mach number it would be desirable to overcome it without recourse to such mechanisms. "Natural" longitudinal damping can be provided by the addition of a tailplane, and the consequences of doing this have, therefore, been investigated.

The fitting of a tailplane of any size would result in an increase of weight and therefore in an increase of take-off weight for a given range, or alternatively in a reduction in range for constant amount of fuel. In either case the height over the target will be lower. At this stage it is not possible to determine exactly the minimum size of tailplane necessary to meet the stability requirements and, in fact, this must await an appreciation of the magnitude of the loss of damping obtained by analysis of the flight tests on the 707A.

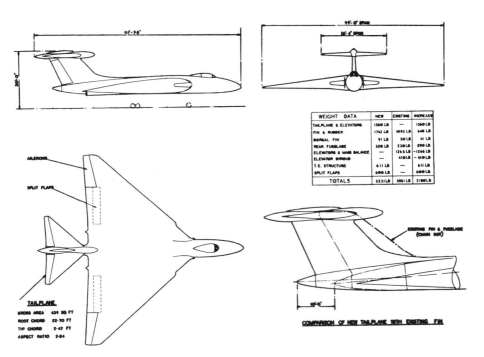

WEIGHT DATA	NEW	EXISTING	INCREASE
TAILPLANE & ELEVATORS	1560 LB	—	1560 LB
FIN & RUDDER	1743 LB	1095 LB	648 LB
DORSAL FIN	91 LB	50 LB	41 LB
REAR FUSELAGE	520 LB	230 LB	290 LB
ELEVATORS & MASS BALANCE	—	1266 LB	-1266 LB
ELEVATOR SHROUD	—	410 LB	-410 LB
T.E. STRUCTURE	611 LB	—	611 LB
SPLIT FLAPS	600 LB	—	600 LB
TOTALS	5231 LB	3061 LB	2180 LB

TAILPLANE.
GROSS AREA 639 SQ FT
ROOT CHORD 22.70 FT
TIP CHORD 2.42 FT
ASPECT RATIO 2.84

COMPARISON OF NEW TAILPLANE WITH EXISTING FIN

PROPOSED TAILPLANE ON AVRO TYPE NO 698

It will be noted that the tailplane is placed wholly aft of the wing trailing edge. This is considered essential to its effectiveness and involves an extension of the fuselage and an increase in size of the fin. The tailplane is fitted with elevators for the normal control of the aircraft. In addition, the whole tailplane is movable to provide trimming. What advantages offsetting the loss of performance can be obtained from such a tailplane if its fitment becomes essential. These are not very great since the present design of the Avro 698 is considered to be the optimum.

Increased wing span

The existing aircraft can be developed in two ways - towards increased range or increased bomb load and these two objects will be considered as separate issues.

Firstly, to increase the range, the most obvious way is augmenting the existing fuel capacity by fitting extended auxiliary tanks, but this leads to increased drag, requiring still more fuel and furthermore is impractical, due to lack of ground clearance. Use of tank nacelles has been considered, but the most economical way of increasing range is by increasing the span and extending the fuselage this retaining all the fuel within the airframe.

This naturally leads to a larger and hence heavier aircraft, considerably reducing the operational height particularly over the target. For this aircraft, therefore, we have replaced the Olympus Mark 2 engines of 9750 lb. static thrust with Olympus Mark 3 engines of 12,000 lb. static thrust. Although the new engines in their turn further increase the aircraft weight, the result on balance is to restore the height lost.

The extra fuel is then carried partly in extra wing tanks and partly in increased fuselage tankage, so as to avoid a large change in centre of gravity. The outer wing structure is retained almost identical, but the centre section has its span increased and now houses the undercarriage. In addition the front spar has been swept forward to give a longer bomb bay to cater for a probable increase in length of the 'special' bomb.

Secondly, to increase the military load at the expense of range, it would be necessary to lengthen the fuselage in order to provide for a larger bomb bay. The fuel carried would then be cut down to avoid increasing the overall weight of the aircraft.

At 140,000 lb. take-off weight, the fuel at present carried amounts to 8300 gallons or 67,000 lb. If the bomb load was increased from 10,000 lb. to 40,000 lb. and allowing for the increase in fuselage drag due to the extended length, the range would be cut from 4700 nautical miles to 2000 nautical miles.

Should it be required to increase both range and military load a combination of the above two schemes would be necessary, the limiting factor would then be engine power and structural strength.

The provision of more engines in itself rarely results in the necessity for increase of operating speed or height in order to fly above the minimum drag speed at the maximum continuous cruise revs, and hence most economical conditions. Increasing operational speed entails an increase in critical Mach number to avoid compressibility troubles and could entail serious redesign of the wing.

An increase in operational height would require some of the extra power in profile drag due to lower Reynolds number, but this could be offset by a reduction in speed, which in turn affects the range adversely.

The performance of the Avro type 698 due to increasing the wing span by 8 ft. 3 ins. and the length by 7 ft. is shown opposite.

		3350 NAUTICAL MILES.	MAXIMUM RANGE.
Hangar Weight	lb.	130,500	172,067
Take-off Weight	lb.	129,500	171,067
Start of Cruise Weight	lb.	124,500	165,567
Start of Cruise Height	ft.	47,100	40,600
Distance to Target	N.M.	1,675	2,832
Weight over Target	lb.	102,300	118,300
Height over Target	ft.	50,930	48,250
Weight (bare) over Aerodrome	lb.	82,157	82,157
Height over Aerodrome	ft.	55,000	55,000
Fuel Consumed	lb.	48,343	89,910
Range	N.M.	3,350	5,660

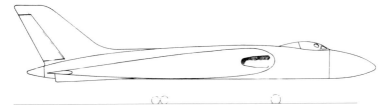

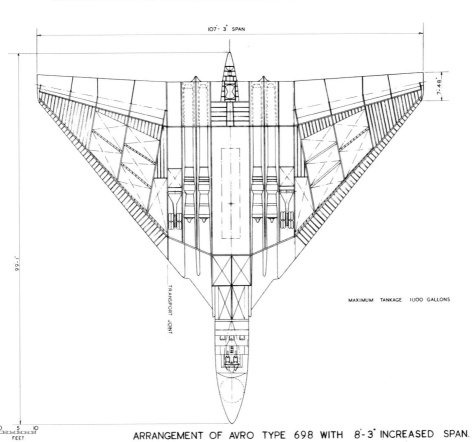

107'- 3" SPAN

7·48"

99'-1"

TRANSPORT JOINT

MAXIMUM TANKAGE 11,100 GALLONS

5 10
FEET

ARRANGEMENT OF AVRO TYPE 698 WITH 8'-3" INCREASED SPAN.

Roly Falk joins 707 test programme

Roly Falk seen here pictured at his Woodford office on 19th November, 1952.

Wing Commander Roland 'Roly' John Falk OBE, AFC and bar, joined Avro in 1950 and took over the test flying of the 707's from the late Eric Esler.

After a distinguished flying career he became Chief Test Pilot at R.A.E. Farnborough in 1943 where he flew jet and rocket propelled prototypes including captured German aircraft. In 1946 he became Chief experimental test pilot for Vickers Armstrong.

In 1951, Falk married Leysa Hanson the daughter of Avro's Chief Test Pilot Bill Thorn who was tragically killed in the Tudor crash in 1947. On 1st March, 1954 Falk was promoted to the unique position of Superintendent of Flying.

Avro Type 707B - VX790

Following the loss of the first Type 707, a second experimental Type 707B was manufactured as a replacement, a new nose and ejector seat was fitted and airbrakes fitted to top of the wing. This aircraft was resonance tested and completed in January 1950. It first flew from Boscombe Down on the 6th September, 1950 in the capable hands of "Roly" Falk.

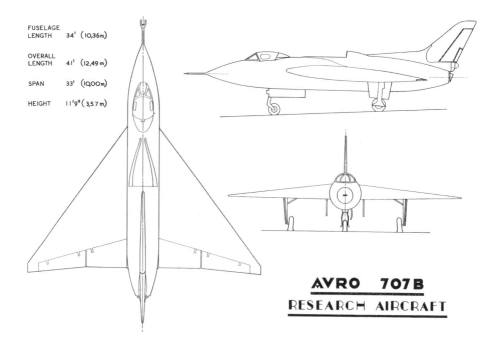

FUSELAGE LENGTH	34' (10,36m)
OVERALL LENGTH	41' (12,49 m)
SPAN	33' (10,00m)
HEIGHT	11'9" (3,57 m)

AVRO 707B
RESEARCH AIRCRAFT

707B Description

At Boscombe Down 6th September, 1950 on the day of its its first flight.

The 707B was primarily for research into the control and stability characteristics of the swept back wing aerofoil at low speeds. Power was supplied by a single Rolls-Royce Derwent V turbo-jet engine, which was housed in the rear section fuselage and given a nominal thrust of 3,600 lb. at sea level conditions. A tricycle undercarriage was fitted with the nose wheel retracting rearward into the fuselage structure and the two main wheel units retracting inward into the wing.

The fuselage is constructed of three jig-built sections comprising a nose and a rear section which is divided into front and rear portions. The nose accommodates the pilot's cockpit, nose-wheel undercarriage and automatic observer; the front portion of the rear section houses the fuel tank and engine air intake, and incorporates the wing spar attachment points; the rear portion forms the engine installation structure and the jet pipe outlet and carries the rearward sloping fin and rudder. A tail skid is fitted or the undersurface of the fuselage below the jet pipe and housing for a G.Q. anti-spin parachute is located below the rudder.

Each wing is of the two spar, stressed skin type, having a leading edge sweepback of 52 degrees 43 minutes. Ailerons and elevators are hinged on brackets attached to the rear spar with the elevators inboard, the two components forming the wing trailing edger The Lockheed main wheel undercarriage units are supported by front and rear beams located between the spars. Each beam is attached to the front portion of the rear section fuselage at the inboard end and to the inner face of the front spar at the outboard end. Air brakes are fitted forward of each undercarriage bay in the wing upper and lower surfaces.

A simple stick type control column, mounted centrally in the cockpit and operating in the natural sense, is used to control the movement of the ailerons and elevators. Two pedals mounted on a pivoted tube located below and forward of the instrument panel, control the rudder movement. Tubular push-pull rods are used throughout the control runs, the aileron rods running on the starboard side of the fuselage and those for the elevators or the port side, The rudder controls run centrally, passing through the engine air intake support and the fairing before connecting to the rudder post. Both ailerons have geared tabs, the port aileron has an electrically-operated trim tab, the elevators have spring tabs and mechanically-operated trim tabs and the rudder has a servo-tab and a yaw damping tab. The servo-tab is convertible to a geared tab, fitted in the anti-balance sense if desired.

The Derwent 5 turbo-jet engine is housed in the aft portion of the rear section fuselage with the jet pipe assembly protruding slightly aft of the fuselage. Four locating points are used for the engine mounting and comprise two forward side trunnions and two rear suspension points constructed of tubular struts on each side, forming a diamond mounting. The trunnions locate in bearers fitted to the inner wall of the engine bearers and the tubular struts pick up with attachment points on a rear mounting assembly. The jet pipe shroud is supported in a channel assembly attached to the section structure or each side. A large detachable panel below the engine is used for removal and servicing purposes.

Basic structure of the engine comprises:-
(1) A wheel case (2) Compressor (3) Nine straight-flow combustion chambers surrounding the centre and rear bearing casings (4) A discharge duct assembly (5) Axial flow turbine (6) A jet pipe assembly.

An oil tank is mounted on the wheelbase, the engine lubrication system being of the dry sump type. The air intake assembly is located on top of the front portion of the rear section fuselage and forms part of the aircraft structure. Aviation kerosene, contained in a single tank below the air intake, is sprayed at high pressure into the combustion chambers and burns continuously with approximately 25% of the total airflow, the fuel supply being controlled by the throttle lever working in conjunction with a barometric pressure control capsule.

Three control levers are located in a box on the port side of the cockpit floor.
These levers operate:-
(1) The throttle which varies the fuel flow and consequently the engine speed and thrust.
(2) High pressure shut-off cock for stopping the engine.
(3) A low pressure cock for isolating the tank during servicing or in the event of fire in the air.

All three levers utilise push-pull rods in the control runs.

The engine is started electrically, using a ground starter battery as the power supply. A starter motor on the engine and the engine master switch, starter button and fuel tank pump switches in the cockpit comprise the aircraft starting equipment. A push-button switch, fitted in the top of the high pressure cock lever, operates the torch igniter for relighting in the air. Oil pressure and oil temperature connections are located on the engine and the jet pipe is fitted with thermo-couples for recording the jet pipe temperatures. A Rotol auxiliary's gearbox, driven from the engine wheel case by a connecting shaft, is mounted on the forward face of the engine firewall and drives the following accessories:-
(1) One Dowty live-line hydraulic pump (2) One generator (3) One Pesco vacuum pump.

Extension and retraction of the main and nose wheel undercarriage units is affected by a high-pressure hydraulic system, using a single live-line hydraulic pump. In addition the air brakes are hydraulically operated. Approximately 6 pints of hydraulic fluid are contained in a reservoir located in the nose section fuselage, the: reservoir being pressurised from the pneumatic system. An emergency air system can be brought into use to lower the undercarriage units in the event of hydraulic failure. The emergency air pressure is stored in a steel, cylindrical air bottle, located aft of the pilot's rear bulkhead.

The pneumatic system operates the following:-

(1) The main wheel brake units.   (2) The pressurisation of the hydraulic reservoir.

The pneumatic air supply is also contained in a steel, cylindrical air bottle located aft of the pilot's rear bulkhead, and charged from a ground supply connection, there being no engine driven pump to maintain pressure. The pneumatic and emergency air systems can be connected to each other via a cock controlled by the pilot. As air pressure in the brakes bottle is used up or exhausted through leakage, the air supply to the brakes can be supplemented by using the pressure in the emergency air storage bottle.

Power supply for the operation of the electrical services is obtained from a single generator rated to give 100 amps. At 3,0 volts driven by the engine auxiliaries gearbox. The generator also charges the two Type C batteries which are connected in series. A voltage regulator maintains the system line voltage at 28 volts and cut-out controls reverse current flow to the generator. The main circuit is fed through a circuit breaker on the port power panel and is controlled by a reset and cut-out push-button switch located on the starboard console in the cockpit. A heavy duty GROUND/FLIGHT switch, also fitted on the starboard console, operating in conjunction with a Type K relay on the port panel, provides for disconnection of the aircraft batteries when an external supply is used. Indication of generator failure is given by a red warning light on the pilot's instrument panel.

An automatic observer panel is enclosed in a box fitted in the nose section of the fuselage. Instruments on these panels record the handling and performance of the aircraft in flight. At the forward side of the box are two electrically-operated cine-cameras controlled by the pilot, which photograph the instruments when required, to give a permanent record of flight performance. The pilot's instrument panel contains the necessary engine system, and flying instruments. A V.G. recorder is also installed.

The six main items of emergency equipment are:-

(1)   Hood jettison gear (2) Ejector seat (3) Emergency air system (4) Engine fire
       extinguisher (5) Anti-spin parachute (6) Emergency oxygen system.

In the event of an emergency exit becoming necessary, the pilot can release the hood catches and hinge points, allowing the hood to blow away and leave a clear passage for exit. For a high speed exit a Martin Baker ejector seat is fitted. Emergency air can be used to lower the undercarriage and to operate the air brakes, in the event of a hydraulic failure. The pneumatic system can be operated from the emergency air system should the pneumatic system become exhausted. Fire outbreak around the engine is covered by a Graviner Mk5 fire extinguisher system which is operated by a push-button in the cockpit, or in the event of a crash landing, by an inertia switch. A jettisonable anti-spin parachute, housed in the fuselage below the rudder, can be streamed in the event of the aircraft entering a spin or for braking purposes when landing. An emergency oxygen system is incorporated in the pilot's dinghy pack and is turned on automatically when the ejection seat is used, or may be turned on by the pilot without seat ejection.

Wing Data	
Sweepback (leading edge)	52 deg. 43 min.
Aerofoil section	N.A.C.A 0010. to 80% chord
Chord form centre line of fuselage	21ft 8in
Incidence	2 deg. 30 min.

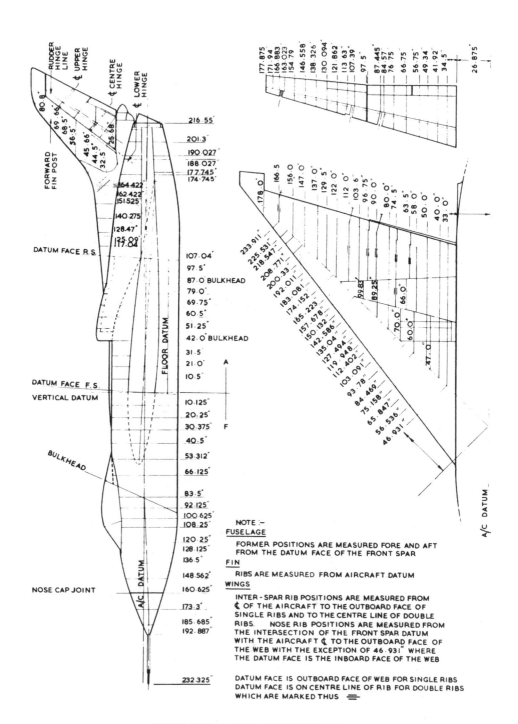

NOTE :—

FUSELAGE

FORMER POSITIONS ARE MEASURED FORE AND AFT
FROM THE DATUM FACE OF THE FRONT SPAR

FIN

RIBS ARE MEASURED FROM AIRCRAFT DATUM

WINGS

INTER - SPAR RIB POSITIONS ARE MEASURED FROM
₵ OF THE AIRCRAFT TO THE OUTBOARD FACE OF
SINGLE RIBS AND TO THE CENTRE LINE OF DOUBLE
RIBS.   NOSE RIB POSITIONS ARE MEASURED FROM
THE INTERSECTION OF THE FRONT SPAR DATUM
WITH THE AIRCRAFT ₵ TO THE OUTBOARD FACE OF
THE WEB WITH THE EXCEPTION OF 46.931" WHERE
THE DATUM FACE IS THE INBOARD FACE OF THE WEB

DATUM FACE IS OUTBOARD FACE OF WEB FOR SINGLE RIBS
DATUM FACE IS ON CENTRE LINE OF RIB FOR DOUBLE RIBS
WHICH ARE MARKED THUS ══

FORMER & RIB POSITIONS

Delta wing development review

A meeting was held on 21st April, 1950 with Government agencies Chaired by Mr E. T. Jones, Principal Director of Scientific Research P.D.S.R. (Air) at the Ministry of Supply to discuss current delta wing designs and to the value of having these projects.

The Avro Type 698 and Gloster F4/48 (Javelin) were left out of the discussion as they were to be operational types. The discussion concentrated on the experimental types that were in progress. This included the Avro 707 aircraft E.15/48 (707B) and E.10/49 (707A).

Information was sought on the reasons for building a low speed aeroplane and why work had continued after the first one crashed, it was stated that a low speed model could be built more rapidly and also the low speed case needed as much investigation as the high speed. After the first E.15/48 had crashed the second one was continued as parts had already been made and construction could be made more quickly, especially as the design of the E.10/49 could not be completed until that of the Type 698 had been finalised. The R.A.E. had suggested changes to the thickness/chord ratio (t/c) and wing section for the latter and a similar wing would go on the E.10/49 model although the relatively large fuselage on the model would alter conditions at the inboard part of the wing. It was believed the models were valuable because sweep back was increased to 53°. It was commented that the catastrophic changes in low speed characteristics, which were feared, were likely to occur between this amount and 60°.

The E.15/48 was so far advanced that only the cancellation of the E.10/49 could be considered as an economy measure. It was pointed out that the high speed model was the more valuable of the two and of tremendous importance in designing the Type 698. There was general agreement about this. The conclusion was eventually reached that there was no opportunity for any cancellation of the projects considered.

VX790 under construction at Chadderton

Modified nose and canopy 18th August, 1950.

Finishing touches being applied before first flight.

Experimental Depatment at Chadderton 18th August, 1950.

Start of intensive flight test programme

VX790 pictured on the 6th September, 1950 the day of its first flight from Boscombe Down. It made its first public appearance at the September S.B.A.C. Show at Farnborough in 1950.

Streaming parachute 2nd November, 1950.

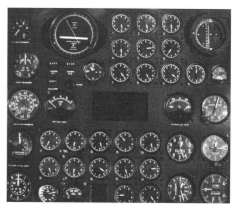

Instrument recording unit 15th August, 1951.   *Auto observer panel initial configuation.*

VX790 pictured in November 1950.

Landing at Boscombe Down during a series of high angle approaches on 2nd November, 1950.

Shown above are rare colour pictures of VX790 at Boscombe Down during early test flying.

Type 707B - VX790 with modified intake

A revised intake to help improve the airflow at higher speeds, pictured below on 6th March, 1951, the original was built for low speed investigation. It was decided to improve the ram efficiency so that higher speeds could be investigated.

Modified air intake 6th March, 1951.

VX790 pictured at Woodford on 6th March,1951. Sir Roy Dobson inspects the cockpit.

An excellent side view taken 13th April, 1951, taken from an Avro Lincoln aircraft of Experimental Flight from Farnborough, piloted by Squadron Leader Ashworth.

Boscombe Down 16th July, 1951.   *Wing appendages.*

Roll to starboard. Top and bottom pictures were taken by Cyril Peckham, Hawker Siddeley Group, chief photographer.

On display to the press at Dunsfold 1st August, 1951.

Press day at Dunsfold

Roly Falk being greeted by Stuart Davies at a press day at Dunsfold airfield near Guildford which Hawker Siddeley had taken over. It was held to inform the press on the merits of Delta design, this included British Movietone News and Charles Gardner from the BBC.

The aircraft had flown from Boscombe Down on 31st July, 1951, where it was involved in an intensive flying programme. It returned to Boscombe Down on 3rd August to complete its test programme. Total flying to date was 176 flights, 323 landings and about 94 hours 35 minutes flying.

Roland Falk's aerobatics were a revelation, the rate of roll appearing especially high. During the afternoon the machine did some high-speed work, which included immaculate upward rolls and inverted flying.

The Avro 707 at Dunsfold on 1st August, 1951. The aircraft had a lot of admirers and created a lot of interest with the press, who had no knowledge of the Type 698 programme at the time.

Type 707B - VX790 progress 1950 - 1951

From its arrival at Boscombe Down the 707B (VX790) started an intensive flight programme and by 22nd December 1950 it had completed 160 landings and take-offs and completed 32 hours 40 minutes flying time. These were mostly concerned with stability and control problems, the longest flight made at that time was one hour with 35 gallons of fuel left. The unstick speed favoured by the pilot was 100 to 105 knots. The aircraft was locked in the hangar over Christmas period with flight test resuming on the 29th December, 1950. On flight 74 after modifications the aircraft reached an altitude of 43,000ft

On 21st March, 1951 engine surging again became apparent at 33,000ft and above at approximately 14,300 r.p.m. this led to a change of engine on 3rd May 1951, with a modified Derwent V engine. A flight test report on (air intake efficiencies) was sent to Mr Ewans and a design sketch was supplied by him for the report.

In April 1951, Roly Falk produced a report summarising the up-date development for assisting the physiology of high altitude flying. Roly was in the habit of taking a surfeit of oxygen for an hour or so before high altitude flights and then putting up with discomfort for short periods at upwards of 40,000ft. The 707B was not a pressured aircraft.

Report 92, covering 6th to 8th April, 1951 showed an improvement in cruising speed due to the new intake. On 11th April, the pilot inadvertently, exceeded the Mach No. this being 0.83 (0.86 - 0.87 true). Shortly afterwards the M-limitation was given as 0.81 indicated unless specific request was received to raise it to 0.82. On Friday 13th one flight was made for publicity photographs. By this time the aircraft had flown 51 hours and completed 210 landings. Report number 99 issued on 1st May, 1951 stated that a first flight was made by a pilot other than Roland Falk, namely Avro test pilot Jimmy Nelson. The latter found the aircraft unconventional on take-off technique which presented some difficulty. Handling in the air between 120 and 360 knots (at low Mach number) and also approach and landing were stated as easy and conventional.

On 26th January, 1956 the aircraft went to the Empire Test Flying School (ETPS) for test pilot training (coded 19). On 25th September 1956 it suffered a landing accident and went into storage. It was later used for spares at R.A.F. Bedford.

In April, 1951 the directors of A.V. Roe Co Ltd., presented a scale model of the 707B to the South Kensington Science Museum.

Sqn. Ldr. Jimmy Nelson was the second test pilot to fly the 707B Delta aircraft. Nelson was born in America and joined the famous R.A.F. No.133 (Eagle) Squadron flying Hurricanes and later Spitfires. In 1943 he became a Test Pilot at R.A.E. Farnborough where he later lost one leg as a result of the flying accident. He joined Avro in 1948 after three years as a test pilot for Miles Aircraft and returned to America in 1953.

Type 698 aerodynamic drawings
Fuselage contours

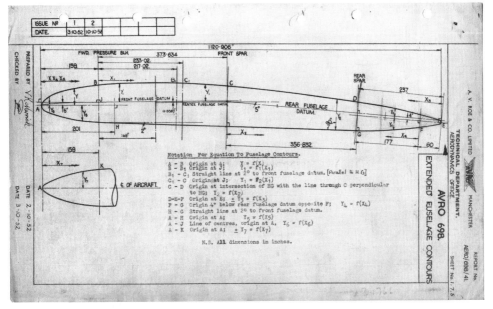

Above are the fuselage contours issued on the 3rd October, 1952.

Wing plan form

The Avro 698 wing section was derived by the Aerodynamics Office after extensive research into high speed properties of Delta wings, with view of keeping the drag rise with Mach number at a minimum.

As a result, the following sections were adopted. Wing section at the transport joint (162.5" from the aircraft centre line) - normal N.A.C.A. 0010. Wing section at 57" from the aircraft centre line (body side) is a specially designed section with a t/c of 12.3% of the chord, the trailing edge angle being the same as that at the transport joint (N.A.C.A. 0010) and the nose radius being double that as defined by the normal N.A.C.A. notation.

Wing section at the tip (49.0 ft from aircraft centre line) - Squire "B" with a t/c of 8%. aft of the rear spar inboard of the transport joint the physical depth of the section remains constant.

Aft of the rear spar inboard of the transport joint the physical depth of the section remains constant. As a further aerodynamic refinement this portion is also set up 2° measured from the chord line.

Shown overleaf are the principle wing dimensions first issued on 15th August, 1950. These drawings were produced as early as October 1950, by the aerodynamics office.

The General Arrangement (GA) drawing was prepared by A. D. Chapman and checked by a young Heinz Vogel, whose father had been a prisoner during the Second World War.

The principle wing dimensions drawing clearly show the triangle shape adopted by the Type 698.

Wing dimensions

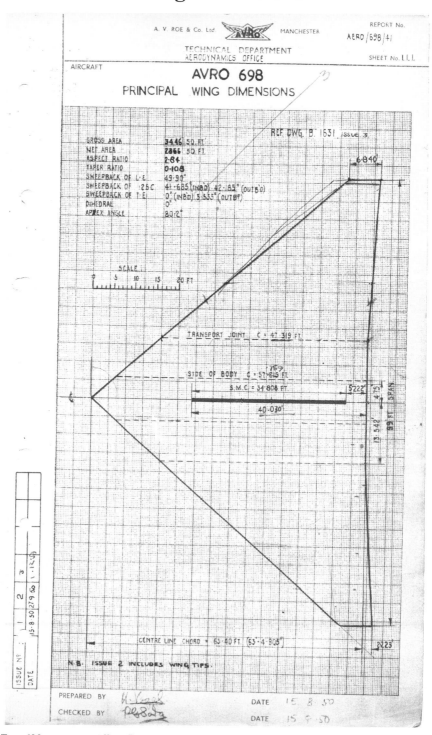

The Type 698 was essentially a flying wing, bended to the fuselage, as can be seen by this drawing issued in August 1950.

General arrangement & rudder drawing

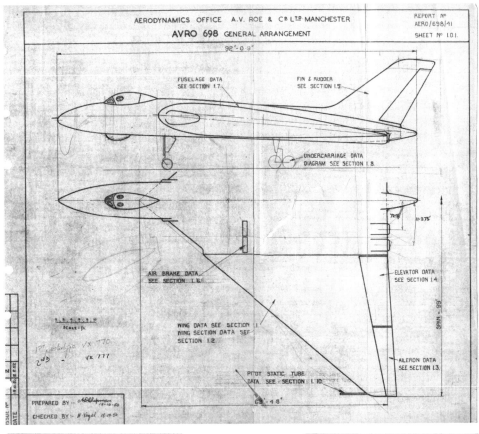

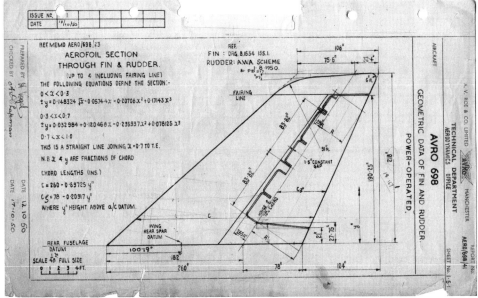

These two drawings were issued on 18th October, 1950.

Type 698 brochure - January 1951

INTRODUCTION

Since issue three of this brochure dated January 1950, a number of developments necessitated a further issue of the brochure.

In the first place detailed design of the aircraft has progressed to the state at which considerable reliance can be placed on the weight estimate, and it is desirable to base performance analysis on the latest figures.

Secondly, a number of high speed wind tunnel tests have been made at the Royal Aircraft establishment at Farnborough, in which wing section modifications similar to those adopted on the 698 were investigated. The results of these have given definite confirmation of the assumptions previously made, namely, that at the design cruising lift coefficient, there would be no compressibility drag rise at least until the specified cruising Mach number of 0.873 was reached.

Wind tunnel tests in the Compressed Air Tunnel of the National Physical Laboratory at Teddington on various models of delta wing aircraft, including the Avro 707B, have shown that for this planform the induced drag factor does not exceed 1.1 at all moderate lift coefficients. This figure has, therefore, been adopted in the new performance calculations instead of the more pessimistic value of 1.25 previously assumed.

On the engine side, a prototype of the Bristol Olympus) Mk.1/2. engine, which is a Mk.1 engine with the Mk.2 rating, has now been running over 80 hours and is already developing thrust and fuel consumption figures within a few percent of those predicted. In the present brochure the use of either the Mk.2 or the Mk.3 Olympus engines is considered. The former is aerodynamically similar to the Mk.2 and gives a sea level static thrust of 9,750 lb. The Mk.3 engine is similar to the Mk.2, but has an increased mass flow, and is estimated to give a sea level static thrust of 12,000 lb. together with somewhat improved fuel consumption. The increased thrust of the Mk.3 engine results in improved take-off performance and in a higher altitude over the target.

Since January 1950, slight changes have been made to the external layout of the aircraft, notably an increase of 2 feet in the span, alterations to the wing tip, and the addition of a bomb-aimer's cupola. The effect of all such items has been included in the new performance estimate.

The Avro 707B, which is the second of the 1/3rd scale delta aircraft, has been designed to explore the flying qualities of this type of aircraft at low Mach number. It has now flown for some 57 hours at speeds between 380 knots E.A.S. and the stall at 82 knots, and 177 landings have been made. A considerable body of flight test evidence has been obtained which shows that over the conditions tested a tailless aircraft can have entirely satisfactory flying qualities. Direct confirmation has been obtained of the following which are applicable to the 698:- Neutral point and static margin, dynamic longitudinal stability, effectiveness and power of all three controls, behaviour in sideslips and at high rates of roll, dynamic lateral stability, stalling behaviour, approach and landing including cross-wind landing, and air brake size.

It was found initially on the 707B, that due to the abnormally far forward position of the c.g. relative to the rear wheels on this aircraft, the pilot was unable to raise the nose wheel until after the normal take-off speed was reached. This led to a take-off in which careful judgement was necessary, and the take-off distance was also greater than it should have been. A longer nose wheel strut, giving a higher ground incidence, was fitted and led to the adoption of a normal take-off technique in which the nose wheel leaves the ground before the minimum take-off speed. There was a corresponding reduction in take-off distance. This effect is less important on the 698, but it has been decided to lengthen the nose wheel strut on this aircraft also to give the same ground incidence as on the 707B.

In order to cover the behaviour of the tailless Delta configuration at high Mach number another 1/3rd. scale aircraft, the 707A, is now nearing completion. The wing, including the flying controls, air brakes, and engine air intakes, is a replica of that of the 698, and it will therefore, be possible to deduce the behaviour of the latter aircraft directly from flight tests on this model.

Structure

The production breakdown has various components into which the aircraft is split for ease of manufacture, handling, and transport, and in the following description these components will be described separately.

Fuselage

The fuselage is broken down into pressure cabin or front fuselage, nose cap and tail cone.

As will be seen from the cockpit layout, the pressure cabin containing crew and equipment is essentially a cylindrical faired shape bounded at the front end by a hemispherical un-stiffened bulkhead with the scanner mounting attached to its forward face. In the centre of this bulkhead is an access hole.

The rear bulkhead consists of a flat circular panel, the two heavy nose wheel beams on the rear face serving as reinforcing in addition to numerous "top hat" stiffeners.

The cabin shell is made up of deep circular arc formers with longitudinal "top hat" stringers covered with 18 S.W.G. light alloy sheet formed to the required shape. At the top and bottom of the shell the openings for canopy, bomb aimer's blister and the crew an entrance door are strengthen by stiff edge members formed to shape and riveted in. Internally, the loads from the pilots and navigators floors are transmitted downwards by struts to three main longitudinal beams which distribute the loads to formers and hence into the shell itself.

The nose cap consists of a faired shape made of Onazote covered with glass cloth and is un-stiffened apart from the rear attachment ring. Moulded into the nose cap are the glide path aerial and localiser and an earthing strip carrying the aerial feeds.

The rear end of the aircraft is completed by a tail cone constructed of Onazote and glass cloth in a similar manner to the nose cap.

Centre Section

The centre section, which is the largest structural item of the aircraft, includes the main portion of the body containing the bomb bay and the engine compartments.

The centre section is essentially a two-spar structure and is built around the very large bomb bay. The latter is bounded on each side by parallel ribs and by the main spars; the roof is constructed of arched formers to conform with the outer body lines and the lower surface is made up by large double-skinned bomb doors.

The two spars are continued outboard of the both bay over the part of the spar occupied by the engines. They are constricted of flat plate webs, together with light alloy booms to take the main end loads. Holes are cut in the webs where necessary for air intakes and jet pipes and suitable local stiffening added. Large chord-wise interspar ribs made up of plate webs and booms are positioned at the body sides, between the engines and at the span- wise extremities of the centre section which is the transport joint.

Forward of the front spar the leading edge of the wing is completely taken up by the engine air intakes which are formed of light alloy skins attached to and stiffened by formers.

The intakes continue aft in the engine bays which occupy the whole of the inter-spar space and forming the engine bays.

The centre section wing surface is formed by 20 S.W.G. light alloy skin and span wise stringers, and where cut for access doors, e.g. to the engines, is reinforced by edge formers.

Forward of the front spar is built a torsion box, the sides of which are extensions of the bomb bay ribs. The wing skinning and stringers form the top and bottom of this box, whilst a bulkhead, completes the box at the front end. This torsion box houses two of the fuselage fuel tanks.

The continuation of the skin and stringer shell forward forms the nose wheel compartment. In addition to the nose wheel and its retracting mechanism this contains two further fuselage fuel tanks supported from the roof structure. This compartment is completed at the forward end by a transport joint to which is attached the pressure cabin.

The trailing edge of the centre section is made up of the normal skin stringer and rib combination described above and is attached by bolting to a subsidiary spar. This trailing edge finishes in a circular ring to which the Onazote tail cone is attached and in which the tail warning scanner is mounted.

Outer wings

The outer wings, which house the main undercarriage, fuel tanks, ailerons and elevators, are constructed on two swept back spars with a stressed skin assisting in the carrying of end loads.

The spars are constructed of plate webs and light alloy booms and are joined by six inter-spar ribs on each side, of which four at the control hinges lie normal to the control hinge line, while the two end ribs lie chord wise to form the transport joint, and the wing tip. These main ribs are formed of plate webs with booms to take the end loads from the control hinges. Subsidiary ribs spaced between the six main ribs maintain the shape of the section and provide support for the 16 S.W.G. skins which forms the surface covering.

Five fuel tanks in each outer wing occupy the space between the spars and the ribs at each end of the elevator, each tank being supported by an elliptical section container built into the subsidiary ribs. Inboard of the fuel tanks and between the transport joint and inboard elevator ribs, is housed the undercarriage. The remaining space in this bay is utilised for nitrogen bottles, Green Satin aerial and camera.

Forward of the front spar, the structure is formed by a multiplicity of nose ribs covered by a span wise corrugated 26 S.W.G. skin, and an outer 14 S.W.G. skin which serves the double duty of provided a load carrying torsion box and ducting for the hot air thermal de-icing system.

Aft of the rear spar the control surface shrouds are supported by ribs attached to the rear spar, the top and bottom surfaces being made up of a corrugated double skinned section. The lower surface is arranged to hinge downwards for access to the control surfaces end the hydraulic control jacks.

Ailerons and Elevators

There are four trailing edge control surfaces on each wing, the outer pairs acting as ailerons and the inner pairs as elevators. They are made up of a stout light alloy D spar, with light trailing edge ribs covered with magnesium alloy sheet. The light alloy nose skin is extended forward to form a balance plate. A sealing strip of rubberised fabric is attached between the forward edge of the latter and the shroud skin.

Fin and Rudder

The fin is constructed on a base of two fin posts with light alloy ribs covered with magnesium alloy skin. Forward of the front fin post the structure is double skinned with corrugated internal stiffening, the corrugations running chord wise so as to form a duct for hot air thermal de-icing. The structure of the rudder is similar to that of the other controls and consists of a light alloy D spar and ribs covered with magnesium as alloy sheet.

Production breakdown

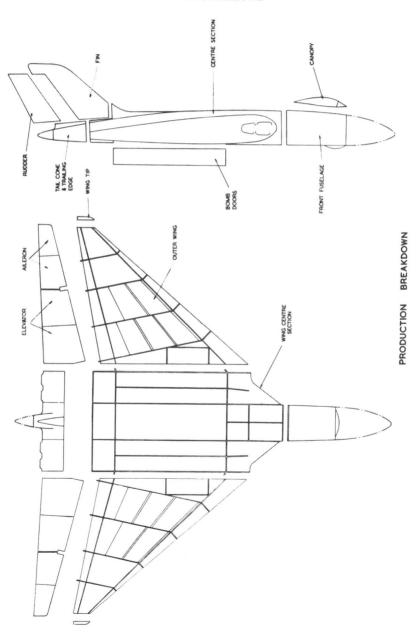

Engine installation

The aircraft is powered by four Bristol Olympus axial flow jet engines. The engine bays have, however, been designed so that the fitting of Rolls-Royce Conway or Avon engines as alternatives is relatively simple. (Use of Avon engines is intended only on the first prototype). The installation described here will be that for the Olympus.

Air for the engines is taken in through two large intakes one in each centre section wing leading edge, and swept back to conform to the wing shape. Each intake is split into two by a dividing wall just aft of the intake mouth, and the four separate ducts continue aft to the faces of the engines. Boundary layer air is removed from the inboard intake walls by bleeds which exhaust into the upper and lower air flows over the wing, and an external lip is provided at the inboard end of the mouth to remove the fuselage boundary layer.

The jet pipes are supported by rollers at each end. They are not lagged, but are contained within a metal tunnel connecting to the engine bay at its forward end. Cooling air is drawn from the engine bay through this annular space by means of an injector system at the rear end.

In order to cater for the variation in pitching moment between power off end power on conditions, the jet pipe has been cut off at an angle at the rear end so that the resultant thrust moment about the normal centre of gravity balances the moment acting at the air intake.

To avoid the necessity for cutting the upper surface load bearing wing skin, the engines are installed from below, four men are required each having control over a manually operate lifting jack which hooks into prepared, positions on the wing structure. It will thus be seen that the operation of engine installation and removal has been made simple and rapid and eliminates the need for special long beam cranes and slinging gear.

The engine accessories provided consist of four 112 volt 22.5 kilowatt output D.C. generators and four Dowty hydraulic pumps delivering 5 G.P.M. at 4,000 lb. per sq. inch. One electrical and one hydraulic generator are fitted directly to each engine, thus eliminating the need for an accessory gearbox.

Bristol Olympus engine layout

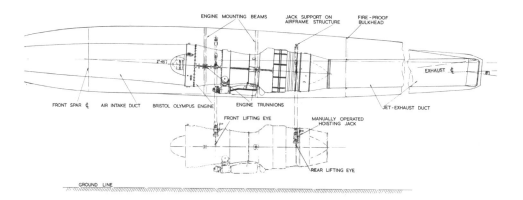

ENGINE MOUNTING BEAMS   JACK SUPPORT ON AIRFRAME STRUCTURE   FIRE-PROOF BULKHEAD

EXHAUST

FRONT SPAR   AIR INTAKE DUCT   BRISTOL OLYMPUS ENGINE   ENGINE TRUNNIONS   JET-EXHAUST DUCT

FRONT LIFTING EYE   MANUALLY OPERATED HOISTING JACK

REAR LIFTING EYE

GROUND LINE

ENGINE INSTALLATION & HOISTING DIAGRAM

SPECIFICATION B.35/46

Bomb arrangement

The large and roomy bomb bay on this aircraft is designed to cater for the greatly diversified bomb arrangements required. These range from a single 10,000 lb. special bomb to twenty-one 1,000 lb. bombs. The following different bomb arrangements are possible.

One	10,000	lb.	Special Bomb.
Two	10,000	lb.	H.C. Bombs.
Two	10,000	lb.	B.B. Bombs.
Three	5,000	lb.	H.C. Bombs.
Two	5,000	lb.	B.B. Bombs.
Five	2,000	lb.	Mines.
Twenty-one	1,000	lb.	H.C. Bombs. or L.C.
Twenty-one	1,000	lb.	B.B. Bombs.

The unrestricted space in the bomb bay measures 29 feet long by 7 feet wide and 6 feet deep making a total volume of 1218 cubic feet. The roof formers which act as beams to transfer the loads to the main centre section ribs are spaced so as to cater for all the necessary variations of carrier slinging points.

To avoid undue drag on opening and improving the bomb dropping characteristics, the very large bomb doors have each been split longitudinally, making effectively four doors in all. The outer portions are hinged to the wing structure along their outer edges, while the inner portions are hinged to the outer portions along the inner edges of the latter. This arrangement gives the minimum of protrusion outside the fuselage lines.

As in the case of the engines the need to preserve the strength of the upper wing skin precludes the use of the normal bomb hoisting gear and the new method has been devised. The bombs complete with their beams and carriers are brought to the aircraft on a special trolley. Two hydraulic jacks are fitted to the bomb beams and extended to hook up into prepared positions in the aircraft. The jacks are then retracted, raising the complete array into position. The carriers are attached to the slinging points by wedge shaped slides after which the jacks are removed and applied to a further array.

It will thus be seen that the scheme provides for an easy and rapid method of bomb loading which is applicable to any bomb arrangement without restriction.

Bomb loading arrangement

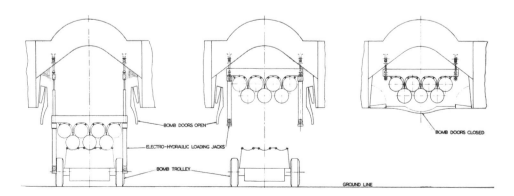

Crew accommodation

The arrangement of the accommodation for the crew consists of the whole of the pressurised portion of the fuselage and provision is made for a crew of five, namely,

First pilot
Second pilot
First navigator/Bomb aimer
Second navigator/radar operator
Signaller

The entrance is an outward opening door in the lower surface of the fuselage reached by means of a ladder. A fixed ladder is also provided in the cabin for access to the pilots' position.

The two pilots are seated side by side on ejector seats on a raised platform at the forward end of the cabin, forward view being through a large curved windscreen. This windscreen is faired by a metal covered canopy in which sideways vision is provided by circular glass portholes in either side at head level. The canopy is jettisonable.

A large instrument panel illuminated by ultra-violet and red lighting, contains the flight instruments which apart from the tail warning indicator, clock and N.B.C. bombing directional indicator, are all duplicated for the second pilot.

Conventional control wheels and rudder bars are provided. The remaining flying controls operated by the pilots are carried on three consoles, one on the port side, one central between the pilots and the other on the starboard side. The centre console, accessible to either pilot, houses the controls for the engines, air brakes, undercarriage, automatic pilot and control trimming together with the low pressure fuel switches and the fuel capacity indicators. On the port console are housed the controls for engine starting, high pressure fuel cocks, bomb door opening and bomb jettisoning, V.H.F. radio, G.4.B. compass, tail warning, instrument landing system and navigation lights. The starboard console carries the switches and instruments for operation of the heating, pressurisation and de-icing system.

The other three members of the crew are positioned to the rear of the pilots, and face aft, being seated side by side at a chart table of generous proportions spanning the width of the aircraft. These crew members are provided with 25g seats and like the pilots carry back type parachutes.

At the rear edge of the table a full width instrument panel carries the radio and radar presentation together with navigational instruments, while two periscopic sextant positions are to be found in the cabin roof one on either side of the aircraft, and situated just aft of the pilots. Thus these sextants give an azimuth range of 360 degrees.

For visual bombing the bomb aimer lies prone on a padded mattress inside a cupola situated in the lower fuselage surface just forward of the entrance door. A flat glass screen in the forward end of this cupola enables a good view to be obtained when using the visual sighting head for the N.B.C. equipment.

In case of emergency the canopy is jettisonable uncovering the type H dinghy stored at the rear end, while each member of the crew also carries a type K seat dinghy. For emergency exit in the air the pilots are provided with ejector seats while the rest of the crew bale out through the entrance door which is held open by powerful pneumatic jacks.

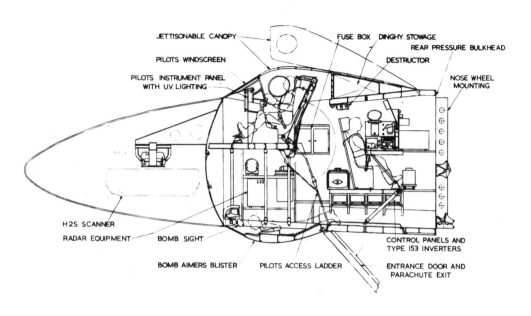

JETTISONABLE CANOPY

PILOTS WINDSCREEN

PILOTS INSTRUMENT PANEL
WITH U.V. LIGHTING

FUSE BOX   DINGHY STOWAGE

REAR PRESSURE BULKHEAD

DESTRUCTOR

NOSE WHEEL
MOUNTING

H.2S SCANNER

RADAR EQUIPMENT   BOMB SIGHT

BOMB AIMERS BLISTER   PILOTS ACCESS LADDER

CONTROL PANELS AND
TYPE 153 INVERTERS

ENTRANCE DOOR AND
PARACHUTE EXIT

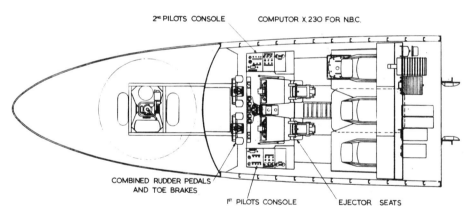

2ND PILOTS CONSOLE   COMPUTOR X.230 FOR N.B.C.

COMBINED RUDDER PEDALS
AND TOE BRAKES

1ST PILOTS CONSOLE   EJECTOR SEATS

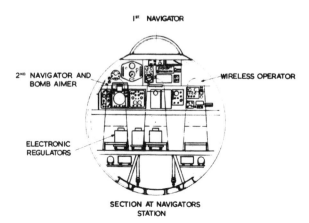

1ST NAVIGATOR

2ND NAVIGATOR AND
BOMB AIMER

WIRELESS OPERATOR

ELECTRONIC
REGULATORS

SECTION AT NAVIGATORS
STATION

Undercarriage

The aircraft is fitted with a hydraulically operated tricycle undercarriage, all three legs of which retract completely into the normal aircraft contour.

Each main undercarriage unit is a four wheeled bogie, consisting of two groups of two wheels each, mounted in tandem, each wheel carrying twin tyres. The units are mounted in the inboard end of the outer wings just aft of the front spar, and retract forward under hydraulic power. Thus air drag assists in lowering the undercarriage.

The main undercarriage doors are sequence operated to allow them to close after the lowering operation is completed, thus reducing undercarriage drag on take-off. Provision is made for these doors to be opened on the ground for maintenance and servicing purposes. This is effected by means of a switch which by-passes the sequence valve, thereby allowing the doors to be opened by means of a hand operated hydraulic pump.

Tyre pressure for the 27 - 6.50 - 15 main wheels is 130 lb. per sq. inch in the normal case rising to 156 lb. per sq. inch for overload cases. Braking is provided by automatically operated hydraulic plate brakes one to each wheel.

The nose wheel undercarriage is of conventional form utilising a levered suspension unit operating on a liquid spring shock absorber, and is arranged to retract aft under hydraulic power. The undercarriage leg itself consists of magnesium casting which includes the side bracing and thus gives a very rigid and light structure. Twin wheels of 30 - 9.00 - 15 size are fitted and operate at a normal tyre pressure of 102 lb. per sq inch. Hydraulic steering power is provided for the nose wheel to facilitate manoeuvres on the ground.

In order to enable the both trolleys to clear the rear fuselage with the existing lengthened nose wheel strut it may be necessary to provide a reduced ground attitude while bomb loading. This is accomplished by bleeding the hydraulic fluid from the liquid spring strut in the nose wheel leg, thus shortening the effective leg length.

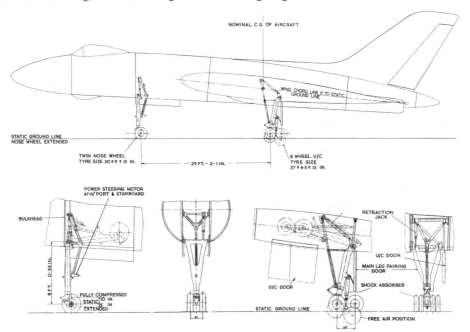

UNDERCARRIAGE ARRANGEMENT

Flying Controls

The flying control surfaces, namely, the ailerons, elevators and rudder are power operated and have forward sealed balances of the Westland- Irving type. Prototype aircraft will have electro-hydraulic Boulton Paul type power units driving hydraulic jacks and the control surfaces will be mass balanced. On production aircraft it is intended to use mechanical irreversible screw jacks in place of the hydraulic jacks so that the mass balance weights can be deleted.

The aileron and elevator control surfaces are divided into two portions, each operated by its own jack and controlled from its own power unit, so that there is no connection between the two sections and their power units other than the common pilot's control on the input side. Failure of a power unit or jack will cause the corresponding section of the control surface to lock in the position it occupied at the time of failure. The other three sections remain unaffected so that control of the aircraft at three-quarters of the full normal rate is then obtainable.

In the case of the rudder, splitting the surface into two sections would result in the power units being placed high on the fin and in an awkward position for maintenance purposes. Duplicated power units at the base of the rudder have therefore been adopted. Either of these power units is powerful enough to operate the whole of the control surface and one will normally be controlling the rudder while the other is idling. In the event of failure the second unit is automatically brought into operation.

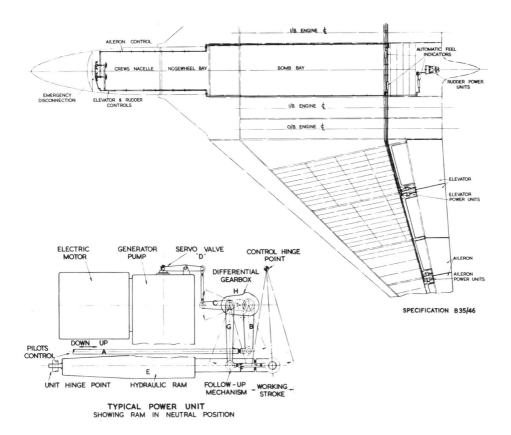

Conventional push-pull rods connect the control column and rudder bar to the power units. Artificial feel is provided to give a variation of stick force with control movement from the trimmed position. In order to give pleasant control forces and harmonisation over the speed range, the stick force per degree of control movement increases as the one and one-half power of the indicated air speed in the case of the ailerons and as the square of the indicated air speed in the case of the elevators and rudder.

In addition a 'g' restrictor is provided in the pilots control circuit to the elevator, to guard against over-stressing of the aircraft.

Each unit consists of an assembly of an electric motor, a three bank hydraulic pump of the variable stroke type and a hydraulic jack. The electric motor drives the hydraulic pump and is in continuous operation. One bank of the pump supplies oil at a base pressure to operate a servo mechanism. The remaining two banks deliver oil to the jack in response to the servo mechanism.

The power unit diagram on the previous page shows the input lever (B) and the follow-up lever (G) are on opposite sides of a differential gear operating the servo lever (C). The pilot demands a control surface movement by moving the push-pull tube A. which rotates the input lever (B). This motion is transmitted through the differential gear to the servo lever (C) and operates a pilot valve contained in the pump body. Movement of the pilot valve causes oil at the base pressure to be fed to the servo valve (D) moving it in the same direction as the pilot valve. Movement of the servo valve increases the stroke of the pistons in the pump and causes oil to be delivered to the jack (E). The side of the piston to which oil is delivered and therefore the direction of the control movement is determined by the direction in which the servo valve has been moved. In order to cancel the signal to the servo valve, the ram is connected to the follow up lever (C). Movement of the ram is therefore fed back to the differential gear box and returns the servo lever (C) to neutral when the control surface is in the position demanded by the pilot.

Air Brakes

The air brakes are situated in the centre section just aft of the front spar and perform three main functions:

(a) To allow the aircraft to achieve high rates of descent without exceeding the speed and Mach number limitations laid down from strength considerations. This is particularly necessary at high altitude both for operational purposes and to reduce altitude rapidly in case of pressure cabin failure.

(b) To effect rapid deceleration from high air speeds.

(c) To give additional drag on the approach and landing.

In addition, the automatic operation of the air brakes from the Mach meter so as to prevent the limiting Mach number being exceeded is under consideration.

The number of air brakes used is eight in all, mounted in four pairs each pair comprising an upper and lower brake. Light alloy stiffened panels form the main slats of the air brakes and each is supported by two stiff tubular columns which pass either side of the air intakes. Operation is effected through a system of balancing chains driven through sprockets by shafts coupled to a central gearbox, which is in turn driven by duplicated electric motors. By this means all the air brakes act simultaneously.

The operating lever is a gated control with three positions. In the retracted position the slats lie flush with the wing surface. In the first extended position, corresponding to the gate, the slats are extended into the airstream, but remain along the line of air flow; in the second, they are turned through 90° to give a much higher drag coefficient. The first position is used at high speeds and the second at low speeds and for landing.

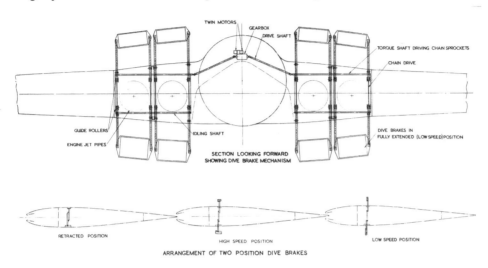

ARRANGEMENT OF TWO POSITION DIVE BRAKES

Pressurisation and Anti -Icing
Pressurisation

The air required for pressurising the aircraft is obtained by tapping high pressure air off each engine at the last stage of the compressor and feeding it through mass flow controllers into a common duct situated in the nose wheel bay.

Prior to entering the cabin the flow of air is controlled and regulated by means of an automatically operated control unit. This unit allows the air either to pass through or by-pass

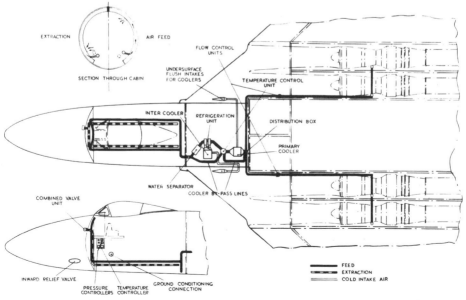

AIR CONDITIONING

an air to air cooler and/or a refrigerator, depending on the atmospheric conditions in which the aircraft is operating. The cabin air temperature range is from -50°C to +25°C and air is delivered at the rate of 10 lb./min.; the used air is not re-circulated but is discharged to heat the radar equipment in the nose.

A cabin altitude of 8,000 ft. is maintained up to a height of 47,400 ft., corresponding to a pressure differential of 9 lb./sq. inch. Above this altitude the same differential is maintained. Provision is made for increasing the cabin altitude to 25,000 ft. under combat conditions, whilst emergency decompression is obtainable by fully opening the discharge valve. Air conditioning without pressurisation is also provided for low level flight. A "Flood Flow" is automatically provided in the event of excess leakage, e.g. following damage to the cabin in combat.

Anti - Icing

A hot thermal anti-icing system provides protection again at ice accretion on all leading edges. The hot air required for this system is obtained from the same source as the pressurisation air. It is mixed with cold air by means of an injector and then fed to the wing and fin at a controlled temperature of 150°C. Distribution through the wing is by means of a leading edge duct around the corrugations under the wing leading edge skinning, thence into a collecting duct and out to atmosphere.

Bomb Bay Heating

A separate paraffin fired combustion heater is provided for heating the bomb bay, this method being considered the most economical in view of large surface areas involved.

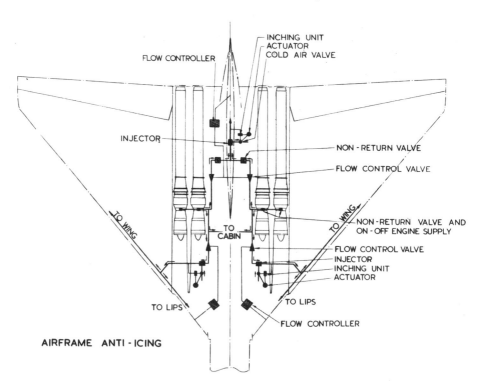

Fuel System

The total quantity of fuel carried by the aeroplane is 8,300 gallons. This amount is distributed between 14 flexible crash proof tanks, four of which are situated in the nose wheel bay of the fuselage, the remainder being in the wings. To cover the overload range of 5,000 nautical miles an additional tank of 360 gallons capacity, making 8,660 gallons, can be fitted at the forward end of the bomb bay roof.

The fuel tanks are arranged in groups so that each engine is fed by a particular group of tanks. The outboard engines are fed by tanks 1, 4, 5 and 7, whilst the inboard engines are fed by tanks, 2, 3 and 6. Under normal conditions each engine is fed by its own group of tanks, but emergency cross feed cocks are provided so that any engine may receive fuel from any tank or group of tanks. For short-range operations, the aircraft will normally be flown on tanks No.1, 3, 4, and 6 only.

All the tanks are fitted with electrically operated fuel pumps which normally run at half current. Under take-off conditions all pumps run at full power. Throughout the flight each tank is selected in turn by a cam-selector mechanism driven by a constant speed motor, and the pump in the respective tank is boosted to full capacity for a time proportionate to the fuel capacity of the tank. The pressure built up by other pumps running at half current is not sufficient to overcome the resistance of the non-return valves in the system so that one pump running at full power is feeding each engine throughout the flight. If, however, the fuel capacity of the one pump is not sufficient to supply the engine with fuel, the pressure in the in feed line falls and the non-return valves can open, thus allowing the idling pumps to empty some fuel to the engine. In this way the tanks are allowed to empty at an even rate and the balance of the aircraft is maintained between the desired limits.

An electrically operated fuel transfer pump is fitted in the forward fuselage tanks (number 1), and the outboard wing tanks (number 7) so that fuel may be transferred from one to the other to balance the aircraft in an emergency.

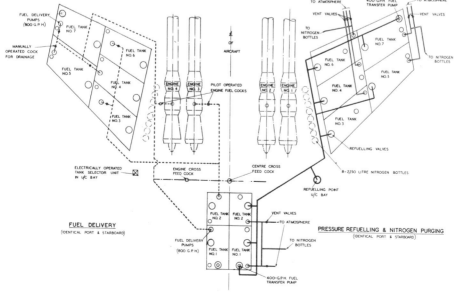

FUEL SYSTEM – DIAGRAMMATIC

The controls for the fuel system are remotely operated by switches under the control of the pilot. The presentation of these switches is in the form of a diagram showing the layout of the aircraft with each switch positioned relative to the unit it controls, The total quantity of fuel available is shown on the pilot's panel while the amount of fuel available to each engine (without operation of cross feeds) is indicated on the fuel control panel. Individual tank contents are available by depression of a switch relevant to the particular tank, the reading being presented on the gauge appropriate to the group to which the tank belongs.

The tanks are pressurised by means of a nitrogen purging system which assists in preventing the fuel boiling.

Pressure re-fuelling and de-fuelling is provided, the charge points being situated in the main undercarriage bays.

Electrical System

Main electrical power for the aircraft and its equipment is generated by four 112 volt 22.5 kilowatt D.C. generators, one on each engine. Two power panels are mounted one for each side at the forward end of the bomb bay, and each contains voltage regulation and thermal protection equipment for the generators in one wing. The voltage regulators are remotely trimmed from the generator panel at the signaller's position in the crew's cabin.

The supply is fed from these power panels to the common busbar in the 112 volt distribution panel located on the aft face of the front spar in the boat bay. Feeders also run from the power panels to energise the two 'power operated flying control' panels mounted aft of the bomb bay on the rear spar. The feeds from these latter panels to the individual flying control actuators and their control equipment are duplicated for safety purposes.

Conversion of the 112 volt supply to the more normal 28 volt supply is accomplished by means of three rotary transformers situated at the rear end of the nose wheel bay. The input to these transformers from the distribution panel is 112 volt D.C. and the output is 3 kilowatts each at 28 volts D.C. The power panels for these units are mounted on the forward face of the rear nose wheel bay bulkhead and feed a common busbar in the 28 volt distribution panel which is mounted close by.

The 112 volt and 28 volt distribution panels feed into the main fuse panels mounted on either side of the fuselage in the pressure cabin, distribution to normal services etc. taking place through these fuses.

Five 214 volt 4.0 ampere hour batteries are installed in a battery box mounted on the port side of the nose wheel bay. Four of these batteries, nominally 96 volts, are coupled to the busbar on the 112 volt distribution panel and one feeds to the busbar on the 28 volt distribution panel.

A 112 volt D.C. ground supply plug for ground testing and engine starting is fitted at the rear end of the nose wheel bay on the starboard side and connects to the 112 volt distribution panel. Only one ground supply plug is provided, and if a 28 volt supply is required for ground testing it is obtained by starting up one of the rotary transformers.

Engine starting is effected by 112 volt D.C. motors controlled through starter relays, and the main supply to each motor in turn is through a starter panel situated adjacent to the 112 volt distribution panel. For starting the engines from the aircraft batteries, the five batteries may be coupled in series giving a total of 120 volts 4.0 ampere hours. As soon as one engine is started the batteries are recoupled in their original 96 volt and 24 volt circuits and the other engines started from the normal 112 volt system.

The radar equipment receives its electrical power through three AD/DC rotary converters mounted on the starboard side of the nose wheel bay. Each converter operates on 112 volt

D.C. input and gives A.C. outputs, one of one kilowatt at 115 volts 3 phase 4.00 cycles per sec. and the other of two kilowatts at 115 volts single phase 1600 cycles per sec. The output of these converters is controlled from a relay panel situated on the rear cabin bulkhead with switches and manual circuit breakers on the signaller's transverse panel.

Four further rotary converters mounted under the cabin floor on the starboard aide, provide electrical power for the instruments. These converters operate under a 112 volt DC. input, two having an output of 750 watts 115 volt- 4.00 cycles and the other two a 200 watt 115 volt 400 cycle output.

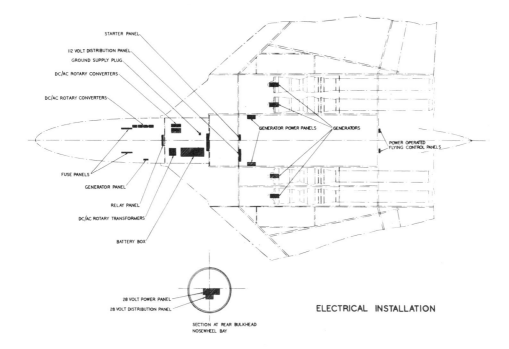

ELECTRICAL INSTALLATION

Radio and Radar installation

Main radio communication is made by a remote controlled high frequency transmitter and receiver (T.1570/R.1511) for H/T and W/T which is operated by the signaller. The receiver output is presented to the signaller only, and a change-over switch permits him to select H.F. equipment or intercom, as required. The main radio units are housed on the starboard side of the nose wheel bay and the suppressed aerial of the loop excitation type and its associated tuning unit are fitted in the dorsal fin behind a di-electric cover.

An intercom, amplifier is provided for the crew stations and for several ground servicing points, including the undercarriage bays and the bomb compartment.

The V.H.F. installation is provided with a total of 20 crystal controlled channels and consists of T.R.1934/1935 fitted in the tail end of the fuselage. Both these sets are controlled by the first pilot, the controller being fitted on the port console, where switches are provided to prevent both sets being used at the same time.

The two pilots have "Press to Transmit" switches incorporated in their control columns, and microphones which can be connected to the V.H.F. equipment. A single aerial with a change-over switch is housed in the Onazote cap of the fin.

For instrument landing a type S.R.14. localiser and marker receiver and S.R.15 glide path receiver are fitted in the cabin, being under the control of the first pilot, to whom both aural and visual presentation is provided. The output from these sets may be fed into the type "D" auto-pilot if desired for blind landings.

The localiser and glide path aerials are moulded into the Onazote nose of the aircraft, and a suppressed marker aerial of the slot type is fitted in the underside of the forward fuselage.

Provision is also made for a radio compass and a suppressed loop for automatic direction finding equipment.

The two navigators control the H.2.S. Mk.9 and N.B.C. Mk.2 equipment. The H.2.S. is housed in the Onazote nose of the aircraft which gives the maximum possible forward view and a rearward view which is cut off at an angle of approximately 40° from the horizontal over a small sector about the aircraft centre line.

The N.B.C. equipment includes various emergency computers and controls and a visual sighting head to permit accurate visual bombing.

The tail-warning signal and transmitter-receiver forms one complete and easily removable unit located in the tail fairing of the fuselage. The signaller has a cathode ray tube for presentation and also the main control of this equipment. The pilot also has a cathode ray tube and a secondary control is fitted in the port console.

Standard Mk.3 I.F.F. equipment is fitted together with its suppressed slot aerial being controlled from the signaller's station.

The first navigator's station is fitted with a Gee indicator, as a short range navigational aid. A combined indicator and controller for Green Satin is provided at the navigator's station whilst the aerial is housed behind a di-electric window aft of the port undercarriage bay.

A high range radar altimeter presents its information on a cathode ray tube at the second navigator's station, its two aerials and T.R. unit are mounted close by.

RADIO INSTALLATION

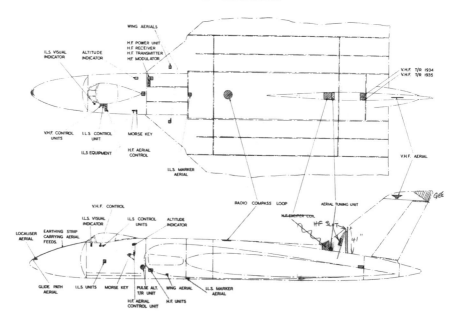

The aerial for Blue Boar is fitted within the Onazote nose of the aircraft, with controls and an indicator at the first navigator's station.

On the navigator's panel are switches and indicators for controlling three inverters which provide A.C. supplies for the radar equipment.

The switching is arranged so that in the event of failure on one unit, power can be maintained to the H.2.S. and N.B.C. equipment.

RADAR INSTALLATION

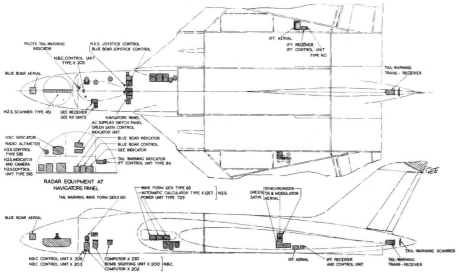

Performance

Authors note:- This section of the brochure gave the performance of the aircraft under various operational conditions, and assumptions made in estimating the performance. Not shown are all the graphs but some relevant information is included.

Throughout, the alternative use of the Bristol Olympus B.OL.2 or of the Bristol Olympus B.OL.3 was considered, the appropriate data being taken respectively from Bristol Aeroplane Company brochures T.C.202/4 and T.C.210. A summary of the engine thrust and fuel consumption of the MK.3. engine is substantially better than that of the MK.2. (i. e. 0.962 lb/lb/hr. as against 1. 02 lb/lb/hr for the case of 500 knots at 50,000 ft). It is understood that this is due to a modification (as yet untested) which will be incorporated in the MK.3. engine, and could be incorporated in the MK.2. engine. Its effect is not, however, included in the performance data for the MK.2. engine which is used throughout this brochure.

The maximum range on a jet-propelled aircraft flying in the stratosphere is obtained when it is flown at all times at the maximum altitude possible. The air speed is determined by the avoidance of the compressibility drag rise and there is ample evidence to show that at the low cruising lift coefficient (namely, 0.20) which is characteristic of the Delta layout, there is no drag rise at the cruising Mach number of 0.873, corresponding to a true air speed of 500 knots in the stratosphere. In the standard flight plan, therefore, the aircraft takes-off, accelerates to the best climbing speed, climbs to the altitude at which there is no rate of climb at the above Mach number, and thereafter cruises at constant Mach number. As fuel is consumed on the cruise, the altitude increases.

Flight Plans

Flight plans have been estimated for the standard case in which a 10,000 lb. bomb load is carried throughout, (i. e. it is not dropped at the target), and are given on graph (A) for the MK. 2. engine and graph (B) for the MK. 3 engine. Flight plans are given for operating radii of 500, 1,000, 1,500, 2,000 and 2,325 nautical miles, corresponding to still air range of 1,350, 2,350, 3,350 and 5,000 nautical miles. It is assumed that the additional still air range of 350 nautical rules represents a fuel allowance for diversion, stand-off and landing. In order to illustrate the effect of the allowance of 350 nautical miles still air range, the figures shown on graph (C) have been prepared and indicate that for the full 3,350 nautical miles still air range case and using an average glide technique the fuel remaining in the tanks after landing, will be in the order of 150 gallons. For 3,000 nautical miles still air range and using the same glide technique, the fuel remaining will be 576 gallons for the Mk.2. engine and 546 gallons for the MK.3. engine.

The normal range quoted in the specification, and for which the aircraft is designed, is 3,350 nautical miles and at the weight corresponding to this range, the full structural factors specified are obtained. A range of 5,000 nautical miles represents the maximum for which internal fuel is provided and is regarded as an overload case.

In the case of the MK.2. engine, the corresponding amount of fuel is 8,660 gallons of which 8,300 gallons are carried in the "built in" wing and fuselage tanks, and 360 gallons are carried in a tank fitted at the forward end of the bomb bay roof. The fitting of this tank does not conflict with any of the bomb arrangements. This tank is not required for 5,000 nautical miles range with the MK.3. engine.

It will be noted that the hangar weight exceeds the take-off weight by 1,000 lb, comprising an allowance of fuel for starting up the engines and taxiing out to the take-off point.

Take-off and landing

In both take-off and landing cases, the technique used, has been based on techniques developed during the course of flight testing on the Avro 707B. For instance, the lift coefficient at take-off, climb away, and on the approach and touch-down, have been based on an average of those obtained on the 707B and thus represent what an operational pilot can achieve on the majority of the occasions. In the case of the landing run, the provision of automatic brakes on the 698 enables the assumption to be made that a friction coefficient of 0.3 represents the average value that will be obtained during the ground run.

Effect of typical engine failures

The effect on height and range of typical engine failures on the aircraft fitted with Bristol Olympus B.OL.3 engines an estimated drag increment of 30 lb. at 100 ft/sec. has been used for a stopped engine. This increase in total drag of the aircraft, together with the decrease in available thrust necessitates a reduction in cruising speed.

The optimum cruising speed for one engine stopped has been found to be approximately 430 knots True Air Speed. At this speed, for an engine failure one hour after take-off, the range reduction is 626 nautical miles (12.5% the maximum reduction allowed in the a specification is 1,000 nautical miles (20%).

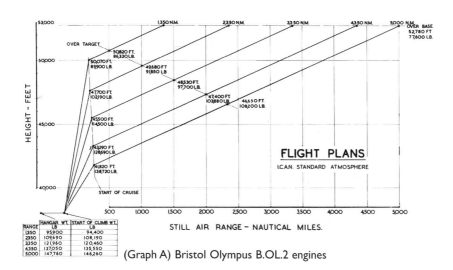

RANGE	HANGAR WT. LB	START OF CLIMB WT. LB
1350	95,900	94,400
2350	109,690	108,190
3350	121,960	120,460
4350	137,050	135,550
5000	147,760	146,260

(Graph A) Bristol Olympus B.OL.2 engines

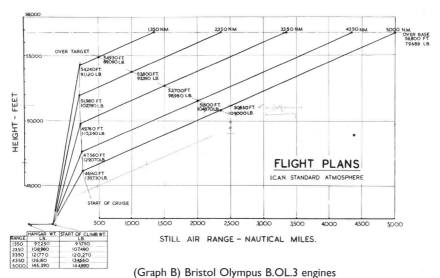

RANGE	HANGAR WT. LB	START OF CLIMB WT. LB
1350	97,250	95,750
2350	108,980	107,480
3350	121,770	120,270
4350	136,160	134,660
5000	146,390	144,890

(Graph B) Bristol Olympus B.OL.3 engines

(Graph C) Bristol Olympus B.OL.3 engines

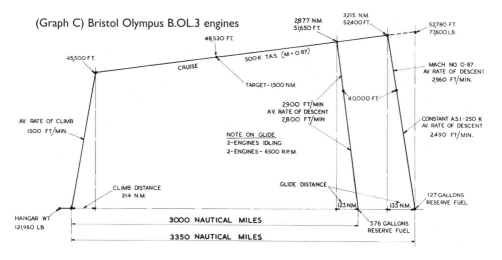

The use of Landing Parachutes

Practical experience with the Avro 707B aircraft has shown the beneficial effect of the use of brake parachutes for landing. Over 30 landings have been made with an 8 ft. diameter parachute. The normal procedure is to stream the parachute at a height of about 20 feet when using the normal approach technique. There is no effect on the trim of the aircraft and the subsequent flatten out and landing is made in the usual way.

In view of the above, a scheme has been considered for the fitting of two 16 ft. diameter parachutes on the Avro 698. It is expected that these would be used chiefly in circumstances in which the landing run would be greater than normal, i.e., for landing at higher weights or on a small aerodrome, or under conditions when ice is on the runway. Parachutes are also of value in reducing wear and tear on the wheel brakes and tyres.

In order to show the effect of parachutes on landing distance, calculations have been made, assuming two 16 ft. diameter parachutes open at a height of 20 feet and used in conjunction with the normal wheel braking.

These landing calculations assume that the approach speed has a normal value as obtained on the 707B. The parachutes are of considerable value in compensating automatically for increased approach speeds since the braking effect of the parachutes increases as the square of the speed. Thus the adverse consequence of an approach with excess velocity are considerably reduced.

Development to give increased bomb load and/or range

This section describes the proposed fitment of nacelles, one on each wing, so as to make possible a considerable increase in the Bomb load at the expense of range. Alternatively, additional fuel may be carried in the same position giving a considerably increased range with the 10,000 lb. special bomb. The load cases considered are :-

45 x 1,000 lb.	H.C. or L.C. bombs, at reduced range.
53 x 1,000 lb.	H.C. or L.C. bombs, at reduced range.
4 x 10,000 lb.	H.C. bombs, at reduced range.
1 x 10,000 lb.	Special bomb at increased range.

The low wing loading and the large thrust weight ratio with the proposed Olympus MK.3. engine, make the Avro 698 relatively insensitive to considerable increases of load. For normal bomber use, however, the aircraft must operate from existing airfields which sets a limit to take-off distance to a height of 50 ft. of 2,500 yds, in still air, and I.C.A.N. standard conditions. The corresponding take-off gross weight is 162,500 lb. and this is, therefore, adopted as the maximum weight for the first three cases listed, above, namely, those of increased bomb load. This weight limitation, therefore, fixes the range at which any of the above loads can be carried.

The proposal for increasing the range when carrying 1 - 10,000 lb. special bomb is in a different category. For this type of operation, it should be possible to make use of one of the larger aerodromes, permitting a further increase in take-off weight to the value of 173,900 lb. at which the take-off distance, to a height of 50 ft. is 2,860 yds. At this weight, a special bomb can be carried for still air range of 6,150 nautical miles.

The above, of course, assumes unassisted take-off. The layout of the 698 makes it relatively easy to apply rocket assistance to the aircraft, should this be acceptable to the Service.

For all these cases, it is proposed to meet the full factors when carrying any of the above loads plus 2/3 of the fuel associated with the above take-off weights. This will lead to slightly reduced factors for the first part of the flight, but full factors will be obtained before reaching the target areas. Since the extra loads on the wing, namely, the weight of the nacelle and bombs or fuel, provide relief loads on the main flight cases, the corresponding structure weight increase will not be large. It is made up as follows:-

Strengthening of Wing & Fuselage Structure.	1,100 lb.
Strengthening of Undercarriage.	450 lb.
Attachment points for the Nacelles.	50 lb.
Total	**1,600 lb.**

A number of arrangements of nacelle were studied, e. g, suspended on a strut from the wing, but the design shown was considered to give the smallest increase of drag at high Mach numbers. The fineness ratio is about 7 and the maximum thickness is placed well forward in relation to the maximum thickness of the wing. Detailed wind tunnel tests are in hand to investigate the effect of nacelle shape on critical Mach number and it is expected that these will lead to further improvements on the shape shown.

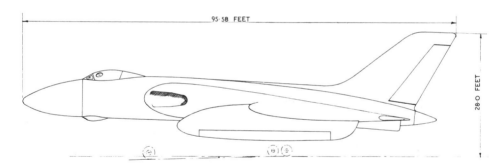

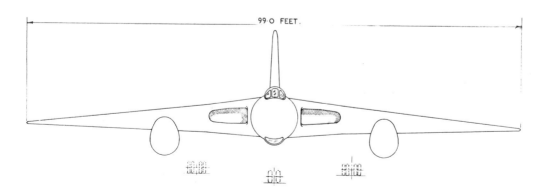

Photographic Reconnaissance (PR) Version

It is visualised that when the Avro Type 698 is in operational use a bomber, that there will be a need for a long range high performance photographic reconnaissance aircraft to seek out and photograph possible targets and also to photograph the effects of previous raids by bombers. This version of the 698, will have a maximum range of 6,520 nautical miles at a take-off weight of 171,900 lbs. At this weight, the take-off distance to a 50 ft. screen is 2,800 yds. which, although high by normal standards, may be acceptable for a few specialised aircraft operating from particular aerodromes. Rocket assisted take-off, for which the 698 is ideally suitable, will, of course, reduce this distance, and make possible operation from normal Bomber Command aerodromes.

It is proposed to meet the full factors when carrying 2/3 of the fuel associated with the above take-off weight. This will lead to slightly reduced factors for the first part of the flight, but full factors will be obtained before reaching the target area.

The increase in structure weight is not large, and is made up as follows:-

Strengthening of Wing & Fuselage Structure	1,150 lb.
Strengthening of Undercarriage	450 lb.
Total :	1,600 lb.

The modifications to a standard 698 to convert it to this duty have been kept to a minimum. The alterations are confined to the bomb bay and fuel system. As will be seen the only appreciable items are the substitution of the alternative bomb doors, a fairing in place of the centre part of the bomb door and the provision of special mountings for the camera crate, for the both bay fuel tanks and for the pyrotechnic carriers.

The following at present proposed, are illustrated below.

10	-	F.X.96	Cameras.
2	-	70 m.m.	Cameras.
1	-	F.49.	Camera.
2	-	70 m.m. (Night) Cameras.	

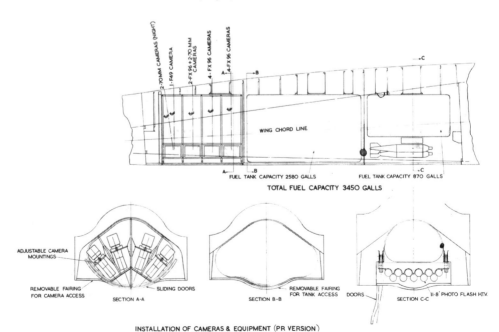

INSTALLATION OF CAMERAS & EQUIPMENT (PR VERSION)

Target Marker version

When the Avro Type 698 is in operational use with the Service as a long range high speed bomber it is visualised that an aircraft of comparable range will be required to seek out and mark precise targets for the bomber. A development of the 698 as a target marker aircraft is therefore, proposed. The target marker aircraft must, of course, have the same range as the 698 but differs from the latter in that it is required to descend to low altitudes for location and marking of targets. The 698 has been designed for maximum efficiency at high altitudes and some strengthening of its structure will therefore, be necessary if its potential performance is to be exploited fully when flying at low altitudes. Apart from this strengthening and from certain modifications which are required by the role of target marking, the aircraft will not differ much from the standard 698 and all the modifications would be incorporated on the normal production line.

The increased structure weight and the considerable increase in fuel load necessitated by high speed operation at low altitude, lead to an appreciable increase in take-off weight. If required, the target marker aircraft could, of course, be used as a bomber, but the increased structure weight and the consequent increase in fuel weight, lead to a take-off weight which is greater than that of the standard aircraft.

There are, at the moment, no requirements for a target marker aircraft with a performance and range comparable to the Avro 698, and the requirements of Specification B.104.D. have therefore, been studied with a view to laying down a comparable specification.

The increase in structure weight required to meet the above flight envelope conditions is estimated to be as follows:-

Mainplane.	1775 lb.
Fuselage.	70 lb.
Fin and Rudder.	625 lb.
Landing gear.	14.5 lb.
Total	**2615 lb.**

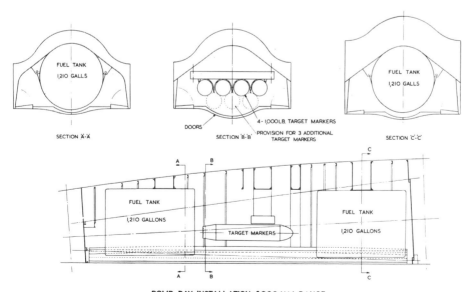

BOMB BAY INSTALLATION- 5,000 N.M. RANGE
TARGET MARKER VERSION

Type 707A - WD280

Contract 6/acft/3395/CB/6(a) for this aircraft was issued on 6th May, 1949 to specification E.10/49. The air intake was more representative of the 698 and was mainly used to test the high speed envelope confirming that buffeting at high Mach numbers would be a problem.

On 23rd May, 1951 Avro 707A (WD280) arrived at Boscombe Down to be assembled. Fitting of the components started on 24th May and by the 28th May, the wings had been attached. The first flight of WD280 was on the 14th June, 1951 eleven months after the Type 707B. Continuing the bright colour schemes adopted for the small Delta aircraft WD280 was painted a shade of orange/red.

AVRO 707
RESEARCH AIRCRAFT
____

AN AVRO PHOTOGRAPH
BY STAFF PHOTOGRAPHER
PAUL CULLERNE
A.I.B.P.
Issued with the compliments of
A. V. ROE & CO. LTD.,
MANCHESTER - ENGLAND.

This picture was used as a colour handout and was taken by Avro's staff photographer Paul Cullerne

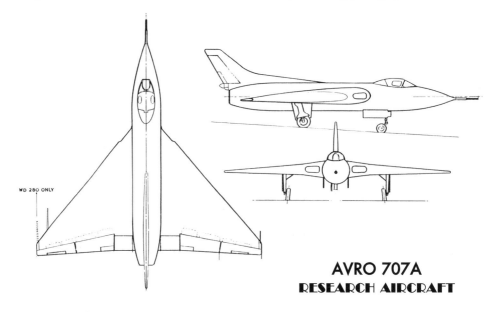

WD 280 ONLY

AVRO 707A
RESEARCH AIRCRAFT

707A Cockpit 16th July, 1951.

Rolls-Royce Derwent 5 engine in-situ.

707A at Boscombe Down 16th July, 1951.

Rear view of WD280 at Boscombe Down, pictured in July 1951.

AVRO 707A AND 707B S.M.C., C.G. & N.P., DATA DIAGRAM

Data diagram produced by the Aerodynamics Department 2nd November, 1950 shows the differences between the Type 707A and 707B development aircraft.

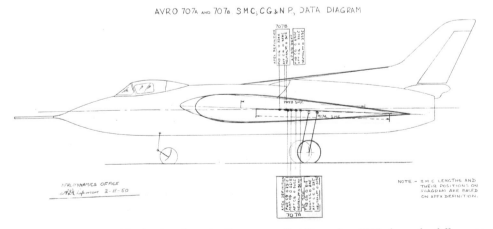

This view shows the delta wing to its best advantage, photographed in September, 1951.

A description on the 707A delta design is shown in a later section later of this book on the second 707A aircraft WZ736.

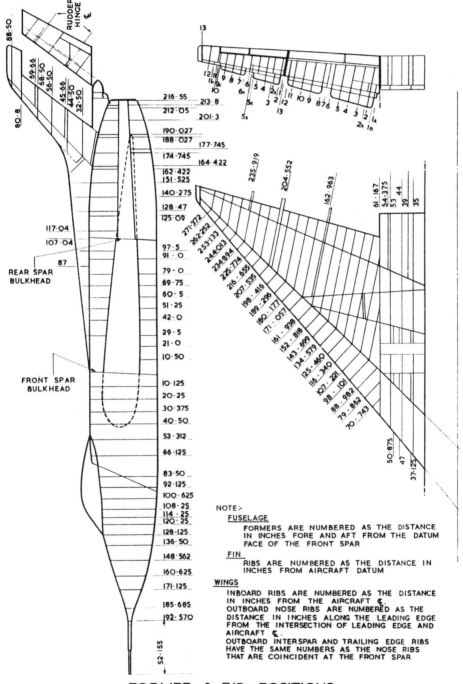

NOTE:-

FUSELAGE
FORMERS ARE NUMBERED AS THE DISTANCE IN INCHES FORE AND AFT FROM THE DATUM FACE OF THE FRONT SPAR

FIN
RIBS ARE NUMBERED AS THE DISTANCE IN INCHES FROM AIRCRAFT DATUM

WINGS
INBOARD RIBS ARE NUMBERED AS THE DISTANCE IN INCHES FROM THE AIRCRAFT ℄.
OUTBOARD NOSE RIBS ARE NUMBERED AS THE DISTANCE IN INCHES ALONG THE LEADING EDGE FROM THE INTERSECTION OF LEADING EDGE AND AIRCRAFT ℄.
OUTBOARD INTERSPAR AND TRAILING EDGE RIBS HAVE THE SAME NUMBERS AS THE NOSE RIBS THAT ARE COINCIDENT AT THE FRONT SPAR

FORMER & RIB POSITIONS

Avro flight research unit at Boscombe Down

A. V. Roe established a flight research unit at Boscombe Down, Amesbury, Wiltshire which was a complete organisation able to collect information, analyse and issue reports on the results. The unit was headed by Mr Z. Olenski with the help of W. Gilmour, F. Basset and S.I.R. Nicol plus a staff of over forty people.

Boscombe Down was the home of the Avro flight research unit, WD280 pictured in July 1951.

Reports were sent by teleprinter to Woodford on progress at Boscombe Down. Later as more aircraft were built and early experimental problems were overcome the unit moved to Woodford and became part of the normal flight organisation.

Progress Summary May - July 1952

Various reports were produced on the progress of WD280 and VX790 in early 1952, shown below are extracts from those reports.

Avro 707A (WD280) on flight (No.166) gave a demonstration to Imperial Defence College delegates in early May. The subject of flights (No.168 and 172) between 9th to 11th May were concerned with vibrations up to 450 knots E.A.S. In the same month Roly Falk laid down clear requirements of handling properties for power controls to minimise delays in future development and in early June issued report Aero/misc9 on power control system requirements. On the 12th May WD280 was flown to Woodford for major modifications (powered controls and pressurisation). From 12th May since its first ferry flight (No.173) which took 30 minutes, WD280 was flying at Woodford up to 20th May. It made five flights at Woodford (No.174 to 178) and made five landings totalling one hour thirty five minutes. Total flying time to that date was 92 hours 40 minutes in 178 flights and 197 landings.

Avro 707B (VX790) since its very short flight (No.200 first after rebuilding) made on 12th May 1952, the aircraft had been grounded and remained at Woodford. This non flying period was fully utilised for catching up with items delayed due to intensive 707A flying prior to the 12th May. On 5th June VX790 flew to Dunsfold where on 6th June three flights were made (No.202 to 204) to improve lateral trim control and demonstration of the aeroplane before returning to Boscombe Down. On 1st July (flights 222-224) the aircraft made a transit flight to and from Boscombe Down and a demonstration flight given at the combat fighter establishment at West Raynham. By July 1952 after rebuilding it had completed twenty seven flights, twenty eight landings totalling nine hours fifty minutes.

Generations apart - Type 707B, the last Anson and Lancaster pictured at Woodford 16th May, 1952

Roy Ewans

John Roy Ewans succeeded Stuart Davies as chief designer to A. V. Roe and Co., Ltd. in June 1955.

Born on 21st December, 1917, Ewans completed a post-graduate course in aeronautics that led to an appointment, in 1938, at the R.A.E., where for six years he concentrated on aerodynamic research. In 1944 he was a member of a team of investigators sent to France and Germany, and in 1946 he joined the Blackburn Aircraft Company as head of the aerodynamics section of the design office. In October 1949 he was appointed chief aerodynamicist to A. V. Roe and Co., and in May 1955 became deputy chief designer.

By 1960, Roy Ewans was Chief Designer at Avro and is seen here with one of his projects, the Avro 748 turboprop airliner.

Aerodynamics of the Delta

By J. R. Ewans, Avro's Chief Aerodynamicist
For an article published 10th August, 1951
Twelve months before the Type 698 first flight.

So far as can be ascertained, the idea of using a triangular plan-form for aircraft wings, now known as the delta wing, was first put forward in 1943 by Professor Lippisch, who will be remembered for his association with the Messerschmitt Company. His studies had led him to think that this form was most suited for flight at speeds in the region of the speed of sound, where conventional aircraft designs were already known to be in trouble. By the end of the war, he had a number of delta wing projects in hand, including an un-powered wooden glider intended to explore the low-speed properties of the wing. This was by then partly built, and was later completed under United States orders. The idea of the delta wing was studied by many other aeronautical experts and a strong recommendation for its use was given, for instance, by Professor Von Karman, of U.S.A., at the 1947 Anglo-American Aeronautical Conference.

At the time of writing, three British delta aircraft and two American are known to have flown, and it is pretty certain that others are on the way. In the date order of their first flight, these are: Consolidated-Vultee XF-92, Avro 707, Boulton Paul P111, Douglas XF4D-1, and Fairey FD-1.

Authors note: The Boulton Paul P111 was built to specification E.27/46 as a delta wing transonic aircraft. Following a belly landing by Sqn. Ldr. Jimmy Harrison of the Aero Flight at R.A.E. Farnborough, the P111 was near to being shelved when the idea for variable gearing between stick and surfaces was successfully incorporated into the design of the re-designated P111A. The Fairy FD1 was built to specification E10/47 by Fairy Aviation at Heaton Chapel, Stockport, near Manchester. The aircraft made its first flight from Boscombe Down on 12th May, 1951. It was also seen as an attractive insurance policy should it be required for the Avro delta research program.

With the exception of the last-named, which is fitted with a small fixed tailplane for the first flights, all the above aircraft are tailless.

The following notes are intended to give a logical explanation of why there is this considerable interest in the delta wing, and just what advantages it promises the aircraft designer. But consideration must first be given to the type of aircraft the designer is trying to produce.

The delta wing is of value only for very-high-speed aircraft and at the present stage of engine development this implies the use of jet engines. When projecting his high speed aircraft, the designer will attempt to produce something carrying the greatest payload for the greatest distance, at the highest speed, and for the least expenditure of power (i.e., using the least amount of fuel). This applies to all types of aircraft, whether they be bombers, in which the payload is bombs, or civil aircraft in which it is passengers or cargo, or fighters in which it is guns and ammunition.

The most fundamental factor determining the ultimate achievement is the height at which the aircraft flies. As height increases the density of the air is reduced, so that drag is less; it is possible to fly at a given speed at say, 40,000ft, for an expenditure of only one quarter of the power required at sea level.

The advent of the jet engine has enabled the aircraft designer to get his aircraft up to considerable altitudes and take advantage of the reduced drag, but a new factor is coming in to limit the speed of the aircraft. This is the speed of sound.

The speed of sound occupies a fundamental position in the speed range of aircraft. It is roughly 760 m.p.h. at sea level and falls off to a value of 660 m.p.h. at heights above 36,000ft. Because the speed of sound is of such importance, aircraft speeds are commonly related to the speed of sound, using the term Mach number (the ratio of the speed of an aircraft to the speed of sound at the same height). As an aircraft approaches the speed of sound—in fact, for conventional aircraft when a speed of about 70 per cent of the speed of sound (Mach 0.7) is reached—the effects of compressibility become important, for the characteristics of the airflow change fundamentally. There is a very large increase in the air resistance, or drag, and an excessive expenditure of power becomes necessary to increase the speed any further.

For transport and bomber aircraft the speed at which the drag starts to increase (known as the "drag rise" Mach number) becomes the maximum cruising speed, because, if the aircraft is flown at higher speeds, the disproportionately higher thrust required from the engine means excessive fuel consumption and loss of range. At a rather higher Mach number there will be changes in the stability of the aircraft and in its response to the pilot's control— leading, possibly, even to complete loss of control.

In order to progress to higher speeds it is, therefore, necessary to design aircraft so as to postpone and/or overcome these effects.

We have noted that with an "old-fashioned" type of aircraft design, i.e., that of jet-propelled aircraft current in 1945, the limiting speed in steady cruising flight is likely to be a Mach number of 0.7 (higher speeds have, of course, already been achieved and a number of aircraft have exceeded the speed of sound, but only for short periods, either by diving or by use of rocket power). However, from the knowledge now available, it appears possible, by careful aerodynamic design, to postpone the rise in drag until a Mach number in the region of 0.9 is reached, and this figure is likely to be the practical limit of cruising speed for transport aircraft of all types for many years to come.

The designer of a civil aircraft, a bomber, or a long range fighter, will, therefore, spend all his energies to achieving a Mach number of this order without any drag rise. In addition, he must pay attention to the changes of stability or lack of control which might occur in this region, and this will occupy his attention to the same extent as the purely performance aspect of the drag rise. It is quite easy to design a fuselage shape which is relatively immune from Mach-number effects. It is the design suitable for high speed must also give satisfactory flying properties at low speeds for take-off and landing.

As air flows past a wing its speed is increased over the upper surface to a considerable extent and over the lower surface to a less extent, so that there is a greater suction on the upper surface than on the lower surface. Thus, at whatever speed an aircraft is flying, the speed of the air around the wing will, in fact, be higher. In the case of an aircraft flying at a Mach number of 0.8 the speed around its upper surface may be equal to the speed of sound, or may easily exceed it. At this stage, the airflow pattern round the wing will be considerably changed and it is, in fact, this change which gives rise to the drag and stability effects mentioned above. It is essential, therefore, to keep the velocity above the wing as little in excess of the speed of the aircraft as possible. There are four ways of improving the behaviour of a wing.

They are different methods of keeping down the air velocities, and all can be applied simultaneously: (1) sweep-back; (2) thinness; (3) low wing-loading; (4) low aspect-ratio.

(1) Sweepback.—The amount of sweep-back is measured by the angle by which the tip of the wing lies behind the centre line. The extent of the gains possible from sweepback is very considerable, and sweeping back a wing may easily lead to a postponement of the compressibility effects by a Mach number of 0.1. illustrated in Fig.1, which compares the drag rise of the former occurs at 0.7, and the latter at 0.83. Fig.2 shows the way in which the drag-rise Mach number is increased by sweep-back.

(2) Thinness.—Keeping a wing thin leads to a reduction in the amount of air that must be pushed out of the way by the wing, and this helps the passage of the wing through the air. The thickness of a wing is measured by the thickness/chord ratio, which is the maximum depth of the wing divided by its length in the line of flight. In the past, the thickness/chord ratios of aircraft wings have ranged from 21 per cent down to perhaps 12 per cent. Now values of 10 per cent down to 7 per cent are becoming common.

(3) Low Wing-loading.—The wing loading is the weight of aircraft carried by a unit area of wing, measured in pounds per square foot. Mach-number effects are postponed by keeping the wing loading as low as possible, i.e., by supporting the weight of the aircraft with a large wing area. This is particularly important for flight at high altitudes where the low air density puts a premium on keeping the wing-loading low. In fact, flight at high altitudes becomes virtually impossible unless this is done.

(4) Low Aspect-ratio.—Aspect-ratio is the ratio of the span of a wing to the average chord. For moderate speeds, a high aspect-ratio, i.e., a large span relative to the chord, gives greatest efficiency. At high Mach numbers this consideration is no longer important—in fact, some alleviation of compressibility effects is given by reducing aspect ratio.

There is another reason for choosing a low aspect-ratio. One of the disadvantages of sweeping a wing back is that the flying characteristics at low speed become poor. A typical symptom is that the wing tip of a swept wing stalls, giving violent behaviour if the speed is allowed to fall too low. Research has, however, shown that this bad characteristic of highly swept wings may be overcome relatively easily. Fig.3 is a graph of sweep-back versus aspect-ratio, compiled from a very large number of tests of wings of various plan-forms. Each of these forms has been classified as giving good or bad characteristics at the stall, and the line shown is the boundary between the good and the bad characteristics. It will be noted that although almost any aspect ratio can be accepted with an unswept wing, for wings of 45 deg sweepback an aspect-ratio of little over 3 is the most satisfactory.

There is yet a third reason for choosing a low aspect ratio— the behaviour (as regards stability, etc.) in the high Mach number region. Compressibility effects are minimized and a transition from speeds below that of sound to the speed of sound and above is much more readily accomplished if the aspect-ratio is low, say in the order of 2 to 4.

Put the above four requirements together and the result is an aircraft highly swept back, with a thin wing, a moderately large wing area and a low aspect-ratio. A little consideration of geometrical properties and possible plan-form of wings lead to the conclusion that the delta wing is the only form which satisfies these requirements. It possesses high sweep-back and low aspect-ratio. The wing area will, of necessity, be generous for the size of aircraft and, for reasons which will be detailed later; it is easy to build it with a low thickness-chord ratio.

Next, how does the delta plan-form, indicated from considerations of aerodynamic performance, line up with practical design requirements and, in particular, the overriding necessity for keeping weight and drag low in order to obtain maximum performance. A preliminary question is whether a tailplane is necessary.

From the earliest days of flying, the question has been raised as to whether aircraft can be flown satisfactorily without a tailplane. Confining attention only to the case of the high-speed jet aircraft, each of the functions of a tailplane will be examined in turn in relation to the delta wing aircraft. The functions are:-

(a) To trim out changes of centre of gravity position according to the load carried and the consumption of fuel.—Investigation shows that a control surface at the trailing edge of the wing, provided that the latter has a large root chord (as has the delta), can cater for all but extreme c.g. movements.

(b) To deal with trim changes due to landing flaps, etc.—With the low wing-loading associated with the delta wing, take-off and landing speeds are moderate without the use of flaps, and this question does not, therefore, arise.

(c) To provide damping of pitching oscillations.—The reduction of damping of the pitching oscillation has led to difficulty on some tailless aircraft, but it does not arise on the delta, since the large chord near the root gives adequate damping.

(d) To deal with loss of stability or control power consequent on distortion of the wing structure at high speed. ("Aero elastic distortion").—At very high speeds, all aircraft structures distort to a greater or less extent under the high loads imposed, and this distortion alters the aerodynamic form. In extreme cases this leads to loss of stability or control power, making the aircraft dangerous or impossible to fly at high speeds. An aircraft with a high aspect-ratio, swept-back wing would need a tailplane to deal with this, but the shape of the delta wing makes it extremely stiff, both in bending and in torsion, and a tailplane does not appear to be necessary.

(e) To provide for spin-recovery.—Although this point has not been proved, it is expected that the controls on a tailless delta wing would not be powerful enough to ensure recovery from a fully developed spin. A tailplane appears to be the only way of dealing with the problem. This restriction is of small significance for transport or bomber-type aircraft.

It can, therefore, be concluded that for a delta-wing aircraft of the transport type a tailplane is unnecessary. Its deletion leads immediately to a considerable saving of weight and drag, and to a major gain in performance.

We have now shown that, compared with a conventional aircraft, the delta-wing aircraft will be simpler by the omission of the following items: the tailplane; the rear fuselage necessary to carry the tailplane, and wing flaps and other high lift devices such as the drooped wing leading edge. There is a saving of weight, of design and manufacturing effort and of maintenance when the aircraft is in service. These economies will have a considerable bearing on the initial cost and the man-power necessary to produce and maintain a number of aircraft.

Because of its shape, and the large root chord, the delta wing provides a large internal volume in relation to its surface area, even when using the thin sections which, as noted above, are essential for high-speed aircraft. Simple calculations show that for the same wing area, the delta wing has 33 percent more internal volume than an un-tapered wing, while, if the inboard half of the wing only is considered (as this represents a more practical case from the point of view of the aircraft designer) the internal volume of the delta wing is more than twice that of the corresponding un-tapered wing.

It is found that without exceeding a wing thickness of as little as 8 to 10 per cent, it is possible on a moderate-sized delta-wing aircraft to bury completely the engines, the undercarriage, and sufficient fuel tanks for long range. The fuselage also has a tendency to disappear into the wing at the root.

The result is the attainment of an aircraft consisting only of a wing, a fin and a rudimentary fuselage, representing a degree of aerodynamic cleanliness which has never before been reached. In fairness, it must be pointed out that this is achieved at the expense of a rather larger wing area than usual, but investigation shows that the drag of this area is less than that due to a conglomeration of items such as engine nacelles, tailplane, etc.

From the design point of view, the shape of the delta wing leads to an extremely stiff structure without the use of thick wing skins, and strength becomes the determining feature rather than structural stiffness. This avoids the inefficiency of conventional swept-back wings where the wing has to be made stronger than necessary in order that it shall be stiff enough. Summing-up, it can be said that in order to meet the requirements of large loads for a long range, at high speed, the high performance transport or military aircraft of the future will cruise at a considerable altitude, at a speed not much below that of sound. The delta wing provides the only satisfactory solution to these requirements, for the following reasons:-

(1) It meets the four features necessary for avoiding the drag rise near the speed of sound, i.e., it is highly swept back, it can be made very thin, the wing loading is low, and the aspect ratio is low.

(2) Extensive wind-tunnel and flight tests have shown that the low-aspect-ratio delta wing gives minimum changes in stability and control characteristics at speeds near the speed of sound.

(3) In spite of the wing being thin, its internal volume is large, so that the engines, undercarriage, fuel, and all the necessary equipment can be contained within the wing and a rudimentary fuselage.

(4) Adequate control can be obtained by control surfaces on the wing, thus eliminating the need for a conventional tailplane. Together with item 3, this leads to a considerable reduction in the drag of the aircraft, and, therefore, to high performance.

(5) Auxiliary devices such as flaps, nose flaps, or slots, and the all-moving tailplane, are unnecessary, thereby saving weight and design effort, and simplifying manufacture and maintenance.

(6) The delta wing is very stiff and free from distortion troubles.

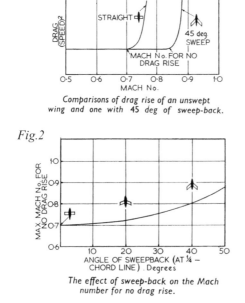

Fig.1

Comparisons of drag rise of an unswept wing and one with 45 deg of sweep-back.

Fig.2

The effect of sweep-back on the Mach number for no drag rise.

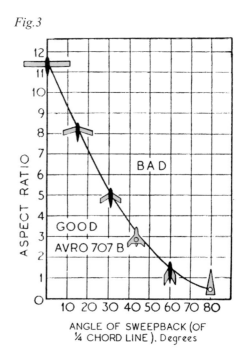

Fig.3

Effect of fitting tips & increased centre section

EXISTING AEROPLANE

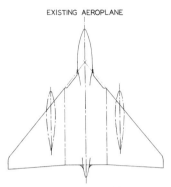

EXISTING AEROPLANE

FUSELAGE LENGTH	92·1 FT.
SPAN	99 FT.
WING AREA	3446 SQ.FT.
ASPECT RATIO	2·84
SWEEPBACK OF ¼ CHORD O/W	42·2°
ROOT CHORD	63·4 FT.
TIP CHORD	6·84 FT.
T/C AT JOINT	10%
T/C AT TIP	8%

WITH EXTERNAL FUEL TANKS

HEIGHT OVER TARGET- FEET	50,850	47,850
STILL AIR RANGE- NAUTICAL MILES	5,000	6150
CRUISE SPEED - KNOTS T.A.S.	500	500
HANGAR WEIGHT- LBS.	146,390	174,918
FUEL WEIGHT- LBS.	66,702	92,230
WEIGHT LESS FUEL- LBS.	79,688	82,688
TAKE- OFF WING LOADING LBS/SQ.FT.	42·2	50·4
TAKE- OFF DISTANCE TO 50FT-YARDS	1980	2860

EXISTING AEROPLANE WITH TIPS

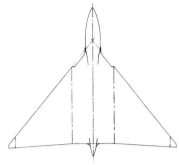

CONFIGURATION 1

FUSELAGE LENGTH	92·1 FT.
SPAN	107 FT.
WING AREA	3483 SQ.FT.
ASPECT RATIO	3·29
SWEEPBACK OF ¼ CHORD O/W	42·2°
ROOT CHORD	63·4 FT.
TIP CHORD	2·25 FT.
T/C AT JOINT	10%
T/C AT TIP	8%

HEIGHT OVER TARGET- FEET	51,820
STILL AIR RANGE- NAUTICAL MILES	5390
CRUISE SPEED - KNOTS T.A.S.	500
HANGAR WEIGHT- LBS.	147,030
FUEL WEIGHT- LBS.	66,702
WEIGHT LESS FUEL - LBS.	80,328
TAKE- OFF WING LOADING LBS/SQ.FT.	41·92
TAKE- OFF DISTANCE TO 50FT-YARDS	1980

INCREASED SPAN CENTRE SECTION WITH EXISTING OUTER WING

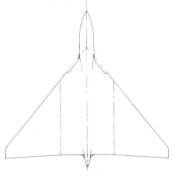

CONFIGURATION 2

FUSELAGE LENGTH	99·1 FT.
SPAN	107·25 FT.
WING AREA	3989 SQ.FT.
ASPECT RATIO	2·88
SWEEPBACK OF ¼ CHORD O/W	42·2°
ROOT CHORD	68·3 FT.
TIP CHORD	6·84 FT.
T/C AT JOINT	10%
T/C AT TIP	8%

HEIGHT OVER TARGET- FEET	49,040	50,500
STILL AIR RANGE- NAUTICAL MILES	6340	5000
CRUISE SPEED KNOTS T.A.S.	500	500
HANGAR WEIGHT- LBS.	173,857	150,200
FUEL WEIGHT- LBS.	89,910	66,253
WEIGHT LESS FUEL- LBS.	83,947	83,947
TAKE- OFF WING LOADING LBS/SQ.FT.	43·58	37·70
TAKE- OFF DISTANCE TO 50FT-YARDS	2420	1800
TAKE- OFF DISTANCE TO 50FT-YARDS	1700	

(WITH 20,000LBS OF ROCKET THRUST FOR 30SECS)

INCREASED SPAN CENTRE SECTION WITH EXISTING OUTER WING PLUS TIPS

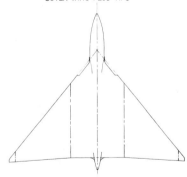

CONFIGURATION 3

FUSELAGE LENGTH	99·1 FT.
SPAN	115·25 FT.
WING AREA	4025 SQ.FT.
ASPECT RATIO	3·29
SWEEPBACK OF ¼ CHORD O/W	42·2°
ROOT CHORD	68·3 FT.
TIP CHORD	2·25 FT.
T/C AT JOINT	10%
T/C AT TIP	8%

HEIGHT OVER TARGET FEET	50,000	51,650
STILL AIR RANGE- NAUTICAL MILES	6660	5000
CRUISE SPEED KNOTS T.A.S.	500	500
HANGAR WEIGHT- LBS.	174,497	145,800
FUEL WEIGHT- LBS.	89,910	61,213
WEIGHT LESS FUEL- LBS.	84,587	84,587
TAKE- OFF WING LOADING LBS/SQ.FT.	43·35	36·20
TAKE- OFF DISTANCE TO 50FT-YARDS	2420	1730
TAKE- OFF DISTANCE TO 50FT-YARDS	1700	

(WITH 20,000LBS OF ROCKET THRUST FOR 30SECS)

Effect of fitting new outer wings to existing centre section

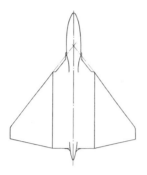

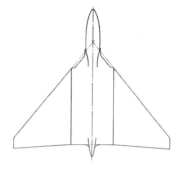

CONFIGURATION A		CONFIGURATION B	
		EXISTING AIRCRAFT	
SPAN	80 FT.	SPAN	99 FT.
WING AREA	2920 SQ.FT.	WING AREA	3446 SQ.FT.
ASPECT RATIO	2·19	ASPECT RATIO	2·84
SWEEPBACK OF ¼ CHORD O/W	42·2°	SWEEPBACK OF ¼ CHORD O/W	42·2°
ROOT CHORD	63·4 FT.	ROOT CHORD	63·4 FT.
TIP CHORD	6·84 FT.	TIP CHORD	6·84 FT.
T/C AT JOINT	10%	T/C AT JOINT	10%
T/C AT TIP	8%	T/C AT TIP	8%
HEIGHT OVER TARGET	49,300 FT.	HEIGHT OVER TARGET	50,850 FT.
STILL AIR RANGE	5000 N.M.	STILL AIR RANGE	5000 N.M.
CRUISING SPEED (M·0·87)	500K.T.A.S	CRUISING SPEED (M·0·87)	500K.T.A.S.
HANGAR WEIGHT	150,800 LB.	HANGAR WEIGHT	146,390 LB.
FUEL WEIGHT	74,600 LB	FUEL WEIGHT	66,702 LB.
WEIGHT LESS FUEL	76,200 LB.	WEIGHT LESS FUEL	79,688 LB.
TAKE-OFF WING LOADING	51·3 LB/SQ.FT.	TAKE-OFF WING LOADING	42·2 LB/SQ.FT.

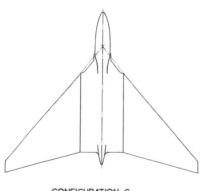

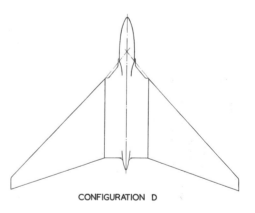

CONFIGURATION C		CONFIGURATION D	
SPAN	120 FT.	SPAN	140 FT.
WING AREA	4000 SQ.FT.	WING AREA	4550 SQ.FT.
ASPECT RATIO	3·6	ASPECT RATIO	4·3
SWEEPBACK OF ¼ CHORD O/W	42·2°	SWEEPBACK OF ¼ CHORD O/W	42·2°
ROOT CHORD	63·4 FT.	ROOT CHORD	63·4 FT.
TIP CHORD	6·84 FT.	TIP CHORD	6·84 FT.
T/C AT JOINT	10%	T/C AT JOINT	10%
T/C AT TIP	8%	T/C AT TIP	8%
HEIGHT OVER TARGET	52,600 FT.	HEIGHT OVER TARGET	53,300 FT.
STILL AIR RANGE	5,000 N.M.	STILL AIR RANGE	5,000 N.M
CRUISING SPEED (M·0·87)	500K.T.A.S	CRUISING SPEED (M·0·87)	500K.T.A.S
HANGAR WEIGHT	142,400 LB	HANGAR WEIGHT	145,400 LB
FUEL WEIGHT	58,500 LB	FUEL WEIGHT	57,200 LB
WEIGHT LESS FUEL	83,900 LB.	WEIGHT LESS FUEL	88,200 LB
TAKE-OFF WING LOADING	35·4 LB/SQ.FT.	TAKE-OFF WING LOADING	31·8 LB/SQ.FT.

PART TWO

CONCEPT TO REALITY

Type 698 in Experimental at Chadderton. This area of Chadderton was screened off to the workforce, with passes having to be shown to security guards before entering the area. In the background can be seen the wooden mock-up of the 698. A great amount of time was saved by use of mock-ups for establishing pipe templates, electrical runs and looms etc., care was taken that the mock-up was a true reproduction of the aircraft structure.

In the background of the above picture shows a full scale mock-up of the "special bomb" - Blue Danube which was Britain's first atom bomb. The casing was the joint work of the Armament Design Establishment (ADE) and Armament Research Establishment (ARE) at Fort Halstead and subcontractor and manufacturer Hudswell, Clarke & Co. Ltd., at their Leeds factory. The latter Company was involved in various post war secret projects, including Britain's nuclear weapons programme.

April - August 1952

There was much speculation in the press, to what seemed to be an aeroplane, when the main fuselage structure left Chadderton on its way to Woodford in April 1952.

The rare pictures shown below were taken at Woodford Flight Sheds, where the first prototype was assembled, in great secrecy from parts manufactured at Avro's factory at Chadderton. The wing outboard of the wing transport joint on production aircraft were manufactured at Woodford, with the leading edge manufactured in an "envelope" jig at Chadderton. The first prototype wings were manufactured at Chadderton.

Immediately after being moved to No.5 hangar 24th July, 1952.

Resonance set-up at Woodford flight sheds 25th July, 1952.

On the move...

On the way to the paint shop 3rd August, 1952.

On the move 22nd August, 1952. Close inspection of the photograph shows Roly Falk pictured in his white shirt and sunglasses.

...22nd August, 1952

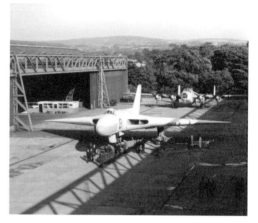

Type 698 pictured with the Avro Ashton WB493 research aircraft on 22nd August, 1952.

Looking at the future, 22nd August, 1952. Pictured above L to R walking away is Group Captain Dearth, Avro's Security Manager; Jack Green Maintenance Director; Teddy Fielding Works Director; Sir Roy Dobson Managing Director and J. A. R. Kay Director.

Engine test - 29th August, 1952

Pictured above a close up of the tail taken on the 29th August, 1952. The Avro logo had still to be completed on the tail. Unusually the logo was painted black and yellow.

Type 698 pictured the day before the first flight on the 30th August, 1952. It is seen here prior to its engine test. The team worked twenty four hours a day so that the aircraft could appear at the 1952 S.B.A.C. Show at Farnborough. This included Sir Roy Dobson who went to the cafeteria to get coffee to keep the workers awake.

The Avro 698 at that time had a black anti-dazzle panel in front of the windscreen, after the first flight it was found that the panel was not required.

First flight Saturday 30th August, 1952.

Avro type 698 on its way to its first flight, note the black anti glare panel under the cockpit window.

First Flight pilot

Wing Commander Roland Falk was an experienced pilot, having served with the RAF, 1939-1946 and was chief test pilot at Farnborough in the beginning of 1943 and had flown over 300 different types of aircraft at the wars end. He typically flew the first flight of the 698 wearing a lounge suit. The aircraft at the time was only equipped for one pilot to fly with no second pilots seat, it also had no cockpit pressurisation or wing fuel system.

Falk liked his Savile Row suits and was also known as "man in a pin stripe suit"! Well, most pilots will tell you that the cockpit is their office!

Drama in the sky

It was reported by a local newspaper on Saturday 30th August, 1952 that after 35 minutes in the air a giant plane landed perfectly back at the airfield where it was assembled at Woodford, Cheshire. Later the test pilot, Wing Commander Roland Falk, was recorded to have said the aircraft was "First Class".

"The four-jet plane-the world's first big delta aircraft-made an impressive sight as it roared over the Cheshire fields.

There was only one slight hitch. Five minutes after taking off Wing Commander Falk lowered the undercarriage in a routine test. Two metal pieces, later learned to be the nose-wheel doors, ripped away from the underside of the aircraft.

As the huge, silver-painted *(sic)* machine circled the aerodrome at a low altitude, the pilot tried further tests, lifting and lowering the 10-wheeled undercarriage. Then the watching crowd saw the tiny Avro 707A tangerine-painted research aircraft take off to join the circuit. With the second machine flying low beneath the spread of the bomber's wings, an inspection of the damaged undercarriage was carried out in the air. Later, a Vampire fighter with another Avro test pilot aboard took-off from Woodford to fly beneath the bomber still circling the airfield. Thirty-five minutes after take-off the great bomber made a perfect landing, using a huge parachute to slow down its run on the runway. The machine rolled to a standstill halfway up the runway and taxied round to the flight sheds with the parachute streaming out behind.

Police closed Old Hall Lane, which runs from the main Chester Road at Woodford to the perimeter track of the Avro aerodrome, for a 90-minute period immediately following the take-off of the new aircraft.

Most pedestrians and cars were held up until the machine had landed safely and been towed away inside the experimental sheds out of sight from the road. In the sheds engineers immediately, started to put right the damaged nose-wheel doors".

In actual fact it was the main undercarriage leg fairings that had become detached; the aircraft flew in that condition at the SBAC show at Farnborough ten days later. Company photographs at that time were retouched to show the fairings in place.

Roly Falk recalled that before he made his first flight he did one fast taxi to satisfy himself with regard to ground handling, wheel shimmy and nose wheel lifting. He reduced the number of taxi runs to avoid overheating the brakes. When he was at the end of the runway he noticed a large flock seagulls in front him and a vehicle was sent to frighten them away, the rest is history.

Avro 698 completes its fast taxi proir to its first flight, from a photo taken by the Company's Chief Inspector at the time, A. C. "Sandy" Jack. On the previous day it had completed its first fast taxi.

Avro Type 698 (VX770) first flight

Rare pictures of VX770 high speed taxi and first take-off. Its first flight began at 9.45 a.m. at Avro's Woodford airfield on Saturday 30th August, 1952. It took off from the Poynton end of runway (25) and flew to a height of 10,000 ft before landing back at Woodford 35 minutes later.

Pictured left - the 698 on it's maiden flight taken by Cyril Peckham, Hawker Siddeley Group, chief photographer.

The Type 698 takes off on its first flight on Saturday 30th August, 1952.

Nose up on fast taxi.

Take-off sequence.

This rare first flight take-off sequence was taken by Sandy Jack.

U.F.O.!

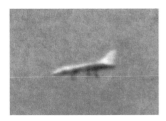

707A (WD280) takes-off during the first flight of VX770, to inspect the undercarriage, it was flown by Avro test pilot Jimmy Nelson. The 707 had to land after ten minutes due to lack of fuel, when another Avro test pilot Jack Wales also went to inspect the undercarriage in his No.613 (City of Manchester) Squadron Vampire.

Landing safely back at Woodford after first flight minus undercarriage doors. Despite ground tests the combination of air loading on the fairing and slight over-swing of the undercarriage in its fully retracted position caused the failure of the main undercarriage fairing attachment.

After first flight, note the group of figures surrounding the main undercarriage.

Commenting on the flight, Mr. Duncan Sandys, Minister of Supply, said that the advent of the 698 might well have a profound influence upon future development not only in air warfare but in civil transport. "The Government decided recently to order an appreciable number of these new bombers without waiting for the prototype to carry out the usual flying trials," he continued. "I am confident that both on military and economic grounds our decision will prove to be justified." The bold decision to adopt the triangular wing for an aircraft of this size and to dispense with the tailplane was an act of faith for which the designers and manufacturers deserve the highest praise.

Development summary

To summarise this part of the development of the 698 it is interesting to note how much effort was made by the work force to achieve its first flight.

Between 1947, and the first flight of the 698 in 1952, Avro was involved in the design and manufacture of a variety of aircraft, these included the production of four hundred sixty six Anson's with the last twenty four being delivered in 1952, they also produced eighty six Shackleton's, five Ashton's, twenty two Athena's, five Lancastrian's, twenty eight Tudor's, twenty York's and three Type 707 delta research aircraft during that period.

This output put enormous pressure on the design and production departments and to the skills and talent employed by Avro at that time. The design and production of the 698 was a huge risk taken by all those concerned with a lot of reputations being at stake. The fact that the 698 became the spearhead of bomber command and their biggest threat during the Cold War is a great testament to those pioneering achievements.

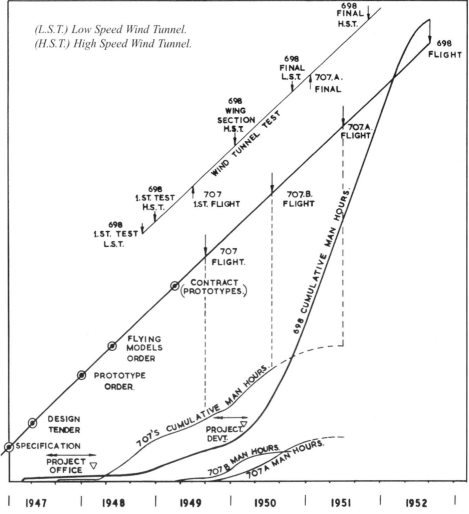

The actual time from issue of the first manufacturing drawings to the works to the first flight of the first prototype was twenty three months; this was due to unconventional configuration which was responsible for at least half the total time in the design of the prototype.

Prime movers

Prime movers - in the design and production of the Type 698. Pictured from left to right Mr J. A. R. "Jimmy" Kay (Director), W/C R. "Roly" Falk (Test Pilot), Sir William Farren (Technical Director), Mr S. D. "Stuart" Davies Chief Designer, Sir Roy Dobson (Managing Director),Gilbert Whitehead (Project Designer) and C. E. "Teddy" Fielding (Works Director) in front of the first prototype Vulcan.

First public appearance

The aircraft flew to Boscombe Down on the 1st September, 1952; the Avro team are pictured here at Boscombe Down on Monday 8th September, 1952.

S.B.A.C. Airshow September 1952

The Society of British Aircraft Constructers', S.B.A.C., held an annual Airshow at Farnborough Hants, usually in September to show case U.K. company products. This was an excellent opportunity for aircraft companies to meet and display their wares to the press, government organisations and general public. In the early years this was entirely confined to U.K. manufactures, but changing times has meant that the Show is now held once every two years and open to all manufactures worldwide.

This air to air picture was taken on Monday 8th September, 1952. Note the black anti dazzle panel under the cockpit window had disappeared by the time of the S.B.A.C. Show.

The 698 made its first public debut at the S.B.A.C. Farnborough Airshow on the 2nd September, 1952, on Tuesday afternoon; it was just its fifth flight and appeared on seven occasions. It did not appear on the Monday due to an undercarriage problem and returned to Boscombe Down. The two Jimmies, Orrell in the 707B and Nelson in the 707A kept the delta flag flying with their synchronized performances in the little research machines.

It was described as being the day of days - the day which will always be remembered for one of the most significant flying demonstrations in the whole history of British aeronautics. "Imagine a late-summer afternoon, with woolly clouds strewing the sky and, beyond Laffan's Plain, three triangular silhouettes orbiting low on the horizon. Joining formation, they headed for the airfield-in the lead a white triton, with a red minnow on the left and a blue one on the right. Low and fast they came sweeping in the 698 at last, in all its white beauty, with the red 707A and blue 707B. Then one remembered a certain evening in 1949 when S. E. Esler brought the very first delta, the original Avro 707, over the same airfield on a similar occasion. The tri-coloured formation broke. The bomber wheeled like some great yacht and came scudding across at a speed which, despite its size, it was utterly amazing in view of the fact that this was but its fourth flight. Indeed, the 707s, when they sought to tag along, appeared to find themselves hard-pressed. Then Falk (for he was, of course, the pilot of the 698 and was, incidentally, flying alone) really got into his stride and, except for aerobatics, flew the brand-new bomber exactly as he is accustomed to fly one of his little stable of "hack" 707s. That is quite literally the truth, and it is a truth in which everyone in this country (and, especially, a few people Manchester-way) may take comfort and pride".

The aircraft was based at Boscombe Down and did not land at Farnborough during the Show. It is interesting to note that this was the same year that the De Havilland 110 crashed, which caused much concern back at Avro as they believed the crash might have been the 698.

At the end of its initial flying period the aircraft was grounded for fitment of revised undercarriage fairings, a second pilots seat and some miscellaneous alterations to the instruments, with the total flying time until Flight Eleven being seven hours and forty minutes. It resumed its flying on 24th November, 1952.

The above picture shows VX770 before its appearance at the S.B.A.C Show in September 1952, it was part of a series of pictures taken for publicity purposes. The aircraft was minus its undercarriage doors and due to the fact that it would be flying the few hours of its life under speed limitations it was decided to carry on flying without these fairings. In fact Avro retouched some photos to show the fairings in place.

The first public appearance of the 698 at the S.B.A.C. Show at Farnborough, yet to be named Vulcan. Seen here with the red 707A (WD280) flown by Jimmy Nelson. The Blue Avro 707B not pictured here was flown by Avro test pilot Jack Wales.

Roly Falk shows the delta wing to best advantage during this flypast at the 1952, S.B.A.C. Show at Farnborough.

What's in a name debate?

Quoted below is a feature article that appeared in Flight and Aircraft Engineer in the 19th September, 1952 publication on the naming of the Avro Type 698.

"Like others who recognize that the naming of a new aircraft may be of far-reaching importance, they considering at odd moments a suitable appellation for the 698. Names being a matter of individual taste, (by which is implied the present writer) advance our proposals with diffidence. Reactions will be both varied and violent. In the first place, we are of the opinion that, other things being equal, alterative names such as Vickers Valiant are most desirable, and one that leaps to mind for the 698 is Avenger. That this was conferred upon an Avro fighter of long ago need not prejudice its acceptance today, for the fighter was a little-known 'one-off'; it is, however, firmly ruled out by the continuing employment of similarly entitled carrier-borne Grumman's. For a similar reason Apollo must be discounted, and in any case, the names of mythology are not ideally suited to this unique British achievement.

Following the Javelin, of course, Assegai calls for serious consideration. But, having duly pondered these and several other names, alternative and otherwise, we offer Albion-the ancient name of Britain, easy on the tongue, resonant and noble on the ear (and in this choice we were in no wise influenced by the parrot-croak "perfidious"). For a commercial development we consider Aurora to be beyond reproach".

The debate finally came to a close when Sir John Slessor, Chief of the Air Staff (CAS) ruled that the Avro type 698 would have a name beginning with "V" to follow the Vickers Valiant. The name Vulcan was revealed to the public during the week ending 24th October, 1952. Sir John Slessor was a major proponent of Britain developing a nuclear deterrent force, retiring from the RAF in 1952.

In the same publication the 698 was described as being one of the most photogenic machines ever to take the air.

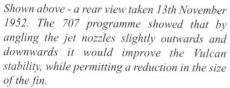

Shown above - a rear view taken 13th November 1952. The 707 programme showed that by angling the jet nozzles slightly outwards and downwards it would improve the Vulcan stability, while permitting a reduction in the size of the fin.

PART THREE

PROGRESS
THROUGH DEVELOPMENT

The second prototype VX777 takes-off from a snow covered runway at Woodford on 23rd February, 1955 for an air test and demonstration flight for the Australian Minister for Air.

Progress through development

Following its demonstration at the S.B.A.C. Show at Farnborough VX770 carried out its initial programme of test flying. In general, the flying qualities confirmed the results predicted from the information acquired as a result of flying the 707 models.

It became apparent however, that the actual physical arrangements of the flying controls and instrument panels in the cockpit could be improved. Also the extension of the nose wheel, which had been incorporated at a late date in the design, led to rather complicated retraction sequences and it was thought desirable to increase the length of the nose wheel bay in order to simplify the nose wheel itself. This brought in its train, re-arrangement of the electrical and hydraulic systems and increases in the fuel tankage in the wing in order to balance the increased tankage in the fuselage.

The net result of all these changes amounted to very considerable internal redesign, although the external appearance of the aircraft was apparently unaltered. It was decided to bring the second prototype in line with all these projected alterations so that the production aircraft which would be identical with the second prototype could start off on a fully tested basis. At the same time, advantage was taken of these decisions to increase the strength and stressing weight of the aircraft to make the long range case (5,000 n.m.) a "normal' instead of on "overload" condition.

These decisions were taken during the autumn of 1952 and resulted in a re-issue of approximately 75% of the Vulcan drawings for the second Prototype.

Runway trials in extreme weather conditions 21st November, 1952 using the original ribbon type braking parachute.

The first prototype used a small trailing-static 'bomb' during low speed calibration of the static pressure sources of the aircraft on 21st December, 1952. The device is trailed at a distance which places it in the air undisturbed by the presence of the aircraft and pressures sensed at the 'bomb' transmitted to test instrumentation in the aircraft.

Development potential brochure - October 1952

**AVRO
VULCAN
DELTA BOMBER**

BROCHURE INTRODUCTION

The AVRO VULCAN formerly known as the AVRO 698 was designed to carry a 10,000 lb. bomb and various other bomb loads up to 39,000 lb. could be carried in the bomb bay and by fitting nacelles on the wing a total load of seventy-five 1,000 lb. bombs could be carried for short range missions.

The photographic reconnaissance version has a still-air range of 7,000 nautical miles for day operation. For night operation, ranges up to 4,700 nautical miles were offered depending on the photoflash load carried.

The above performance is based on the thrust and fuel consumption ratings of the Bristol Olympus 3 engine. Since the development of this engine was not yet complete, the first few production aircraft will be fitted with four Olympus 101 engines which give a slightly lower level of thrust and greater specific fuel consumption.

The foregoing is a brief statement of the capabilities of the first production series of AVRO VULCAN aircraft. There is, however, a large development potential in the delta wing configuration and the purpose of this brochure is to indicate some lines of development that could be incorporated in subsequent production aircraft.

In addition to its other advantages such as simplicity and structural stiffness, the delta wing form possesses two features which make a considerable extension of the performance of the aircraft possible at the expense of only minor changes in design and therefore in jigging and tooling. These features are the relatively large wing area and therefore low wing loading, and the large internal volume available for fuel.

Two limitations exist for the maximum altitude a given aircraft can attain; the first is the engine thrust available relative to the weight of the aircraft and the second is the lifting ability of the wing. High Mach number reduces the maximum lift of a wing and it may be accepted that for aircraft flying at Mach numbers around 0.9 the cruising lift coefficient should not exceed about 0.4 in order to ensure an adequate degree of manoeuvrability. This value is already closely approached by the conventional swept wing aircraft, which has therefore little reserve for development to higher altitude. Due to its larger wing area, however, the AVRO VULCAN cruises at a lift coefficient of 0.25 at 500 knots at 50,000 ft. with Bristol Olympus 3 engines, and therefore has a considerable margin of lift in hand.

This potential of increased lift can be utilised by increasing the thrust of the engines, thereby raising the cruising and target altitudes. The AVRO VULCAN can be developed to absorb a thrust rating equivalent to 20,000 lb. from each of four engines giving a target altitude approaching 60,000 ft. The advantage in placing the aircraft above the operational ceiling of enemy fighters is obvious.

The increase of thrust can be obtained in a number of ways:-

    (a) By increasing the working temperature of the basic engine.

    (b) By fitting two additional engines in nacelles on the outer wing.

    (c) By redesigning the centre section to accommodate three Sapphire 7 engines.

Flying with more powerful engines reduces the air miles per gallon of fuel, so that for the same range an increase in fuel capacity is necessary. Alternatively increased fuel capacity may be required to obtain additional range. By modifications to the internal structure of the outer wing to increase the fuel space and by making a comparable increase in fuselage fuel, the total capacity can be increased from 9,000 gallons to 11,300 gallons. This increases the range in the basic case to 6,000 nautical miles.

An alternative development is in the direction of increased speed. By fitting to the existing fuselage new wings with the thickness chord ratio reduced to 5% but with the planform unchanged, the cruising Mach number can be raised from 0.87 to 0.92 with no loss of performance in other respects.

Finally, if a range of the order of 7,500 to 8,000 nautical miles at increased target altitudes is required with the standard bomb load, this can be offered by designing a wider centre section which attaches to the standard outer wings and fuselage. This centre section will accommodate the larger undercarriage made necessary by the increase in all-up-weight together with either four 20,000 lb. thrust engines or six Olympus 3 engines. The increased wing area ensures that the cruising lift coefficient is kept low, thus retaining the possibility of further thrust augmentation.

It must be emphasised that all the developments presented retain unchanged the major part of the design and production effort, namely the fuselage containing the cockpit, the bomb bay and bomb gear, and all the hydraulic, electrical, radio and pressurisation services. Furthermore, the proved flying qualities will remain unaltered.

STANDARD PRODUCTION AIRCRAFT

AVRO VULCAN aircraft of the first production series carry a 10,000 lb. bomb 5,000 nautical miles at 500 knots T.A.S. (M = 0.873) and fly over the target at a height of 50,000 feet. The four Bristol Olympus 3 engines each give a static thrust of 13,500 lb. at sea level.

A large bomb bay is situated between the front and rear spars of the wing and can accommodate all the alternative loads. Aft of the rear spar a single photoflash is carried in a separate compartment. The rear fuselage supports the vertical fin and houses the tail warning radar and a 24 ft. diameter ribbon parachute, which is used as an aid to landing. Forward of the bomb bay are fuselage fuel tanks, the nose wheel and the pressurised crew cabin. The latter accommodates a crew of five, namely two pilots, a radio operator and two navigators. The simplicity of the cockpit layout is illustrated by the fact that the first prototype AVRO VULCAN was handled on its early flight trials by a single pilot only. Forward of the crew cabin is the H2S scanner.

The engines are located side by sides in the wing centre section outboard of the fuselage, so that they are completely buried except for the aft part of the jet pipes; the air intakes are in the wing leading edge. The main undercarriage is located outboard of the engines. The major part of the fuel is carried in tanks in the outer wing and the remainder in the forward fuselage. The tanks are so arranged that the aircraft centre of gravity is maintained as fuel is consumed. The total fuel capacity of the first production aircraft will be 9,350 gallons which is appreciably in excess of the fuel required for 5,000 nautical miles range with the cold engine even when using wide cut gasoline. No external tanks are therefore necessary.

The trailing edge of the outer wing is occupied by ailerons on the outboard part and elevators inboard. Each control surface is split into two halves and each half is operated by its own separate power unit. In the event of failure of one or even two power units, adequate control remains. The rudder is also power operated by duplicate units. Airbrakes are provided on the wing centre section just aft of the front spar on each side and on both top and bottom surfaces of the wing.

The only change which the pilot can make in the external configuration, apart from the usual ones of operating the flying controls, undercarriage and bomb doors, is extension of the air brakes. Items which would be necessary on a conventional swept wing aircraft, such as a tailplane (probably of variable incidence), landing flaps and nose flaps or slats, are not required. The AVRO VULCAN is thus built from a smaller number of main items, leading to greater ease of production and in particular - since the number of major moving parts is fewer - to reduced maintenance.

Every emphasis has been laid on obtaining the maximum performance. The wing sections have been chosen as a result of considerable wind tunnel research and give a drag divergence Mach number approaching 0.9 at the normal cruising lift coefficient of 0. 25. At the fuselage side the wing section is built up to a thickness chord ratio of 12.3% at 15% of the local chord. This has the effect of bringing the maximum suction line forward near the centre of the aircraft to delay the loss of effective sweepback at high Mach numbers. The standard N.A.C.A. 0010 section is retained at the transport joint outboard of the engines, but the tip thickness is reduced to 8% and the tip section changed to Squire 'B' in order to reduce peak suctions towards the tip.

Although the first few production aircraft will probably be fitted with Bristol Olympus 101 engines of 11,000 lb. sea level static thrust, the performance has been calculated utilising the Olympus 3 engines of 13,000 lb. sea level static thrust since these will be fitted to subsequent aircraft. Provision is made on all aircraft for the retrospective fitting of the Olympus 3.

The performance of the standard aircraft cruising at height at maximum continuous power for I.CA.N. standard conditions was quoted as being with a 10,000lb bomb load and a take-off weight 156,700 lb would require a take-off distance of 1970 yards, (50ft obstacle), would give it a still air range 5000 nautical miles at a ceiling of 55,000ft.

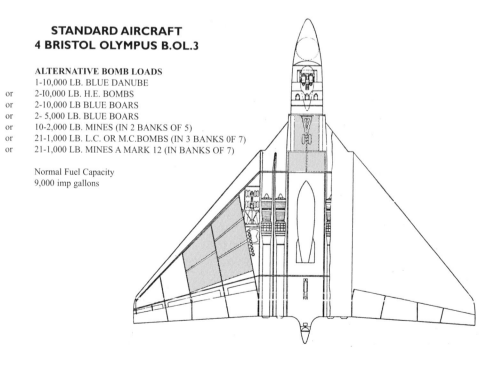

STANDARD AIRCRAFT
4 BRISTOL OLYMPUS B.OL.3

ALTERNATIVE BOMB LOADS
1-10,000 LB. BLUE DANUBE
or   2-10,000 LB. H.E. BOMBS
or   2-10,000 LB BLUE BOARS
or   2- 5,000 LB. BLUE BOARS
or   10-2,000 LB. MINES (IN 2 BANKS OF 5)
or   21-1,000 LB. L.C. OR M.C.BOMBS (IN 3 BANKS 0F 7)
or   21-1,000 LB. MINES A MARK 12 (IN BANKS OF 7)

Normal Fuel Capacity
9,000 imp gallons

PHOTOGRAPHIC RECONNAISSANCE AIRCRAFT

The standard AVRO VULCAN heavy bomber is readily convertible to a very long range reconnaissance and survey aircraft for both day and night operation. The bomb doors and their associated hydraulic mechanism are removed, and a camera unit is fitted in the bomb bay. Alternative camera units incorporating small sliding doors which open to uncover the camera windows are provided for the Day and Night reconnaissance roles. The Survey role utilises a similar unit to the Day version.

In the Day or Survey versions, the camera unit is mounted on the centre container stowage supports and the remainder of the bomb bay is filled by two 2,000 gallon fuel tanks.

By this means a maximum range of 7,000 nautical miles is obtained.

In the Night version the camera unit is mounted on the rear container stowage supports and a large number of photoflashes are carried in the following alternative arrangements:-

(a)   116 - 8" photoflashes in the bomb bay
(b)   26 - 161/2" photoflashes in the bomb bay or
(c)   26 - 161/2" photoflashes in the bomb bay plus
      36 - 161/2" photoflashes in external nacelles.

AIRCRAFT WITH CONTAINER STOWAGE

The standard production AVRO VULCAN can be fitted for the carriage of a heavy load of 1,000 lb. bombs in container stowage.

Utilising the special AVRO containers, 39 x 1,000 lb. bombs may be carried in the bomb bay, 13 bombs in each of three containers. In addition, 36 x 1,000 lb. bombs are carried in two wing nacelles holding 18 bombs each, giving a total bomb load of 75,000 lb. Special attention has been given to simplifying production of these items. The three fuselage containers are identical items as are the containers for nine bombs, a pair of which comprises one nacelle. In addition a large number of items such as the bomb doors and their operating mechanism, and the bomb crutching and release gear are identical.

The nacelle shape and position were developed as a result of extensive wind tunnel research and give the minimum loss of stability and performance for the greatest load. An important feature is that the number of bombs carried in the nacelles is nearly equal to that carried in the bomb bay and a good pattern is therefore produced when area bombing. The loading of the containers follows the standard AVRO practice using hydraulic legs. All the containers are loaded without raising the aircraft from its normal attitude on the ground.

EFFECT OF OLYMPUS ENGINE DEVELOPMENTS

The performance predictions so far presented have been based on the original rating of the Bristol Olympus 3 engine. This rating is known for convenience as the "cold" rating since the turbine entry temperature at maximum continuous thrust is 960°K. The commonly accepted limiting temperature for continuous cruising is 1050°K and this can be obtained by a reduction in the diameter of the jet nozzle. The corresponding "hot" rating has a maximum continuous thrust some 25% greater at the expense of a 5% increase in specific fuel consumption.

It should be emphasised that the use of the alternative rating involves no change in the airframe or engine but only in the jet pipe nozzle.

By fitting a variable jet pipe nozzle which can be set to the area required for either the cold or the hot rating, the advantage of the hot rating in giving maximum altitude over the target area can be obtained at the expense of very little loss of range where the hot rating is used for a radius of 500 miles from the target, giving 4,000 ft. gain of altitude at the expense of some 70 nautical miles of range.

Since the low wing loading of the AVRO VULCAN makes it able to absorb these increases of thrust, it would appear that the hot rating should be adopted. If the complication of variable area nozzles is not acceptable an improvement in the range of the aircraft with the hot nozzle can be obtained by throttling the engine over the majority of the flight and opening up to the hot rating only in the target area.

An alternative to the variable nozzle is a form of after-burning known as Thermodynamic Area Control (T.A.C.). In normal after-burning, thrust is increased by burning additional fuel in the jet pipe and enlarging the nozzle size. With T.A.C. fitted to a "cold" (i.e. 960°K) Olympus 3 engine, it is possible to obtain a limited amount of after-burning at the same nozzle size.

The specific fuel consumption under these conditions is of course greater than for the normal engine but is very much less than that for normal after-burning. A maximum engine thrust at 50,000 feet and 500 knots T.A.S. of 2,700 lb. with a specific fuel consumption of 1.2 lb/lb./hr. is likely to be achieved with T.A.C. This gives an even greater increase of altitude over the target at the expense of a further loss of range.

It is emphasised that neither of the above mentioned forms of thrust augmentation affect the maximum take-off thrust, which will remain at 13,500 lb. for both "cold" and "hot" Olympus 3 engines. Take-off distances are quoted at this rating, but the possibility of a later increase to 14,500 lb. exists.

In the following pages of this brochure any combination of the above Olympus 3 ratings may be assumed although data is presented only for the "cold" or the "hot" engines as described above. It is emphasised that only "maximum continuous" ratings have been used, and no account has been taken of the further increased performance available for short periods at the "maximum" rating.

EFFECT OF FITTING SIX ENGINES

Despite the encouraging improvement in cruising thrust at altitude that can be expected from the development of existing engines, there still remains a sufficient margin to permit utilisation of even more thrust. As an interim measure, if the tactical situation should demand it, a relatively simple way of achieving this would be to fit two additional engines, which could be conveniently installed under the outboard wings. Each engine is mounted on two beams which pick up on the front spar and on the heavy hinge rib which separates the elevator and aileron. By adopting this outboard position conflict with the location of the wing bomb nacelles is avoided.

As is usual the increase of thrust means a reduction of range and unless this reduction can be accepted an increase in fuel tankage is necessary. The large internal volume of the delta wing makes this possible without resorting to external tankage. By redesigning the wing ribs so that the tanks occupy a greater depth of the wing and by extending the fuselage three feet the fuel capacity can be increased to 11,300 gallons.

As an interim measure and pending the introduction of the Olympus 3 engine a useful gain of performance is obtained with six Olympus 101 engines.

The fitting of external nacelles has of course led to an increase of drag which has been allowed for in the performance estimates. This drag increase can be avoided by installing the six engines internally in the centre section, in place of the present four engines. The design and development effort involved is of course considerably greater than in the alternative of external nacelles.

The small diameter and length of the Armstrong Siddeley Sapphire engine makes it possible to install six of these engines in the present width of centre section.

Six Olympus engines could be installed internally in a similar way, but some increase in centre section width would be necessary.

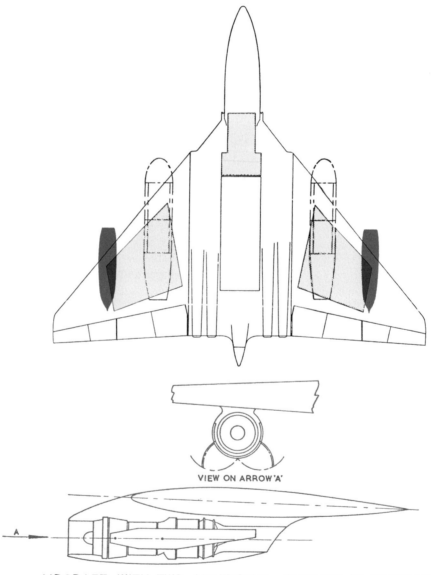

VIEW ON ARROW 'A'

AIRCRAFT WITH TWO ADDITIONAL ENGINES IN NACELLES
ENGINES — 6 BRISTOL OLYMPUS B.OL.3

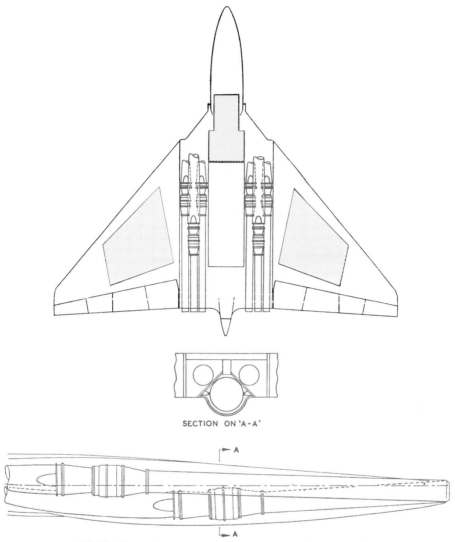

SECTION ON 'A-A'

AIRCRAFT WITH 2 ADDITIONAL BURIED ENGINES
ENGINES - 6 ARMSTRONG SIDDELEY SAPPHIRE A.S.Sa.7

EFFECT OF WING TIPS AND TAIL ARMAMENT

Increasing the span of an aircraft is a well known method of reducing the induced drag at high altitude, and a study has therefore been made of the effect of fitting wing tip extensions to the AVRO VULCAN. These are estimated to increase the weight of the aircraft by 100 lb. and to increase the target height - other things being equal - by 1,400 ft. This order of difference is large from the military point of view, but it is a small effect aerodynamically and it is not possible to say from wind tunnel tests that the whole or the advantage will be obtained in practice. However, full scale flight tests on the AVRO 707A are planned to investigate this.

The addition of the wing tips increases the stability margin by 3% which, although acceptable from the point of view of handling qualities, would result in some of the gain of performance being lost. Ideally; therefore, the centre of gravity should be moved aft at the same time by re-disposition of equipment. One item which would fit in conveniently with this is the proposed adoption or tail armament which gives a corresponding aft movement of the centre of gravity.

Alternatively it may be argued that the increase in operating altitude already indicated in will keep the AVRO VULCAN above the operating height of all but rocket-propelled interceptors, and the need for tail armament will become less.

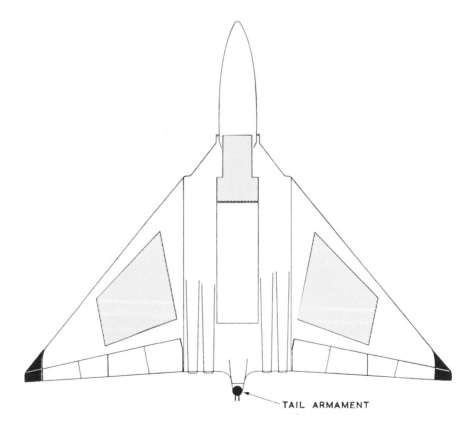

TAIL ARMAMENT

AIRCRAFT FITTED WITH WING TIPS AND TAIL ARMAMENT

DEVEL0PMENT FOR INCREASED SPEED

An alternative development is in the direction of increased cruising speed, since the sweepback of the AVRO VULCAN represents the best compromise between the inter-related factors of aspect ratio and sweepback; it is not possible to increase the critical Mach number of the wing by increasing sweepback except at the expense of a considerable loss in range. Increased Mach number must therefore be obtained by reducing the wing thickness.

The drawing shown is an indication of how this would be done. The existing planform of the wing and the existing fuselage are retained intact, while the outer wing has its thickness chord ratio reduced to 5% at the wing joint and at the wing tip. By this means, the drag rise Mach number is raised to at least 0.92. The outer wing construction is of the sandwich skin type and the fuel tanks are of the bag type occupying the full depth of the wing. The total fuel capacity obtained, namely 8,500 gallons, is sufficient for the normal range of 5,000 nautical miles with "cold " Olympus 3 engines.

As in the case of the standard aircraft it is possible to take advantage of the alternative "hot" rating of the engines to obtain 4,000 feet increase in cruising height at the expense of 400 miles of range. The reduction in wing thickness reduces the available internal fuel volume so that this type of development is not suitable for extended ranges unless drop tanks are fitted.

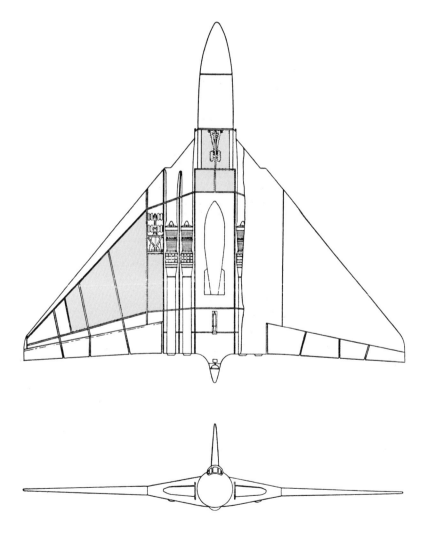

DEVELOPMENT FOR INCREASED SPEED

DEVELOPMENT FOR VERY LONG RANGE

As will have been noted in the section dealing with increased engine power, the lift coefficient necessary for flight at high altitude sets an eventual limit to the development of the aircraft. Furthermore, the range which can be obtained is limited by fuel capacity.

A development is therefore proposed in which the centre section is widened so as to accommodate either four engines of around 20,000 lb. static thrust or six Bristol Olympus 3 engines. The aircraft consists of a standard VULCAN fuselage and bomb bay and a standard outer wing, the only major difference being the new and widened centre section which picks up with the other components. The undercarriage is moved from its position in the outer wing to the widened centre section, and is redesigned to accommodate the increase of all up weight. The space in the wing at present allocated to the undercarriage is devoted to fuel, so that with some additional fuselage tankage the total capacity becomes 17,000 gallons.

It will be seen that with engines which have a specific consumption no better than that of the "cold" Olympus 3 but with a total thrust per aircraft increased by 50% a range of 7,700 nautical miles is obtained as a bomber and over 9,000 nautical miles as a photographic reconnaissance aircraft. For these ranges the target height is above 53,000 ft. and it can be raised to 57,000 ft. at a slight expense in range by the use of the "hot" rating. At shorter ranges the target altitude is of course greater.

Apart from this change in performance the aircraft has exactly the same equipment and will perform the same operational functions as the standard VULCAN. The use of the same wing for a long range civil aircraft is under consideration.

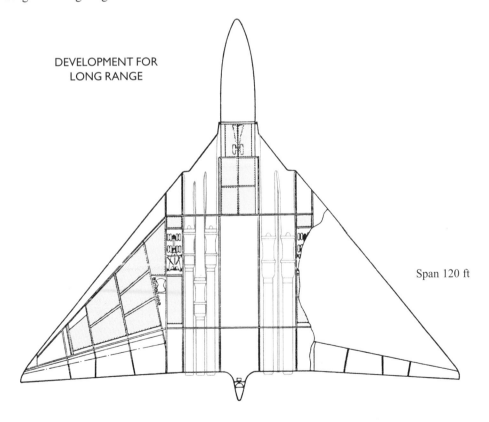

DEVELOPMENT FOR
LONG RANGE

Span 120 ft

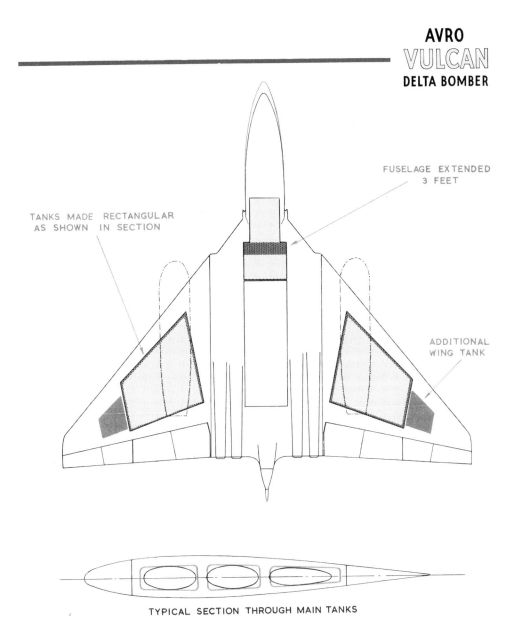

AVRO
VULCAN
DELTA BOMBER

FUSELAGE EXTENDED
3 FEET

TANKS MADE RECTANGULAR
AS SHOWN IN SECTION

ADDITIONAL
WING TANK

TYPICAL SECTION THROUGH MAIN TANKS

INCREASED FUEL CAPACITY
NORMAL TANKAGE OF 9,000 GALLONS INCREASED TO 11,300 GALLONS

Type 707A - WZ736

The first 707A had turned out to be such a useful and reliable aircraft that the Royal Aircraft Establishment (R.A.E.) expressed a wish for one for its own purposes and a second 707A was built to contract 6/Acft/7470/CB.6(c) dated 13th November 1951. It was part of a contract which also included the duo 707C aircraft. WZ736 was assembled at the Avro facility at Bracebridge Heath and first flew from RAF Waddington on the 20th February, 1953.

Following the introduction of powered flying controls and other modifications and since the new control system differed extensively from that already fitted to aircraft WD280 the provision of a separate publication became unavoidable. When the new system was introduced on WD280 the original publication was to be withdrawn, but in the meantime both manuals were in existence together and care had to be taken to distinguish between them.

WZ736 pictured on 14th March, 1953. Avro test pilot Jimmy Nelson first flew the aircraft from R.A.F. Waddington on 20th February, 1953.

DESCRIPTION (second edition)

The aircraft was powered by a single Rolls-Royce Derwent 8 turbojet engine which provided a nominal thrust of 3,600 lb. Tricycle alighting gear was fitted, the nose wheel retracting rearwards into the fuselage and the main wheels inwards into the respective wing housings. Cockpit heating and pressurisation were incorporated, the latter being automatically operative and maintained at altitudes above 10,000 ft.

The fuselage was constructed of three jig- built sections:- nose section, centre section and rear section. The nose section accommodated the cockpit, nose-wheel unit, radio and auto observer. The centre section housed the fuel tank, auxiliary's gearbox and the internal passages of the air intake ducts and also incorporated the wing attachment points. The rear section housed the engine jet pipe and carries on its upper surface the swept back fin and rudder; immediately below the rudder the anti-spin parachute is housed in its container.

The aircraft flying controls, except the rudder, were equipped with hydraulic rams which provided the power required to operate the ailerons and elevators through a normal stick-type control column and tubular push-pull rods, the control column was mounted centrally in the cockpit. Two pedals mounted on a pivoted bar below and forward of the instrument panel, were used in the normal manner to operate the rudder, which is not power operated.

Artificial feel was automatically introduced into the control column under powered control conditions by spring feel units, and the pilot, although relieved of the actual control surface hinge moments experiences stick forces which, for the elevators, are varied with the speed of the aircraft. Release units enable the pilot to revert to full manual control if this should become necessary, re-engagement of the powered controls is not permitted in the air.

Two methods of flying control trimming were provided whilst flying under powered controls; separate electrical actuators are used to move the control column position relative to elevator or aileron artificial feel; in addition orthodox mechanical control hand-wheels are coupled to auxiliary tabs. The port aileron and the elevators are equipped with combination variable geared-cum-trim tabs, and the starboard aileron embodies a plain geared tabs.

Provision was made for the installation of an auto-observer in the nose-wheel bay for the purpose of recording handling characteristics. In addition, the aircraft incorporated strain gauge recording equipment which was used to obtain data effecting control surface and control rod forces.

The Derwent 8 turbo-jet engine was housed in the rear section of the fuselage with the jet pipe protruding at its extremity. Leading edge air intakes supplied the engine with air via ducts in the wings and centre section. The basic structure of the engine comprised:-
(1) A wheel case. (2) Compressor. (3) Nine straight flow combustion chambers surrounding the centre and rear bearing casings. (4) A discharge flow turbine. (5) Axial flow turbine. (6) Jet pipe assembly.

An oil tank was mounted on the wheel case, the engine lubrication system being of the dry sump type. Aviation kerosene, contained in a single bag tank located in the lower part of the centre section, was sprayed at high pressure into the combustion chambers and burned continuously with approximately 25 per cent of the total airflow. The fuel supply was controlled by the throttle lever in conjunction with a barometric pressure control capsule on 707A aircraft, the engine control levers were located on the port console and included:-
(1) The throttle which varied the fuel flow and consequently the engine thrust and aircraft speed. (2) High pressure fuel cock for stopping the engine. (3) A low pressure fuel cock for isolating the tank during servicing or in the event of fire in the air. All three levers operate the push-pull rod control runs.

The engine was started electrically, using an external ground supply battery as the power supply. A starter motor on the engine and the engine master switch, starter button and fuel tank pump switches in the cockpit constitute the aircraft starting equipment. A push-button switch fitted in the top of the high pressure cock lever operates the torch igniter for relighting in the air. Oil pressure and oil temperature connections were located on the engine, and the jet pipe was equipped with thermo-couples for recording the jet pipe temperatures. A Rotol auxiliary's gearbox, driven from the engine wheel case by a connecting shaft, was mounted on the forward face of the engine firewall and drives a Dowty Vardel hydraulic pump and a generator.

Extension and retraction of the alighting gear units was affected by a high-pressure hydraulic system and the wing air brakes, the trim flaps and the powered flying controls were also hydraulically operated. An emergency air system could be used to lower the alighting gear if the hydraulic system failed. The main-wheel brake units were pneumatically operated and the air supply was contained in a cylindrical air storage bottle. In an emergency the wheel brakes could be operated from the emergency air system supply, also stored in a cylindrical air bottle. There was no air compressor and the air storage bottles were charged through a ground connection before flight.

Power supplies for the operation of the electrical services was obtained from a single generator mounted on the auxiliary's gearbox and two batteries connected in series. A heavy-duty GROUND/FLIGHT switch on the cockpit side at the rear of the starboard console, operating in conjunction with a relay, Type K, on the power panel, provided for the disconnection of the aircraft battery when a ground supply was used. Batteries could be stowed in the nose or wing root stowage's respectively according to the particular research

WZ736 - development history

On the 16th June, 1953 WZ736 was delivered to the R.A.E at Farnborough. Powered controls were fitted by Avro in 1954. On 12th December, 1954 it was delivered to National Aeronautical Establishment (N.A.E.) at Bedford for automatic approach trials, automatic landing trials were also carried out at the Aircraft and Instrument Experimental Unit (A.I.E.U.) Martlesham Heath in the same year.

In 1957, it was used for automatic throttle trials at R.A.E. Bedford (B.L.E.U.). On the 24th May 1962 it was delivered to R.A.E. Farnborough for source spares for WZ744.

In 1964, it was allotted to RAF Colerne as 7868M for preservation, it later went to RAF Finningley and then to RAF Cosford. It is now on loan by the RAF Museum to the Museum of Science and Industry in Manchester.

WZ736 was assembled at Bracebridge Heath and made its first flight from RAF Waddington on 20th February, 1953. Waddington was only a few miles down the road.

Pictured at a Family day at Woodford alongside its big brother and an Avro 504.

WZ736 at RAF Cottesmore in 1961 resplendent in its yellow colour scheme.

In a sorry state at RAF Colerne.

Refurbished WZ736 is now display at Air and Space gallery at the Museum of Science and Industry (MOSI) in Manchester.

Type 707C - WZ744

The Avro Type 707C was a two seat delta wing aircraft powered by one Rolls Royce Derwent 8 turbine engine, designed for research and familiarisation of pilots with characteristics of tailless aircraft of delta planform.

Two Type 707C aircraft were allocated serial numbers in 1952, but the first WZ739 was never built. The second WZ744 was flown for the first time on 1st July, 1953 from R.A.F Waddington, with Sqd Ldr Jack Wales at the controls. By this time the policy had changed and the other 707C aircraft were not proceeded with. The aircraft incorporated flying controls which were operated by two separate circuits, manual control by the port control column and rudder pedals and hydraulic operation with electrical control by the starboard column and rudder pedals. Conversion to dual manual control was possible by the installation of a conversion kit. Accommodation was provided for first and second pilots in the form of two standard type seats located side by side. Whilst the aircraft also catered for pressurised flight, full cockpit heating and ventilation incorporated.

The aircraft joined the R.A.E. in January 1956 and made a substantial research contribution into the development of fly-by-wire controls. The aeroplane flew with the R.A.E. until September 1966 and after a long and distinguished career it was selected to be saved, to be put on display at the RAF museum at Cosford near Wolverhampton.

Nose section under construction 15th April, 1953.

The all silver two seat trainer was built at Bracebridge Heath and transported to RAF Waddington where it made its first flight on the 1st July, 1953.

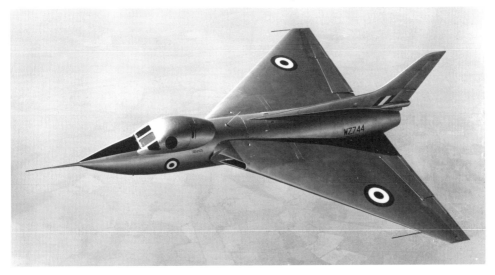

Air to air taken 3rd July, 1953.

This view shows the side opening canopy at Woodford, 12th August, 1953.

Because of the cramped space ejection seats could not be fitted.

Shown above various views of WZ744 at Woodford, 12th August, 1953.

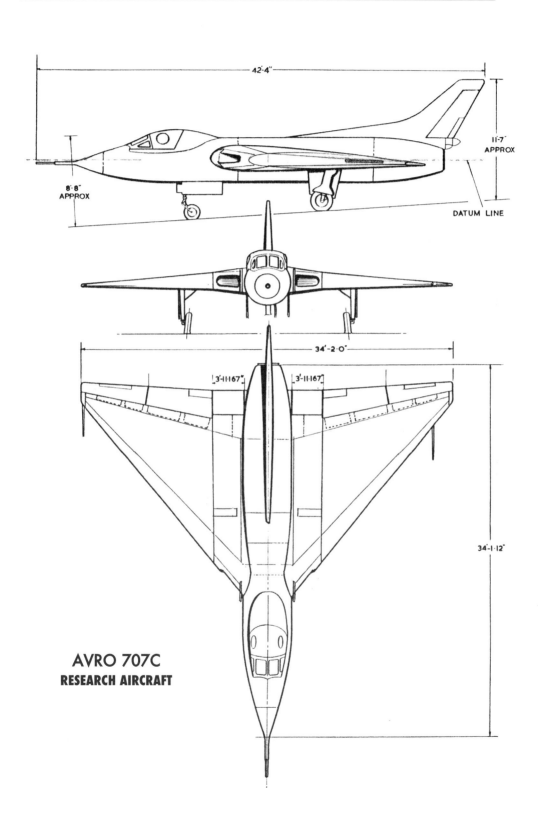

AVRO 707C
RESEARCH AIRCRAFT

In flight refuelling receiver and tanker

A second issue of Operating Requirement OR 229 was published in January 1953 to cover the Vulcan and Victor being built. With the addition of flight refuelling requirement a third version was issued on the 2nd June, 1954. A brochure was produced for the conversion of the Vulcan B.Mk1 with four Olympus 101 engines. The proposals were based on the requirements laid down in a letter from the ministry dated 16th January, 1954 and a meeting held at A. V. Roe, at Chadderton and Woodford on the 14th December, 1953 and at Chadderton on 8th January. Basically the requirements were for :-

(1). A Receiver to cater for a rate of flow of 500 g.p.m. (2). A Receiver to cater for a rate of flow of 1,000 g.p.m. (3). A Tanker to cater for a rate of flow of 1,000 g.p.m. and a transfer capacity of at least 10,000 Imperial gallons.

Additional to the above requirements a Tanker version was offered catering for rates of flow of 500 or 1,000 g.p.m. and a transferable capacity of approximately 5,000 gallons, with a large increase in range and endurance on the proposal (3) above.

The modifications required to embody the fixed fittings for this version are of a relatively minor nature, involving the bomb bay only and can be embodied retrospectively.

It is assumed that this modification will be introduced at some stage in the production line. Retrospective action could be taken, but would involve a large increase in labour time. It is suggested that this would be a Class B/C Mod. (embodied on the production line or by Contractor during repair or overhaul).

The estimated time to convert a Standard Bomber to the Refuelling version by R.A.F. personnel, assuming that the modification to introduce the fixed fittings is embodied, is:-

(1) Receiver 500 g.p.m. - 24 hours. (2) Receiver 1,000 g.p.m. - 24 hours. (3) Tanker 10,000 Imperial gallons - 3 days. (4.) Tanker 5,000 Imperial gallons - 2 days.

Details of the Refuelling Units for the Tanker Version could be found in a separate brochure supplied by Messrs. Flight Refuelling Limited.

In flight receiver

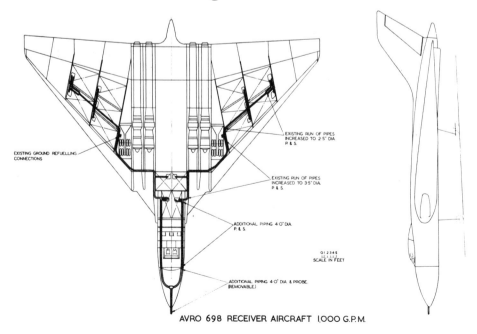

EXISTING RUN OF PIPES
INCREASED TO 2.5" DIA
P. & S.

EXISTING GROUND REFUELLING
CONNECTIONS

EXISTING RUN OF PIPES
INCREASED TO 3.5" DIA
P. & S.

ADDITIONAL PIPING 4.0" DIA
P. & S.

0 1 2 3 4 5
SCALE IN FEET

ADDITIONAL PIPING 4.0" DIA & PROBE
(REMOVABLE)

AVRO 698 RECEIVER AIRCRAFT 1,000 G.P.M.

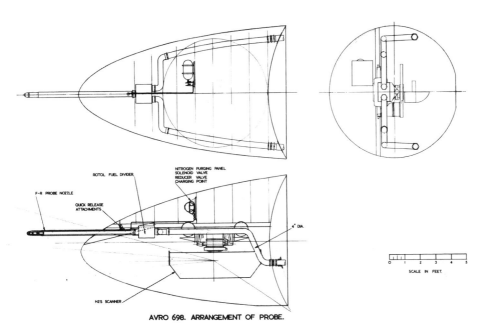

AVRO 698. ARRANGEMENT OF PROBE.

In flight tanker

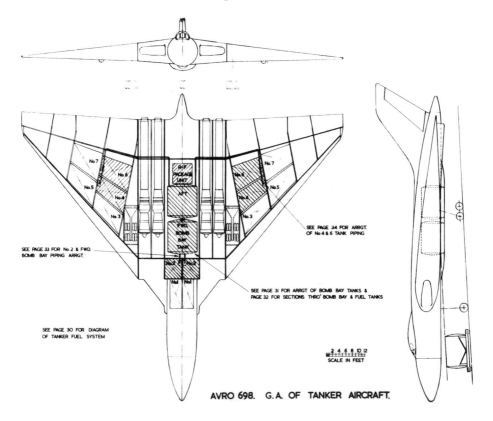

SEE PAGE 34 FOR ARRGT.
OF No 4 & 6 TANK PIPING

SEE PAGE 33 FOR No. 2 & FWD.
BOMB BAY PIPING ARRGT.

SEE PAGE 31 FOR ARRGT. OF BOMB BAY TANKS &
PAGE 32 FOR SECTIONS THRO' BOMB BAY & FUEL TANKS

SEE PAGE 30 FOR DIAGRAM
OF TANKER FUEL SYSTEM

SCALE IN FEET

AVRO 698. G. A. OF TANKER AIRCRAFT.

Sapphire power

Ground shot 3rd, August 1953.

Take-off 3rd August, 1953.

Landing 3rd August, 1953.

September 1953.

The Sapphire replaced the Avon shown above.

During one of VX770 high altitude test flights in February 1953, Roly Falk was extending the airbrakes when the port outer airbrake under the wing fractured. With the aircraft grounded it was decided to take the opportunity to change the engines to the more powerful Armstrong Siddeley Sapphire Sa6 of 8000 lb static thrust.

A full wing fuel system had been fitted and on 27th June VX770 now fitted with the Sapphire engines flew with Roly Falk at the controls to test the new fuel system up to 30,000 ft.

Leading particulars

The Sapphire engine air was delivered through an annular intake at the front of the engine into a multi-stage axial flow compressor. After compression the air passed into an annular combustion chamber. The engine had a two stage turbine and fixed area nozzle. The turbine was directly coupled to and droved the compressor rotor. The fuel was delivered by one fuel pump. The fuel flow to the burners were controlled by a full range flow control unit which incorporated a manually operated throttle valve and a high pressure cock, an automatic acceleration control was fitted.

Engine Limitations

Rating	Speed R.P.M	J.P.T.	Estimated Static Thrust lb
Take-off (5 min limit)	8,600 ± 50	665	8,000
Operational necessity limit (5 min)	8,700	665	(note.b)
Intermediate (30 min. limit)	8,400	625	7500
Max. continuous	8,200	585	6900
Min.idling on ground	3,000 + 200	570	

NOTE: (a) The overriding engine limitation is the one first attained either R.P.M. or J.P.T.
(b) Due to control system characteristics the maximum r.p.m. will vary with altitude. Up to 20,000 ft max. r.p.m. will increase to approximately 8,700 and above this altitude will decrease to approximately 8,350 at 50,000 feet.

As can be seen from this picture the Vulcan was highly manoeverable for an aircraft of its size, especially at high altitude, where it could out manoeuvre even the most modern fighter.

VX777 second prototype

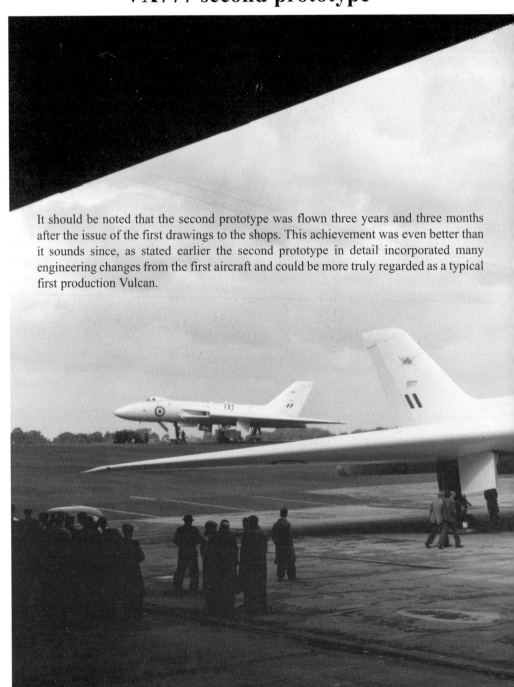

It should be noted that the second prototype was flown three years and three months after the issue of the first drawings to the shops. This achievement was even better than it sounds since, as stated earlier the second prototype in detail incorporated many engineering changes from the first aircraft and could be more truly regarded as a typical first production Vulcan.

Second prototype Vulcan VX777 with VX770 in the background at Woodford flight sheds, September 1953.

After a long and extensive test flying career which continued to the end of 1960, VX777 working life went on for another two years at Farnborough. It was finally scrapped in 1963 after the airframe had been used for ground based armament and equipment trials.

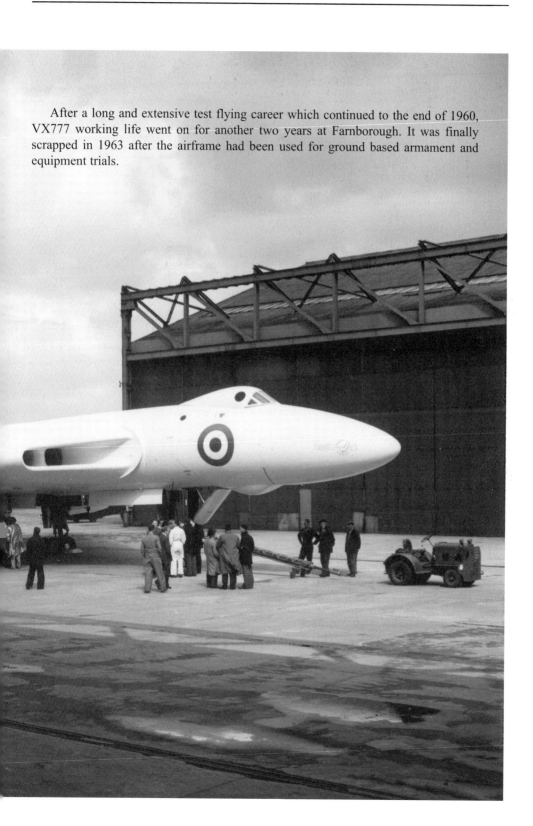

Olympus power - first flight VX777 prototype

September 3rd, 1953 saw the initial flight of the second prototype Vulcan with Roly Falk at the controls. It was powered by four Olympus 100 engines, these were later changed to the more powerful Olympus 101 engines following a heavy landing at Farnborough in July 1954. As with VX770 it was just in time to make it's first public appearance with the first prototype Vulcan at the memorable 1953, S.B.A.C. Show.

VX777 landing back at Woodford after first its flight. The twin airbrakes underneath the wing can be clearly be seen, these were later altered to single airbrakes on production Vulcan's.

S.B.A.C. Airshow September 1953

"A record number of exhibitors filled the two acres of tent showing everything from batteries to guided missiles, paints to radar sets, electrical fittings to ejector seats. Following the crash the previous year which killed a number of spectators the flying display had to meet strict regulations and safety procedures, but this did not stop the show being one of the most iconic events in the Shows history.

The Show was stolen by the Avro Deltas, led by Roly Falk in the second prototype Vulcan VX777 and Jack Wales in the first prototype VX770. They lined up for take-off looking like two swans and their brood. After some time during which they formed together all eyes were turned to the Laffin's Plain end of the runway when the deltas flew past. This was followed by slow and fast fly-past by the individual aircraft and the climb performance of the Olympus powered Vulcan was noted". *Extract from Flight.*

Squadron Leader Jack B. Wales D.F.C. T.D., O.B.E. pictured in his office on 4th January, 1952. He flew the first prototype Vulcan at the 1953 S.B.A.C. Show. He was tragically killed test flying an Avro Shackleton on 7th December, 1956.

The two prototypes with Avro ground staff. Seen landing is the Gloster Javelin delta aircraft.

The pilots who flew the six delta aircraft on Saturday, Left to Right J. B. Wales (Avro), F/L J.E. Burton, F/Lt W. J. Laidler, S/L W. J. Potocki, Lt. W. Nobel, R. J. Falk (Avro).

The Avro delta aircraft steal the Airshow

Delta line up Saturday 12th September, 1953.

Four 707s preparing to take-off 12th September, 1953.

Fly past S.B.A.C. show 12th September 1953.

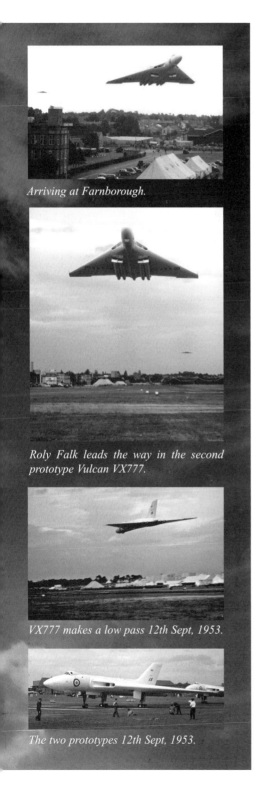

Arriving at Farnborough.

Roly Falk leads the way in the second prototype Vulcan VX777.

VX777 makes a low pass 12th Sept, 1953.

The two prototypes 12th Sept, 1953.

'V' formation - when this historic photograph was taken by Avro staff photographer Paul Cullerne, the pilots were: Vulcan (W/C. R. J. Falk, A.F.C.); 707As (S/L. H. T. Murley, D.S.C., A.F.C., and F/L. J.K. Hough); 707B (S/L. W. J. Potocki, D.FG.); 707C (F/L. J. E. Burton). The service pilots were all from R.A.E. Flying as passenger in the 707C was G/C. S. W. R, Hughes, O.B.E., A.F.C., in charge of experimental flying at Farnborough.

Delta formation taken Friday 11th Sept, 1953.

Diamond formation 12th September, 1953.

Models, post cards, adverts, & cigarette cards...

AVRO
707. B.

Interceptor fighter aircraft capable of flying faster than the speed of sound.

The Science Museum, London.
No. 340

"TURF" CIGARETTES

AVRO 707B DELTA WING (JET)

BRITISH AIRCRAFT — SERIES OF 50   N°32

"TURF" CIGARETTES

AVRO VULCAN (JET)

BRITISH AIRCRAFT — SERIES OF 50   N°4

"TURF" CIGARETTES

AVRO VULCAN B.1 (JET)

BRITISH AIRCRAFT — SERIES OF 50   N°53

THE VIRTUES OF THE AVRO VULCAN

3.   *Exceptional*

Simplicity of controlling the Avro Vulcan is due not only to the absence of high-lift devices, but a smooth and progressive high Mach number effect. In addition, the low wing-loading ensures low stall speed, while docility of the stall and the most natural stall warnings add to the safety of an aircraft fairly described as the most effective bomber in the world.

A. V. ROE & CO., LIMITED / MANCHESTER

AVRO

Member of the Hawker Siddeley Group | Pioneer . . . and World Leader in Aviation

5.   *High Altitude Flight*

Low wing-loading and reduced drag are major factors in the unequalled high-altitude performance of the Avro Vulcan, the most effective bomber in the world.

1. *Aerodynamic Simplicity.*
2. *Easy Landing.*
3. *Exceptional Safety.*
4. *Great Range.*
5. *High Altitude Flight.*
6. *High Speed Flight.*
7. *Servicing Simplicity.*
8. *Fighter-like Manœuvrability.*
9. *Large Carrying Capacity.*
10. *Great Development Potential.*

AVRO
A. V. ROE & CO., LIMITED,
MANCHESTER

*Member of the Hawker Siddeley Group
Pioneer . . . and World Leader in Aviation*

...the Vulcan captures the public imagination

Shown left one of the rarest Dinky models produced was of the Avro Vulcan produced in 1955.
Below is the now rare FROG plastic kit of the Avro Vulcan B.Mk1.

THE VIRTUES OF THE AVRO VULCAN

2. Easy Landing

The Delta configuration of the AVRO VULCAN offers excellent handling qualities at low speeds. The technique of approach and landing is exceptionally simple. The landing attitude is normal and approach speeds may be selected over a wide range. Powerful air brakes and the absence of trim changes from air brakes or undercarriage are other welcome features of this, the most effective bomber in the world.

A. V. ROE & CO., LIMITED / MANCHESTER

AVRO

Member of the Hawker Siddeley Group | Pioneer . . . and World Leader in Aviation

1. Aerodynamic Simplicity.
2. Easy Landing.
3. Exceptional Safety.
4. Great Range.
5. High Altitude Flight.
6. High Speed Flight.
7. Servicing Simplicity.
8. Fighter-like Manoeuvrability.
9. Large Carrying Capacity.
10. Great Development Potential.

A series of adverts produced on the virtues of the Vulcan.

Press photographs

Publicity pictures were much sought by the media. These were part of a series taken in September 1953 to meet this requirement. The photographs were able to get these dramatic shots from the rear of a USAF Fairchild C-119 Packet.

Nice air to air picture of VX770, a distinguishing feature was the lack of bomb blister which was not specified for the first prototype also note the single pitot on the nose.

Prototype development

By December 1952 VX770 had completed twenty seven take-off and landings, and twenty one hours and five minutes in the air.

It is interesting to note that the Handley Page Victor which was built to the same B35/46 specification as the Vulcan was its main competitor made its first flight on the 24th December, 1952 nearly three months after the Vulcan. Like the Vulcan in April 1953 the Victor was powered by four Armstrong Siddeley Sapphire (Sa.6) engines.

The first prototype Vulcan was a very basic aircraft at the time, which was more or less suggested in the September 1948 report to speed up the testing programme.

By April 1953 the first prototype VX770 had four Armstrong Siddeley Sapphire (Sa.6) engines installed, the wing fuel system was fully operative and the cockpit pressurisation was also made operative. By August 1953, after an intensive flight programme, which included demonstrations, sixty flights had been completed. The flight tests covered an extensive field, engine handling and installation tests, fuel tests, trim curves, strain gauge tests on wing and structure and air brakes. Position error tests and drag measurements were also carried out.

During this period, the second prototype Vulcan VX777 was fitted with Bristol Olympus 100 engines and made its initial flight on the 3rd September, 1953. The aircraft immediately thereafter had a number of engineering changes, including modifications to the Olympus engine control systems. Additional systems were also completed, the object being to carry out handling trials at the highest possible altitude. This work continued to spring of 1954.

The first prototype during this period was carrying out extensive handling tests. The tests included trim changes due to airbrakes both at high Mach numbers and in landing configuration. Manoeuvring stability, trim points, handling tests with engines stopped and with power controls switched off, were also carried out.

On the 27th July, 1954, the second prototype VX777 was damaged during a heavy landing at Farnborough. During the subsequent repair work, Olympus 101 engines were installed. Also as the preliminary results from the structural test specimen were becoming available, a number of strengthening modifications were incorporated.

Second prototype VX777 takes-off from Woodford on 31st March, 1954. It made a heavy landing at Farnborough on 27th July, 1954.

Engine development

June 1954 saw the issue of document I.P.D.56 which gave more information on the performance of the Avro Vulcan as described below in the original report. This enabled a comparison to be made on the performance with various engine developments.

Two limitations exist for the maximum altitude a given aircraft can attain; the first is the engine thrust available relative to the weight of the aircraft, and the second is the lifting ability of the wing. The maximum lift of a wing is reduced at high subsonic Mach numbers and it may be accepted that for aircraft flying at Mach numbers around 0.9 the cruising lift coefficient should not exceed about 0.14 in order to ensure an adequate degree of manoeuvrability. This value is already closely approached by the conventional swept wing aircraft, which has therefore little reserve for development to higher altitude. Due to its larger wing area, however, the Avro Vulcan with Bristol Olympus 101 (11,000 lb. rating) engines cruises at 500 knots and 50,000 ft, at a lift coefficient of only 0.26 and therefore has a considerable margin of lift in hand.

This potential of increased lift can be utilised by fitting more powerful engines, thereby raising the cruising and target altitudes. The advantage in placing the aircraft above the operational ceiling of enemy fighters is obvious.

At the outset of the Vulcan design provision was made for the installation of any jet engine having a diameter up to a maximum of 46" and prototype Vulcan aircraft had already flown with Rolls-Royce Avon, Armstrong Siddeley Sapphire and Bristol Olympus 100 engines. At the same time the air intake design was based on the air consumption of engines having a dry thrust of 15,000 - 17,000 lb. and the jet pipe tunnel was capable of accepting jet pipes suitable for thrusts of this order.

The Brochure also gave the performance of the Vulcan with Bristol 01.101 engines (11,000 lb. sea level static thrust). These engines could then be fitted to the first five or so production aircraft and would be superseded by developed engines having ratings of 12,000 lb. and 13,000 lb. sea level static thrust. Performance with the latter engine with 12,000 lb. rating may be assumed to be intermediate between that and the 11,000 lb. rating.

The time scale for the completion of the order for pre-production aircraft roughly coincided with the flight stage in the development of the Olympus to the B.01.6 (16,000 lb. rating) and the Rolls Royce Conway R.Co.6 (15,000lb. rating) engines. *The performance of the Vulcan with these engines was given later in the brochure.*

The higher ratings of the B.01.101 were obtained without any installation changes. The installation of the B.01.6 or the Rolls-Royce Conway 6 engines necessitated detailed alterations to the engine mountings and to the accessories and services in the engine bays. The engine air intakes and the aircraft structure remain unchanged.

On the basis of the ratings offered by the engine manufacturers at the time of writing the Conway 6 had lower fuel consumption than the B.01.6 and therefore showed an advantage in range performance. The lower altitude thrust of the Conway 6, at the cruising rating however, gives a height over the target less than the Olympus 6.

FOUR BRISTOL OLYMPUS B.O1.101 ENGINES
(11,000 LB. RATING)

Engine Data

The Bristol Olympus B.01.101 is a jet propulsion engine employing compound axial compressors individually driven by separate single-stage turbines in conjunction with an annular combustion chamber with separate flame tubes. This engine has a mass flow of 175 lb./sec. under I.S.A. sea level static conditions. Details of engine performance have been extracted from the Bristol Aeroplane Company brochure T.C.204/4.

Thrust boosting is available for this engine in the form of Bristol Simplified Reheat (B.S.R.) or water injection, or a combination of both.

With the Bristol Simplified Reheat system a substantial increase in thrust is obtained without the complications of a full reheat system e.g. bigger jet pipe diameters, mechanically variable final nozzle etc. A simple aerodynamic control is used to vary the final nozzle area. The use of B.S.R. has been confined in this brochure to boost the take-off thrust although the cruising thrust can also be augmented by this method.

Water injection is only used for take-off. The engine is over speeded and water is injected into the combustion chamber in order to reduce the high temperatures thereby produced under tropical summer conditions the amount of thrust boost available by this method is the same as can be obtained by using B.S.R. in I.C.A.N. conditions the gain is less.

Finally, since the two systems are independent a combination of both methods may be used in order to produce even higher thrust.

A summary of the sea level static thrusts under I.S.A. and Tropical summer conditions is given below:-

	Take-off thrust lb.	
	I.S.A.	Tropical summer
Without thrust boosting	11,000	8,600
With B.S.R.	13,400	11,000
With water injection	12,100	11,000
With B.S.R. and water injection	14,700	14,100

FOUR BRISTOL OLYMPUS B.01.101 ENGINES
(13,000 LB. RATING)

Engine Data

The B.01.101 (13,000lb rating) engine is a direct development from the lower 11,000 lb. rating engine. There will be an interim higher rating of 12,000 lb. thrust which will be obtained by the addition of another stage to the compressor. This will later be developed to the full 13,000 lb. thrust for the production engines.

As on the 11,000 lb. rating engine thrust boosting is again available in the form of B.S.R. and water injection. The sea level static thrusts with and without thrust boosting are given below: -

	Take-off thrust lb.	
	I.S.A.	Tropical summer
Without thrust boosting	13,000	10,200
With B.S.R.	15,800	13,000
With water injection	14,300	13,000
With B.S.R. and water injection	17,500	16,600

The weight data for the aircraft fit with the 13,000 lb. engines is assumed to be the same as for the 11,000 lb. engines since the difference in engine weight is very small and no further data is available.

FOUR BRISTOL OLYMPUS B.01.6 ENGINES
(16,000 LB. RATING)

Engine Data

This engine was originally designated the Bristol Olympus B.01.4 engine with a thrust rating of 14,000 lb. The present engine has been developed by increasing the air mass flow into the engine without alterations to the compressor dimensions. Hence, with the exception of the jet pipe, the B.01.6 is outwardly similar to the B.01.4.

Two speed compressors are employed as on the B.01.101 and this arrangement enables high pressure ratios to be achieved which are not possible with the single shaft compressor.

Due to the possibilities of over speeding the low pressure compressor the maximum thrust rating is defined by:-

Turbine entry temperature = Maximum

Or

L.P. Compressor r.p.m. = 100%

The maximum cruise rating of the engines at 94% maximum turbine r.p.m. which corresponds to 100% L.P. compressor r.p.m.

Thrust boosting can be applied to the engine and water injection will restore the I.S.A. conditions in the Tropics.

Under sea level static conditions the thrust produced by the B.01.6 engine is:-

	I.S.A.	Tropical Summer
Net jet thrust lb.	16,000	12,800

Performance figures were derived from the Bristol Aeroplane Company's brochure T.C.213/2.

FOUR ROLLS-ROYCE CONWAY R.Co.6 ENGINES

Engine Data

The Rolls-Royce Conway R.Co.6 is a by-pass turbo-jet engine which has been specifically designed to give high cruising economy for bomber aircraft.

It features multi-stage axial flow compressors which deliver air into a single stage high pressure turbine and a multi-stage low pressure turbine. The combustion chamber consists of an annular air casing housing separate straight flow flame tubes. A by-pass duct surrounds the engine in the region of the H.P. compressor inlet and continues rearward to the exhaust unit. A particular feature is the cool exterior of the engine which avoids the necessity for separate shielded fire zones.

The engine has a water/methanol injection system supplied through an aircraft-mounted high pressure turbo-pump driven by compressor delivery air.

Performance figures were extracted from Rolls-Royce publication T.S.D.522.

The sea level static ratings of the engine are given below:

	Take-off thrust lb.	
	I.S.A.	Tropical Summer
Without water/methanol	15,000	12,200
With water/methanol	17,500	15,000

Boundary layer experiments

It became apparent that at high altitudes and speeds on the early test flights with the 707A and VX777 that the wing was suffering from buffet problems and affecting the performance. On the 11th March, 1954 Roly Falk took VX777 with wool tufts fitted on the starboard wing tip, Chief Aerodynamicist Roy Ewans was occupying the co-pilots seat so that he could observe the tufts on the wing to study the breakdown in airflow at high speed.

In the summer of 1954, new test pilot Jimmy Harrison had flown WD280 trying wing fences, vortex generators and notches to help find a solution to the boundary layer problem.

The R.A.E. at Farnborough in the meantime proposed the fitting of a kink leading edge and a experimental mock-version of the leading edge extension was tested on WD280 using a technique of applied 'g' to simulate the correct Vulcan Mach No C_L relationships. The wind tunnel prediction was confirmed by flights in early 1955 and modification to the B.Mk1 Vulcan was authorised.

Boundary layer wing fence end on WD280, pictured 12th April, 1954. Due to undesirable wing buzz caused by airflow over the wing tips, large wing fences were fitted. It was not enough to solve the problem and led to the redesign of the outer wing leading edge.

707A, WD280 with Vortex generators pictured 17th June, 1954.

In January 1955, it was decided to evaluate the new kink wing on WD280.

B. Mk1 Brochure

In July 1954 Avro produced a detailed brochure on the Vulcan B. Mk1 powered by four Olympus turbo-jet engines having a sea level thrust varying between 11,000 lb and 16,000 lb each according to which engine installed. This is an abridged version of the brochure as parts are repeated from the 1951 specification already printed in this book.

Centre section

The width of the centre section encompasses the four engines and bomb bay and its length extends from the rear of the pressure cabin to the rear fuselage. The main load bearing structure is bounded by the front and rear spars and main wing transport ribs, all of which are constructed on the extruded boom/shear web principle. The rear spar bottom boom is cut away to allow the jet pipes to pass, the end loads being carried round the pipes by forged steel rings.

Two strong ribs form the side walls of the bomb bay separating it from the inboard engine bays. The engine bays on each side of the centre section are divided by a central rib so that each engine is housed in its own compartment, a feature which localises fire risks. Forward of the front spar the ribs at the side of the bomb bay are extended to enclose a box structure housing two large fuel tanks. Between this structure and the pressure cabin is the nose undercarriage bay, housing the pressurisation control gear, much of the radio and radar equipment and two additional fuel tanks. The air intakes form the structure forward of the engine bays.

The bomb bay is a single large compartment occupying the full section of the fuselage. The roof, which is also the upper surface of the fuselage, is supported by strong arch-shaped members which carry the bomb load. Two pairs of doors, which fold with a concertina action, extend the full length of the bomb bay.

Outer wings

Each outer wing is of two-spar construction with ribs running between spars and lying normal to the control surface hinge line. In each wing six of these ribs, reinforced to carry the control surface hinge loads, are of extruded boom and double web construction. Each inboard rib also carries a proportion of the main undercarriage reaction. The ribs forward of the elevators between the spars carry five fuel tank bays which are elliptical in cross section. The skin covering is of aluminium alloy stiffened by Z-section and T-section stringers. The main undercarriage units are housed in the inboard portion of each outer wing between the inboard elevator hinge rib and the transport rib. The leading edge structures incorporate thermal anti-icing. They are formed of nose ribs covered by an aluminium alloy skin with a thin inner skin corrugated chord-wise.

Aft of the rear spar the control surface shrouds are of corrugated sandwich construction with rib let's attached to the spars. The lower surface shroud panels are hinged along the spar for access to the control surfaces.

Four strong points are fitted in the outer wing for attachment of wing nacelles. Access to aileron power control units, fuel tanks, pumps, contents gauges, etc., is from the undersurface of the wing. No servicing is required on the top surface.

Ailerons and elevators

There are four trailing edge control surfaces on each wing, the outer pairs acting as ailerons and the inner pairs as elevators. They are made up of a strong light-alloy D-section spar with light trailing edge ribs covered with magnesium-alloy sheet. The light-alloy nose skin is extended forward to form an aerodynamic balance and it carries also the mass balance. A sealing strip of rubberised fabric is attached between the forward edge of the latter and the shroud skin.

Fin and rudder

The fin is constructed in a similar manner to the wing, i.e. two spars and inter-ribs, but the skinning is of magnesium alloy. The leading edge construction is again similar to the outer wing for anti-icing purposes. The fin cap is constructed of material which is transparent to radar signals. The rudder is constructed similarly to the elevators and ailerons.

Crew accommodation

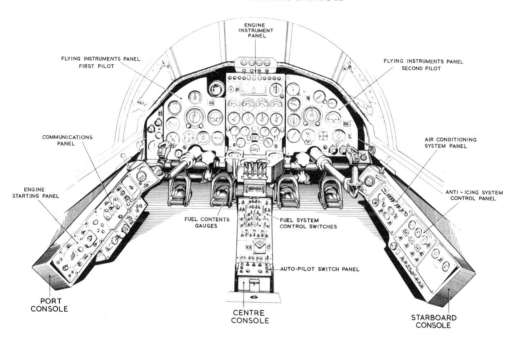

The arrangement of the accommodation for the crew consists of the whole of the pressurised portion of the fuselage and provision is made for a crew of five, namely: First Pilot, Second Pilot, First navigator/air bomber (visual), Second navigator/radar operator/air bomber, Signaller

Access

The only entrance is an outward opening door in the lower surface of the fuselage reached by means of a ladder. A further ladder is also provided in the cabin for access to the pilots' position.

Pilots' controls

Single-grip-type control handles and conventional rudder bars are provided at each pilot's position. Further controls are housed on three consoles and a centrally disposed throttle quadrant. A console on the port side of the cockpit houses engine starting, wireless, bomb door and radio altimeter switches. On the starboard side of the cockpit a console with three panels houses controls and indicators for the cabin conditioning, anti-icing and the fuel tank nitrogen pressurisation systems. Between the pilots' seats is a retractable console housing the fuel system controls, artificial feel unit switches and an auto-pilot control unit.

Flying controls

The flying control surfaces, namely, the ailerons, elevators and rudder are power operated and have forward sealed balances of the Westland-Irving type. The power controls are electro-hydraulic units which actuate each control surface.

Aileron and elevator controls

The aileron and elevator control surfaces are divided as shown below. Each section is operated independently by its own jack and controlled from its own power unit, which is actuated by the common pilot's control on the input side. Failure of a power unit or jack will cause the corresponding section of the control surface to trail in the neutral position. The other three sections remain unaffected so that control of the aircraft at three-quarters of the full normal rate is then obtainable.

Rudder controls

Duplicated power units are installed at the base of the one-piece rudder, this position providing good accessibility for maintenance purposes. Either of these power units is powerful enough to operate the whole of the control surface, and one will normally be controlling the rudder whilst the other is idling. In the event of failure the second unit is automatically brought into operation.

Control feel

Conventional push-pull rods connect the control grips and rudder bars to the power units. Artificial feel is provided to give a variation of stick force with control movement from the trimmed position. In order to give pleasant control forces and harmonisation over the speed range the stick force per degree of control movement increases as the square of the indicated air speed in the case of the ailerons and elevators and as the cube of the indicated air speed in the case of the rudder.

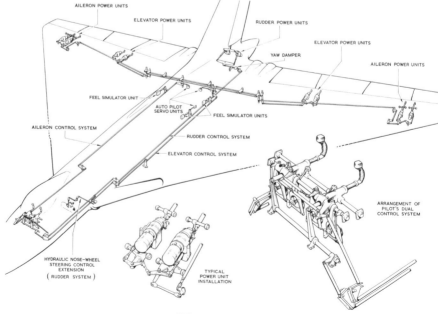

FLYING CONTROLS

Power units

The power units consist of an assembly of an electric motor, a three-bank hydraulic pump of the variable stroke type, and a hydraulic ram. The electric motor drives the hydraulic pump and is in continuous operation. One bank of the pump supplies oil at a base pressure to operate a servo mechanism. The remaining two banks deliver oil to the jack in response to the servo mechanism.

Air brakes

Eight efficient air brakes situated in the centre section wing extend above and below the aerofoil. They are actuated simultaneously by a centrally mounted actuator with duplicated electric motors controlled by a three-position lever in the cockpit.

Braking parachute

One 24-foot diameter ribbon parachute is installed on the starboard side of the tail fuselage below the rudder. It is provided primarily for use in emergency landings such as return to base soon after take-off or landings at aerodromes with short runways. It is also valuable in reducing wear on wheel brakes and tyres but its use in this manner will depend on the technique adopted in service.

Undercarriage

Main-wheels

Each main-wheel unit consists of a Dowty liquid spring leg with a bogie having two axles carrying four Dunlop wheels. Each wheel is fitted with two tyres. Retraction and extension are controlled by an UP and DOWN push-button type selector switch on the pilots' centre panel.

The plate type wheel brakes are operated by two independent hydraulic supplies, which are controlled by foot motors on the pilots' rudder pedals. Maxaret anti-skid units are also fitted. Either of the two hydraulic supplies will operate the brakes. A parking control handle is located on the port side of the centre console.

Nose wheel

The nose wheel unit consists of a liquid spring leg with levered-suspension mounting for two wheels each having a single tyre. Retraction and extension are controlled by the pilots' push-button type switch. The nose wheel unit is provided with a hydraulic steering mechanism controlled by movement of the rudder pedals. A steering control press switch on either pilot's control handle must be depressed before the steering mechanism can be brought into operation. A centring jack on the leg unit which allows castor action, normally tends to hold the nose-wheels in a fore-and-aft direction.

Undercarriage doors

Hydraulically operated doors which close the wheel compartments are controlled electrically so that they operate in the correct sequence with the leg units. The doors are mechanically locked in the closed position so that damage to the hydraulic system cannot cause inadvertent extension of the undercarriage.

Emergency operation

Emergency lowering of all the wheels is effected by pulling a single control located at the starboard side of the pilots' centre console. This action releases compressed air from two independent systems which operate respectively the nose wheel unit and the main wheel unit.

In the event of failure of the main hydraulic system to the wheel brakes, duplicated supplies are available from hydraulic accumulators. These units are charged on the ground and the reserve of pressure is sufficient to bring the aircraft to rest after landing and for a normal amount of subsequent taxiing.

Engine alternatives

The engine bays have been designed so that various engines may be installed without major structural re-design. This will enable the full potential of the aircraft to be developed as more powerful engines become available.

The engines considered are as follows:-		Manufactures brochure references.
B.01.101	11,000 lb.	T.C. 204/4
B.01.101	13,000 lb.	Factored increase on T.C.204/4. With simplified reheat.
B.01.6	16,000 lb.	T.C. 213/2
Rolls-Royce Conway R.Co.6	15,000 lb.	T.B.D. 522

The B.0l.101 engines, at both the lower and higher ratings, are scheduled for installation in the first production batch of aircraft. The information in the following paragraphs of this section, although dealing specifically with the B.0l.101 engine, is generally applicable to the others.

The engines are housed in pairs inside the main plane centre section between the front and. rear spars. Each leading edge air intake divides into two ducts just aft of the intake mouth. Boundary layer air is exhausted from the inboard intake walls to the upper and lower surfaces of the wing and an external lip at the inboard end of each intake diverts the fuselage boundary layer.

Each engine bay is divided into zones by bulkheads in order to localise engine fire and inflammable vapour which might accumulate in these zones is ventilated to atmosphere. The design also ensures that the cooling air flow is restricted to the minimum. Extensive precaution has also been taken to prevent the collection of liquid fuel during a wet start by the use of baffles and drains. Fire precaution in the form of self resetting detector units and Methyl Bromide fire extinguishers is supplied for each zone of each engine. In the case of a fire in flight, a red light is visible to the pilots in the fire buttons which control the extinguishers. If the aircraft should crash land the fire extinguishers are detonated automatically by inertia switches.

Engine-driven aircraft accessories

A 112-volt, 22.5 kilowatt D.C. generator is mounted on the nose of each engine and on three of the engines there s a Dowty hydraulic pump which delivers 5 gallons per minute at 4,000 lb. per sq. in. As all these accessories are mounted directly on to the engines the need for accessory gearboxes is eliminated.

Engine controls

Four throttle levers, mounted on the centre console in the cockpit, are connected to the engine by light-alloy push-pull tubes. The levers also operate the H.P. fuel cocks in the initial 10° of movement. The engine starting and electrical controls are mounted on the port console.

Engine mounting

Each engine is mounted within the main plane on three self-aligning mounting points secured to fixtures on each engine rib and the top structure. Installation of the engines has been made rapid and simple by the use of four manually-operated winches from underneath the aircraft. This method not only enables the upper surface of the wing to be maintained as a smooth unbroken surface but also avoids the use of large long-jib cranes and slinging gear.

Olympus engine November 1956 showing special hoist looking foward.

Engine bay 3rd April, 1956.

The Olympus engine was continuously developed throughout the career of the Vulcan, this led to internal and external changes to the Vulcan's airframe.

Fuel tanks

Fuel is carried in fourteen bag-type tanks contained in light-alloy compartments as shown on the opposite page. Port and starboard systems are identical. Each tank is equipped with contents gauge transmitters, electrically operated fuel pumps, a maximum fuel level cut-off switch and refuelling valves. In addition the wing tanks have a small pump for internal transfer of the fuel. Fuel transfer may also be effected between the outboard wing tanks and the forward fuselage tanks by supplementary transfer pumps.

The tanks are arranged in groups so that each engine is normally fed by a particular group of tanks. Cross feed cocks are provided so that in emergency any engine may receive fuel from any tank or group of tanks. The tanks are pressurised to prevent loss of fuel by boiling due to rapid climb in the tropics with highly volatile fuel. This is done with a nitrogen purging system controlled from the starboard console in the cockpit. If the nitrogen supply becomes exhausted air pressure from the engine compressors is automatically supplied to keep the tanks pressurised.

Fuel control

The control of the fuel supply is arranged so that the balance of the aircraft is maintained between the desired limits. This is done by two electric automatic sequence timers connected to the tank pumps. The timers allow the pumps to operate in sequence so that the fuel is delivered from the tanks in equal percentages of the contents of each tank. The system is remotely operated by switches under the control of the pilots and the presentation in the cockpit is arranged to simulate the fuel installation. Four gauges show the total fuel available in each group of tanks and a press switch for each tank enables the contents of any one tank to be shown on the gauge for its group. In the event of a failure in the sequence timers the pilot can select the tanks for delivery by using the appropriate switches on the centre console. At any time during a flight trim adjustment is possible by transferring fuel from the No.1 to the No.7 tanks and vice versa.

Fuelling arrangements - ground

Pressure fuelling is carried out at four fuelling points, two in each main-wheel bay. Each fuelling valve is rated at 150 gallons per minute. Even distribution of the fuel load is automatically ensured by utilising the electric output of the contents gauge transmitter units to control the fuelling valves in each tank. The desired capacity is registered on the fuelling control panel in each main-wheel bay as a percentage of the total. On completion of the fuelling sequence the system is automatically cut off.

Fuelling arrangements - air

Avro Vulcan aircraft may be equipped either as receiver or tanker aircraft using the well-known probe and drogue system. As a receiver the fuel system will accept fuel initially at a rate of 500 gallons per minute. Later this will be increased to 1000 gallons per minute. The probe, which may be quickly detached, is on the nose of the aircraft.

As a tanker the aircraft delivers 5000 gallons from a tank in the bomb bay which also houses the drogue and its associated equipment.

Fire protection

A methyl-bromide system protects all fuel tanks, the extinguishers being automatically discharged by pyrotechnic flame switches. In the event of a crash landing the extinguishers are also discharged automatically by inertia switches.

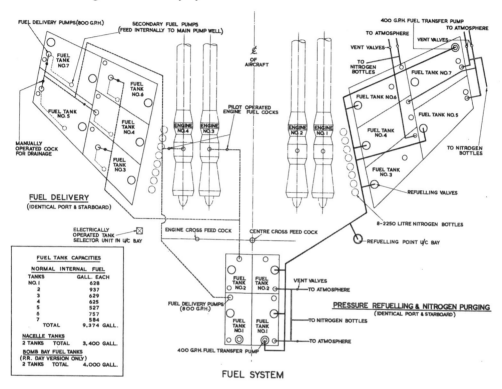

FUEL SYSTEM

Services

Hydraulics

The hydraulic system is served by three pumps, which deliver oil at 4,000 lb. per sq. in. maximum to a main feed line, from which connections are made to the following hydraulic services:-

> Alighting gear and associated doors.
> Nose wheel steering.
> Main wheel brakes.
> Bomb doors.

The controls for all these services are located at the pilots' station as follows:-

(1)	Undercarriage selector switch	UP and DOWN push-button type, centre panel.
(2)		
(a)	Steering control	By use of rudder controls.
(b)	Steering ON push-button	Pilots' flying control handle.
3)	Brake foot motors	Four, one on each rudder pedal.

(4)   (a) Bomb door selector Port console: single switch (normal) pole 3-position switch.
               (b) Bomb door selector Port console: rotary switch (emergency) 3-position switch.

To avoid possible accidental retraction of the alighting gear on the ground, a solenoid-operated lock integral with the selector switch prevents the wheels UP push button being depressed whilst the wheels are on the ground. The lock is controlled by micro switches associated with the torque links of the main wheels. Under emergency conditions it is possible to retract the alighting gear whilst on the ground after rotating an EMERGENCY RELEASE on the selector switch through 90 degrees.

In the event of any failure of the hydraulic system an electrically-driven hydraulic power pack is available to operate the bomb doors. The power pack is controlled by the bomb door emergency selector switch on the pilot's port console.

The emergency power pack may also be used to recharge the brake accumulators when the engines are not running and when the aircraft is away from normal base servicing equipment. The power pack shuts off automatically when the outlet pressure reaches 4,000 lb. per sq. in.

If failure occurs in the hydraulic system for the undercarriage, the main wheel and the nose wheel units may be lowered by emergency air obtained from two bottles which are charged on the ground to 3,000 lb. per sq. in.

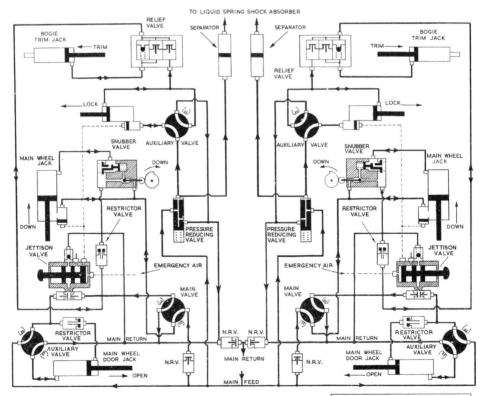

HYDRAULIC CIRCUIT DIAGRAM

THIS MAIN WHEEL CIRCUIT IS SHOWN AS A REPRESENTATIVE PART OF THE HYDRAULIC SYSTEM

Electrical system

The electrical power in the AVRO VULCAN is supplied by four 22.5 Kw. 112-volt D.C. engine-driven generators connected in parallel to a common bus-bar. Five 24 - volt batteries provide reserve power at 96 volts and 24 volts.

The 112-volt system also supplies D.C. power at 28 volts through rotary transformers and A.C. power at 115 volts through rotary inverters. Four of the batteries are connected across the 112-volt supply and one across the 28-volt supply.

All services use single pole wiring, the negative return being taken through the airframe. An extensive voltage regulation and generator protection system is provided and all services are protected by fuses and, in some cases, by circuit breakers.

The location of the main items of electrical equipment is shown below.

Two three-pin international ground supply plugs are installed on the port side of the fuselage, one for 112 volts and the other for 28 volts.

In the event of the unlikely failure of all four generators the primary concern would be the power operated flying controls. Sufficient power to maintain control for a limited period would be available from the 96 volt battery.

Control panels for the electrical system are located on the port side of the crew's cabin adjacent to the signaller's position.

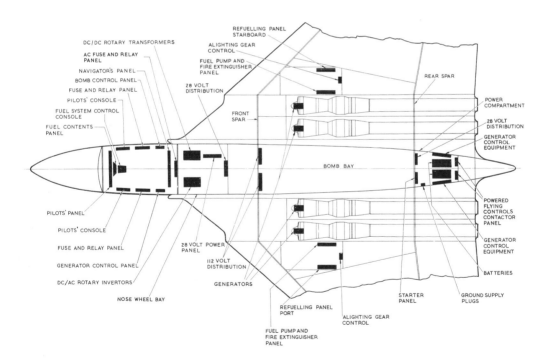

The power supplies are used for the following services:

112-volt D.C. (Generators)   Engine starting, flying controls, fuel pumps, air
                                    brakes, radar and hydraulic power pack (emergency)

96-volt D.C. (Battery)	Engine starting (one to three starts) Ground Hydraulic power pack Ground Flying controls (air-borne emergency)
28-volt D.C.	Instruments, fuel cocks, generator controls, electro-hydraulic system, radio, bomb gear and lighting
115-volt, 400 cycles, A.C.	Radar, fuel pump control, cabin atmosphere control, bomb bay heating control, anti-icing control and U/V and fluorescent lighting.
115-volt, 1,600 cycles, A. C.	Radar

Pneumatic

Two air storage cylinders, each charged to 2,000 lb. per sq. in. from a ground supply, feed air to two simple pneumatic systems which provide power for the following services:

Crew's entrance/escape door

The crew's entrance/escape door opens under its own weight for normal ground use, and is raised by two pneumatic jacks fed by air at 400 lb. per sq. in. through a reducing valve. When the door is to be used as an escape hatch the opening lever is moved into the emergency position. Air at 1,200 lb. per sq. in. is fed into the down side of the jacks which force the door open against the airstream, thus forming a wind-break for emergency exit.

Canopy jettison

Canopy jettison is initiated by two small pneumatic jacks which lift the leading edge of the canopy into the airstream. This system operating at 1,200 lb. per sq. in. is controlled by a valve operated by the canopy release lever.

Pressure seals

Both the canopy and the entrance door are sealed by pressure seals inflated to 25 lb. per sq. in. through a reducing valve from the 300 lb. per sq. in. system. In each case the control valves, for inflation or deflation of either seal, are operated automatically by opening or closing the canopy or entrance door.

Windscreen de-icing

A tank containing de-icing fluid for the wind-screen and air bomber's window is pressurised at 7 lb. per sq. in. when de-icing is selected.

Engine oil system

Each engine has its own independent integral oil system, (oil capacity 7 gallons with 3 gallons air airspace) four oil pressure gauges are on the engine instrument panel.

Oxygen

The normal installation consists of five storage cylinders and provision is made for a further three. The cylinders are charged to a pressure of 1,800 lb. per sq. in. and the capacity provided is sufficient for missions of medium or long duration.

The cylinders are mounted on each side of the bomb bay and the high pressure system from each side normally supplies all members of the crew. In the event of damage to one half of the system non-return valves will close the affected line and oxygen will still be available from the other half of the system.

A regulator is provided at each normally occupied station and also the air bomber's position. "walk-around" oxygen set is stowed on the back of the navigator's seat. It can be recharged at two points from the main system, one at the radar navigator's position and the other at the air bomber a position.

The regulators are known as the pressure demand type. They are designed for high altitude flying and automatically mix air and oxygen, the ratio depending on altitude, and deliver the mixture at the appropriate oxygen pressure to the mask on inhalation.

Anti-icing

A thermal anti-icing system provides protection against ice accretion on wing, fin and engine air-intake leading edges. Hot air for this system is bled off the engine compressors, mixed with cold air to give a controlled temperature of 150°C., and then distributed to ducts in the leading edges of the wings and fin. The hot air flows in a chord wise direction between the outer skin and an inner corrugated skin, and is finally exhausted to atmosphere. The system can be automatically or manually operated as desired by means of electric controls.

Cabin atmosphere control

Cabin atmosphere control in the AVRO VULCAN is a combination of pressurisation, temperature control and ventilation. The air for pressurisation and heating is obtained from the engine compressors at an automatically controlled mass flow and before it enters the cabin its temperature is adjusted to maintain the crew's compartment at a comfortable level over the whole range of conditions likely to be encountered in flight.

Continuous change of air is ensured throughout the cabin by exhausting used air through discharge valves in the pressurised compartment. This air is then utilised to cool radar equipment in the nose of the aircraft.

Control

The controls for the air conditioning system are grouped on a panel on the starboard console in the pilot's cockpit. The cabin atmosphere is controllable, either manually or automatically, from this panel according to the selection which may be made at any time during flight. The cabin can also be pressurised or de-pressurised at any time as required.

A cabin altitude of 8,000 ft. is automatically controlled up to a height of 47,000 ft. giving a maximum differential pressure of 9 lb. per sq. in. For altitudes in excess of 47,400 ft. the same differential pressure is maintained.

Under combat conditions the cabin altitude can be increased to 25,000 ft. and should the pressure fall to a dangerous level, due to combat damage, the mass flow control valves open automatically and provide "flood flow" to counteract decompression. A manual control is provided which enables partial resetting of the system to give control of the "flood flow" condition. If the need for "flood flow" ceases, the system can be reset to normal mass flow.

Emergency decompression is provided by operating either pilot's NO PRESSURE switch or the entrance door opening lever. These controls operate the decompression valves electrically. Manual operation of the valves is accomplished by the lever in the cabin roof above the crew's table.

Temperature control and ventilation

The temperature of the air entering the crew's compartment is controlled by the Avro Conditioning Unit. This unit is primarily a heat exchanger which receives its cooling air from a ram air intake in the port leading edge between the fuselage and the engine air intake boundary layer fence. When cooling of the cabin is required the compressed air, after passing through the heat exchanger, is fed through a turbine refrigeration unit before entering the cabin. The Avro Conditioning Unit operates automatically to maintain the selected cabin temperature, and a manual control is also provided.

The air is fed into the crew compartment through small louvers at floor level after, circulating between the outer skin insulation and inner trimming panels. Branch pipes feed air to the windscreen and air bomber's window to prevent misting.

Ventilating air for low-level un-pressurised flight is tapped from the air intake for the Avro Conditioning Unit.

A five inch ground conditioning connection is located on the starboard side of the aircraft.

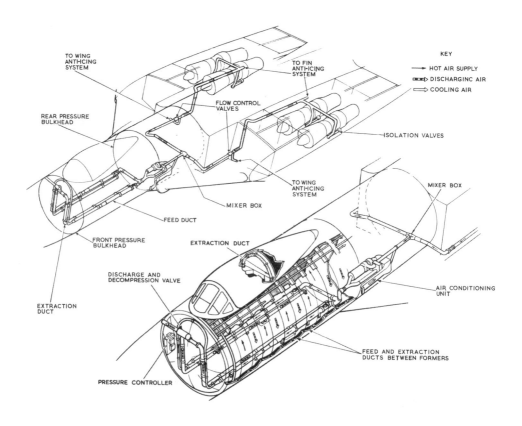

CABIN ATMOSPHERE CONTROL

Armament and Cameras

Bomber (basic aircraft)

The bomb bay is 29 feet long, 7 feet wide and 6 feet deep and has a total capacity of 1218 cubic feet. It can, therefore, accommodate a wide variety of bombs and the following are typical examples:

1	- 10,000 lb.	Special bomb
2	- 12,000 lb.	"Tallboys"
2	- 10,000 lb.	H.C. bombs
14	- 2,000 lb.	Mines
30	- 1,000 lb.	E.C. or L.C. bombs

A predetermined temperature is maintained inside the bomb bay by a number of electric sensing elements. The average output of these elements is amplified and operates hot and cold air valves to govern the temperature of the mixed air. Hot air is obtained from all four engine compressors and cold air from an intake in the dorsal fin.

Bomber (with external nacelles)

In order to extend either the range or the bomb load built-in attachment points are provided for the fitment of two external nacelles. There are two designs of nacelle, one for bombs and the other for fuel. The illustrations overleaf show details of the bomb nacelles. The fuel nacelle is considerably smaller both in length and diameter and each type is designed for quick attachment and removal.

Attachments for jettisoning the bomb nacelles have been provided but the gain in performance which would result from jettisoning does not justify the loss of substantial and expensive equipment. The fuel nacelles may be jettisoned about two hours after take-off, resulting in a worth-while gain in performance. Each fuel nacelle has a capacity of 1,700 gallons.

Each bomb nacelle is designed to carry a maximum of 14 x 1,000 lb. H.C. or L.C. bombs or, 1 x 10,000 lb. H.C. bomb or 3 x 2,000 lb. mines. These loads may be carried in addition to any of the standard loads carried in the main bomb bay of the aircraft.

When the external bomb nacelles are fitted a substantial improvement in load at reduced range is achieved and when the external fuel nacelles are fitted a greatly increased range is obtained with a minimum bomb load of 10,000 lb.

The bomb nacelles are, bombed up in a similar manner to the main bomb bay. Clusters of bombs are loaded on to trolleys complete with their carriers and beams, wheeled under the nacelles and hoisted into position by hydraulic jacks.

The following carriers and associated equipment, comprising one aircraft set, are required when the bomb nacelles are supplied.

Bomb carriers

AV.215	7-way unit for 1,000 lb. bombs	4 off
AV.216	Triple unit for 2,000 lb. mines	2 off
AV.217	1 unit for 10,000 lb. H.C. bomb	2 off

Removable aircraft fittings

AV.251	Crutch assembly for AV.217	2 sets Ground equipment

No additional ground equipment is required for loading the nacelles but the setting and lifting sling AV.249 (supplied for use with AV.22 in the main aircraft set) is used for loading the 7-way unit AV.215.

The fuel nacelles may, of course, be fitted to AVRO VULCAN aircraft which are equipped for either day or night photographic reconnaissance roles.

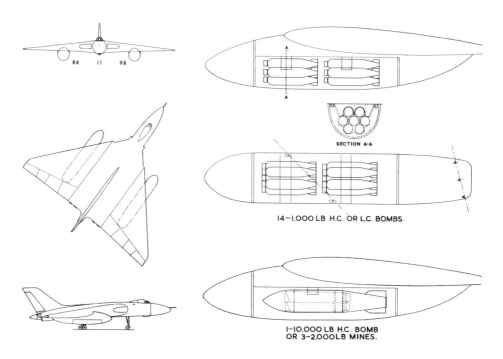

SECTION A-A

14–1,000 LB H.C. OR L.C. BOMBS.

1–10,000 LB H.C. BOMB
OR 3–2,000LB MINES.

BOMB NACELLE ARRANGEMENT

Loading arrangements

The AVRO system of bomb carriage has been developed in order to make full use of the large volumetric capacity of the bomb bay. It has several important advantages over previous methods.

In the first place no access panels are required in the skin panelling of the bomb-bay roof so that smooth unbroken contours are maintained. Secondly, as all loading is done from underneath the aircraft, the use of cranes with long jibs and other slinging gear is avoided. A secondary advantage is the weather protection afforded to the armourers by the aircraft.

Thirdly, the assembly of the bomb cluster does not have to be carried out during the actual bombing-up operation as this work is completed at the bomb stores.

Fourthly, the arrangement of carriage in clusters reduces the number of bomb carriers.

The diagrams opposite show three stages in the bombing up process. The bombs in complete clusters on trolleys are wheeled under the aircraft. Two hydraulic jacks are placed under each end of the beam surmounting a cluster and then extended through holes in the beam to hook into prepared positions in the bomb bay arches. The jacks are then retracted, raising the complete bomb cluster into position. The carriers are crutched to the slinging points and locked in position by wedge shaped slides. The jacks are then removed and applied to the beam of a further cluster. A ground supply power pack operates the jacks.

The complete system provides an easy and rapid method of loading which is applicable to any bomb arrangement without restriction.

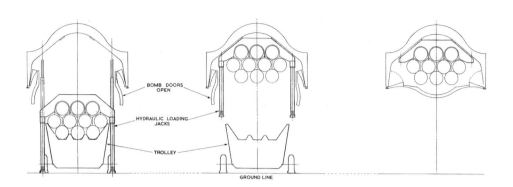

BOMB DOORS
OPEN

HYDRAULIC LOADING
JACKS

TROLLEY

GROUND LINE

Bomb carriers 5th December, 1955.

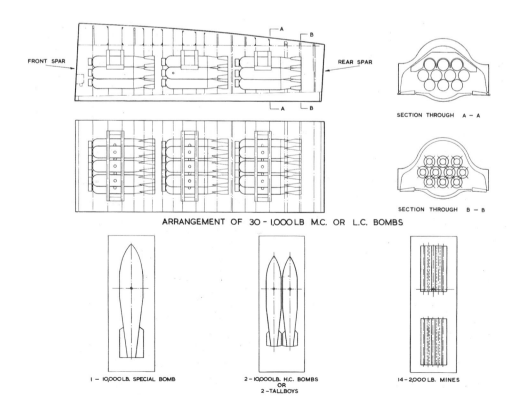

FRONT SPAR

REAR SPAR

A

B

A

B

SECTION THROUGH A – A

SECTION THROUGH B – B

ARRANGEMENT OF 30 – 1,000 LB M.C. OR L.C. BOMBS

1 – 10,000 LB. SPECIAL BOMB

2 – 10,000 LB. H.C. BOMBS
OR
2 – TALLBOYS

14 – 2,000 LB. MINES

Photo reconnaissance aircraft

The AVRO VULCAN may also be used as a day or night photographic reconnaissance aircraft. Additional fuel is carried in the bomb bay (day version only) and in wing nacelles so that very long range may be achieved. The cameras are secured in mountings which are adjustable for angle and the camera containers are provided with temperature control and window demisting.

Day version

Cameras fitted with lenses of various focal lengths are installed in special - containers which are disposed forward and aft of a centrally mounted fuel tank in the bomb bay, as shown in the illustration below. Above the forward container there is a supplementary fuel tank strapped to the structure. The forward camera container is divided into two compartments containing a total of three F.96 cameras, two of which are mounted to take oblique photographs to port and starboard. The third camera is mounted to take vertical photographs. The oblique cameras are fitted with a 6 in. or 24 in. lens and the vertical camera with a 6 in. lens. The container at the after end of the bomb compartment houses eight F.96 cameras which are fitted with 36 in. or 48 in. lenses. They are installed in pairs on adjustable mountings.

The standard doors for the bomb bay are removed and replaced by metal fairings, except in the positions for the containers which have built-in electrically actuated doors. The containers complete with cameras are hoisted into the bomb bay by the method used for the bomb carriers. An F.49 camera, mounted in a compartment aft of the starboard main undercarriage bay, is remotely adjustable. This camera takes a 6 in., 12 in., or 24 in., lens. Adjustment and control of this camera and control of all the fixed cameras is effected electrically from a panel on the instrument panel at the starboard side of the crews' compartment.

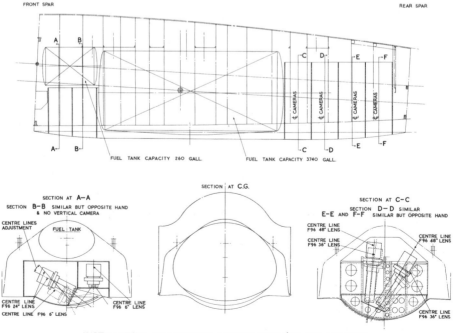

INSTALLATION OF CAMERAS & EQUIPMENT (P.R. DAY VERSION)

Night version

The cameras for night photography are fitted in a single container mounted at the aft end of the bomb bay. They include five F.89 Mk.3 units, taking 24 in. or 36 in. lenses, and two F.24. units with 5 in. lenses, all fitted fanwise.

Three P.89 Mk.3 cameras with 36 in. lenses plus three F.89 Mk.3 cameras with 24in. lenses can be fitted as an alternative arrangement. In addition to the cameras the container holds six photo-cells installed in pairs.

The remainder of the bomb bay interior is used for the carriage of photoflash stores as follows:-

96 x 8 in. stores on two carriers

OR

20 x 16 in. stores on two carriers

The camera container is provided with its own electrically actuated doors and the photoflash compartment of the bomb bay has shortened doors of similar design to those fitted on the standard bomber.

Radio and Radar Equipment

Radio

General purpose H.F. radio communication is provided by a remotely controlled, 24-channel transmitter-receiver. This equipment has a frequency range of 2.8 to 18.1 Mc/s. It is installed at the navigation station and is under the control of the signaller. A suppressed aerial, tuning unit and matching unit are installed in the dorsal fin.

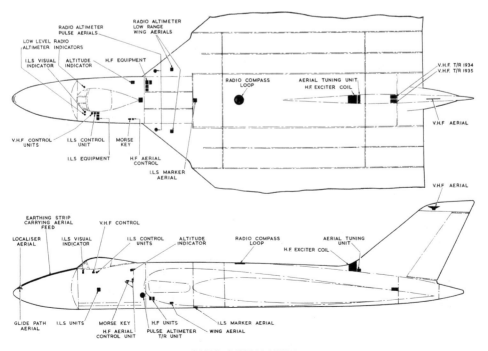

RADIO INSTALLATION

Twin V.H.F. transmitter-receivers are provided. These are 10-channel sets installed in racks in the rear fuselage. Separate remote control units-and a common volume control are mounted on a panel in the pilot's port console and a press-to-transmit switch is fitted to each pilot's control handle. Both sets may be switched on together but the facilities of one set only can be used at a time. The entire crew can receive V.H.F. The radio transmission available to the pilots is verbal only. A suppressed aerial is installed in the top of the fin.

An A.D.F. Radio Compass system is installed with a master indicator and controls at the master navigator's station. A repeater, visible to both pilots, is fitted to the pilot's panel. The receiver is mounted in the rear fuselage and the loop and its drive mechanism in the roof of the bomb bay. The V.H.F. aerial is used for "sense".

On the port console in the pilots' cockpit is a controller for the Instrument Landing System. Both pilots are provided with visual and aural signals. The localiser and glide path receivers are installed in the nose of the aircraft, and a suppressed marker aerial of the slot type is fitted under No.2 tank bay. Localiser and glide path suppressed aerials are fitted in the wing tips.

Eight mic/tel sockets are fitted at convenient positions. In addition to one at each of the normal crew positions, one is fitted for use by the air bomber when he is in the prone position and one is located near each periscopic sextant. To facilitate ground servicing two inter-communication points are fitted, one in the nose-wheel bay and one in the tail warning bay.

On each of the port and starboard consoles in the cockpit is a 3-position toggle switch which enables either pilot to select V.H.F./intercommunication, H.F., or crew-call facilities.

The signaller has a 2-position toggle switch for H.F. and intercommunication. On H.F. he has both R.T. and W.T. facilities.

The master navigator also has a 2-position toggle switch for selecting either A.D.F. or intercommunication. If the master navigator and signaller are switched to A.D.F. and H.F. respectively either pilot can call them through the intercommunication system using the CALL switch.

If failure of the normal amplifier occurs, emergency intercommunication can be brought into operation by a change-over switch at the signaller's station. This introduces the modulator amplifier of the selected V.H.F. set.

Radar

Radar equipment includes bombing, navigational and landing aids, tail warning equipment and an I.F.F. installation.

The Navigational and Bombing System (NBS) comprises H_2S Mk.9A and the Navigational and Bombing Computer (NBC) Mk.2. It is controlled from the navigation station and it enables both 'blind' and visual bombing to be accomplished. For the latter, a Visual Sighting Attachment is fitted to the equipment at the prone position for the air bomber. The scanner is fitted in the nose of the aircraft. An additional aid to bombing, known as Blue Study, is provided by equipment which controls the aircraft automatically on a defined track.

An Mk.3 Gee installation is fitted at the navigation station for short range navigation. The copper foil suppressed aerial is installed in the fin.

Two radio altimeters are fitted. The Mk.5 equipment, under the control of the first pilot, covers the height range of 0 to 5,000 ft and includes two indicators, one for each pilot. The Mk.6 equipment, covering the range of 500 to 50,000 feet, is controlled by the radar navigator and he only is provided with an indicator. Both systems indicate true height above the local ground.

Tail warning radar which indicates the range and direction of fighters approaching from the rear is installed as a complete unit in the tail fairing of the fuselage. The equipment, known as Red Garter or Orange Putter, is controlled from the signaller's station and indicators are provided for the signaller and the pilots.

I.F.F. Mk.10 equipment is fitted, the transmitter - receiver being installed in the nose-wheel bay along with the omni-aerials. A control unit is mounted on the signaller's panel.

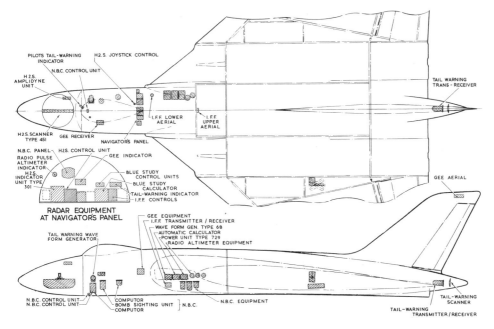

RADAR INSTALLATION

Strength and weight data

The AVRO VULCAN has been designed to a gross weight of 160,000 lb. However, subject to strength test confirmation, it is clear from current stress analysis that a weight in excess of 165,500 lb. can be achieved; this latter weight will therefore be assumed and referred to as the Normal Gross Weight. At the normal gross weight and with a bomb load not exceeding 30,000 lb. the maximum normal acceleration coefficient $n1$ is 2.7 increasing to 3.0 by the time the aircraft has reached one quarter of the normal still air range. Throughout the subsequent flight the value of $n1$ does not fall below 3.0.

A factor of safety is associated with the above values of the normal acceleration coefficient so that the ultimate load factor is 4.05 rising to a value of 4.5.

The design diving speed VD is 415 knots E.A.S. from sea level up to an altitude (approximately 19,000 ft.) at which this speed corresponds to a Mach number of 0.90. Between 19,000 ft. and 25,000 ft., the value of VD decreases by 5 knots E.A.S. per 1,000 ft. to 385 knots E.A.S. at 25,000 ft. (M = 0.95). At higher altitudes, VD is the speed corresponding to a Mach number of 0.95.

The maximum design landing weight is 109,350 lb. The landing under emergency conditions can be made at reduced factors and at increased weights up to the normal gross weight of 165,500 lb.

The aircraft is designed throughout in accordance with the requirements of A.P. 970. The full structural strength testing programme was being undertaken as this specification went to print and calculations showed that the factors specified above would be met in full up to a weight of 170,000 lb. At this weight a limit is set by the present design of the undercarriage and it was assumed that, for the time being, higher weights will be achieved only by flight refuelling after take-off. The normal development of the structure in due course will enable higher normal gross weight to be achieved.

Addendum

Information provided by Rolls-Royce in October 1954 showed that the first Conway's offered to the Vulcan would be the R.Co.5 which had a lower rating than the R.Co.6.

As the weight of each engine was the same all references to weight under the heading R.Co.6 was applicable to the aircraft powered by R.Co.5.

Internal arrangement - July 1954

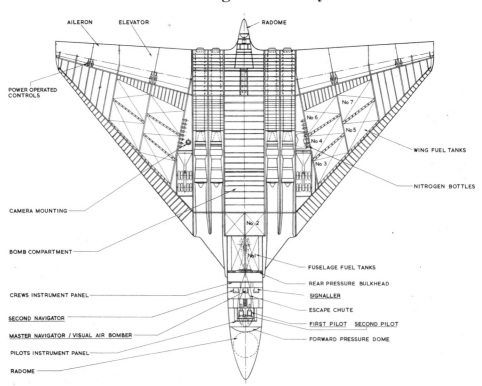

Specification

Normal gross weight:	165,500 lb.
Normal cruising speed:	500 knots
Cruising altitude:	45,000-55,000 ft.
Bomb capacity, normal:	10,000-30,000 lb.
Bomb capacity, overload:	58,000 lb.
Range (10,000 lb. bomb)	4000-5,000 nautical miles
Range (58,000 lb. bombs)	1,200 nautical miles
Range (photo-reconn.)	5,600 - 7,200 nautical miles

General Arrangement

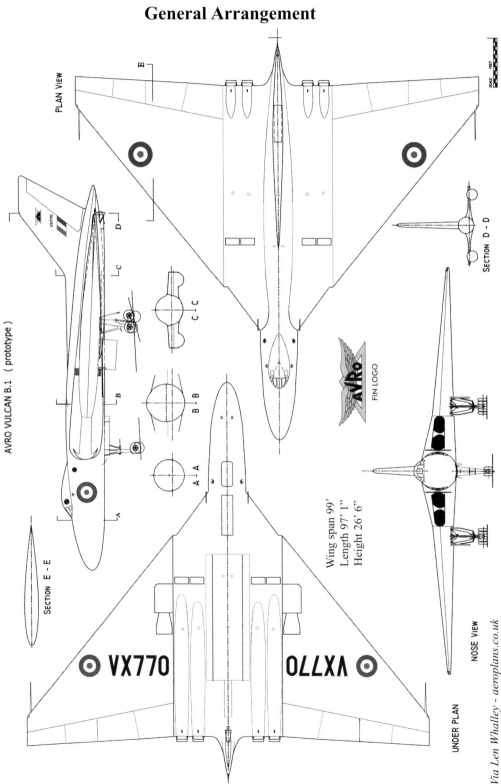

AVRO VULCAN B.1 (prototype)

PLAN VIEW

SECTION D - D

SECTION E - E

FIN LOGO

Wing span 99'
Length 97' 1"
Height 26' 6"

UNDER PLAN

NOSE VIEW

Via Len Whalley - aeroplans.co.uk

Development trials incident

VX777 taken 1954.

The development trials were not without incident, on a test flight carried out at Farnborough on 27th July, 1954, the second prototype Vulcan VX777 was involved in an accident. Investigation showed that the primary cause of the accident was jamming of a spring link in the rudder control circuit following coarse use of the rudder during recovery from a stall.

The aircraft was flown by Roly Falk (First Pilot) and the R.A.E. pilot, Squadron Leader Potocki plus three observers. It was only due to the excellent flying skills that the aircraft succeeded in landing back at Farnborough.

The failures included starboard upper outer brake, jamming of rudder (12 degrees starboard) tail parachute and port wheel brake fading. During a second stall procedure recovery a violent side slip and difficulty in directional control occurred. On levelling out it was found the aircraft was still turning to the right with the controls at neutral. Roly could observe no movement of the rudder indicator following movement of the rudder pedals.

Due to lack of fuel it was decided to make an emergency landing at Farnborough. After descending to 6000 ft it became more difficult to keep straight, by this time it became necessary to fly the aircraft with both starboard engines at take-off power and both port engines idling. Because of the shortage of fuel it was decided a landing at Farnborough should be made as soon as possible. The first approach was abandoned as it was impossible to turn in towards the runway. By considerable over banking to port, it was found possible to turn and the aircraft was eventually lined up with the runway, but further reduction in speed resulted in loss of ability to keep the aircraft straight. By continuing the approach with the port wing well down and with considerable sideslip, it was possible to maintain the correct track along the runway.

Just before the wheels touched down the parachute was streamed. It developed satisfactory and this straightened the aircraft sufficiently for an immediate touch down to be made by pushing the stick forward. Unfortunately the parachute disintegrated almost immediately. The aircraft was held straight with the brake wheels, but the port brake which had to be used more violently, faded early during the run. This meant that there was no means of stopping. When about 100 yards from the end of the runway, Roly observed workmen crossing in front of the aircraft, so applied starboard brake, which was still working and swung on to rough ground. The undercarriage collapsed with all four engines running when the aircraft came to a rest. The canopy jettison handle was then pulled and the pneumatic jack lifted it immediately. Roly then held it up whilst the three observers left the aircraft. It was impossible to discard the canopy and Roly had to hold it up by hand until the fire tender crew arrived and help could be provided.

It has been stated that Sir Roy Dobson was extremely unhappy about this incident and spoke to Falk about the situation. Sir Roy thought the safety of Vulcan and Victor aircraft might be of question within Ministry circles. The Handley Page Victor prototype had also crashed on a test flight at Cranfield in the same month during a low level high speed fly past, killing all the crew. The first prototype Valiant was also lost in a crash on 12th January, 1952.

Showing tyre marks.

The aircraft was fitted with Olympus 100 engines at the time, of 9,500 lb thrust. The opportunity to fit the more powerful Olympus 101 engines rated at 10,000 lb thrust was taken. The aircraft was soon repaired and was used for a preliminary assessment of the Vulcan by the A.&A.E.E. in May 1955.

Vulcan development 1954 - 1955

In December 1954 a brochure was produced to put forward proposals for developments of the AVRO VULCAN which possessed greatly increased performance and operational capability, but which could be obtained with the minimum of new tooling and design effort. Shown are extracts from issue 3 of that report dated February 1955.

INTRODUCTION

The first prototype Vulcan flew in August 1952 and the preliminary phase of flight development on this and on the second prototype aircraft has now been completed. The second prototype will be delivered to Boscombe Down for preview handling trials in the course of the next month. The first production Vulcan has now been successfully flown and a total test flying time on Vulcan aircraft of 230 hours has been accumulated to date.

The structural test specimen has been loaded without failure up to 100% of the ultimate load for the 10,000 lb. both case and up to 95% of the ultimate load for the 30,000 lb. bomb case.

The experience accumulated in flight and during ground test work on Vulcan and 707 aircraft, together with new aerodynamic and structural knowledge, enables the Vulcan to be developed in a manner that provides greatly enhanced performance while utilising the major part of the existing engineering.

It should be clearly understood that the development of a high subsonic bomber (such as the Vulcan) is restricted to certain directions. For example, the cruising Mach number is definitely limited by the drag rise due to compressibility, which is a function of the sweepback and thickness of the whole wing. A complete re-design of the whole wing would enable the cruising Mach number to be increased from 0.87 to 0.92, but this is regarded as being unprofitable since, at the present level of fighter development, a gain in cruising speed of this order would be unlikely to decrease the vulnerability of the bomber. In any case, it is possible to have a new and fully supersonic bomber in service within the next six or seven years.

The other important performance feature of the Vulcan, namely the cruising altitude, the range and the load carrying capacity, are, however, capable of improvement and this brochure describes the methods by which these improvements may be obtained.

A major factor in the development of the Vulcan is the availability of much more powerful engines, for instance the Conway 5 and the Olympus 6 series of engines, which can be installed without any alterations to the aircraft structure, or to the air intakes or jet pipe tunnels. For full advantage to be taken of their greater thrust in increasing the cruising altitude, an increase in usable lift coefficient from the wing and/or an increase in wing area are required. In an interim development known as Phase 2, the leading edge of the outboard wing is modified to increase the usable lift coefficient, and Bristol Olympus 12 or the Rolls-Royce Conway 5 engines are fitted.

In the Phase 3 development further improvements in altitude and range are obtained by fitting a new outer wing of increased span and area.

The new outer wing is of the multi-spar type with honeycomb sandwich skins. Compared with the present outer wing the structure is more efficient in terms of weight per square foot and although the thickness: chord ratio is reduced to give better aerodynamic performance, a considerably greater internal fuel capacity has been provided.

The Phase 3 wing is designed for a take-off weight in the region of 200,000 lb. and to meet the existing eight-wheel bogie undercarriage is replaced by a new four-wheel bogie unit with provision for "Runway Brakes".

The net effect of these improvements on the Vulcan is to give, with Olympus B.0l.6 engines, a still air range without external fuel of about 5,900 nautical miles with a half-range height of over 55,000 ft; alternatively a half-range height of 56,500 ft. can be obtained for a shorter range of, say, 4,500 nautical miles.

These very considerable advantages in performance are obtained without sacrificing any of the basic advantages of the Vulcan in respect of simplicity, reliability, ease of maintenance and facility of bomb loading. It should also be emphasised that this development utilises the entire centre section of the present Vulcan, comprising the fuselage with the bomb bay, cockpit, radar installation, fin and rudder, and the inboard parts of the wings containing the complete power plant installation. The number of fresh jigs and tools required is small, being confined to those for the outer wing.

This brochure also contains a proposal for a further development of the Vulcan (known for convenience as Phase 4), in which small modifications are made to the lower part of the fuselage to permit the carriage of an inertia navigated stand-off bomb. This increases the effective range of the aircraft and at the same time reduces vulnerability by enabling it to avoid heavily defended targets.

This bomb is being developed by the Weapons Research Division of A.V. Roe & Co. Ltd., but further studies are also being carried out on the installation of stand-off bombs designed by the Royal Aircraft Establishment. This type of bomb could be carried by suitably modified aircraft to either Phase 2 or Phase 3 standard, without affecting their capability of carrying all the normal range of bombs.

Phase 2

The 26th production aircraft will be fitted with Bristol Olympus B.0l.12 (13,000 lb. rating) engines in place of the B.0l.l0l (11,000 lb. rating) engines, raising the target height by 3,000 ft.

To permit the use of the greater lift coefficients associated with increased thrust, the wing on the Phase 2 aircraft has been modified over the outer 50% semi-span by extending the leading edge forward and incorporating a small amount of forward camber or "droop". The change in wing section has been confined to the portion ahead of the front spar, thus allowing the whole of the modification to be carried out in the leading edge envelope jig, the front spar itself and the remainder of the wing structure being unaffected.

This leading edge modification has been tested in flight on an AVRO 707A (WD280), which has an exact one-third scale model of the Vulcan wing and these tests indicate that the Vulcan will be capable of a buffet-free trimmed lift coefficient of over 0.30 at the cruising Mach number. Furthermore, the already good low speed flying qualities of the aircraft have been enhanced by the wing modifications, and it behaves in an extremely docile manner down to the minimum flight speed.

It is expected that early production Rolls-Royce Conway R.Co.5 engines (13,000 lb. sea level static thrust) will be available for fitting into the last few of the present production order of AVRO Vulcan's. This engine may be followed by a development of the Conway having an increased by-pass ratio that gives reduced specific fuel consumption and increased cruising thrust. Production Conway engines fitted to the Vulcan will have built-in Sundstrand units driving 40 K.V.A. alternators, making possible the change-over to a fully A.C. electrical system.

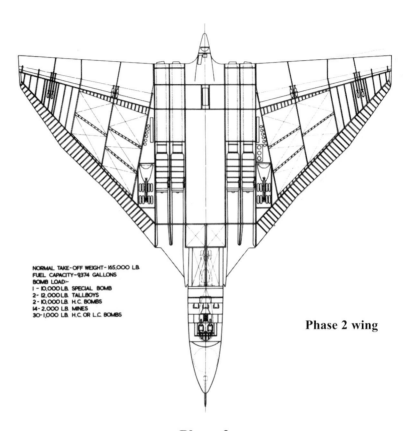

NORMAL TAKE-OFF WEIGHT - 165,000 LB.
FUEL CAPACITY - 9374 GALLONS
BOMB LOAD:-
1 - 10,000 LB. SPECIAL BOMB
2 - 12,000 LB. TALLBOYS
2 - 10,000 LB. H.C. BOMBS
14 - 2,000 LB. MINES
30 - 1,000 LB. H.C. OR L.C. BOMBS

Phase 2 wing

Phase 3

With only minor modifications to the mountings, fuel system etc., the existing Vulcan engine bays can accommodate any one of the following types of engines, the Olympus B.0l.6 (16,000 lb. rating) the Olympus B.01.7 (17,160 lb. rating) the Conway R.Co.5 (13,000 lb. rating) or the Conway Development (14,200 lb. rating). If full advantage in terms of operating height is to be taken of the increased thrust available from these engines, then the usable wing lift coefficient must be increased to about 0.4 (based on the original wing area of 3,446 sq.ft.) increases in range are also obtainable by carrying more internal fuel and these considerations have led to a re-design of the wing outboard of the existing transport joint. The aircraft with this new outer wing is known as Phase 3.

The span has been increased by 14 ft. and the wing tip chord by 5 ft. giving the modified planform shown in the Phase 3 illustration overleaf. The wing thickness: chord ratio at the existing transport joint has been maintained at 10 but that at approximately 50% semi-span is reduced to 6%, and the thickness: chord ratio at the tip to 4%. The wing area has been increased from 3,446 sq. ft. to 4,060 sq. ft. and the aspect ratio from 2.84 to 3.14.

The new outer wing has the following advantages:

(i)   Increased manoeuvring power at high altitude and Mach number,

(ii)   The reduction of wing thickness increases the critical Mach number of the wing, thus offsetting the drag rise associated with operation at high lift coefficients at high subsonic speeds,

(iii) The tankage within the wings has been increased by taking the wing fuel tanks out to the inner surface of the metal sandwich, giving an overall increase in tankage from 9,374 gallons, to 12,950 gallons.

(iv) The wing weight per square foot of area has been substantially reduced by the use of multi-spar construction with sandwich skins, the comparative figures for the standard and Phase 3 wings being 7.6 and 6.8 lb/sq.ft. respectively, based on the gross wing weights and areas. This has enabled the increase in wing area from 3,446 to 4,060 sq. ft. to be achieved for an increase in total wing weight of only 1,330 lb.

2. Aerodynamic considerations.

The planform of the new outer wing is designed to reduce the loading over the tip sections, and the wing section in this region will be capable of carrying lift up to much higher incidences than the more restricted modification of Phase 2. The actual degree of camber and twist to be used on the outer wing is not yet finalised and will be determined by the results of a programme of wind tunnel and rocket launched model tests which is being carried out at the Royal Aircraft Establishment, the National Physical Laboratory and in the Avro Transonic Wind Tunnel.

3. Design details - Phase 3
3.1. Wing
The outer wing is of multi-spar construction with sandwich skins. This type of structure has the following advantages: a smooth and accurate exterior finish, a smooth interior surface which enables the full internal volume of the wing to be used for fuel tanks, minimum weight for the required strength and stiffness and low production costs.

Except for strengthening the booms of the front and rear spars, it has not been found necessary to modify the existing wing centre section.

3.2. Fuel system
It should be noted that the group of tanks adjacent to the undercarriage rib are bag tanks, whereas the remaining wing tanks are of integral construction. It should be noted that the new fuel tankage has been located so that the centre of gravity of the total fuel remains close to the centre of gravity of the aircraft. No alteration to the fuselage fuel tanks is necessary.

3.3. Undercarriage
The Phase 3 Vulcan is designed for operation at weights in the region of 200,000 lb. and a new undercarriage is therefore required. It is proposed that this should be of the four-wheel bogie type incorporating "Runway Brakes" and this unit has already been studied in some detail by Messrs. Dowty Equipment Ltd. The new undercarriage gives a load classification number of 56 for an equivalent single-wheel load of 39,600 lb. at an all-up weight of 196,000 lb. and a tyre pressure of 153 p. s. i.

3.4. Control system
The control system on the basic Vulcan consists of separate ailerons and elevators occupying the whole of the wing trailing edge outboard of the engines. This system has been replaced on the Phase 3 wing by one elevon on each wing occupying the inner 70% of the outer wing. Each elevon is divided into three separate surfaces and each surface is operated by a separate and independent irreversible power control unit. The deletion of the outboard part of the trailing edge as a control simplifies the construction of the outer wing as this is no longer required to accept a high torsional loading on its very thin section. Compared with the present Vulcan, the use of elevon enables the net pitching and rolling powers to be increased to more than cover the corresponding increases in inertias and damping.

4. Weights

Extensive experience on the design of metal sandwich structures has been accumulated by A.V. Roe & Co. in connection with the design of the AVRO 720 rocket fighter and the weight analysis of the new outer wing to be made with some confidence. The improvement in wing weight per square foot has already been discussed in Section 1. Total structure weight of the Phase 3 aircraft will only be about 1,600 lb. greater than the standard Vulcan.

It will be seen that the fuselage weight of the Phase 3 aircraft is less than that of the standard aircraft; this is due to weight savings on fuselage components which will be introduced at the same time.

It is assumed that all Phase 3 aircraft, irrespective of the type of engine used, will be fitted with full A.C. electrical system.

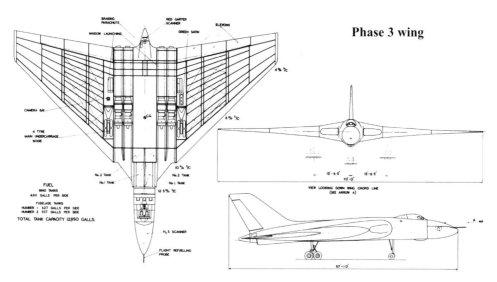

Phase 3 wing

AVRO VULCAN WITH THIN WING

Phase 4

THE CARRIAGE OF STAND-OFF BOMBS

1. General

The effect of carrying a stand-off bomb under the AVRO Vulcan has been investigated in relation to the Phase 2 and Phase 3 aircraft.

The Weapons Research Division of A.V. Roe & Co. Ltd., Woodford, are developing a winged, rocket-propelled stand-off bomb, and details of this weapon are given in a separate brochure (A .V .Roe WRB.1). Three stages of development of the bomb are envisaged:

(1)   14,000 lb. bomb.   Range 100 n.m.   at M= 2.0
(2)   15,500 lb. bomb.   Range 200 n.m.   at M= 3.0
(3)   16,000 lb. bomb.   Range 300 n.m.   at M= 3.5

In this brochure only the second stage, the 15,500 lb. has been taken to show the effect on the Vulcan performance.

As shown the bomb which is 35 ft. long and 48 ins. diameter, is carried half-buried in the bomb bay, since this position gives minimum drag and straightforward release. The modification necessary to the Vulcan to utilise it as a stand-off bomb carrier consist of the removal of the bomb doors and a small part of the operating mechanism, these being replaced by a light metal fairing. This fairing is of streamline shape, corresponding to the upper surface of the bomb, so that it is not necessary to provide bomb doors to close the opening exposed by release of the bomb. The bomb release gear is attached to strong points which will be built into the front spar and it is envisaged that whole change-over from normal bombing roles to the role of stand-off bomb carrier could be undertaken in service in less than 48 hours.

2. Weights

It is estimated that there will be a weight saving of 521 lb. on the basic operational weight of the aircraft when the aircraft is converted to the stand-off bomb role, due to the replacement of the bomb doors by a simple fairing.

3. Drag

High speed tunnel tests have been carried out at the Royal Aircraft Establishment on a similar bomb installation on the Vulcan model and those tests have been used to obtain the value for the drag increment due to the bomb used in evaluated the range performance. On the Phase 2 aircraft an increment of 7% on the zero lift drag coefficient has been taken, i.e. 21 lb at 100 ft/sec. The same drag increment has been used on the Phase 3 aircraft, but in this case the percentage increase is reduced to 6.3%. All range estimates assume that the bomb is released at the target and a drag increment of 9 lb. at 100 ft./sec. has been taken to cover the return flight with the modified undersurface of the fuselage exposed.

Tests are now being carried out in the AVRO low speed tunnel to assess the release characteristics and the effect of the bomb on the aerodynamic behaviour of the Vulcan.

4. Performance

The range performance of the Phase 2 and Phase 3 Vulcan data is based on the normal fuel tankage of the two aircraft, i.e. 9,374 and 12,950 gallons respectively, but it should be noted that the installation of the bomb at the bottom of the bay enables extra bomb bay tanks to be used if required. A typical increase in fuel tankage obtained by this means is 1,800 gallons which would increase the range by approximately 5%, with a slight reduction in mid-range height.

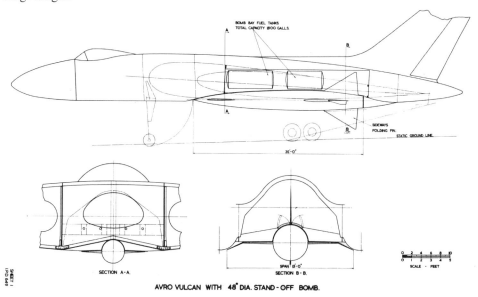

AVRO VULCAN WITH 48" DIA. STAND-OFF BOMB.

Engine combined with wing development

In June 1955 a report was issued which summarised the performance of the Vulcan Development which showed the effect of various engines. The Vulcan development programme was divided into various Phases, these being known as.

Phase 1

The basic airframe as exemplified by the 2nd Prototype Vulcan and the first few production aircraft.

Phase 2

The aircraft fitted with a drooped 20% chord wise extension of part of the outer wing.

Phase 2A

A further increase in the extension of the outer wing sections affecting the whole of the outer wing, together with an increase in span. This series of aircraft would be fitted with a strengthened undercarriage to allow operation at take-off weights up to 190,000 lb.

Phase 3

An entirely new and thinner outer wing constructed of honeycomb sandwich which incorporates a new main undercarriage capable of operating up to take-off weights of 220,000 lb. and an increased fuel capacity. This development was fully described in AVRO brochure I.P.D. 59 Issue 3. dated February 1955.

It should be noted that none of the above phases of development were tied to any particular engine or the ability to carry a Stand-off Bomb, as the centre section of the aircraft which contains the bomb bay and the engines remains substantially the same in all aircraft.

The performance given in the report for a still-air range of 5,000 nautical miles assumed that a 48 in. diameter, 15,500 lb. Stand-off Bomb was carried and released at half range.

The engines considered for the Phase 2A were the Bristol Olympus B.01.12 (13,000 lb. S.L.S.T.) the Bristol Olympus 6 (16,000 lb. S.L.S.T.) and the Rolls-Royce Conway development (15,400 lb. S.L.S.T.). The Conway development engine had a normal cruise rating of 2,200 lb. thrust at 50,000 ft. and 500 kts. but capable of giving an intermediate rating in the target area for one hour of 2,400 lb. at 50,000 ft. and 500 knots, the specific consumption increasing from 0.883 to 0.90 lb/lb/hr.

The Phase 3 engines considered were the Olympus 6 (16,000 lb. S.L.S.T.); the Olympus 7 (17,000 lb. S.L.S.T.) the "Super" Sapphire and the Conway Development. The Super Sapphire engine had been taken as giving 50% more thrust at 50,000 ft. and 500 knots than the Sapphire Sa.9.

Below gives a summary of the performance the Phase 2A and Phase 3 aircraft fitted with the appropriate engines. The height at half range, the fuel for 5,000 n.m. S.A.R. and the corresponding all-up weight are given.

Still air range 5,000 nautical miles. 15,500 lb. 48" diameter "Stand-off" Bomb released at target.

Phase 2A

Engines	B.01.2	B.01.6	R.Co.5 Development
Weight less fuel (lb.)	100,466	99,925	97,984
Normal fuel	72,200 (max)	72,200 (max)	*71,050
Overload, fuel	17,949	17,564.	-
All-up weight	190,615	189,689	169,042
Target height (ft.)	49,100	53,400	*53,400
1g C_L	0.286	0.351	0.327

*R.Co.5 Development at intermediate rating for one hour before target.

Phase 3

Engines	B.01.12	B.01.6	Super Sapphire	R.Co.5 Development
All-up weight	184,893	191,771	187,771	165,668
Target height (ft.)	54,100	56,960	56,600	54,200

Note normal fuel = 99,715 lb.

Phase 2 & 2C wing development

INTRODUCTION

Shown below is a further report produced in August 1955 on wing development proposals.

The altitude that can be obtained at high subsonic Mach number is limited by one of two factors. The first is the maximum thrust that can be obtained from the engines and the second is the product of the wing area and the lift coefficient at which flow break-down over the wing causes buffeting. Given engines of sufficient power it is necessary to avoid buffeting in level flight and in gentle manoeuvres.

The buffet-free lift coefficient obtainable from a wing depends on the distribution of local loading over the span and in particular on the ratio of the maximum local lift coefficient to the mean wing lift coefficient. It depends also on the ability of the wing sections in the critical region to withstand high loading without flow breakdown.

The Vulcan was originally designed for a cruising lift coefficient of 0.2 at the cruising Mach number and it had been found that the first measurable onset of buffeting is at a slightly greater lift coefficient. To utilise the increase of altitude made possible by more powerful engines it is necessary to raise the lift coefficient at which buffeting starts. This can be done both by reducing the of the maximum local lift coefficient to the mean lift coefficient of the whole wing and/or by improving the wing sections in the critical region. With the delta wing of the Vulcan, the maximum local lift coefficient occurs near the wing tip and is some 1.55 times the mean coefficient. Furthermore the wing sections in this region are 9% thick where as it is now known that a thickness ratio of it to 5% is more suitable for Mach numbers of 0.87 to 0.9.

Buffeting is caused by flow separation from the wing this separation may occur either at the leading edge or further back on the wing section. The leading edge separation is fundamentally a function of the nose shape and camber of the section and can only be postponed to higher lift coefficients by modification of these parameters. Its effects are most pronounced in the region of 0.7 to 0.85 Mach number. If the wing section is much thicker than about 5%, shock-induced rear separation occurs at higher Mach numbers, but this separation can be alleviated by fitting vortex generators to the wing.

The first modification of the Vulcan wing, known as "Phase 2", obtains the maximum improvement for the minimum structural alteration, and the modifications have been confined to the outer wing ahead of the front spar, The wing chord near the tip is extended by 20%; the shape of the nose of the section is that of a 5% R.A.E. 101 series and some droop has been incorporated. Flight tests on the AVRO 707A fitted with this wing modification have shown an increase in mean lift coefficient at the buffet threshold of some 50 - 60% up to a Mach number of about 0.86. Beyond this Mach number the gain drop off rapidly but the addition of vortex generators maintains the buffet threshold (on the Vulcan) at a lift coefficient of at least 0.32 at Mach numbers up to 0.89, the maximum which could be tested on the AVRO 707A.

This will enable engines of 12 to 13,000 lb. sea level static thrust to be accommodated in the Phase 2 Vulcan, but as more powerful engines become available a more extensive modification is required. During recent months new information been obtained on buffeting phenomena, and a method of calculating the wing sections to give the best pressure distribution has been developed at the R.A.E. As a result of these studies, developments of the Vulcan known as Phase 2A and 2B were considered, but these have been superseded by the Phase 2C proposal. The latter seeks to obtain the highest possible buffet threshold by a combination of chord wise and span wise extensions of the outer wing and the use of very thin (41/4% to 5%) cambered wing sections in the critical region.

Previous proposals
The development phases of the AVRO Vulcan so far proposed are:-

(a) **Phase 2:** This is a modification to the outer portion of the wing leading edge forward of the front spar and will introduced into early Service aircraft. The Phase 2 modification had been fully tested on the AVRO 707A (WD280) and a Vulcan incorporating the new leading edge was soon flying within the year of this report.

(b) **Phase 2A:** This modification has been described in Report Aero/698/243, and consists of a further modification to the existing outer wing. This modification is similar in principle to that of the Phase 2, but the structural changes are taken back to the maximum thickness of the sections. The main restriction of this type of modification is that the rear portion of the wing section is unaltered and therefore any flow separation dependent upon the surface slopes aft of the maximum thickness would be unchanged.

(b) **Phase 2B:** An interim development of Phase 2A but has not been officially submitted and is no longer considered relevant.

(d) **Phase 3:** In the Phase 3 modification the outer wing was replaced by new unit of reduced thickness and increased span and area. With this modification the flow separation from the rear of the aerofoil sections was eliminated but it involved a complete redesign of all the control surfaces, the undercarriage, and the fuel system. Advantage was taken of metal honeycomb sandwich construction to increase the internal fuel capacity, thus bringing considerable benefits in terms of range for the same engines.
The Phase 3 wing would be capable of accepting any engine up to the Bristol Olympus B.0l.6 rating at 16,000 lb. and the ability to use the thrust of these engines gave large increases in the altitude over the target.

(e) **Phase 2C:** The major disadvantage of the Phase 3 modification was the amount of redesign necessary, and therefore an investigation into the possibility of obtaining the same order of improvement in buffet threshold without the extensive structural modifications was made. This investigation has led to the Phase 2C modification. In general it can be said that the Phase 2C has an altitude performance very similar to that of the Phase 3 aircraft and is capable of accepting all the engines associated with the Phase 3, but it does not possess the outstanding range characteristics of the latter.

Since the Phase 2 modifications affect only the outer portion of the wing it will be appreciated that the normal bomb carrying capabilities of the Vulcan are unchanged. Provision will be made in production Vulcan's for the carriage of winged stand-off bombs and the performance of the Phase 2C with this type of weapon and with the internally carried 10,000 lb. special bomb are considered.

A very important feature of the Phase 2C is that the time required for the modification is such that it can be introduced into the production line of Vulcan's at about the same time as suitable engines would be available for it.

A new phase

Comparison of wing planforms.

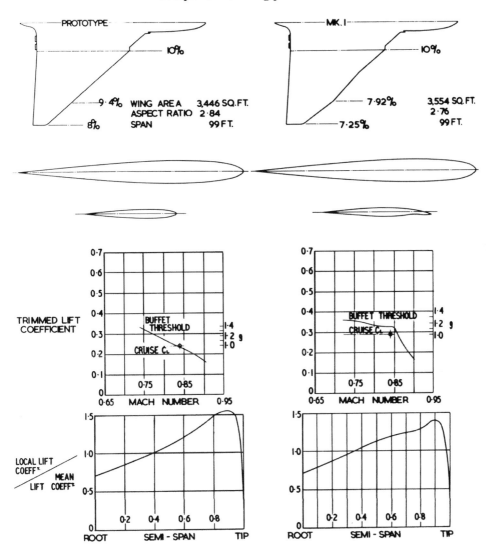

Comparison of wing planforms for early production B.Mk1 aircraft and the first prototype showing the improvement to buffet characteristics due to the new leading edge.

A fully engineered outer wing leading edge modification was fitted to the second prototype VX777, during 1955. This modification was for the Phase 2 wing which was incorporated on later B.Mk1 production aircraft. A larger and thinner kink wing was fitted to Vulcan B.Mk2 aircraft, further details on this Phase 2C wing are shown later in this book.

These diagrams were taken from Manchester Branch of the Royal Aeronautical Society, 14th Roy Chadwick memorial lecture, on 12th March, 1969 by Stuart. D. Davies., B.Sc. (Eng.) C.Eng. F.R.Ae.S. Who had by this time had left the Hawker Siddeley Group as Technical Director and re-joined Dowty Rotol Ltd. as Technical Director.

Preliminary assessment

3rd Part of Report No. A.A.E.E./910.

13th SEP 1955

Aeroplane and Armament Experimental Establishment Boscombe Down
Vulcan VX777 (Second Prototype)
(4 x B.01.101)

Preliminary assessment
A.& A.E.E. Ref: AAEE/5701, n/1
Period of Test: 7th - 25th May, 1955.

A brief preliminary assessment has been made on the second prototype Vulcan flying at an intermediate c.g. position and medium weight. This aircraft was non-representative of production in respect of engine thrust and outer wing geometry.

In view of the non-representative state of the aircraft a full assessment of the type's flying qualities and operational potential could not be made. Although the aircraft has certain outstanding features, serious deficiencies are present, particularly in and above the cruising Mach number range, and until these are rectified the Vulcan cannot be considered satisfactory for Service use.

The features requiring most serious attention are:-

(a)   Inadequate buffet boundary at high Mach number and serious associated aileron oscillation.
(b)   Longitudinal instability and poor damping in pitch at high Mach number.
(c)   Inadequate high altitude performance.
(d)   Tendency to yaw uncontrollably near the 'stall'.
(c)   Serious external reflections in the windscreen panels during night landings.
(f)   Poor engine handling characteristics.

Providing the action already in hand to rectify these deficiencies is successful, and making allowances for changes in weight and thrust, it is believed that the Vulcan will be a satisfactory bomber subject to functional clearance of the bombing and associated installations.

This report is issued with the authority of

Ronald A. Ramsey - Rae
Air Commodore,
Commanding A.& A.E.E.

1. Introduction

A preliminary flight assessment has been made on the second prototype Vulcan in 17 sorties totalling 27 hours flying. This aircraft did not have the intended wing modifications incorporated and the Olympus 101 engines had been derated from 11,000 lb. to 10,000 lb. thrust for take-off. At the time of test the runway length available at Boscombe Down had been reduced to 2000 yards by resurfacing work and it was not feasible to fly the aircraft at a representative operational weight to which it had been cleared (165,000 lb).

The non-representative state of the aircraft limited the scope of the assessment possible and it should be borne in mind that same of the characteristics reported herein may be materially altered in production aircraft. It is not possible at this stage to predict the extent of such alterations.

The opportunity is taken to acknowledge the very considerable assistance afforded this Establishment by the manufacturer during these tests. The aircraft was serviced and maintained by the Firm, their test pilot gave excellent pre-flight briefing and type conversion, their technical staff provided all necessary information and assistance, and considerable use was made of the Firm's test instrumentation. The intensity achieved reflects well their efforts.

2. Condition of aircraft

The second prototype Vulcan, serial number VX777, differed from production aircraft in the following respects:

(a) Drooped leading edge and vortex generators not fitted to outer wing. (b) Olympus 101 engines deficient in thrust by 1000 lb. at take-off and 200 lb. at cruising conditions (per engine). (c) Certain aspects of cockpit layout.

During these tests the aircraft was flown at a mid c.g. position and take-off weights of 119,000 lb. and 130,000 lb. The expected operational take-off weight of production aircraft is about 165,000 lb.

3. Scope of tests

The test programme as based on the requirements of Instruction No.317 of the A.&A.E.E. Handbook of Test Methods, with the main object of assessing the aircraft's flying qualities and operational potential for the bomber role. Within the scope of those tests it was not possible to investigate the characteristics in flight with asymmetric thrust, extreme sideslip or reduced power control output.

4. General appreciation

Initial production Vulcan aircraft will be fitted with a drooped leading-edge and vortex generators on the outer wing, Olympus 101 engines rated at 11,000 lb. take-off thrust, and will have an operational take-off weight of about 165,000 lb. The absence of the all-important wing modifications together with the non-representative engine thrust (10,000 lb.) and take-off weight (130,000 lb. maximum) on VX777 prevented a full evaluation of the Vulcan's flying qualities and operational potential, but certain serious deficiencies adversely affecting the acceptability of the aircraft for service use were shown up by the tests.

The expected cruising Mach number is 0.87 M (500 knots T.A.S.) and the design Mach number is 0.95M. Above 0.86 M a nose down change of trim occurred, which became pronounced with increase of Mach number towards the limit, making the aircraft difficult to fly accurately and requiring great care on the part of the pilot to avoid exceeding the maximum permitted Mach number. This characteristic is unacceptable; the Firm propose to eliminate it in production aircraft by the introduction of an artificial stability device.

With increase of Mach number above 0.89 M the damping in pitch decreased to an unacceptably low level, particularly near the maximum permitted. Mach number and the aircraft was difficult to fly steadily. The Firm propose installing a pitch damper in production aircraft.

As tested the Mach number/buffet characteristics were unacceptable for a high altitude bomber, but considerable improvement is hoped for with the drooped loading edge and vortex generators. Associated with the buffet were oscillating aileron hinge moments which in these tests imposed severe manoeuvre limitations from considerations of structural safety. These conditions should be alleviated by the aforementioned wing modifications and strengthening of the aileron circuit now in hand by the Firm.

The Firm are currently investigating the possibilities of increasing the design Mach number above 0.95 M, but unless a substantial increase can be achieved Service aircraft, even with the aforementioned provision of artificial stability, may require automatic extension of the airbrakes to avoid exceeding the maximum permitted Mach number.

While the stall has no operational significance on V-class aircraft, the tendency of the Vulcan to yaw uncontrollably at high incidence and develop large angles of sideslip is unacceptable for Service usage. In the event of present proposals to limit the available elevator angle - and so prevent the attainment of such high angles of incidence - being impracticable, it will be necessary to impose a minimum speed restriction in Service; and some artificial low speed warning may also be required.

Judgement of take-off attitude by night is not easy and if the aircraft were pulled off at a steep angle the acceleration and climb away would be very slow. At full load this would be dangerous. Further investigation is required to determine a take-off technique for Service use at high weights. Fair weather landings by day were straightforward, but in poor visibility, rain or by night the view was very poor. By night there were also dangerously confusing and unacceptable multiple reflections of the approach lights in the windscreen.

The general handling qualities under conditions other than those mentioned above were very pleasant, apart from high friction in the elevator control and an excessive aileron break-out force. The airbrake characteristics were unpleasant, but development action is proceeding with a view to improving the transient trim changes with brake operation and buffet with brakes in the 'high drag' setting. With the expected improvements in manoeuvre/buffet characteristics and pitch damping it is believed that the aircraft will be an adequate high altitude bombing platform, though the effects on bombing equipment of the buffet with bomb doors open is unknown.

Making due allowance for the differences in engine thrust and aircraft weight between the aircraft as tested and the production version the performance, in terms of attainable altitude, was not outstanding. The likely target height with a 10,000 lb. bomb will only be about 43,000ft. with 11,000 lb. thrust engines and the high altitude turning performance will be poor. This level of performance is considered to be inadequate for an unarmed subsonic bomber, even under cover of darkness and R.C.M. The projected more powerful engines should be introduced as soon as possible to raise the cruising altitude band. It should be noted that the engine handling characteristics experienced during the tests were unsatisfactory.

The cockpit was generally well laid-out and the best yet seen in this class of aircraft, Certain criticisms were made of the comfort aspects and power control switching and warning arrangements, but remedial action is under-stood to be in hand.

It is not known what effects, if any, the wing modifications will have on those characteristics other than the Mach number/buffet boundary, but it will be seen from the foregoing that urgent action is required if the aircraft is to reach an acceptable standard for Service use within a reasonable time.

4.2 Aerodynamic qualities
4.2.1 Taxiing, take-off and landing

(a)   The view for taxiing was not good but was considered to be adequate. Taxiing was easy and the nose wheel steering, selected by a push button on the stick and controlled through the rudder pedals, was excellent. Pilots of average stature found it difficult to apply full rudder and too brake simultaneously because of inadequate rearwards adjustment of the pedals. The turning circle using nose wheel steering alone was rather large, but with the assistance of differential braking was satisfactory.

(b)   Pre-take-off vital actions were simple and the magnetic indicator presentation of essential services was excellent. However, the lack of individual power control switches and indicators was unsatisfactory (see para. 4.4). In general, take-off was straightforward, the change of trim with undercarriage retraction was negligible, and the trim change with acceleration was satisfactory. Judgement of attitude during the ground run at night was not easy; the aircraft could be pulled up to a steep angle without losing sight of the runway over the nose. When the aircraft was taken-off in a steep nose up angle attitude at 130,000 lb. acceleration was very poor and the aircraft did not climb out of the ground "cushion" until attitude was reduced, It should be noted that the thrust loading of production aircraft under operational conditions will be 3.75 lb./lb. thrust compared with 3.26 lb./lb. thrust during these tests, and this behaviour can be expected to deteriorate. These characteristics could constitute a definite hazard and further investigation at representative thrust and wing loadings is required.

(c)   The field of view in the circuit was marginal, and under conditions of bad visibility and by night was poor, the major obstruction occurring over an arc centred at 45° from dead ahead. The windscreen wipers were quite ineffective and forward vision was totally obscured in light rain. Effective wipers are essential. By night there were, multiple images of the approach path lights in the windscreen panels which, being of apparently similar intensity, made discrimination of the real approach lights difficult. These were dangerously confusing and this feature is unacceptable and must be remedied on production aircraft. With the direct vision panels open either singly or together, with or without cabin pressurisation, a strong draught entered the cockpit. With the pilot's head in a position to look through the opening the draught blows directly onto his face. Rain entered with considerable force and prevented the panels' use under such conditions, when, should the windscreen wipers have failed, they would be essential. The possibility of fitting a suitable deflector should be investigated.

(d)   With the air brakes in the "high drag' setting, as recommended for depression of the minimum drag speed, there was continuous buffet throughout the circuit, approach and touchdown. Such buffet is undesirable. All controls were effective throughout the circuit and approach, with adequate response. Speed in the final stages of the approach was about 1 .1 $V_i$md and no difficulties were experienced in controlling the approach path. When thrust was reduced and the stick eased back on crossing the runway threshold speed fell off rapidly but the landing itself was always smooth. The undercarriage shock-absorbing qualities were excellent. Landings in moderate cross-winds (up to 15 knots) presented no difficulty, though the braking parachute produced the usual marked weather cocking tendency which on occasions required full rudder and differential brake to control. On occasion's harsh judder or shimmy of the nose wheel occurred towards the end of the ground run when speed had fallen to about 5 to 10 knots.

(e)   Landings under instrument flight conditions using G.C.A. were straightforward, apart from the previously mentioned vision defects which were embarrassing when changing from instrument to visual conditions prior to touchdown,

(f)   Using higher approach speeds landings were made with the airbrakes retracted both under visual and G.C.A. conditions. Control was satisfactory. Although touchdown speed was high (130 knots I.S.A.) a reasonable ground run could be obtained by use of full maxaret braking or the landing parachute.

(g)   The changes of trim with thrust and configuration during an overshoot from a baulked landing were small, and acceleration and climb away at weights between 105,000 and 110,000 lb. were adequate.

4.2.2 Behaviour at high incidence

(a)   The minimum attainable speed with the aircraft in the test configuration (e.g. 0.301 c, maximum elevator angle -19°) was about 95 knots I.A.S. in the "clean" condition and 100 knots I.A.S. with undercarriage down and airbrakes extended. The aft most c.g. position likely in Service will be about 0.32c.

(b)   As speed was reduced lateral rocking began at 1.3 to 1.4. times the minimum speed, (as in (a), the wings dropping alternately through 10°-15° and requiring continuous aileron movement in an endeavour to maintain steady flight. The aircraft also tended to yaw as the wing dropped. With airbrakes extended buffet was present at all times, and with brakes in buffet was also present at speeds below that for the onset of wing dropping. This lateral rocking is presumably duo to asymmetric flow breakdown, which spreads progressively inboard from the wing tips as incidence is increased. As minimum speed was reached the aircraft became directionally unstable (- nv) and tended to yaw uncontrollably. It is also believed from work elsewhere that it becomes laterally unstable (+ lv), but this was not apparent during these tests. On two occasions a wing drop occurred as minimum speed was reached, resulting in a steady marked sideslip. At minimum speed response to elevator was poor and the aileron effectiveness was very low. No tendencies towards longitudinal instability were apparent down to minimum speed,

(c)   Controlled flight was easily regained by easing the stick forward, and it was found advantageous to roll the aircraft in the direction of sideslip as the nose dropped. If rudder was applied in an endeavour to check the yawing motion considerable care was necessary during recovery to prevent large angles of sideslip developing when stability became positive with reduction of incidence.

(d)   In turning flight at 150 knots I.A.S. buffeting and alternate wing dropping began at 1.2g, becoming marked with increase of 'g' together with a noticeable increase in drag. These characteristics combined to make the aircraft extremely difficult to control accurately) but as pilots are unlikely to use more than 300 of bank (1.15g) for turns in the circuit no serious embarrassment is envisaged.

(e)   Whilst the "stall" has no operational significance on V-class aircraft there may be a case for pilot familiarisation, to some extent, with the slow speed flying qualities. The tendency to yaw uncontrollably at minimum speed and develop large angles of sideslip is unacceptable for Service use and it will be necessary to restrict the aircraft to some minimum speed above this condition. Ideally the aircraft should be made incapable of reaching the instability point by restricting the available up elevator angle, but this solution may be precluded by considerations of elevator power for landing at forward c.g. positions and under conditions of reduced power control output. The Firm are understood to be considering this solution and the possible introduction of variable elevator stops controlled by c.g. position. The desirability and reliability of this latter proposal must receive very careful consideration from the safety aspect. If a minimum speed restriction is to be imposed a satisfactory figure would be that for the onset of lateral rocking, but it is understood that tests on the Avro 707 research aircraft (1/3rd scale model of the Vulcan) have shown that the proposed outer wing modification markedly reduces the speed for the onset of the lateral rock. Further tests will be required on a Vulcan when so modified to assess the adequacy of the warning margin over the instability point. In the event of the warning margin being found insufficient it is considered that artificial warning will be required. This should be assessed as soon as possible.

4.2.3 Longitudinal stability and control

(a)   At low altitudes the aircraft was statically stable throughout the speed range, with moderate stick forces to hold changes in speed. Trimming was not easy due to rather high friction in the input circuit. The friction, measured on the ground, increased from 3 lb. to 8 lb. in the course of the trials and was thought to be somewhat greater in the air with the cabin pressurised. The cumulative effect was one of a high breakout force with poor self-centring qualities. This shortcoming is understood to be due to a material defect in the input push rods which is being rectified in production. Results of stick force per 'g' measurements at 10,000 ft. The considerable scatter, particularly at the lower airspeeds, is thought to be due to the high circuit friction, but the value of stick force per 'g' at the test c.g. position of 0.301c is about 28 lb., which is probably satisfactory. The aft c.g. limit is 0.32c and the minimum required value of stick force per 'g' is 23 lb.

(b)   At high altitudes the aircraft was statically unstable at Mach numbers greater than 0.86 M; a curve of elevator angle to trim against Mach number for heights between 40,000 ft. and 42,000 ft. Trimmed at M.0.85 a 30 lb. pull force was required to hold the aircraft at 0.92 increasing to 50 lb. at 0.94. The aircraft was extremely difficult to trim at Mach numbers above 0.85 due to the static instability and the aforementioned high control friction. Manoeuvre limitations precluded any checks for pitch-up tendencies at constant Mach number, but, self-tightening tendencies in turns with decreasing Mach number above M.0.85 can be expected from the stability characteristics. A full investigation could not be made (see para. 4.2.5.).

(c)   Damping of the short period oscillation deteriorated rapidly at Mach numbers greater than M.0.90. This behaviour is characteristic of the tail-less delta configuration. Too much reliance should not be placed on the numerical values quoted for the damping for the following reasons:

(i)   The control circuit friction may have resulted in inaccurate re-centring of the stick following initial displacement.

(ii)   The difficulty in trimming the aircraft at high Mach numbers.

(iii)   Suspected fuel surging in the tanks, which were unbaffled. A sensation akin to surging was felt in all manoeuvres involving change of attitude or speed. The fuel load at take-off was only 54% of the total capacity. There is some support for this suspicion in the scatter of the periodic time of the motion.

(iv)   The elevator angle measuring equipment was too insensitive to detect possible small movements of the controls during the oscillation, these, even when very slight, can materially affect the aircraft's motion.

The low damping at high Mach numbers resulted in pitching oscillations being triggered off by any air disturbances or control movements. Pilots were unable to prevent or control such oscillations, and on at least two occasions in the region 0.92 to 0.94. their efforts only served to produce a divergent oscillation.

(d)   The combination of static instability and low damping in pitch made the aircraft difficult to fly accurately at high Mach numbers and high altitude. The varying nose-down change of trim and extreme case with which Mach number increased constituted a real risk of exceeding the maximum permitted Mach number. It must be noted that the design cruising speed of 500 knots T.A.S. (M.0.87) is inside the region of instability. These characteristics are unacceptable for Service use and must be improved. The Firm intend to introduce artificial stick free stability by an auto-trimming device activated by a contacting Mach meter, and to improve the characteristics of the short period oscillation by fitting a pitch damper (It will have to be considered whether or not duplication is required). It is essential that these developments be pursued as quickly as possible,

(e)   Very serious consideration must be given to the likely Service maximum permitted Mach number of the Vulcan. The present design limit of M.0.95 is understood to be set by elevator loads, but the Firm are currently investigating the possibility of increasing this figure. Unless it can be increased to the region where a rapid drag rise occurs it is likely to be fairly easy to exceed the limiting speed in Service in only a shallow dive at high altitude. The introduction of a nose up trim change by artificial means is not an acceptable high Mach number deterrent because of its adverse effects in a spiral, where it can cause a sudden increase in normal acceleration. Apart from structural design considerations any increase in maximum Mach number must be considered in the light of possible consequences of failure of the pitch damper should the natural oscillation become divergent at higher Mach numbers, In the event of it being impossible to increase the design, and hence Service, Mach number to a value where a natural barrier exists it will be necessary to introduce automatic air brake extension to limit the aircraft to the selected maximum value. Development of this system should proceed forthwith as an insurance against the aforementioned possibility. Should failure of the auto-trimmer occur in Service it will be necessary to restrict the aircraft under such conditions to M.0.85 Failure of the pitch damper might result in a restriction to M.0.90.

4.2.4. Lateral stability and control

(a)   The characteristics of the lateral oscillation without auto-stabilisation at 10,000 ft. and 45,000 ft. At both altitudes the natural damping was below the minimum A.P.970 requirement for a logarithmic decrement of 0.693. In the landing configuration the lateral oscillation becomes divergent at speeds below 150 knots E.A.S., i.e. on the approach. However, the rate of divergence was slow and the period so long (approx 7 secs.) that pilots found no undue embarrassment in controlling the aircraft. At high altitude it was considered that a reasonable bombing run could be made without auto-stabilisation (see para, 4.2.6).

(b)   With auto-stabilisation the damping of the lateral oscillation just met the auto-pilot bombing requirement for an attenuation ratio of 0.3 laid down in AP.970 Chap. 602. The results obtained were between 42,000 ft. and 44,000 ft.

(c)   At all normal flying speeds aileron electiveness and response were very good and adequate for the role of the aircraft. A full assessment of aileron effectiveness could not be made at high Mach numbers because of hinge moment limitations under buffet conditions (see para. 4.2.5). At low speeds (on the approach and near minimum speed) aileron effectiveness and response deteriorated to a marked extent, but appeared to be adequate. Apart from an excessive break-out force (about 6-8 lb.) the ailerons were pleasantly light, and the 'q' controlled "spring-stop" system for limiting permissible aileron angle with speed was excellent. The aileron break-out force should be reduced to a minimum in production.

(d)   The rudder was very heavy at normal flying speeds by virtue of the V_i3 feel system which appeared to constitute an adequate structural safeguard. In the time available no sideslips tests were made to investigate the possibilities of fin stalling at low airspeeds nor were systematic tests made in flight under asymmetric thrust. No handling difficulties are anticipated in those latter conditions.

(e)   It must be emphasised that it was not possible to test the handling qualities of the aircraft with typically immobilised control surface segments. This must be done as soon as possible to establish the adequacy of control under such conditions.

4.2.5. Buffet boundary characteristics

(a)   Under conditions of buffet at high Mach number oscillation of the ailerons occurred, presumably under the influence of shock-induced separation on the wing ahead of the control surfaces. The frequency of the aileron oscillation was about 20cps (cycle per second) with hinge moments of sufficient magnitude to give considerable concern for fatigue damage to the aileron control output circuit under flight conditions well within the design envelope. Random peak hinge moments in excess of the un-factored design value for the aileron circuit were also indicated under only mild to moderate buffet. This phenomenon severely limited the extent of the high Mach number testing possible. It was necessary to place a restriction on the duration of buffet sustained in any one sortie, and to monitor the aileron hinge moments in flight to ensure that excessively high values were not inadvertently attained. It should be noted that very heavy oscillatory hinge moments were encountered at 1.3g at high Mach number and precluded the application of design values of normal acceleration (2.0g at M.0.95).

(b)   Although the wing of VX777 was non-representative of production some brief measurements of the buffet boundary characteristics were made between 40,000 ft. and 43,000 ft., The reasons for the difference between the two sets of results for the onset of buffet are not known, but may be due largely to variations of human discrimination of buffet. It will be seen that the cruising values of C_L at the specified cruising speed (500 knots T.A.S., M.0.87) lie above those for severe aileron hinge moments in the present configuration. It must be stressed that at no time during these tests was the level of buffet encountered assessed qualitatively as more than "mild to moderate",

(c)   As tested the manoeuvre/buffet characteristics were unacceptable for Service use. Production aircraft will have a drooped loading-edge extension and vortex generators on the outer wing, which should result, as already shown on the Avro 707 aircraft, in considerable improvement of the buffet threshold. It is considered that under cruising conditions over the target the aircraft should be capable of executing a 30° banked turn (1.15g) before buffet commences and in assessing the manoeuvring C_L available from the modified wings it will also be necessary to consider the ability of the aircraft to utilise more powerful engines and cruise at higher altitudes,

(d)   The aileron behaviour should be alleviated to some extent by the aforementioned wing modifications and by general strengthening of the control circuit now in hand by the Firm, even so the problem of aileron oscillation and associated high loads under conditions of buffet must receive urgent attention in view of similar experiences on other aircraft. It should be noted that the aileron behaviour and its structural consequences may limit the aircraft's evasive manoeuvre capabilities.

4.2.6. Assessment as bombing platform

(a)   With auto-stabilisation in yaw the lateral characteristics of the aircraft were adequate for bombing and, apart from the unpleasant aileron break-out forces, heading corrections could be made easily and accurately. As discussed in para. 4.2.5 the buffet boundary characteristics were inadequate in the condition tested. Without auto-stabilisation in yaw the chances of a successful attack appear reasonable with due concentration on control by the pilot.

(b)   As discussed in para, 4.2.4. static longitudinal stability is negative at cruising Mach number (M.0.87), but should be improved, by the proposed artificial stability device. At M.0.87 the aircraft does not meet the pitch damping requirement of A.P.970 Chapter 602 which calls for an attenuation ratio of not more than 0.3 for bombing. This should be improved by the proposed pitch damper.

(c)   On opening the bomb doors on to an empty bay or with 10 x 1000 lb. MC bombs there was a sharp nose down change of trim. At cruising Mach number this required a 10-15 lb. pull force to counteract, and the deceleration in the first 10 seconds from selecting doors open was of the order of 0.7 ft/sec. The bomb doors took 6 seconds to open, J.A.C, paper 602 states that bombs will normally be dropped within 10 seconds of selecting doors open and proposes that the mean deceleration during this period shall not exceed 0.6 ft/sec2.

(d)   With bomb doors open there was only moderate buffet, but its effect on the bomb sight and associated equipment is not known. This should be assessed as soon as possible with a representative store in the bomb bay.

4.2.7. Airbrake characteristics

(a)   It is not proposed to discuss the airbrake characteristics in any detail as the installation was in an interim state of development. As originally tested there was a very sharp transient nose down trim change with brake extension at high Mach numbers, and in the high drag position there was considerable buffet. Qualitatively, drag appeared to be adequate for the needs of a bomber aircraft.

(b)   Then the brake configuration was altered by removal of the lower outer frames towards the end of the trials period aileron circuit fatigue considerations precluded a re-assessment at high Mach number. An attempt to assess the brakes at high Mach number after return of the aircraft to the Firm was rendered semi-abortive by in-flight un-serviceability, but it can be said that the trim change characteristics on extension had been materially improved. Development of the airbrake installation to reduce the buffet and yet maintain adequate drag is continuing at the Firm, and a full assessment must await completion of this work.

4.2.3. Airspeed pressure error correction

The static pressure error correction to the airspeed system was measured over the approximate range from M.0.82 it to M.0.92 near 40.000 ft., using the "fly-past" method in conjunction with a specially calibrated Venom aircraft of this establishment. It will be seen that the correction is large and negative at cruising Mach number. This will materially affect the accuracy of A.P.I. and other navigation and bombing equipment which utilise static pressure. The need to seek a more accurate static source must receive urgent consideration.

4.2.9. Performance capabilities

No specific performance tests were made, but, making due allowances for the derated engine thrust and non-representative aircraft weight, the performance in terms of attainable altitude was not outstanding. It is considered that the over-target height will only be some 42,000 ft. to 43,000 ft. for aircraft fitted with 11,000 lb. thrust engines, which is inadequate for an aircraft of this class, even under cover of darkness and R.C.M. (Radio Counter Measures). More powerful engines must be adopted as soon as possible in order to achieve target heights above 45,000 ft. at the least. It must be appreciated that the level turning performance at operational heights and weights will be very poor.

4.3. Engine handling characteristics

Detailed engine handling tests were not made, but in the course of the flying done the handling characteristics of the Olympus 101 engines fitted to VX.777 were shown to be totally unacceptable for Service use. Major criticisms were:
  (a) excessive r.p.m. creep with altitude,
  (b) excessive jet pipe temperatures during take-off, high altitude cruise, and on the climb,
  (c) reduction of r.p.m. with increase of speed on take-off,
  (d) poor slam acceleration characteristics.
During the tests the second pilot had to devote almost his entire attention to engine functioning. Two engine changes, due to mechanical failures, were required during the period of these tests.

The importance of easy and trouble-free engine handling characteristics on this class of aircraft cannot be over-emphasised and urgent action is required if such are to be achieved, The unsatisfactory nature of the engine handling features encountered has already been discussed with the engine manufacturer,

4.4. Cockpit layout

The cockpit layout was, in general, excellent and the best yet seen in this class of aircraft. The arrangement was neat and logical and all vital controls fell readily to hand. Action is already in hand to rectify most of the criticisms made, the major faults being
  (a) Inadequate power control switching and warning which is being modified to individual switches and warning lights on production aircraft.
  (b) Inadequate rearwards adjustment of rudder pedals to accommodate even the average pilot.
  (c) Control column too far from pilot's body in normal flying position causing the arm to tire rapidly.
  (d) Insensitivity of control trim indicators.
The layout of the basic flying instruments was not liked, but as this matter is understood to be under review no further comment will be made.

The flat cockpit floor and ability to move the rudder pedals well forward much to alleviate the inherent discomfort of the ejection seat by allowing the pilot to shift in his seat with a fair degree of freedom. In this respect the cockpit was superior to those of other bomber aircraft.

It was not possible to assess the crew stations in the rear compartment because of the non-representative seats and presence of non-standard equipment,

The unsatisfactory nature of the direct vision panels, screen wipers and windscreen transparencies has already been discussed in para. 4.2.1.

Conclusions

Although tested under non-representative conditions of weight and thrust, and without the intended wing modification, the Vulcan was found to have certain serious deficiencies, which, unless rectified, render the aircraft unacceptable for Service use. Urgent remedial action is required in order to reach the standard of flying, qualities required in this class of aircraft, and more powerful engines must be introduced as soon as possible to provide an adequate level of performance. If these deficiencies can be corrected it is believed that the aircraft will be a satisfactory bomber, subject to functional clearance of the bombing and associated installations.

Consideration must be given to the following points and where possible, action taken. It is understood that action is already in hand on all of these features.

(i) Introduction of artificial stability to overcome longitudinal static instability at high Mach number.

(ii) Introduction of a pitch damper for high altitude/high speed flight.

(iii) Possible extension of the design Mach number.

(iv) Introduction of automatic air brake operation to restrict maximum Mach number.

(v) Structural consequences of buffet in high Mach number manoeuvres and associated aileron oscillation.

(vi) Adequacy of revised buffet boundary for evasive action.

(vii) Adequacy of revised buffet threshold for use of more powerful engines and higher operating altitudes.

(viii) Restriction of minimum flight speed by limitation of elevator angle, or possible introduction of artificial minimum speed warning.

(ix) Determination of take-off technique suitable for high weights.

(x) Flying qualities with some control surfaces immobilised.

(xi) Reduction of elevator control friction and aileron breakout forces.

(xii) Elimination of serious external reflections in the windscreen at night.

(xiii) Improvement of vision in rain or poor visibility.

(xiv) Improvement of air brake characteristics and consequences of air brake buffet.

(xv) Improvement of engine handling characteristics.

(xvi) Effect of buffet with bomb doors open on sighting equipment.

(xvii) Acceptability of airspeed pressure error corrections for navigation and bombing equipment.

(xviii) Improvement of certain aspects of cockpit layout.

Details of aircraft and limitations
1. General

The Vulcan is a tailless delta wing heavy/medium bomber designed to Specification B35/46. Production aircraft are covered by Specification B129P.

The aircraft is powered by four turbo-jet engines buried in the wing roots.

Leading particulars of the aircraft as tested were:

Gross wing area	3446 ft²
Wing span	99 ft.
Aspect ratio	2.84.
Thickness/chord ratio at root	12.3%
at wing joint	10%
at tip	8%
Sweepback of 1/4 chord line	
inboard of joint	41,685°
outboard of joint	42.185°

All control surfaces were irreversibly power-operated by Boulton-Paul electro-hydraulic units. Each aileron and elevator was sub-divided into two half controls, each surface having an independent power control unit. A dual power control unit was fitted to the rudder, which was also controlled by a Newmark auto-stabiliser.

All controls were provided with artificial feel the systems being Elevator 'q'. Aileron Spring with 'q' controlled stops. Rudder V_i3.

2. Loading

The aircraft was flown at the following take-off loadings:

Weight	C.G. position
119,355 lb.	30.1% S.M.C., undercarriage down.
130,250 lb.	29,6% S.M.C., undercarriage up.

Flying limitations

The flying limitations observed during the trials were based on R.D.(A). Form 13 of 27th April 1955 and Amendment No.1 thereto of 6th May 1955.

(a) Maximum I.A.S. and I.M.N.

Height (ft)	14,000	21,000	25,000	30,000	34,000	39,000
I.A.S. (kts)	430	420	400	375	350	320
I.M.N.	0.82	0.91	0.93	0.97	0.985	1.0

Raising and lowering undercarriage	220 kts I.A.S.
Operation of airbrakes	350 kts I.A.S.
Opening bomb doors	1.0 I.M.N.
Streaming landing parachute	135 kts I.A.S.
(b) Normal acceleration and buffet	
	Accelerometer reading
	2.5g at speeds up to 374. kts or 0.85 TMN
increasing linearly thereafter to	1.8g at 415 kts or 0.95 IMN

These limitations were to be further restricted under conditions of buffet to prevent aileron hinge moments exceeding their design value. This was achieved by visually monitoring hinge moment records on suitable equipment. Conditions varied with height and airspeed.

VX777 taken 16th July, 1954 showing vortex generators, to help overcome buffeting problems. These experiments led to a new wing planform being designed.

Held up by Stress *by W. G. "Geoff" Heath*

The bitter winter of 1946-7 was exacerbated by a fuel shortage, and many factories (including Chadderton) had a total or partial shut-down. Since Emmanuel Shinwell was then Minister of Fuel and bore the responsibility for this unfortunate state of affairs, the period was dubbed, with typical Northern humour, 'Shinwell's Wakes'. One or two corners of the Chadderton factory could be (inadequately) heated and in January 1947 the Stress Office was singled out for temporary location in one such corner so that the work could continue. Henry Bennett spent this period making some preliminary calculations for a new project to meet the Ministry specification B35/46 and bearing the Avro type number 698. In such unfavourable circumstances the Vulcan had its beginnings.

However, at this stage the 698 (it was not named "Vulcan" until after its first flight) had a markedly different appearance to the version which was finally accepted by the Ministry.

The most noticeable difference was the absence of the central fin and rear fuselage; directional stability was achieved by a fin at each wing tip. The air intakes for the engines were protruding circular ducts feeding engines which were placed one above the other instead of side by side, whilst two bomb bays were included outboard of the engines.

It is interesting to note that, in this original concept, the wing derived much of its strength from a box spar with corrugated sandwich covers, placed well forward. Although this principle was abandoned for the production version, we were to come across it again many years later in the Victor. (Avro/HSA were to convert the Handley Page Victor K2 to the Tanker version in the 1970s.)

I was working on the 698 under Henry Bennett's guidance, and it fell to my lot to draw the structural graphs for the tender brochure which was submitted to the Ministry in May 1947 (things moved faster in those days!). My last conversation with Roy Chadwick concerned the wing bending moment diagrams. The presence of the fin induced a bending moment at the wing tip where one would normally expect a zero value, and Chadwick seemed reluctant to accept my word that the fin could produce such an effect and went away (presumably) to ask more expert advice. Since he never returned and the graphs were published, I can only assume that he was convinced of their validity-or maybe he was just testing me. By September 1948 the design had more or less crystallised into its final configuration with a central bomb bay, a single fin, and four buried engines arranged in side-by-side pairs.

Three V-Bombers

In 1953 I had the privilege of attending the Anglo-American Aeronautical Conference in London. By then all three V-Bombers - Valiant, Victor and Vulcan - were flying, as were the B47 and Boeing 707, and some argument raged between the Americans and the British over the pros and cons of podded and buried engines. George Edwards (then Chief Engineer at Vickers-Armstrong) said he doubted very much whether there was a controversy; there were just two ways of doing a job and one was better! Stuart Davies (who was then Chief Designer at Avro) added that they were really debating high aspect ratio wings versus low aspect ratio, and he often wondered what the Boeing B47 bomber would look like, by any stretch of the imagination, if somebody tried to bury the engines, and he would like to imagine the three V bombers with pods!

The bomb doors, flanked by engine access panels with undercarriage cut-outs immediately outboard of them, cut an enormous hole in the wing lower surface. Davies says:

"It was recognised that the policy of creating large holes in the structure at the centre section would increase weight compared with a fully stressed skin multi-spar type structure, and therefore reduce to some degree the weight advantage obtained from the previous decision to delete the tailplane, etc." Basically, then, the wing was a two-spar structure from the centre-line to about half-span, becoming a full box in the outer wing. For the first time in the Vulcan we met the problem of the "wing root triangle". The analysis of the un-swept centre section was straightforward, as was that of the outer wing; it was where they met that the problem arose.

There were not in those days any of the powerful computer programmes to which we resort nowadays for our difficult analyses. The R.A.E. was regarded as a hive of expert knowledge when difficult problems were met, Henry Bennett and I had several meetings with Dai Williams at Farnborough on the thorny subject of the root triangle. Matters were complicated by the jet pipe rings which cut through the rear spar just inboard of the wing joint. Williams advised us to make some Xylonite (cellulose nitrate) models to study strains and deflections, and this we duly did.

Xylonite models

The first models explored various configurations for the jet pipe rings; one such model had the inboard jet pipe protruding through the lower surface whilst the outboard one breaks through the upper surface. Another model featured oval rings which did not break either of the spar flanges. Later, complete wing models (41 in semi-span) were used to study the effect of rib direction on torsional stiffness. We also consulted our colleagues at Coventry, who had just built the AW 52 "flying wing" project which also had the root triangle problem. In the end, we solved the two easy portions inboard and outboard of the wing joint and joined the bending moment diagrams together with a smooth curve. I should add that we learned how to do things better eventually!

Although the computer had not yet arrived on the scene, the first seeds of finite element analysis were already being sown by Argyris and Dunnell. Their papers in the Aeronautical Journal in 1947 aroused considerable interest, even if the mathematics was beyond most of us. One of my colleagues in the Stress Office was laboriously plodding through the first paper and had come to an equation of which the left-hand side was a huge determinant which filled the whole page. As is usual in mathematics, the right-hand side was written as zero. A foreman from the shop floor had come in about a concession and stood looking at this fine display of flute music. Then he said: "Blimey! Does all that lot come to nothing?" There was no answer to that - until we had access to a digital computer it all come to nothing!

Sweepback was not the only new structural problem. Whereas we had ignored the stringers in the Lancaster wing, those reinforcing the upper and lower skins of the 698 were expected to do some work, especially in the outer wing. Their arrangement was somewhat unusual, since all the stringers were parallel to the front spar except the last four, which were parallel to the rear spar. The skins were in narrow planks, butt-jointed on T-stringers, the remaining stringers being Z-section. For the first time in Avro history, the stringers in the wing were extrusions; previously only rolled sections had been used.

The spars were clearly an extension of the Lancaster design, featuring solid booms and sheet metal webs. However, the penalties of increased weight and reduced strength brought about the numerous long steel bolts which passed through the Lancaster boom to attach the web were noted, and the booms of the 698 were extruded with a small "ear" to allow short rivets to be used instead. Further ears picked up the skin panels, thus (albeit unwittingly) avoiding the hole intersection problem found later on the Shackleton.

The main spar joints were of the Lancaster pattern, with massive shackles and single pin attachments through steel reinforcing plates. However, to accommodate the sweepback and the spar "kink", a four-armed forging was introduced at the outer end of each centre section boom. The 698 was, of course, designed before words like "fail safe" and "damage tolerant" were applied to aircraft structures, but (as we shall see later) the Vulcan's limited damage tolerance was exploited to the full. This was achieved in spite of the extensive use of aluminium-zinc alloys which had a very high strength, but which became notorious for their poor fatigue and fracture behaviour, not to mention their susceptibility to stress corrosion.

The fuel tanks were another problem. Because of the high altitude at which the 698 was expected to operate, the tanks had to be pressurised to prevent the fuel from boiling off.

Unfortunately the tanks were of shapes which tended to distort when pressurised: those in the wing were elliptical, there was a large rectangular box just forward of the front spar and two pendulous tear-drop shaped tanks were squeezed in above the nose wheel.

Further complications arose later, when a saddle tank was required to fit around the "Blue Steel" weapon in the bomb bay. This tank had to be reinforced by a system of internal tie rods, which made construction difficult. We handed this particular problem to our friends at Middleton Sheet Metal, who developed the "pre-pressure jig welding" technique as the solution. Up to this time, the problems of aero elasticity such as flutter had been avoided by the use of an empirical formula which ensured that a wing had adequate torsional stiffness. This criterion had been developed for conventional wings of low speed aircraft and was obviously useless for a high speed delta. The problem had therefore to be solved from scratch, but the mathematics was too complex to be handled without some computational aid. In the absence of a digital computer, we commissioned an analogue. This had just four degrees of freedom; the next model had no less than six!

One cannot talk about the early days of the 698 without mention of the one-third scale models which preceded it - the 707A, B and C. In the interests of rapid design and production, they had very simple (if not crude) structures, using a two-spar wing with closely-spaced ribs. The front fuselage was a welded tubular framework (shades of the Anson!) with light alloy fairings, whilst the rear fuselage (which housed the engine) comprised two steel cantilever box beams. For the first 707 the main undercarriage came from the Athena and the nose undercarriage and pilot's canopy from the Meteor and had a dorsal air intake. The 707B was of similar design, but with improvements from lessons learnt from the first prototype; the A and the two-seater C had intakes in the wing leading edge like their "big brother". We were proud to have a 707A on display alongside the Shackleton in the Air and Space Gallery at the Museum of Science and Industry in Manchester.

No major structural tests were required for the 707 series. This was probably just as well, since we were fully occupied with the test programme for the 698. The first test of significance was the pressure test on the crew's cabin. This was originally conceived as a detachable unit, which could be jettisoned from the wing in an emergency, descending like a modem space capsule on an array of parachutes. Although this idea was quickly abandoned, the separate cabin remained as a convenient production unit.

Remembering the Tudor problems, a sunken water tank was built at Chadderton, and the cabin was tested there in 1952. The crew's cabin was similar to Tudor and York fuselage construction, with inverted" top-hat stringers and light rolled-section frames. However, cleats were used to secure the stringers to the frames.

The rear pressure bulkhead was flat, and carried the nose wheel loads in two vertical beams. A few years later, when the Comet disasters were still fresh in official minds, the static pressure test was followed by a fatigue test. The nose fuselage specimen was placed upside-down in a tank at Chadderton so that the nose wheel loads could be applied more easily. Once the static test was completed, production cabins were proof-tested with air. On one occasion, the rear bulkhead was unfortunately held in place by a few "slave" bolts when the cabin was wheeled outside for its test. At a very low pressure, these bolts gave way and the enormous flat disc went spinning away down the factory yard. The foreman was puzzled by the tremendous forces involved. Said he, "I've got thirty pounds in my tyres and they're quite safe!

Organisational changes

The 698 was responsible for many changes in the organisation at Avro. Not least, it brought about the establishment of a full-scale Structural Test Department at Woodford, up till then, it will be recalled, Farnborough had been the full-scale test centre. Perhaps it was the unusual shape of the 698 which would not fit into the Cathedral at RAE, or perhaps the simultaneous arrival of three huge "V" bombers would have swamped the RAE's resources. Whatever the reason, the early 1950s were a watershed in structural test policy, and since then most major static tests have been conducted by British contractors at their home base. This period also marked the transition from screw jacks to hydraulics; it became clear that it was preferable to control the applied load rather than the deflection.

The 698 thus presented yet another structural challenge in that we now had to design and build our own test facility before testing could commence. Since a building with considerable height and floor space was needed, one half of a flight hangar at Woodford was set aside for this purpose. Basically, the idea was simple: piles were sunk in a regular pattern, and massive beams were laid on the pile caps. This "strong floor" was then equipped with a set of gantries and "gallows" which, bolted down to a convenient set of beams, could apply or react forces great enough for the testing of all conceivable future aircraft. A pump house for the hydraulic power, a control room and offices for the staff completed the installation. This universal facility has been continuously occupied by a succession of aircraft; somewhat ironically, it tested the Vulcan's great rival, the Handley Page Victor.

Structural testing is a business in which it is impossible to succeed. If the specimen achieves its target strength at the first attempt, the Structures Department is accused of conservatism. Structural test engineers suffer the gibe that they are not happy unless they are breaking something, but if there are failures on the way to the desired goal, the Department's capability is called into question. Since there is no middle way, the Department learns to expect and accept criticism whatever happens.

The 698 had its fair share of minor failures during the initial tests which revealed, among other things, a few weaknesses around the infamous root triangle. John Benton, who will always be remembered for his leadership in the Stress Office on both the Vulcan and Nimrod aircraft, earned the nickname "Ten Gauge Benton" after one of his more-than-usually hefty reinforcing plates had been fitted in the region of the wing root joint. The problems were finally solved by Henry Bennett, who introduced an expansion joint in the shape of a tapered gusset of "bowler-hat" section. Sometimes it pays to make things more flexible rather than stronger!

Testing of the original delta wing reached a satisfactory conclusion in 1956. By then, the Mk 2 Vulcan was being designed with its re-vamped wing outline and thinner aerofoil sections. The centre section of the Mk 1 test specimen was therefore fitted with the new outer wings, and testing recommenced in 1959. This time, things did not go so well and the wing suffered a premature failure which was attributed to the fact that the stringers were not parallel to the principal stress direction - a phenomenon which had been evident during the Mk 1 tests. In keeping with Manchester practice, the wing strength had been estimated from the results of compression panels in which the stringers had been parallel to the line of action of the applied load. Yet another series of Xylonite models was made and tested at Farnborough to study the effect of stringer directionality. These tests showed that stringers parallel to the front spar were much less effective than those parallel to the rear spar. Since it was too late to redesign the wing and after more consultations with Farnborough, the compression panels were tested in the skewed condition. These tests enabled a simple strengthening scheme to be devised.

Fatigue considerations began to weigh more heavily in official circles and after the Mk 2 static strength specimen had been repaired and tested satisfactorily, a third Vulcan specimen was installed in the Woodford test frame. This specimen, unlike its predecessors (which were built specifically as test specimens) was originally destined for the RAF and was designated the "tail number" XM596. Since its absence was soon noticed by the "reggie-spotters", the rumour began to spread that it had crashed whilst carrying a nuclear weapon and the accident had been "hushed up"!

Although the Farnborough Cathedral was no longer used for static testing, the RAE continued to develop methods for fatigue testing. The first major specimen (in 1952) was a wing from a retired Lancaster. The test utilised the resonance method, the wing being excited by an eccentric driven by a slipping clutch. The next report concluded that "with certain equipment, wings can be fatigue tested in a matter of weeks by the resonance method." Using a more sophisticated method, the Vulcan fatigue test commenced in 1964 and continued until 1970's. The fatigue tests were followed by a series of residual strength tests, so that the specimen was in the test frame until 1973. Altogether, the three Vulcan specimens occupied the frame for nineteen years.

The fatigue loading sequence included gusts and manoeuvres of various levels plus a ground case. The gusts and manoeuvres were divided into separate blocks, but each individual event was selected in a random manner. These were more realistic conditions than a purely repetitive programme could produce. Additionally, a particularly high level of "g" was simulated every 100th "flight".

In accordance with the system which came into operation about this time, fatigue life consumption was translated into a "Fatigue Index" (Fl), so that 100 Fl correspond to the life required by the aircraft specification. The Vulcan was conceived as a high altitude bomber, which meant that it would spend its life in relatively calm air flying straight and level. These conditions were not particularly severe from the fatigue point of view.

Role change

The role of the Vulcan changed dramatically whilst the test programme was in progress to that of a low-level aircraft. Terrain-following, with its continuous succession of relatively high-g manoeuvres in gusty air, meant that the same life in terms of flying hours needed the demonstration of a much higher Fl. By the end of the test, after the incorporation of some modifications and repairs, the demonstrated life was 320 Fl.

During the fatigue test, cracking of the "ears" of the spar boom caused us to investigate their residual strength in a series of detail tests. Fatigue cracks were started artificially in specimens of the spar extrusion and "grown" to known lengths under cyclic loading. Each specimen was then broken to determine its residual strength. This series of tests was a convincing demonstration that the concentration of all the wing bending loads into one or two solid members was not the best way to combat fatigue. One might have expected that a crack in an insignificant "ear" of a massive spar boom would be quite innocuous, but the loss of only 2.4% of cross-sectional area reduced the strength by 48%.

The linking of the striations on the fracture surface to the events which caused them, thus enabling us to determine for how many 'flights" a crack had been present, was our first serious essay into the developing science of fractography (the study of fracture surfaces of materials, One further new venture was the measurement of stresses in flight for comparison with those measured on the fatigue test specimen. These flight trials enabled final adjustments to be made to the declared fatigue life. For the residual strength tests proper, the repairs to the specimen were progressively removed from the fatigue cracks so that their criticality could be judged. To safeguard the specimen from premature failure, several skin cracks were monitored using the "crack opening displacement" technique to compare their behaviour with that of previously-tested components.

So the structural integrity of the Vulcan was proved, and the satisfactory results enabled it to remain in RAF service throughout 1980's, the few remaining aircraft having been converted to tankers during "Operation Corporate" (the Falklands Campaign). In his Chadwick Memorial Lecture, Stuart Davies said: "The Vulcan is expected to have a useful operational life well into the mid-1970s." I am sure he will not object to me pointing out that he was in error by almost a decade, and it is a remarkable fact that the 698 was first used in anger 30 years after its first flight, the few remaining aircraft having been converted to tankers during "Operation Corporate" (the Falklands Campaign).

The structures department also developed composite items which dated back to the Type 720 and from work producing large glass fibre radomes for the Vulcan. In 1969, after Philips Johnson and Watt at the R.A.E. produced the first carbon fibres, the structures department began to investigate ways of making lightweight components from this new material.

Two airbrake components were made for the Vulcan constructed of aluminium honeycomb with carbon fibre facing, these components were in service for eleven years until the aircraft was withdrawn in 1982. It was found when examined that these components were perfectly sound.

Skin buckles on upper surface of Vulcan Mk1 wing during strength test in 1954.

Vulcan pressure cabin fatigue test specimen at Chadderton in 1957.

Structural test specimen

Test rig display model layout.

In 1954 the third Vulcan B.1 off the Avro production line was subjected to a comprehensive series of structural tests. Two years later these tests were passed with complete success.

Rock-like rigidity for the rig was achieved without exceptional cost by sinking 104 concrete piles 30ft into the ground, each pile having a bulbous foot to resist up-or down-loads of 15 tons. The base of the rig itself comprised a T-shaped assembly of steel beams, measuring 110ft each way and weighing 58 tons. Over this the Vulcan was suspended from 22 hydraulic jacks and it was also anchored to the base at three anchoring points, all the jacks and anchors incorporating load-measuring units. By this arrangement the Vulcan was supported in a zero-g (weightless) condition.

To apply test loads each jack had a partner capable of exerting a force up to a combined total of approximately 700 tons. Under the centralized control of a single remote console forces were applied and deflections up to l00 m measured at 28 stations to an accuracy of a few thousandths of an inch. In addition nine sets of strain recorders received signals from 450 points on the test airframe, which actually had 1,200 strain gauges applied to its surface. The arrangement was such that any unduly high strains were immediately visible.

Towards the end of the programme (which included simulated take-off, landing and a low-speed, high-g pull-out) a major failure was predicted near a wing root. Early in January 1956, loads well in excess of those specified in the design (multiplied by the appropriate factor) were applied, but the major failure did not occur. The only failures had been in secondary structures and have been cleared with insignificant effect on the weight.

In the landing and take-off programmes the Vulcan was mounted at a nose-up angle of five degrees, with the undercarriage down. Not only did this imply a considerably higher landing speed than would be likely in practice, but sideways loads were imposed to simulate a large amount of drift.

As the primary structure was still obstinately remaining intact it was to be fitted with wings of new design for more advanced testing. These tests were the first to prove the characteristics of Avro's composite wings fabricated from light-alloy honeycombs. Not only would the later test programme help in the development of the Vulcan it would also be invaluable to the development of future multi-engine supersonic aircraft.

Structural test rig 27th January, 1955

From slide rule to digital computer

It was 1953, when the stress department used one of the world's first commercially available digital electronic computer's at Manchester University, the Ferranti Mk1 also known as the Manchester Electronic Computer. A development of this machine was installed at Chadderton in 1955. It used a 16,000 word magnetic drum for storage, together with a 256-word cathode ray tube working store. The paper tape input was at the rate of 100 characters per second, output was 33 characters per second.

The Ferranti Mk1 digital computer. It worked out basic calculations swiftly so speeded up the process of reconciling physical possibilities of aircraft theoretical demands.

Systems and ground testing

Engine

Major decisions concerning the structure were influenced mainly by the shape of the aircraft; there were a number of other important points of the initial design to settle.

Perhaps the most important decision concerned the power plant. The original proposals were based on what was then a hypothetical engine whose main characteristic was to be a minimum static thrust of 9,000 lb. coupled with the lowest possible cruising fuel consumption. In fact, the proposed engine was based on a Bristol design study, which eventually became the 'Olympus'. However, during the early development stage in the design of the 698, it appeared probable that it could be ready before the engines, and consideration was given to the fitment of alternative power plants.

The dimensions of the wing root chord enabled the largest engines visualised at that time to be accommodated without embarrassment, so that it was felt that whilst the primary design effort should be concentrated on the 'Olympus', the actual choice of power plant to fly the first prototype could be deferred until the delivery situation of engines was a little clearer.

Flying controls

Another early decision with considerable influence on the eventual satisfactory flight behaviour of the 698 concerned the flying controls. It had originally been hoped to operate all the surfaces manually by means of aerodynamic servo tabs and sealed nose balances; the structure of the control surfaces and control runs were designed accordingly. However, doubts concerning the effects of high Mach No. on control forces and effectiveness led to the view that manual operation was not practicable at either end of the speed ranges.

It was therefore decided to adopt full power control and to study alternative methods of providing automatic integrity of the system in the event of a failure or run away of a single unit. Also the partial aerodynamic balances already schemed were retained to reduce the overall power requirements particularly in low speed manoeuvres.

Ultimately the present system of splitting the controls into four surfaces for ailerons and elevators each with a self-contained power unit was adopted. Each packaged unit comprised an electric motor driving a variable stroke pump, control valves, sealed reservoir and jack. In this system not only was the integrity of the system fully safeguarded, but from a military point of view the power supply via alternative electrical bus bars was felt to be less vulnerable than long hydraulic pipes connecting engine-driven pumps to control valves and jacks at the control surfaces.

Fuel System

In the early days of the design when the acceptable c.g. range was unknown, the possible effects of the movement of the c.g. of the fuel, as it was utilised, was a source of anxiety. This was aggravated by the fact that the fuel was distributed in a number of tanks each of relatively small volume in the interests of reduced vulnerability. At first, a rather elaborate electronic system of control was visualised whereby the selection of tanks was dependent upon signals received from the fuel contents gauge system. Apart from the frightening complexity of the scheme as it was applied to a number of tanks, it was felt that it would also prejudice the reliability of the fuel contents gauge system. Eventually, a simpler but automatic scheme was devised which was based on the cyclical sampling of the tanks in turn, and which enabled the c.g. of the fuel to be kept constant throughout the flight.

Naturally in view of the unconventional nature of the 698 design an extensive ground rig test programme was decided upon. This included hydraulics, powered flying controls, pressurisation and air conditioning, fuel system and engine installations.

With regard to the last two items, these were certainly novel as far as the Company was concerned. The fuel system rig comprised a full-scale structure containing all the tanks, fuel piping and everything appertaining to the fuel system on the port side of the aircraft. This rig was designed to be rotated in pitch and rolls to cover all possible attitudes of the aircraft in flight and has been of inestimable value in eliminating minor snags in the fuel system.

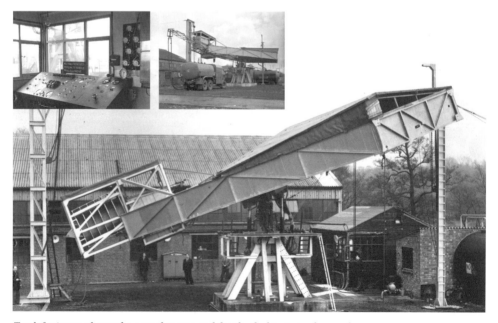

Top left picture shows the contol room used for the fuel test rig shown above.

Engine test rig

The engine installation rig was decided upon in light of experience that there appeared to be more difficulties in getting satisfactory running conditions on the ground with modern high powered jet engines than in the air. In particular, the twin air intake was suspect, since it was thought from experience on another aircraft that one of the pair of engines when running could influence the intake conditions of the other. This rig was also useful in clearing the secondary cooling conditions in the engine bay, for the generator and other accessories. Alterations to ducts and injectors were relatively easy to carry out on this rig and resulted in satisfactory conditions throughout, with the minimum expenditure on cooling air.

This rig incidentally, had been utilised to clear the installation, not only of the 'Olympus', but of the 'Avon' and 'Sapphire' engines used in the 698, with each engine having its own problems when applied to the aircraft. It was considered that this had amply justified the effort and expense of this particular installation rig.

The first Olympus to run in the wing jig was a Olympus Mk 100 in February 1953.

Flying controls

The flying control test rig may also be mentioned, since this was intended not merely to carry out endurance tests on the control system and the power control units, but was also useful in developing satisfactory artificial feel systems. Incidentally, since the power control units were dependent upon ample and reliable supplies of electrical power, it was also thought advisable to run the flying control test rig, from what was virtually an electrical generator test rig of the aircraft.

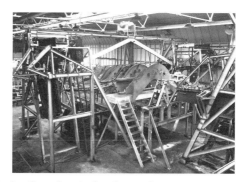

Various test rigs were used to check the structure, hydraulics, electrical and control systems.

Into production

Avro had a tradition of breaking down aircraft structures to relatively small components, both in the interest of rapid and cheap productions and easy repair. It was early appreciated that a multiplicity of transport joints would not only be heavy, but unless very specially jigged would upset the external finish.

It was therefore decided to deal with the problem in two stages. First of all, the prototype breakdown was decided, based on the practical problem of moving the prototype components from the factory to the aerodrome in the ordinary course of business. It still leaved a rather bulky fuselage centre section unit (which however, was in fact transported over seventeen miles of city streets and country roads), but provision was made in the design for the ultimate inclusion of a further transport joint at the junction of the stub wings to the fuselage. By deleting this at the prototype stage, the stub wing sub-assembly jigs with their necessary interchange ability media were saved.

The problem of surface accuracy was solved by a mixture of design decisions and tooling policy. In the first place it was found that the wing skin was not going to be of the paper thickness once visualised; torsional stiffness considerations dictated the wing skin gauges which would be comparable with those already used on existing bomber aircraft.

As far as the leading edges of the main plane and the nose portion of the fuselage were concerned, it was decided to adopt modified forms of envelope jigging by which the outer contour of the aircraft became the main jigging reference, apart of course, from the main pick-up points.

For the main flying controls, the difficult problem of ensuring that the skins did not unduly deform under aerodynamic loading was solved by the widespread use of fairly thick Magnesium Alloy sheet for the skin and many structural details.

The policy of adopting production type jigging assisted in meeting the tight timetable, since it was possible to work simultaneously on a number of components which were scattered to suit the exigencies of the labour situation, with the assurance that all the components would mate together on final assembly at the aerodrome. These jigs, whilst perfectly satisfactory for production were relatively simple, consisting of steel rafts (to keep the structure independent of any floor movements) carrying the minimum number of jigging points which were necessary to ensure interchange ability.

A typical example of such is the rear fuselage jig shown below. This jig was used to construct the rear end of the centre section containing the jet pipe tunnels. From an interchange ability point of view, the forward face of the components must be flat and drilled correctly in relation to the mating holes on the front centre section. Accordingly the jig carries, as its most important fixture, a base plate suitably drilled to locate this transport face. Such details as formers, stringers, etc. were not located on the jig since they did not contribute to the overall accuracy of the components. On the other hand the contour which is important was controlled by detachable scrieve boards, which are not shown in the photograph.

Rear fuselage jig and component.

Prototype wing under construction at Chadderton.

Chadderton production line.

Chadderton production 9th November, 1954.

Scaffolding around the wing jig at Woodford 8th December, 1954.

Chadderton assembly line June 1955.

Hydraulic press at Chadderton.

Heavy Press shop at Chadderton June 1955.

Front centre section spar boom bending.

Wing being transported. Note the Shackleton fuselages, which were also in production at that time.

Chadderton was well equipped for the production of the Vulcan seen here is the Heavy Press at Chadderton

Wing leading edge jig at Chadderton 15th March, 1955. The wing leading edge was manufactured in a novel (Fairey Aviation Ltd patent) reversed "envelope" jig which acted as a mould and into which the sheet metal was formed.

Working on the Vulcans structure at Chadderton 15th March, 1955.

Production potential at Woodford photographed from finals June 1955.

Woodford 15th March, 1956 XA892 is in background.

First production aircraft - XA889

The initial flight of the first production Vulcan B. Mk1 aircraft took place on 4th February, 1955. Initially Bristol Olympus 100 engines were fitted with the wing planform identical to that of the first prototype aircraft.

On 18th June, 1955 (XA889) made a flypast at the Paris Airshow and appeared at the 1955 S.B.A.C. Show at Farnborough. During October 1955 it was grounded to enable the wing leading edge modification to be incorporated and auto-stabilisation system fitted. Flight testing recommenced in mid February 1956. After a series of check flights, the aircraft was fitted with Olympus 101 engines and delivered to the A.&A.E.E. to begin its official trials on 15th March, 1956 for the official C.A. release of the Vulcan B.Mk1. The release was issued by the Ministry of Supply on the 29th May, 1956.

The aircraft was then allotted for Olympus development at Patchway Bristol. On 12th June, 1956 it returned to Woodford for fitment of Olympus 102 engines. On the 3rd January, 1958 it was fitted with Olympus 104 engines and on 4th February, 1958 went to Boscombe Down A&AEE for clearance of the these engines. In April 1958 it went to Bristol's for further development work on the Mk.104 Olympus engines. On 25th November, 1959 it was then re-allotted for engine development and structural strain gauge testing and tests on the revised wing leading edge. In 1965 it was to escort a Buccaneer on a transatlantic flight after being used for conventional armament, radio and navigation trials at Boscombe Down since delivery to the A&AEE in November 1962. After ASV.21 radar trials in 1965 it was struck off charge as scrap at Boscombe Down on 25th August, 1967.

The first production aircraft XA889 prior to its first flight.

First flight of XA889 4th February, 1955 from Woodford.

Different views of the first production aircraft XA889 4th February, 1955. After various trials which included conventional weapon evaluations in 1962, it was struck off charge for scrap in 1967.

The first production aircraft XA889 in finals at Woodford, June 1955. This rare picture also shows Canberra WD391 used for trial installation of a bomb carrier. Avro also built 75 Canberra aircraft under licence. Incidentally Canberra WD952 in 1952 was the first aircraft to be powered solely by the Bristol Olympus and on 4th May, 1953 broke the F.A.I. altitude record reaching a height of 63,668 ft.

Early progress

In parallel with the C.A. release trials on the first production aircraft, the second production aircraft XA890 with an unmodified leading edge, was carrying out the essential radio tests for the initial C.A. release, it was never to be fitted with the revised wing. By this time a number of production aircraft had flown and earlier aircraft were fitted with the kink leading edge and extended engine nacelle intakes which became standard on subsequent aircraft along with essential modifications arising from the prototype and first production aircraft flight trials.

XA889 at Woodford 4th June, 1955.

A nice side view of XA891 flying above the clouds 4th October, 1955.

XA892 at Farnborough streaming the breaking parachute. By using the Vulcan large wing it was found that by using aerodynamic braking there was no need to use the parachute to slow the aircraft.

Shown above a series of pictures showing the third production Vulcan XA891 pictured on 4th October, 1955. It first flew on 22nd September, 1955 with Johnny Baker at the controls. On 31st January, 1957 it went to A.V. Roe at Langar for preparation of the B.O1.6 Olympus series 200 trials. On a test flight from Woodford the aircraft was to crash at High Hunsley, Cottingham, Humberside after major electrical failure on 24th July, 1959. At the time of the crash it had the new kink wing fitted.

1955 S.B.A.C Show -"Roly" rolls the Vulcan

The first public appearance of a production Vulcan caused quite a stir at the 1955 S.B.A.C. Airshow at Farnborough, when "Roly" Falk rolled the second production prototype XA890, which was on loan to Avro from the Ministry of Supply. This caused quite a sensation amongst the crowd, test pilots and Airshow organisers.

Second production aircraft XA890. Note it still had a pair of twin airbrakes beneath the wing.

This extract from Flight magazine gives a flavour of that moment. "The three V-bombers flew one after the other at the show, with J. W. Allam putting up some quite fast runs in the sky-blue second Victor. As he came past the horizontal tail could be seen to flex in the slightly turbulent air. Now in service with the R.A.F., the Valiant B.I was flown by Brian Trubshaw, who, despite the huge under-wing tanks, made some of the fastest passes at Famborough that year".

But it was the Vulcan that practically stole the show on the first three days by completing a splendid upward roll, it was a slow roll made upwards at about 30 deg to the horizontal, each time the commentator stressed that Roly was cautious and calculating. Roly was later told that he was to stop doing this manoeuvre by the Airshow organisers after complaints by Sir Frederick Handley Page and despite his attempts to be allowed to continue as he would have to change his air display routine with the inherent dangers due to lack of rehearsal. Roly had first practised the manoeuvre in XA889 at Woodford on 31st August, 1955 with a surprised Ted Hartley as his observer.

Film footage

XA890 upside down during it's roll at S.B.A.C. Airshow at Farnborough September 1955.

Part of the development programme

The second production aircraft XA890 had a distinguished career in the development programme of the Vulcan. It first flew on 24th August, 1955 and handed over to the M.o.S air fleet at Woodford. On the 27th April it went to A&AEE at Boscombe Down for radio and radar trials. It returned to Woodford on 5th June 1956 for preparation for Phase 2 radio and radar trials; these were continued at the A&AEE at Boscombe Down by September it had returned to Woodford for modifications.

In March 1957 it was performing radio compass trials at Boscombe Down before it returned to Woodford for preparation armament trials. The aircraft was used for trials with 2000, 6000 and 7000 bombs during 1958 at RAE Farnborough. On 2nd February, 1959 it returned A. V. Roe for preparation of Red Beard Mk2 tactical nuclear weapon trials. In 1962 it was re-allotted for 'Rapid Blooming Window' and infra-red decoy trials. On 27th January 1964 it went to RAE Bedford for experimental take-off directors (TODs). It went to A&AEE Boscombe Down for Electromagnetic pulse trials on 26th October, 1968. It was Struck off Charge in 1969 at Boscombe Down for non flying trials and use for fire fighting training.

First prototype development

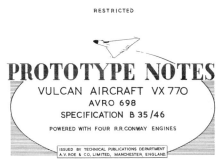

PROTOTYPE NOTES
VULCAN AIRCRAFT VX 770
AVRO 698
SPECIFICATION B 35/46
POWERED WITH FOUR R.R.CONWAY ENGINES

ISSUED BY TECHNICAL PUBLICATIONS DEPARTMENT
A.V. ROE & CO, LIMITED, MANCHESTER, ENGLAND.

This brochure was issued on the 23rd April, 1953 with the last amendment being made on the 27th February, 1958. This included notes on the fitment of four Rolls-Royce Conway power plants.

Since its first flight the first prototype Vulcan was subjected to continuous development to bring it up to production standard.

New engine for VX770

When the Avro 698 design was approved much thought was given to alternative power plants. The projected future development of these engines was one of the augments put forward for using the Bristol Olympus.

On the 18th January, 1955 VX770 was accepted off contract at A.V. Roe. It was then decided to fit the aircraft with Rolls-Royce Conway engines and was allotted for fitment on 8th June, 1956.

Modifications were made to engine mountings for fitment of Rolls-Royce Conway 5 and 11 power plants. The first prototype was never to be powered by the Bristol Olympus.

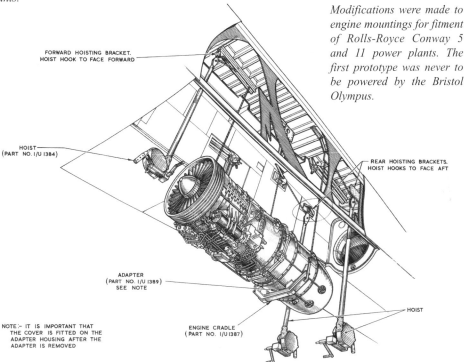

FORWARD HOISTING BRACKET.
HOIST HOOK TO FACE FORWARD

HOIST
(PART NO. I/U 1384)

REAR HOISTING BRACKETS.
HOIST HOOKS TO FACE AFT

ADAPTER
(PART NO. I/U 1389)
SEE NOTE

HOIST

NOTE:- IT IS IMPORTANT THAT
THE COVER IS FITTED ON THE
ADAPTER HOUSING AFTER THE
ADAPTER IS REMOVED

ENGINE CRADLE
(PART NO. I/U 1387)

ENGINE SLINGING – ROLLS-ROYCE CONWAY

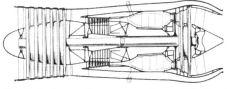

The Rolls-Royce Conway was the world's first by-pass engine.

Rolls-Royce Conway

As an alternative power plant to the Bristol Olympus it was proposed that the Rolls-Royce Conway by-pass engine, which had a similar power rating to the Olympus, could be employed. This led to the first prototype being converted to carry the Rolls-Royce Conway at the Avro Langar facility Nr Nottingham.

The first prototype (VX770) made its initial flight with four Rolls-Royce Conway R.Co5 engines on 9th August, 1957 and was flown to Woodford by Jimmy Harrison for handling tests. On the 24th August, 1957 the aircraft was delivered to the Rolls-Royce test facility at Hucknall, Nr Nottingham for development flying.

The basic concept of a bi-pass (turbofan) engine had been studied from the earliest days of jet engine design. Alan Arnold Griffith working at the Royal Aircraft Establishment had proposed a number of different by-pass engine designs as early as the 1930s. Griffith joined Rolls-Royce in 1939 and progressed these designs after developing the Rolls-Royce Avon. The first of these engines now known as the Conway ran in August 1952 as the R.Co.2 of 9,500lb. thrust. In July 1953, during the development of the R.Co3 a substantial increase in thrust was produced to a value of 11,250 lb. Full type tested approval was gained in July 1955 for the R.Co.5 which gave a thrust of 13,000lb, in fact it was to be flight tested on the Avro Ashton aircraft.

The Rolls-Royce Conway R.Co.11, a military rated version of the R.Co.10, was later selected to power the Handley Page Victor B.2 variant, replacing the Armstrong Siddeley Sapphire of earlier models.

VX770 appeared at the 1957 and 1958 Farnborough Air Shows crewed by Rolls-Royce personnel, but on the 20th September, 1958 it tragically crashed at R.A.F. Syerston during the Battle of Britain Display due to structural failure after being overstressed. The aircraft had built up to 800 hours as an engine test bed before the accident at Syerston.

VX770 arrives at Rolls-Royce, Hucknall.   *Tragic demise at Syerston.*

VX770 arriving at Rolls-Royce, Hucknall. The aircraft had flown from Langar back to Woodford on 9th August, 1957. Avro did a small amount of engine handling with Rolls-Royce pilots in the right hand seat before it was flown to Hucknall.

Proposed revised cockpit layout

This drawing from the prototype notes for VX770 shows the cockpit in a more conventional configuration to that on the original prototype and later aircraft.

Various modifications had to be made to the cockpit for provision of the Rolls-Royce Conway used on VX770. Amongst these was Mod 167 to introduce a flat wind screen in lieu of curved glass. Mod 464 was for an Mk.10 auto pilot - to provide roll error cut-out and change trim circuit from normal to emergency when the auto pilot was engaged.

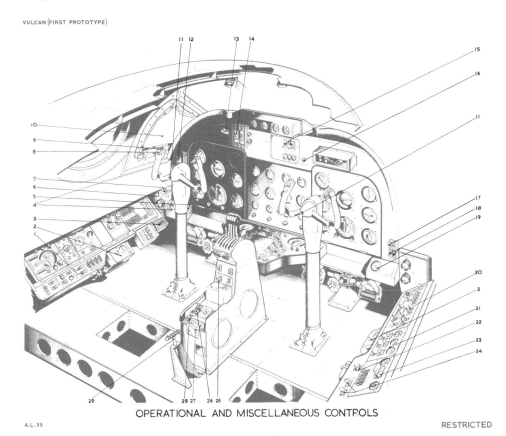

OPERATIONAL AND MISCELLANEOUS CONTROLS

1. Heated clothing switches
2. Oxygen regulator
3. Emergency decompression switch
4. Alighting gear indicator
5. Hydraulic pressure gauge
6. Photoflash door switch
7. Bomb door switch
8. Bomb release switch
9. "Press-to-talk" switch
10. D.V. window
11. Nose wheel steering switch
12. "Alighting gear fully extended" indicators
13. Air brake position indicator
14. Tail parachute switch
15. Windscreen demister switches
16. Tail bumper indicator
17. Windscreen wiper speed control switch
18. Pressure head heater switches
19. Cabin altitude indicator
20. Heating and ventilating control panel
21. Thermal anti-icing control panel
    (Not at present operative)
22. Heated clothing switches
23. Nitrogen control panel
24. Landing lamp switches
25. Air brake motor changeover switch
26. Alighting gear control switch
27. Alighting gear emergency air control
28. Bomb jettison switch
29. Crew's escape hatch handle-pull to close

VX770 structure described

Also in the prototype notes was a useful detailed description of the structure.

MAIN PLANE

This section contains a general description of the outer wing structure. The disposition of the spars and ribs within the structure is given on overleaf.

A descriptive and other details of the centre section, which is integral with the fuselage, have been included since the description of the main plane portion of the structure cannot be conveniently separated from that of the fuselage portion.

DISCRIPTION GENERAL

The delta main plane is a two-spar cantilever structure with main ribs between the spars and is built in two outer portions, port and starboard, which are bolted to the shackles on the centre section.

In plan view the outer planes have a sweep back of approximately 50 deg. on the leading edge to delay the onset of the effects of compressibility; the trailing edge also has a slight sweep back. The complete main plane, which has sufficient depth at the roots to accommodate the power units and alighting gear, tapers in plan and elevation to the wing tips.

In the absence of a conventional tail unit, the elevators are mounted in the outer planes and extend from the centre section/wing transport joint to a main hinge rib slightly more than half way along the wing trailing edge, the ailerons extend from this rib to the wing tips. As a safety precaution, the elevators and ailerons are each divided into two half sections, each half being operated by a separate electro-hydraulic powered control unit. Should a power unit fail its associated surface will trail to a neutral position but the remaining half surface will still be operative. The control surface leading edges are sealed to the main plane with rubberised fabric sheeting to provide internal balances which relieve the control operating loads. Electrically operated air brakes are mounted in the centre section above and below the engine air intakes.

WING STRUCTURE
Front spar

The front spar is built up from an upper and. a lower boom of machined, extruded stepped T-section aluminium alloy with a plate web between. Bolted to the rear faces of the booms are small brackets which form the attachments for the spar ribs. Secured to the root ends of the booms with $1\frac{1}{9}$ in.dia. B.S.F. joint pins are stainless steel reinforcing plates which are bushed to accommodate the centre section shackle pins. On assembly the $1\frac{1}{8}$ in dia. pin nuts are torque loaded to 124 (min) - 170 (max.) ft. lb. and, together with the plates, are coated with protective PX - 9 (Stores Ref. 34,B/923) against rust.

The plate web, in five sections of diminishing thickness outboard and joined together with strengthening plates, is of 9 s.w.g., 13 s.w.g.,13s.w.g.,16s0w.g., and 18 s.w.g., aluminium-alloy sheet from the inboard to the outboard ends respectively. Riveted to the web plates are vertical angle-section stiffeners which also form the attachments for the leading edge nose rib sub-assembly. The spar web has flanged holes towards the outboard end to permit the exit of air from the leading edge de-icing system.

Rear spar

The rear spar is similar in construction to the front spar consisting of machined extruded booms and web plates. Small pressed ribs attached to its aft face support the control surface shroud on the top surface and accommodate the bottom shroud which is hinged for ease of access to the control surfaces.

Ribs

The front and rear spars are joined by six heavy section main ribs flanked by secondary ribs. The main ribs are constructed from an upper and a lower channel-section boom joined by a double web plate and extensively reinforced with top-hat section stiffeners to carry the control surface hinge loads.

Between the three inner main ribs are light-alloy ribs of rolled angle-section edge members joined by a web plate to which vertical, top-hat section stiffeners are riveted. These ribs have large elliptical holes, the edges of which are reinforced with angle members and skinned with light-alloy sheet plate to form the fuel tank tunnels.

Outboard of the third main rib the secondary ribs are constructed of angle-section edge members with plate webs and vertical, top-hat- section stiffeners.

Skin plating

Over the area between the spars the covering consists of sub-assembled skin panels running span wise and having their stringers riveted to the skin plating in the detail production stage. The attachment brackets of the stringers are then riveted to the ribs and the edges of the skin panels butt jointed on T-section stringers.

Leading edge assembly

The leading edge assembly, containing the thermal de-icing ducting, is constructed of pressed channel-section nose ribs riveted to the front spar and covered with a double skin. The inner skin is corrugated to distribute de-icing air and is riveted to the outer skin which is of 14 s.w.g. aluminium alloy.

Trailing edge assembly

Aft of the rear spar is the trailing edge assembly consisting mainly of extensions to the six main ribs which carry the hinges of the control surfaces. Between the hinge ribs and riveted to the rear spar are diaphragm members which, together with transverse angle-section members, form the attachment for the curved portion of the shroud.

On the upper surface of the trailing edge are fixed shroud panels of double skin construction consisting of an outer, light-alloy skin plate with an inner corrugated skin. Below are the hinged portions of the shroud which are again of double skin construction.

AILERONS

Each aileron is divided into two half sections, each section having its own power control unit so that should one unit fail sufficient surface is available to control the aircraft, the failed section will trail to a neutral angle.

Each half aileron is carried on the wing trailing edge ribs by a pin and ball race hinge at each end; the outer half also has a central main hinge of a similar type. The sections are built up of forward and rear spars with pressed ribs between. The front spar which carries beaked nose ribs consists of an upper and a lower stepped T-section extruded boom joined by a plate web with channel-section member reinforcement. The rear spar, a channel-section member, forms the attachment on its forward face for the main ribs; on the rear face are flanged trailing edge riblets. Between the spars the ribs are pressed members with flanged lightening holes and angle section members on their edges for the attachment of the skin plating.

Over the ailerons the covering is of magnesium skin plating. Mass balancing of the ailerons is effected by mild steel and lead plates bolted on the leading edges.

Disposition of spars and ribs within the structure

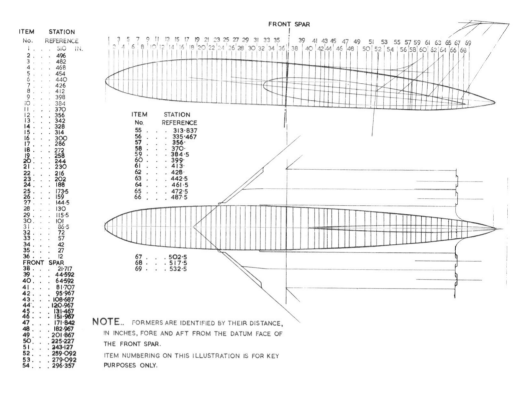

ITEM No.	STATION REFERENCE
1	510 IN.
2	496
3	482
4	468
5	454
6	440
7	426
8	412
9	398
10	384
11	370
12	356
13	342
14	328
15	314
16	300
17	286
18	272
19	258
20	244
21	230
22	216
23	202
24	188
25	173·5
26	159
27	144·5
28	130
29	115·5
30	101
31	86·5
32	72
33	57
34	42
35	27
36	12
FRONT SPAR	
38	21·717
39	44·592
40	64·592
41	81·707
42	95·967
43	108·687
44	120·967
45	131·467
46	151·967
47	171·842
48	182·967
49	201·867
50	225·227
51	243·127
52	259·092
53	279·092
54	296·357

ITEM No.	STATION REFERENCE
55	313·837
56	335·467
57	356·
58	370·
59	384·5
60	399·
61	413·
62	428·
63	442·5
64	461·5
65	472·5
66	487·5
67	502·5
68	517·5
69	532·5

NOTE.. FORMERS ARE IDENTIFIED BY THEIR DISTANCE, IN INCHES, FORE AND AFT FROM THE DATUM FACE OF THE FRONT SPAR.

ITEM NUMBERING ON THIS ILLUSTRATION IS FOR KEY PURPOSES ONLY.

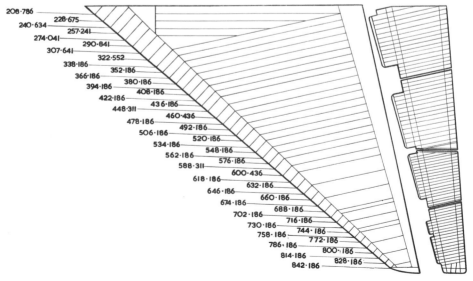

TAIL UNIT

With the exception of a detachable tip of composite construction, and the magnesium alloy webs of the ribs, the fin structure is built, in aluminium alloy, of a front and rear post joined by plate ribs.

Forward of the fin front post is the leading edge assembly, consisting of nose ribs with plate webs and angle- section stiffeners suitably cut away and flanged to accommodate vertical skin plating, which forms the ducting of the thermal de-icing system. The leading edge assembly has an inner skin which is corrugated to distribute de-icing hot air and is riveted to an outer skin.

Fin posts

The fin forward post comprises a port and a starboard machined, extruded, T-section boom joined by doubling plates to a plate web. Top-hat section stiffeners are riveted at intervals along the web. A circular aperture reinforced with a doubling plate and angle-section stiffeners in the lower end of the web provides access to the fuselage attachment bolts.

The fin rear post is similar in construction to the forward post but angle-section stiffeners are utilised along the web plate.

Ribs

Between the fin posts are three main ribs (ribs 3, 11 and 18) which carry the rudder hinge loads and are each constructed from two lipped-channel-section booms joined by two web plates and reinforced with angle-section stiffeners.

Flanking the hinge ribs are secondary ribs consisting of a plate web, containing flanged lightening holes, edged with angle-section members and carrying plate-type skin attachment brackets.

The final rib at the top of the fin (rib 20) is constructed to carry the fin tip and consists of a plate web with angle-section stiffeners. Anchor nuts in the edge members accommodate the securing screws of the fin tip.

Shroud

Behind the rear spar are diaphragm members to which the curved portion of the shroud is riveted. The trailing edge is completed by a port and a starboard Frise fairing which together with the curved shroud form a balance chamber. To facilitate servicing of the hinge attachments and the rudder sealing fabric, the port fairing is mounted on hinges.

Skin covering

The fin is covered by sub-assembled magnesium alloy skin panels having their stringers riveted to the skin plating in the detail production stage. The stringers are then riveted to the rib attachment brackets. Z-section stringers are employed except at the skin butt joints where T- section is used.

Fin Cap

The fin cap is a one-piece moulding constructed of five layers of Durestos, a Phenolic impregnated asbestos felt with reinforcing layers in the crown of the moulding to avoid erosion, or moisture loading due to capillary action, the cap is treated with Neoprene both inside and outside. The lower edge of the tip is reinforced with an extra layer of Durestos bolted between inner and outer plate members. The plates are, in turn, secured by 3/16 in. dia. B.S.F. screws to the anchor nuts on rib 20 of the fin.

RUDDER

The all-metal rudder is constructed in magnesium alloy, with the exception of the main spar which is of aluminium alloy and consists of a main spar and a channel-section rear member joined by plate ribs.

The main spar is built up from an upper and a lower extruded boom with a plate web, which has flanged lightening holes and angle-section stiffeners to form the attachment for the ribs; the rear member is a straightforward channel section.

Between the spar and rear member are the main ribs consisting of a plate web, with flanged lightening holes, fluted for additional stiffness. Riveted to ribs 18 and 35 are forged steel brackets housing roller bearings which accommodate the bolts forming the centre and top hinges to the fin ribs.

Forward of the front spar are D-section nose ribs Channel-section members riveted chord wise to the ribs carry mass balance weights of lead strip and also form the attachment for the fabric sealing to the fin shroud.

The trailing edge is completed by channel-section riblets attached at their forward end to the rear member and at the rear to a trailing edge strip member.

The whole structure is covered with magnesium-alloy skin plating.

MODIFIED AIR BRAKES

A large number of modifications were completed to bring the prototype to B.Mk1. production standard and to allow fitment of the Rolls-Royce Conway.

By this time VX777 had made its first flight in May 1955 with single airbrakes below the wing, this was done to Modification 170 for the deletion of the bottom O/B air brakes and stiffening of access doors and provision for three angles of airbrake, this conversion was extended to all production Vulcan's.

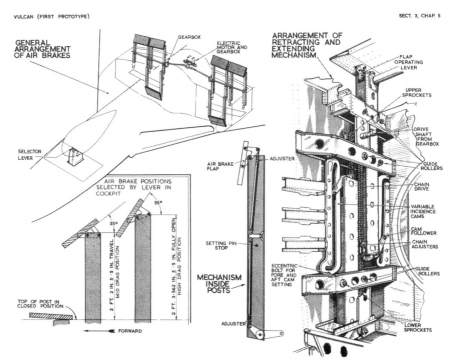

Engine weight change comparison first prototype

Weights	R A'3s *16.3.1947* **Target**	Sa 6's *21.9.1955* **Previous**	R.Co.7's *16.6.1957* **Present**
Total structure	38,054 lb	42,338 lb	42,307 lb
Basic operational	66,286 lb	77,781 lb	80,061 lb

Aircraft sections

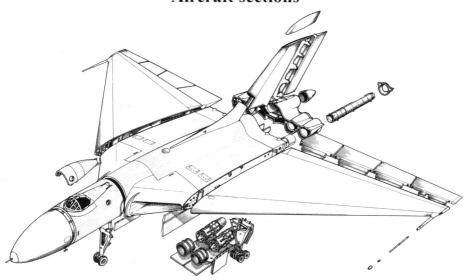

Access panels and doors

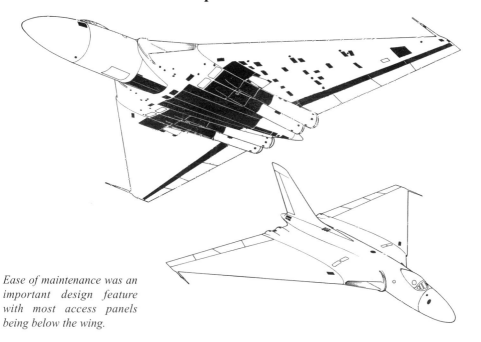

Ease of maintenance was an important design feature with most access panels being below the wing.

Weights and dimensions - B.Mk1

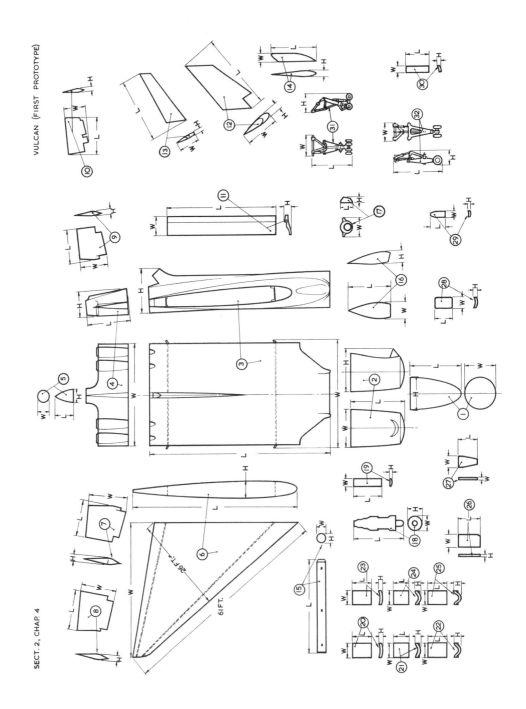

VULCAN (FIRST PROTOTYPE)

SECT. 2, CHAP. 4

ITEM	COMPONENT	LENGTH	WIDTH	HEIGHT	STRUCTURE TARE WEIGHT (lb.)
1.	Fuselage nose	13 ft. 3 in.	8 ft. 2 in.	8 ft. 2 in.	308
2.	Front section fuse]age	15 ft. 3 in.	9 ft. 2 in.	10 ft. 3 in.	2,106
3.	Centre section fuselage (including air intake and dorsal fin)	52 ft. 0 in.	28 ft. 10 in.	12 ft. 0 in.	16,517
4.	Rear section fuselage	9 ft. 0 in.	27 ft. 3 in.	6 ft 0 in.	903
5.	Tail fairing	5 ft. 0 in.	3 ft. 0 in.	3 ft 0 in.	81
6.	Main plane	50 ft. 0 in.	35 ft. 0 in.	5 ft 0 in.	6,007
7.	Inboard elevator section	9 ft. 6 in.	10 ft. 9 in.	1 ft. 8 in.	342
8.	Outboard elevator section	10 ft. 6 in.	10 ft. 0 in.	1 ft. 6 in	312
9.	Inboard aileron section	7 ft. 8 in.	7 ft. 2 in.	1 ft. 1 in.	198
10.	Outboard aileron section	10 ft. 0 in.	5 ft. 3 in.	1 ft. 0 in	231
	Bomb door (each)	29 ft. 3 in.	5 ft. 2 in.	8 in.	706
12.	Fin	21 ft. 0 in.	10 ft. 0 in.	2 ft. 0 in.	996
13.	Rudder	18 ft. 6 in.	7 ft. 0 in.	1 ft. 2 in.	328
14.	Fin capping piece	11 ft. 6 in.	2 ft. 3 in.	1 ft. 0 in.	82
15.	Jet pipe	21 ft. 0 in.	2 ft. 6 in.	2 ft. 6 in.	352
16.	Canopy	10 ft. 6 in.	4 ft. 8 in.	2 ft. 6 in.	195
17.	Jet pipe cap	2 ft. 10 in	4 ft. 2 in.	1 ft. 9 in.	16
18.	Engine, (R R Conway)	10 ft. 8.8 in	3 ft. 8.45 in.	3 ft. 6.2 in.	3,675 (dry weight inc, starter Generator)
19.	Nose-wheel door (each)	9 ft. 6 in	1 ft. 9 in.	$3^1/_2$ in.	96
20.	Inboard engine doors - forward	5ft. 6 in.	4 ft. 0 in.	$3^1/_2$ in.	34
21.	centre	5 ft. 0 in.	4 ft. 0 in.	10 in.	39
22.	aft	6 ft. 3 in.	4 ft. 0 in.	11 in.	57
23.	Outboard engine doors forward	5 ft. 6 in.	4 ft. 0 in.	8 in.	33
24.	centre	5 ft. 0 in.	4 ft. 0 in.	1 ft. 0 in.	37
25.	aft	6 ft. 3 in.	4 ft. 0 in.	1 ft. 1 in.	54
26.	Main-wheel door	6 ft. 6 in.	4 ft. 9 in.	6 in.	$139^1/_2$
27.	Main-wheel fairing	5 ft. 4 in.	3 ft. 8 in.	4 in.	$37^1/_2$
28.	Entrance door	5 ft. 0 in.	2 ft. 9 in.	1 ft. 0 in.	162
29.	Tail-bumper door	2 ft. 8 in.	1 ft. 10 in.	3 in.	5
30.	Photoflash door (each)	7 ft. 0 in.	1 ft. 2 in.	$2^1/_2$ in.	1 2
31.	Main-wheel unit	12 ft. 8 in.	5 ft. 0 in.	6 ft 0 in	2,231 per side
32.	Nose-wheel unit	13 ft. $2^1/_2$ in.	3 ft. 6 in.	3 ft. $1^1/_2$ in.	876

New wing for VX777

In July 1955 VX777 was grounded for fitment of the first 'Phase 2' wing. It made a short circuit of the airfield with this wing on 4th October, 1955 with Roly Falk at the controls. Further flights continued to confirm the results of Jimmy Harrison's testing in the 707A.

The flight trials on the 707A and the earlier tests on the prototype Vulcan had indicated the need to incorporate auto-stabilisation systems. These systems, (yaw damper, pitch damper and Mach trimmer) had been designed especially for the Vulcan and were fitted to the VX777 in November 1955. The flight development of these systems was the major task for the second prototype between November 1955 and June 1956. This work took just over 100 hours flying in approximately 70 flights.

The second prototype VX777 with its new kink wing layout at Woodford 30th December, 1956.

First flight of the second prototype VX777 with the new Phase 2 wing was on 4th October, 1955. It is seen here taking-off from Woodford 10th October, 1955.

B. Mk1 production aircraft with Phase 2 wing

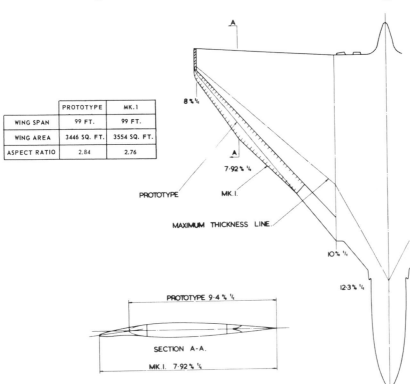

	PROTOTYPE	MK.1
WING SPAN	99 FT.	99 FT.
WING AREA	3446 SQ. FT.	3554 SQ. FT.
ASPECT RATIO	2.84	2.76

It was found that by fitting vortex generators near the wing leading edge it re-energised the boundary layer giving a substantial gain in lift coefficient. They formed a row of sixteen at 25 per cent chord, spaced 22.5 inches apart inboard of the leading edge kink and at half spacing outboard of it. The Phase 2 wing started on the ninth production aircraft, the rest were retrofitted to most of the first eight aircraft. Production halted whilst the leading edge envelope jig was scrapped and sixteen sets of the straight wing leading edge modified to the new version.

XA889 with new kink wing at Woodford 13th February, 1956.

Early production aircraft

XA895 first flew from Woodford on 12th August, 1956 and delivered to 230 Operational Conversion Unit on the 16th August, 1956. On the 5th March, 1958 it returned to Woodford for ECM TI and flight trials. In 1965 the aircraft then went to RRE (Royal Radar Establishment) Pershore for development and trials of Red Steer Mk2. It was sold for scrap to Bradbury Ltd on 19th September, 1968.

Production Vulcan's at Woodford 19th May, 1956. Pictured along with a Vulcan ready to be painted are XA894, XA889, XA891, XA892, XA893 and XA896.

XA895 at Woodford 19th August, 1956.

Bewildered by the size of the Vulcan! A look into the future at Woodford 19th August, 1956.

Early versions of production Vulcan's never entered service with the RAF, they were used by various organisations and were development aircraft throughout their lives.

Post C.A. release summary

Following the initial C.A. release on 29th May, 1956 enabled the R.A.F. to commence essential flight and ground crew training, it was important to develop the Vulcan B. Mk.1 into an effective weapon system as quickly as possible. A number of early production aircraft were therefore used for these tasks.

The first production aircraft were used to clear successively the Olympus 102 and 104 engine installations. Performance and handling tests included the auto-stabilisation systems.

The second aircraft continued with the flight testing of the various radio and radar installations, the original straight leading edge being retained. All other production aircraft had the modified leading edge fitted either retrospectively or during initial build.

The third production aircraft after the incorporation of the drooped leading edge modification carried out various engine installation developments. These included fuel tank pressurisation, nitrogen purging and the clearance tests to use various fuels.

The fourth aircraft was allocated to carry out armament trials at the Aeroplane and Armament Experimental Establishment at Boscombe Down. A further production aircraft was allocated to carry out the clearance tests on the autopilot installation and the airframe de-icing system.

XA889 being flown from Boscombe Down in March, 1956 by Roly Falk during its official trials for C.A. release. The aircraft had vortex generators near the wing leading edge.

Showing the new wing to best advantage XA891 on 27th June, 1956.

Production line up at Woodford 19th August, 1956 shows XA898 with the new Phase 2 wing.

First B.Mk1 development aircraft with new wing

Looking on - Freddie Basset Avro technical representative 10th July, 1956.

Now with the kink leading edge wing XA895 on 20th September, 1956.

Keeping the neighbours happy - the second production aircraft XA890 at the de-tuners at Woodford 6th February, 1957.

XA891 take-off at Woodford in August, 1956.

Pictured here is XA891 the third prototype near Liverpool on 27th June, 1956 with its new wing.

PART FOUR

INTO SERVICE
B.MkI/Mk.IA

Production and support

A total of twenty five B.Mk1/1A aircraft were delivered, including the straight wing version. The successful introduction of the kink wing required sixteen straight leading edge wings to be modified.

The first production Vulcan contract for twenty five B.Mk1 aircraft was placed in 14th August, 1952 and were built to contract 6/Aircraft/8442(CB.6(a). They were allotted serial numbers XA889 to XA913 on 22nd July, 1952.

A further order was placed for thirty seven aircraft in September 1954; there were two amendments to this order. *Amendment (1), April 1956, was for thirty B.Mk1 and seven B.Mk2. Amendment (2), June 1957, was for twenty B.Mk1 and seventeen B.Mk2.* These twenty aircraft, set numbers 26-45 were allocated serial numbers XH475-XH532.

The aircraft were built in three batches, the first batch of five aircraft sets one to five XA889-XA893 were B.Mk1 aircraft. Batch two of twenty aircraft were both B.Mk1 & Mk1A aircraft with serial numbers XA894-XA913, with batch three of twenty aircraft XH475-XH532 sets 25-45 built to B.Mk1A standard.

On the 1st June, 1956 further contracts for eight B.Mk1 aircraft placed on 31st March, 1955 was amended to eight B.Mk2 aircraft and a contract for twenty four B.Mk1 aircraft placed on 26th February, 1956 was also amended to B.Mk2 aircraft.

First production Vulcan B. Mk1 XA889 in finals.

Early production assembly picure showing the second production Vulcan XA890.

Jig centre section at Chadderton 20th December, 1957.

Finals at Woodford 10th December, 1957.

This picture was taken from finals.

First production Vulcan XA889 on the production line 10th December, 1957 - seen here with it's the new wing fitted. Also seen alongside is XA896 which first flew on the 30th January, 1957.

Chadderton production line in full flow 21st November, 1956.

Production cockpit XA892 3rd April, 1956.

Assembly line at Woodford 7th January, 1957.

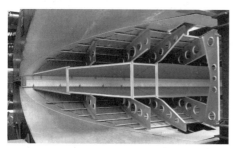

Thermal de-icing duct wing leading edge 15th June, 1956.

Outer wing skinning at Woodford 20th December, 1957.

Main assembly line Woodford 7th January, 1957.

Looking towards finals at Woodford. 10th January, 1957.

An high altitude test chamber was installed at Chadderton and could simulate all the pressure and temperature conditions which would be experienced throughout a flight under tropical, temperate or arctic conditions.

Crew trainer at Chadderton

High flying Vulcan photo feature

In 1956, a series of pictures were taken by chief photographer Paul Cullerne for publicity purposes showing a series of views taken from a Vulcan flying at high level, a role for which it was originally designed. One of these classic pictures was taken of the Isle of Man at approximately 50,000 ft. These pictures were taken on a trip round Britain on 22nd November, 1956. The aircraft was flown by Avro test pilot Johnny Baker. Paul took the pictures from the bomb aimer's position with a hand held camera he had built himself. At the time Paul laid claim that he had taken these pictures at a higher altitude than any other civilian photographer.

This picture of the Isle of Man appeared in the August 1957 issue of Avro news.

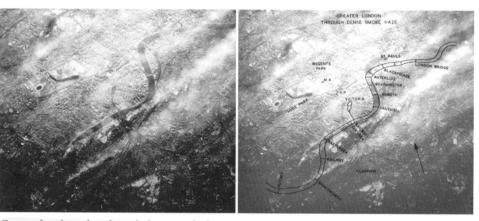

Greater London taken through dense smoke haze.

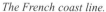

The French coast line.   *Coast line at 48,000 ft.*   *Snow covered area in Scotland.*

Tragic end to a triumphant tour

XA897 comes in to land at R.A.A.F. Avalon airfield in Australia.

The first flight of XA897 was on 10th July, 1956 and was allotted to 230 OCU but was never delivered. The aircraft was the first Vulcan to go overseas when it departed Boscombe Down on 9th September, 1956, staging through Aden and Singapore before landing at Kingsford Smith airport at Sidney in Australia. After some public displays, it went to New Zealand for more demonstrations and back to Australia. The aircraft departed from Darwin after completing a successful and notable visit.

On its return to the United Kingdom on 1st October, 1956, tragedy struck when in low visibility, misty rain and with the worlds press waiting, the aircraft hit the ground 2,000 ft short of the threshold whilst under the control of Heathrow ground approach (GCA) to runway 10L (Left) and in the attempted overshoot the aircraft banked slowly to starboard then dived into the ground at an angle of 20 to 30 degrees. The aircraft with Sq/Ldr Howard at the controls and Harry Broadhurst, who was one of the Vulcan's great supporters, in the second pilot's seat ejected from the aircraft with both surviving the crash. Freddie Bassett, who had only recently been married, was Avro's well respected technical representative perished along with Squadron Leaders A.E. Gamble, J.A.W. Stroud and E. J. James, who without ejection seats and the low level of the aircraft were unable to escape.

XA897 seen here in New Zealand alongside an R.N.Z.A.F. Vampire.

Air Marshal Sir Harry Broadhurst, A.O.C-in-C. Bomber Command survived the crash when he also used his ejection seat. Sir Harry was later to become Managing Director of A.V. Roe in 1961, taking over from J.A.R. Kay. He then became Chairman of the Hawker Siddeley Group. He is seen here pictured above with Jimmy Harrison and Sir Roy Dobson at Woodford on 26th March, 1956.

Squadron Leader "Podge" Howard from R.A.F. Bomber Command was attached to Avro and is seen here at Woodford with Avro Test Pilot Jimmy Harrison on 13th February, 1956. Both pilots survived crashes of a Vulcan.

Crash site at Heathrow.

New Chief Test Pilot

James Gordon Harrison, OBE, AFC
Chief Test Pilot 1958-1970

After serving with the R.A.F. during the Second World War, going on to command No.4 Squadron, in 1949 he joined the elite group of aviators selected to attend the Empire Test Pilots School at Boscombe Down on Course No.8 along with Bill Bedford, Ted Tennant and other famous pilots. Jimmy flew the latest types of the jet age going on to graduate with a distinguished pass and it was his exceptional flying skills that saw his appointment to the Aero Flight at Farnborough. This prestigious unit was engaged in testing all of the experimental aircraft types coming from the manufacturers at that time and his skill, recognised by his superiors, led to him being awarded an A.F.C. in 1952.

His testing of the delta-winged Avro 707 prompted a personal invitation from Sir Roy Dobson for Jimmy to join Avro as a test pilot to assist Falk in development of the Vulcan bomber.

Jimmy joined Avro in February 1954 and became Chief Test Pilot in 1958. In 1968 he was awarded the OBE for his role in the development of the Vulcan.

Jimmy was chief test pilot when pictured on 3rd June, 1960.

J.H. "Jimmy" Orrell
Chief Test Pilot 1947-1956

Previous to Jimmy Harrison being made Chief Test Pilot the post was held by Jimmy Orrell and later Roly Falk. After many nail-biting episodes Jimmy joined Avro in 1942 as a test pilot and helped guide the Avro Lancaster through its development. Between 1942 and 1945 Jimmy flew 900 different Lancaster's from Woodford and then went on to do all of the early test flying on the Lincoln which arrived just too late to see war service.

During 1947 he was made Chief Test Pilot for A.V. Roe and flew many of the new post-war jet aircraft including the Avro 707s, Avro Canada C102 Jetliner and the Vulcan.

In 1955 he became Superintendent of Flying for the Company's Weapon Research Division; Jimmy held that position until he retired in 1969.

In May 1956 he was awarded the O.B.E. for his services to aviation.

Jimmy Orrell left and below pictured with Avro chief test pilot Bill Thorn. Bill was tragically killed in the Tudor crash in 1947.

Olympus development for B.Mk1 Vulcan

The design of the Olympus series of engines can be traced back to a Bristol Aircraft Division requirement in 1946 for a high thrust engine, of 9,000 lb thrust. The design was for a long range, high flying bomber designated Type 172. Engine specification T.E.1/46 was issued by the Bristol Engine Division to meet this requirement. The first engine ran on 6th May, 1950 designated the B.01.1; it weighed 3,600 lb and gave a thrust of 9,140 lb. By November 1950 B.01 1/2 was running on a test bed producing a thrust of 9,500 lb.

The second prototype Vulcan (VX777) made its first flight on 3rd September, 1953 with four Olympus series 100 engines, which had been re-engineered from the derated Olympus 99 that had powered the high altitude, record braking, English Electric Canberra. Engine trials with the Olympus series 100 had began in the summer of 1952, with flight clearance being given in January 1953 at a lowly rating of 9,250 lb thrust.

The first production Olympus for the Vulcan was the Mk. 101 which produced 11,000 lb thrust at an overall ratio of 10.2.1, it received its type test certificate in December 1952.

Development work on the Olympus was also carried out on Avro Ashton WB493, these were 97, 97a, 101, 102 and 104 engines.

The 101 was up-rated to 12,000 lb thrust and re-designated the 102. By raising the turbine entry temperature it was found that a gain of 1000 lb thrust could be achieved and a conversion was made to all existing 102 engines, which were up-rated to 104 standard.

The 104 was initially rated at 13,000 lb thrust and type tested at that rating in December 1956 and flew for the first time in XA889. The aircraft had been delivered to Filton for development work on the 104 in July 1957. When the 104 entered service in the Vulcan B. Mk1 it had a rating of 13,500 lb. These developments of the Olympus were to lead to the re-design of the airframe of the Vulcan to accommodate the extra thrust from these engines.

A further development for the Vulcan was the Olympus 200 series, which was designed in parallel with the first production examples; the first of these engines the B.01 6 developed 16,000 lb of thrust. These new engines were fitted to XA891 at Filton in spring 1958, but development with this aircraft stopped when, on a test flight from Woodford, it crashed due to total electrical failure in 1959. A developed version the B.01 7 produced 17,000 lb of thrust and was produced in quantity for the Vulcan B. Mk.2.

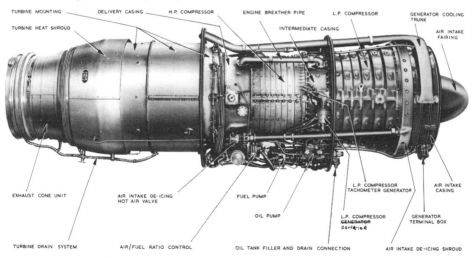

OLYMPUS 101 TURBOJET – STARBOARD VIEW   TP.2892

First production engine for the Vulcan.

Olympus 100 series

The Olympus was a two spool high pressure ratio engine that employed axial compressors individually driven by separate single stage turbines. Up-rated from Olympus 101 the 102 engine had a length from inlet to flange to exhaust outer cone of 152.2 ins with a diameter of 40 ins. Dry weight was 4,040 lbs. The combustion system had straight flow "Cannular" chambers, with ten separate flame tubes.

Section view of the Olympus 101 engine.

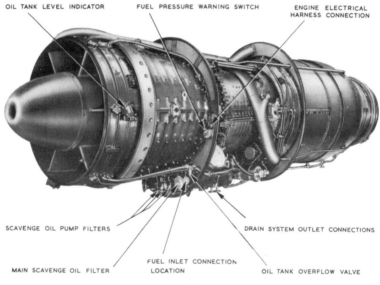

OIL TANK LEVEL INDICATOR   FUEL PRESSURE WARNING SWITCH   ENGINE ELECTRICAL HARNESS CONNECTION

SCAVENGE OIL PUMP FILTERS   DRAIN SYSTEM OUTLET CONNECTIONS

MAIN SCAVENGE OIL FILTER   FUEL INLET CONNECTION LOCATION   OIL TANK OVERFLOW VALVE

Secure embodiment loan compound at Woodford. The Olympus engines were financed to a Ministry of Supply contact and held at Woodford for fitment to the Vulcan.

FLIGHT PLANS WITH BRISTOL OLYMPUS ENGINES.

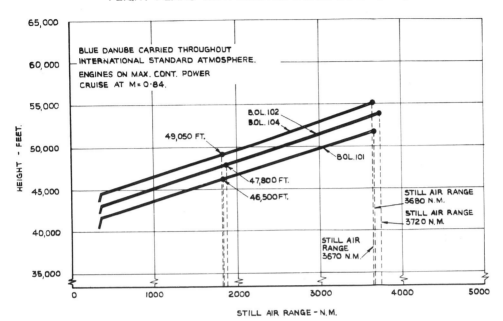

4 Olympus B.O.L 101 Engines (6450 R.P.M. 570°C J.P.T.) *Weight of store 10,000 lb.*
Weight less fuel & store 85,166 lb. Fuel weight 71,533 lb. Hangar weight 168,699 lb.
4 Olympus B.O.L 102 Engines (5890 R.P.M. 580°C J.P.T.) With 24 sq in trimmers.
Weight less fuel & store 85,822 lb. Fuel weight 71,533 lb. Hangar weight 167,355 lb.
4 Olympus B.O.L 104 Engines (6470 R.P.M. 590°C J.P.T.)
Weight less fuel & store 85,906 lb. Fuel weight 71,533 lb. Hangar weight 167,439 lb.

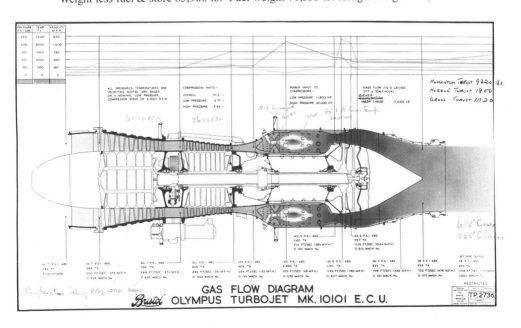

GAS FLOW DIAGRAM
OLYMPUS TURBOJET MK. 10101 E.C.U.

The Australian connection

A meeting was held in London in 1953 of the Commonwealth Advisory Aeronautical Research Council (C.A.A.R.C.), formed in 1946 with the objective of encouraging and co-ordinating aeronautical research throughout the commonwealth to avoid duplication. The committee recommended the approach to the United Kingdom for an appropriate research aircraft. With the reconstitution of the Australian Aeronautical Research Council (A.R.C.C.), in August 1954, a submission was made for an Avro 707 to be used for control of delta aircraft using boundary layer control. Boundary layer research had been carried out in Australia since the 1950's, following a recommendation of the C.A.A.R.C. in 1947.

On 21st March, 1955 discussions were held at A.V. Roe between senior officials of both Governments, which included discussions on obtaining a 707, both Roly Falk and Jimmy Harrison were at the meeting, by this time WD280 had completed an intensive test programme on a new wing planform destined for the Vulcan. By November 1955 it was decided to provided WD280 for further research into low speed handling of a delta wing aircraft and a meeting held at Woodford on 4th November, 1955 looked at the logistics of transferring the aircraft to Australia with provision of a spares package and support.

Following detailed financial discussions, which delayed the progress of the aircraft going to Australia, it was finally decided to loan the aircraft on a two year term.

After a complete overhaul, WD280 departed Woodford on 8th March, 1956 for Renfrew airport in Scotland with Jimmy Harrison at the controls and loaded on board H.M.A.S. Melbourne at King George dock, Glasgow on 9th March, 1956. The aircraft had completed a total of 283 hours 10 minutes flying time before going to Australia. The research programme was directed by the Australian Aeronautical Research Development Unit along with Avro. A 1/8th scale model was also provided and gave useful information on the validation of wind tunnel data. The aircraft flew until 1963 and is now preserved in Australia.

Pictured here on 8th March, 1956 prior to going to Australia.

WD280 leaves Woodford Australia bound 8th March, 1956.

A memorandum produced in March 1959 by the Australian Aeronautical Research Laboratory on wind tunnel tests on the 707A 1/8th scale model for force measurement and flow visual-isation. The report was for future reference of certain wind tunnel tests. The results showed that at high lift coefficients reversed flow occurred out of one of the intakes.

Proposed Vulcan for R.A.A.F.

PROPOSAL

FOR THE SUPPLY OF

AVRO VULCAN
Mark 2 Bombers

TO THE ROYAL AUSTRALIAN AIR FORCE

1ST · MAY · 1956

In 1954, the Australian Air Mission had prepared detailed proposals and costing to purchase twenty eight V-bombers which included the Avro Vulcan. In response to this request Avro produced a brochure on the B.Mk1 Vulcan to meet Operating Requirement OR/AIR/36 for the Royal Australian Airforce in November, 1954. The specification was almost identical to B.35/46 issued by the Ministry of Supply. The Australian requirements were met substantially and in many instances exceeded. The requirement was for an aircraft with a range of 5,000 n.m. with flight refuelling and included a rear firing 2x20mm cannon with automatic lock and follow defensive armament. The Air staff required the aircraft to be in service by mid 1959.

A further proposal was issued on 1st May, 1956 for the B.Mk2 version of the Vulcan. It stated that Avro had the back up of a large production facility and design organisation, extensive research facilities including a large flight test section and subsonic, transonic and supersonic wind tunnels and aerodynamic research establishments. The company also operated a Weapons Division engaged in the design and manufacture of guided missiles.

Avro gave prices for the supply of 25 standard B.Mk2 aircraft with either Olympus or Rolls-Royce Conway phase 3 engines. The total cost of both packages was over £22 million which included spares and ground servicing. The unit price of 25 standard Mk2 aircraft with four Bristol Olympus B.01.6 engines was quoted at £633,000. The Rolls-Royce Conway version was dearer at £693,000; further costs were to be discussed between Australian and U.K. Governments.

On 23rd February, 1955 Mr. A. G. Townley, Australian, Minister for Air and Civil Aviation took over the controls of the Avro Vulcan during a 35-minute flight from Woodford aerodrome.

During his visit he saw the Vulcans in production for the Royal Air Force.

Here he is shaking hands with Mr. R. J. Falk, Avro Superintendent of Flying, with Mr. J. A. R. Kay Avro Sales Director, looking on.

Royal Australian Air Force visit to Woodford 25th April, 1957. Hosted by Prince Emanuel Galitzine and Gilbert Whitehead.

Prince Emanuel Galitzine, was a direct descendant of Catherine the Great of Russia, later became sales manager at A. V. Roe Co. Ltd., in 1960.

Navigation attack system

During the second world war early bombers used new innovations in navigational aids these included Oboe, GEE-H (G-H) and GEE which used high powered transmitters based in the U.K. Limitations on accuracy meant that these aids were not very effective over long distances, so development was concentrated on a self contained radar that could be carried in the aircraft. A breakthrough came with the design of the resonant cavity magnetron in 1940, which was able to produce a pulsed output of 10KW. Further improvements led to the formation of the Telecommunications Research Establishment (TRE) led by (Sir) Bernard Lovell to exploit a technique which was known as H_2S. This radar first used a magnetron transmitter on a 9.1 cm wavelength with a rotating dish scanning aerial under the aircraft transmitting a narrow beam towards the ground. The reflected returns were presented on a long-persistence CRT screen so that an outline of the ground details remained until replaced by subsequent scans. A further innovation, known as Fishpond, was introduced to H_2S which used a second smaller CRT monitor to display radar returns arriving before the first ground returns. These returns which would be from other aircraft flying between the bomber and the ground, would serve as a useful warning of the possibility of attack from below.

At the end of the war there were several versions of H_2S up to Mk VIII. This latter version was superseded by the Mark IXA specifically designed for use in the Avro Vulcan and other V bombers. In the case of the Mk IXA the bombers were designed so that the radar system was an integral part of the nose section of the aircraft. The equipment was known as NBS (Navigational and Bombing System) and incorporated an Mk IXA 1-12 S linked to both an NBC (Navigation and Bombing Computer) and a vertically downward looking Doppler radar system (Green Satin) which calculated accurate ground speed and drift angles. A 6ft long radar reflector was fed by a 3 cm slotted waveguide from a magnetron with pulsed power up to 200 KW. The speed of rotation of the scanner was 8, 16 or 32 revolutions/min and it was both roll and pitch stabilised.

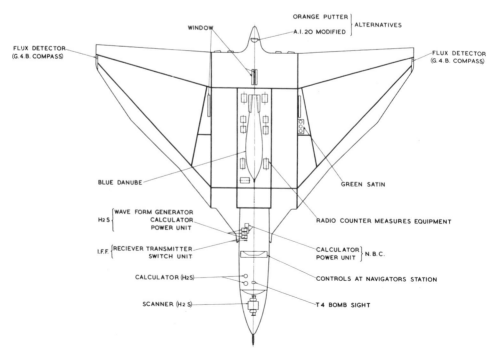

High level role

XA900 viewed from port side climbing to its natural environment.

By 1957 Vulcan's were painted in an anti-flash overall white colour scheme, in order to reflect the harmful effects of rays from a nuclear blast. With the increased high altitude performance of the Vulcan, crews were fitted with equipment suitable for these attitudes. With the introduction of the low level role of the Vulcan in the late 1960's and with the reliability of the pressurised cockpit crews reverted to normal flying gear.

Mk 3K ejector seat with pilot wearing early pressure suit for Vulcan B.Mk1 aircraft, 23rd June, 1954.

Vulcan crew pictured boarding XA889 on 29th January, 1958. The aircraft had returned to Woodford for fitting and clearance of Olympus 104 engines on 3rd January, 1958.

Baxter Woodhouse & Taylor Ltd, based at Woodside, Poynton, Cheshire provided Avro crews with high altitude pressure helmets. Helmets were custom made for each crew member.

Derek Bowyer from Inspection makes some final adjustments. Shown opposite is flight test observer Mike Turner 29th February, 1958.

The Phase 2C wing

In August 1955 the Vulcan B.Mk2 version was proposed and wing leading edge modification designed. The 'Phase 2C' wing as it was known was allotted to be fitted to VX777 and contract 6/Aircraft/13262/CB.6(a) was issued for an aerodynamic prototype on 10th July, 1956. The first flight of VX777 with the new 'Phase 2C' wing was made on 31st August, 1957.

VX777 makes a low pass with the new Phase 2C wing at Woodford on 23rd October, 1957.

VX777 pictured with its Phase 2C wing on 23rd October, 1957. Note the drooped leading edge.

Taken in the week before S.B.A.C. Airshow, VX777 shows the new wing to best advantage on 1st September, 1957.

Vulcan's to the fore

At the 1957, S.B.A.C. Show at Farnborough five Vulcan's were shown. Avro also showed models in the exhibition hall demonstrating the guided missile equipment by the Weapons Research Division. Two Vulcan's were entered by the Company, a production B.Mk1 flown by Roly Falk and the second prototype VX777 that had been converted to be B.Mk2 standard, flown by Jimmy Harrison. The aerodynamic prototype B.Mk2 had flown for the first time at Woodford on the previous Saturday, on a fifteen minute flight with Roly Falk at the controls. A third Vulcan was entered by Rolls-Royce piloted by Jim Hayward their chief test pilot, to demonstrate the power of the Conway engines which had been installed. Two other R.A.F. Vulcan's in company with two Vickers Valiant's flew in box formation.

In formation - XA907 was delivered to No.83 squadron 12th August, 1957 and XA902 from No.230 O.C.U. at Waddington which was later delivered back to Woodford on 2nd December, 1958 after the crash of VX770 for conversion to carry the Rolls-Royce Conway Mk108 engines. The Valiant was to become a familiar site at Woodford as five were allocated for Blue Steel missile development.

B.Mk1 takes-off at the S.B.A.C. Farnborough Airshow, some of the photographers got a bit too close.

B.Mk1 enters service

Air Commodore J. N. H. Whitworth station Commander at R.A.F. Scampton. He is seen here taking delivery of No.617 Squadrons first Vulcan B Mk1 XH482 on 6th May, 1958. He also acted at technical advisor on the 1955 film "The Dambusters"

When Roly Falk made a night arrival at Boscombe Down in the first production Vulcan, a series of acceptance trials began with A.&A.E.E. test pilots of (B) squadron. In fact Tony Blackman who later joined Avro as a test pilot was one of the pilots responsible of getting the best from the aircraft. At the time of the initial trials the first Vulcan station at Waddington was being manned in readiness for the delivery of production aircraft. The officers, N.C.O.'s and airmen were near the end of intensive courses of instruction some of which were conducted in the Avro Technical Training School at Woodford. These trials were completed in May 1956 and the Vulcan was ready to go into service.

The first operational unit was No.83 Squadron along with No.230 Operational Conversion Unit (O.C.U.) with both being based at R.A.F. Waddington. Another squadron reformed on 1st May, 1958 to operate the Vulcan, was the famous No.617 Squadron based at R.A.F Scampton. The Squadron received its first Avro Vulcan aircraft XH482 on 6th May, 1958.

XH504 flying over a snow covered countryside. The aircraft was delivered to No.230 OCU on 31st December, 1958 and No.83 Squadron on 19th November, 1959. It was delivered to Bitteswell for conversion to B.Mk1A in 1961. On the 2nd March, 1962 it was delivered to No.101 Squadron and in 1963 the Waddington Wing. It was struck off charge on 4th January, 1968 for fire fighting duties at Cottesmore.

Flying high - Waddington B. Mk1 Vulcan's before conversion to B. Mk1A standard, in formation XH480 and XA906 were pictured on 22nd August, 1958.

XA900 showing condensation trail caused by water vapour in the engine exhaust.

XA900 first flight was on 16th February, 1957 and entered service with No.230 Operational Conversion Unit (O.C.U.) on 25th March, 1957, it joined No.101 Squadron at RAF Waddington on 22nd June, 1960. It was later allocated to the R.A.F. museum at Cosford and was the last B.Mk1 to be scrapped in 1986. It is seen here pictured on 22nd August, 1958.

In service

The first of many - XA895 was delivered to No.230 O.C.U. at Waddington on 16th June, 1956.

Fine air to air picture of XA900 of No.101 Squadron.

This well known picture taken on 13th June, 1959 shows XH476, XH475 and XA909 from No.101 Squadron based at Waddington. The aircraft were now painted in the overall white anti-flash paint scheme.

B.Mk1 Vulcan
General Arrangement

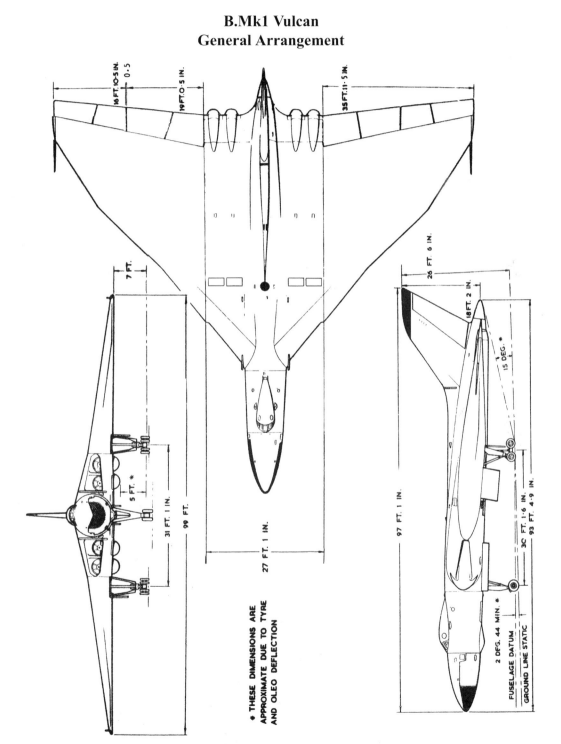

Aircraft dimensions – Mk.1 Aircraft

Weapons Research Division goes to Australia

Advances in the defence of the main targets that "V" bombers were to successfully deliver their weapons and for it to be a valuable deterrent was to lead Avro to look at stand-off weapons for the aircraft to deliver its load to increase its chances of survival. To meet this requirement a Weapons Research Division was established at Woodford in 1954.

Working to operational requirement OR1132, issued by the Air Staff on 3rd September 1954, Avro designed a stand-off missile to meet this prerequisite.

In February 1957 the Avro Weapons Research Establishment had chosen a site at Edinburgh field, Salisbury which was about sixteen miles north of Adelaide, in Australia and about 250 miles south from the test range at Woomera.

The site was chosen for testing the design of a new guided missile being built at Chadderton and at Woodford. The first batch of Avro technicians flew out in October and by the end of that year over fifty personnel had flown there. Trials began in August 1957 with two-fifths scale un-powered models being dropped from a Vickers Valiant; a scale powered model flew in February 1958. Vulcan B.Mk1 XA903 was allotted in May 1957 to carry the full scale version and arrived at Edinburgh airfield on 16th November, 1960. By this time the missile was publicly known as "Blue Steel" supersonic stand-off missile.

Pictured on 23rd January, 1957 beneath a Vickers Valiant is a test missile.

One third scale missile showing interior 13th August, 1959.

Seen here on take-off from Woodford B.Mk1 XA903 with Blue Steel missile on 3rd September, 1958.

Valiant five

In the March 1956 brochure on the B.Mk2 Vulcan, referred to later in the book, reference was made to a special store weighing 13,000 lb. Mission profiles were produced using the Olympus and Conway engines. The Bristol Olympus B.OL.6 profile is shown below, along with the Vickers Valiants used for missile development.

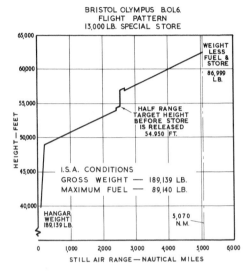

BRISTOL OLYMPUS B.OL6.
FLIGHT PATTERN
13,000 LB. SPECIAL STORE

WEIGHT LESS FUEL & STORE
86,999 LB.

HALF RANGE TARGET HEIGHT BEFORE STORE IS RELEASED 54.950 FT.

I.S.A. CONDITIONS
GROSS WEIGHT — 189,139 LB.
MAXIMUM FUEL — 89,140 LB.

HANGAR WEIGHT 189,139 LB.

5,070 N.M.

STILL AIR RANGE—NAUTICAL MILES

MAXIMUM CONTINUOUS POWER
USED FOR CRUISING, EXCEPT FOR
HALF AN HOUR IN THE TARGET
AREA AT MAXIMUM
INTERMEDIATE POWER.
STORE RELEASED AT HALF RANGE

Vickers Valiant's used for missile development

WP204   Arrived Woodford from Vickers 19th June, 1959. Went to Australia 15th August, 1960. Returned to Woodford 9th January, 1962. Left Woodford for No.4 School of Technical Training (SofTT) St. Athan 1st June, 1962.

WP206   Arrived Woodford from Marshall Aerospace, Cambridge 20th May, 1958. Returned to Marshalls 11th October, 1960. Marshalls to Woodford 7th July, 1961. Went from Woodford to Australia 12th October, 1961. Departed Australia for Woodford 27th May, 1963. Scrapped at Woodford September, 1964.

WZ370   Arrived Woodford from Marshalls 19th September, 1956. Went to Australia 16th July, 1957. Returned to Woodford 17th November, 1959. To Vickers 14th December, 1959.

WZ373   Arrived Woodford from Vickers 26th August, 1959. Went to Australia 27th October, 1960. Returned to Woodford 21st July, 1962. Scrapped at Woodford September, 1964.

WZ375   Arrived Woodford from Marshalls 5th July, 1957. Went to Vickers 25th February, 1959. Returned to Woodford 2nd March, 1960. Went to Australia 24th March, 1961. Returned to Woodford 17th February, 1963. Departed to Marshalls 25th September, 1963.

This rare picture shows Vickers Valiants at Woodford. They were used for early missile test flights.

XA891 incident

A familar sight to Vulcans crews as XA891 flies past Lincoln Catherdral on a early test flight.

On 24th August, 1959, the third production Vulcan B.Mk1 was on a routine test flight from Woodford with Avro test pilot Jimmy Harrison at the controls, when it crashed due to total electrical failure. The aircraft was a development aircraft for the Olympus B.01.6/35 engines, to contract 6/acft.15267/cb(6)a. Up to flight 95 the port two engines had a.c. alternators with Sundstrand drive units. For flight 95 to 100 a production Mk 200 engine was fitted in the port inner position with two B.01.6/3 engines starboard. These were fitted with d.c. generators for aircraft services. The engine air intakes were altered aft of the front spar to curve the airflow up into the new engine, the front of which were raised 5° above the Olympus 101 datum to accommodate the alternators etc.,

On board from Avro were first pilot Jimmy Harrison, second pilot R. G. "Dickie" Proudlove, Radio Operator R. S. "Bob" Pogson, Flight Test Observer E. H. "Ted" Hartley and from Bristol Siddeley Engines Ltd., Phil Christie.

As the Vulcan got into trouble, Harrison called to abandon the aircraft with the three rear crew being the first to leave with the last Bob Pogson just managing to escape due to the door entrance not being fully open. The two pilots managed to use their ejection seats, but all had difficulty due to wearing full pressure gear. The crew were wearing high flying gear at the time. This was one of the few occasions when all the crew were able to escape from a crippled Vulcan. Bob Pogson was no stranger to danger and uniquely he survived the effects of a nuclear blast, when the first nuclear bomb exploded on the Japanese city of Hiroshima on Monday, 6th August, 1945 as, at the time, Bob was a prisoner of war 1500 ft deep in a copper mine. Bob joined Avro's on the same day that XA897 crashed at Heathrow.

The crash of XA891 was caused by the 112 volt d.c. busbar shorting the frame due to installation failure; resulting in the loss of electrical power to all Power Flying Controls (P.F.C.'s).

Shown opposite is the radio recording between Woodford and Avro 4 (Jimmy Harrison) made by English Electric site at Warton, as Woodford did not have these facilities at that time.

Rear crew escape door and crew entrance on XA891.

The remains of XA891 in a field at High Hunsley, Cottingham, Humberside.

TRANSCRIPTION OF RADIO TELEPHONE RECORDINGS (AVRO 4) ON 24.7.59.
22.5mc/s (Recorded by English Electric Aviation, Warton)

Time G.M.T.

10.39.00	Avro 4-Woodford	Landing immediately.
10.40.20	Avro 4-Woodford	Yes, we are, electrical difficulties, trying to land immediately.
10.41.30	Avro 4-Woodford	Mayday, Mayday, Mayday.
		Indicating total electrical failure and flat battery. We are flying towards the East in case of having to bale out unless we can sort it out.
10.42.00	Avro 4-Woodford	Negative, had no time.
10.42.30	Avro 4-Woodford	Get Whitehead on the structural test specimen immediately.
I 0.44.30	Avro 4	Mayday, Mayday, Mayday, to Woodford.
		We are at 14,000 feet 200 knots 112 volt battery flat, half PFCs only. Stick fully forward at 200 knots and No.4 generator only which has already flickered once.
10.45.50		Yes we are going over again now.
10.46.00		Time check injected by Warton A.T.C.
10.46.31		Negative thank you Hucknall.

4-Woodford 123.3 mc/s

10.47.25	Indications are that 28 volts is O.K.
10.47.30	We have lost three rotaries.
10.47.55	That is correct and I have half PFCs working.
10.48.40	Zero on 112 volts.
10.49.38	Stand by.
10.50.40 to 10.51 .25	From Avro 4 to Woodford.

In summary the situation is we have No.4. generator only. We are on half PFCs, the 112 volt battery is indicating zero, the 28 volt battery indicating serviceable, the aircraft is unusually difficult to fly with the stick fully forward for 170 kts. at 16,000, any advice? We are reluctant to attempt a landing because the aircraft is not flying appropriate to the half PFC condition.

10.51.45	Stopped of their own accord & have now been switched off.
10.52.25	Negative, only on rudder when we inadvertently got both off.
10.52.35	It did.
10.53.15	Does Whitehead confirm that we are running half PFCs from one generator only without battery backing?
10.55.35	Say again?
10. 54. 00 to 10.54.15	I still want confirmation of my question, does it appear on the ground as though all PFCs that are working are running off one generator only? that is to say No.4?
10.55.55 to 10.57.20	Roger, our main difficulty the stick is very much further forward than is usual in a little over half PFC case. Will you confirm that the ailerons are standard in this aircraft now.
10.55.55	Now I am in danger of losing No.4 engine.
10.57.15 to 10.57.20	Avro 4 to Woodford. will you alert Waddington.

End of recording made by Warton, aircraft changed to 121.5 mc/s and following passage recorded by Preston Centre.

10.57 .30	Avro-4 to Waddington	Pan Pan Pan. Please give me a steer on this frequency immediately. I am in major electrical difficulty in Vulcan.
10.58.00	Avro-4	One eight zero.
10.59.00	Avro-4	Trying with difficulty to turn on to the course. We are at 13,000ft. Two crew members already gone.
10.59.12		Mayday Mayday Mayday. Baling out. (*End of Messages*)

Vulcan B.Mk.1A

The most visible change to the B. Mk1A was a flat plate antenna which was fitted underneath between the starboard engine jet pipes, a large refuelling probe to allow in-flight refuelling and rear fuselage which accommodated the new radar and Electronic Counter Measures (E.C.M.) equipment.

Other improvements included the higher powered Olympus 104 Series engine. The braking parachute was also repositioned. The main elements of the electronic suite were the Green Palm voice communications jammer, Blue Diver metric frequency jammer, Red Shrimp centimetric jammer, Blue Saga radar warning receiver, Red Steer rear-facing radar (adapted from the night-fighter Meteor) replacing the Red Garter and Orange Putter radar receivers. Decoy chaff dispensers were also fitted. These developments were used for both the B.Mk1A and B.Mk2 aircraft with variations on those aircraft equipped to launch Blue Steel.

B.Mk1A aircraft conversions

After delivery back to Woodford on 5th March, 1958, XA895 was used as a trials aircraft for the new ECM TI equipment, this led to the Vulcan being re-designated B.Mk1A. It first flew in this configuration on 5th January, 1960.

All B.Mk1A conversions were carried out at the Armstrong Siddeley, Bitteswell site at Lutterworth, Leicestershire. The first aircraft delivered for conversion were XH500 and XH505, both aircraft being delivered to Bitteswell on 13th July, 1959. The B.Mk.1A conversions were completed between 1959 and 1962, with the last deliveries in 1963.

Aircraft	Destination	Date Delivered
XH505	RAF Scampton	29.9.1960
XH500	RAF Scampton	19.9.1960
XH506	RAF Scampton	1.11.1960
XH904	RAF Waddington	24.1.1961
XA912	RAF Finningley	6.3.1961
XH481	RAF Finningley	5.5.1961
XH477	RAF Waddington	13.7.1961
XH483	RAF Waddington	25.8.1961
XH501	RAF Waddington	1.11.1961
XA913	RAF Waddington	28.11.1961
XH504	RAF Waddington	1.3.1962
XH478	RAF Waddington	8.2.1962
XH479	RAF Waddington	24.1.1962
XA907	RAF Waddington	3.5.1962
XH476	RAF Waddington	4.5.1962
XH497	RAF Waddington	22.5.1962
XA909	RAF Waddington	22.6.1962
XA910	RAF Waddington	18.7.1962
XA906	RAF Waddington	15.8.1962
XH482	RAF Waddington	31.8.1962
XH475	RAF Waddington	21.9.1962
XH499	RAF Waddington	11.10.1962
XH532	RAF Waddington	14.11.1962
XH480	RAF Waddington	22.11.1962
XA911	RAF Waddington	14.2.1963
XH502	RAF Waddington	22.2.1963
XH503	RAF Waddington	6.3.1963

XH505 at Finningley on 14th September, 1963. It was one of the first B.Mk1 aircraft to be converted at Bitteswell to B.Mk1A. Note the addition of refuelling probe and enlarged rear fuselage which housed the E.C.M. equipment.

XH478 at St.Mawgan. It first flew from Woodford 14th February, 1958. It is seen here with the top surface in camouflage.

Vulcan XH503 first flight was 30th September, 1958 and delivered to No.44 Squadron on 31st December, 1958. It was the last B.Mk1 to be converted to B.Mk1A standard at Bitteswell and was delivered to Waddington on 6th March, 1963.

Pictures via George Jenks

Canned Heat

A point of note is the difference between passive and active radar in aircraft and the beginnings of electronic warfare. For example the GEE navigation system was passive there was no radar transmission from the aircraft itself but only from the ground stations in the UK. However with H_2S the aircraft carried a powerful radar transmitter in the aircraft itself which could be detected by other enemy aircraft equipped a receiver. Famously the Lancaster bomber carried an early warning radar called Monica. The Germans successfully developed a passive radar receiver which managed to intercept the Monica radar emissions and guide German night fighters to their target. This led to advances in electronic counter measures used to confuse enemy radar and radio transmissions, which continued onto the Vulcan.

The new rear fuselage of the B.Mk1A housed the Electronic Counter Measures (E.C.M.) jamming equipment. The transmitters and power units were in large pressurised 'cans' and could get quite hot when in operation, these cans were kept cool by vapour cycle heat exchangers. On the starboard side of the E.C.M. compartment an air intake provided cooling air. Electrical power for the E.C.M. was provided by a Bleed Air Turbine (B.A.T.) powered by air taken from No.3 or No.4 engine and drove a 200 volt, three phase alternator. This was necessary because the B.Mk1 had a 112 volt DC electrical system. The B.A.T. was not needed on the B.Mk2 with its 200 volt AC system and its position, just aft of the starboard main wheel bay, was filled by a Rover gas turbine powered A.P.U.

All Electronic Counter Measures was controlled by the Air Electronics Officer. During one of the E.C.M. test flights a full test was made of the equipment which led to the black out of all radio and T.V. transmissions in the vicinity of the Vulcan. From that day onward cabinet approval had to be obtained before they could test the equipment.

The Red Steer tail warning radar was situated in the rear tip of the compartment and the brake parachute re-located under a hatch just to the rear of the rudder.

Rear counter measures equipment used on B.Mk1A and B.Mk2 aircraft

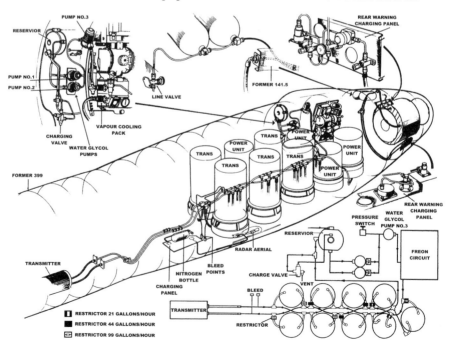

B.Mk1A Vulcan
General Arrangement

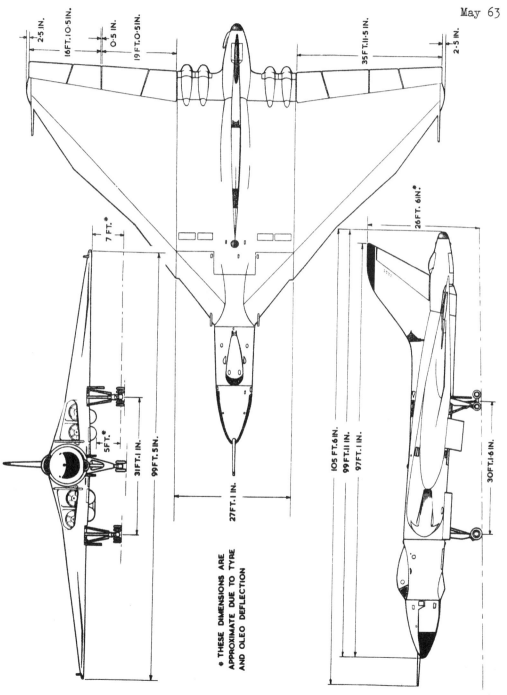

Aircraft dimensions - Mk.1A Aircraft

Vulcan B.Mk1A - Release to service

Copies to:- AD/RAF/B2, RDT.3, OR.1, RTO A.V. Roe (4.).

AEROPLANE and ARMAMENT EXPERIMENTAL ESTABLISHMENT

Our Ref:- APF/Rl.   15th February, 1960.
The Secretary, Ministry of Aviation,
RAF/B1(a),
St. Giles Court,
1-13,St. Giles High Street, London WC2

We recently carried out a series of tests on Vulcan XA895 which has been converted to represent the B.Mk1a version. The aircraft was fitted with the E.C.M. rear fuselage fairing and incorporated modified aileron control linkage. This linkage reverses the sense of aileron float with change of incidence from that on the Mk.1 and while this results in some loss of static stability it increases the elevator angle/g in manoeuvring flight, thereby permitting the use of the more c.g. positions which result from the introduction of E.C.M. equipment. Aircraft XA895 was fitted with Olympus Mk.101 engines and a Mach trimmer with only 6° elevator authority whereas Service Mk.1A aircraft will have Olympus Mk.104 engines and 7.4° authority Mach trimmers. The pitch damper installation was also modified to be effectively a twin limb system.

2.   Handling tests were made at a c.g. position of $0.328\bar{c}$, which is expected to be the practical aft most c.g. limit on Mk.1A aircraft, and in addition to the standard stability and control checks included autopilot functioning and simulated malfunctions of the pitch damper system. Tests were limited to a maximum Mach number of 0.98 I.M.N. from considerations of longitudinal instability. The Mach trimmer characteristics were not investigated because of the aforementioned difference between test and Service aircraft; it will be necessary to check these when a representative aircraft is available.

3.   The salient results are given below:

(a) Longitudinal control.

(i)   Though damping of disturbances in pitch with two or one pitch damper operating is satisfactory at indicated Mach numbers up to 0.98, the aircraft has only a small measure of positive damping at this Mach number with both pitch dampers inoperative. The firm's results show that damping is effectively zero at 0.99 I.M.N. without pitch damper assistance. Failure of both damper limbs must be considered as no warning to the crew of any failure is provided. It is recommended that the maximum I.M.N. be restricted to 0.95 for the Service to ensure sufficient pitch damping under all conditions. Up to this Mach number the consequences of the worst oscillatory fault in the pitch damper system are very mild.

(ii)   The reversal in direction of aileron float with applied normal acceleration has increased the elevator angle per "g" over that of the basic Mk.1 version with the result that the stick force per unit "g" with the c.g. at $0.328\bar{c}$ is now 22 lb at 300 knots and 10,000 ft. This compares with a value of 16 lb. with the c.g. at $0.309\bar{c}$ for the Mk.1 aircraft. In general it can be said that the elevator forces in manoeuvres are slightly greater than those on the Mk.1 for comparable loading cases and are therefore satisfactory.

(iii)   The rearwards movement of the c.g. position and aileron circuit modifications have resulted in some loss of static stability and at the test c.g. the aircraft was unstable above about 250 knots I.A.S. at 10,000 ft. and 0.85 I.M.N. at high altitude. Within the speed limits proposed the loss of stability is not considered to be serious and its chief manifestation is some increased difficulty in trimming the aircraft at cruising Mach number, as stated in paragraph 2, assessment of Mach trimmer effectiveness must await availability of a representative aircraft.

(iv)   The trim change with bomb door operation is small compared with that on the Mk.1, presumably as a result of the E.C.M. fairing and is controllable by a small stick force. The bomb door/elevator interconnection to minimise trim change with bomb doors opening which was necessary for Vulcan Mk.1 aircraft appears to be unnecessary for the Mk.1A. and should be deleted.

(v)   Operation of the airbrakes at high I.M.N. and high I.A.S. results in a strong nose down trim change. This trim change is slightly greater than on the Mk.1 aircraft, but at low I.A.S., the behaviour is very similar to that of the Mk.1. The behaviour is considered acceptable.

(vi)   The take-off, landing and slow speed handling characteristics are substantially similar to those of the Mk.1 version.

(b)   Autopilot Mk.10

(i)   Under autopilot control without height lock the aircraft is more difficult to trim than the Mk.1 and at 43,000 feet an oscillation of up to ± 150 feet and ± .015 I.N. may develop.

(ii)   At all altitudes the height lock controls the altitude precisely and its use is recommended for cruising flight whenever possible. A suitable method of approximating to the optimum cruise-climb would be by use of the height lock in a step-climb profile.

(iii)   At 43,000 feet and 0.88 I.M.N. the pitch change 5 seconds after selecting bomb-doors open was measured as 0.25° nose down, using a bomb door elevator compensation setting of zero. This attitude change is the maximum advised as tolerate by SP.970, leaflet 600/2.

It is recommended that the manufacturers carry out tests to establish the optimum setting for auto-pilot elevator compensation with bomb-doors opening.

(iv)   In view of the increase in elevator angle/g over the basic Mk.1 version it was not considered necessary to investigate pulse or ramp runaways of the elevator channel as these will in consequence be less severe than those already acceptable on the Mk.1. Oscillatory malfunctions of the auto-pilot elevator channel have no significant effect.

4)   **Conclusions and recommendations.**

Subject to checks of the auto-Mach trimmer characteristics on a representative aircraft it is considered that the flying qualities of the Vulcan B.Mk1A are acceptable for Service use subject to the following limitations

Aft most c.g. position	$0.328\bar{c}$ (U/C down)
Maximum airspeed	250 Kts I.A.S. from SL to 20,000 ft.
	300 Kts I.A.S. above 20,000 ft.

Maximum Mach number with Mach trimmer and. pitch dampers functioning.	0.95 I.M.N.
Maximum Mach number with one or both pitch dampers inoperative.	0.95 I.M.N.
Maximum Mach number with Mach trimmer inoperative.	0.95 I.M.N.
maximum Mach number under autopilot control with Mach trimmer and pitch dampers functioning.	0.93 I.M.N.
Maximum Mach number under autopilot control with Mach trimmer or one or both pitch dampers inoperative.	0.90 I.M.N.
Maximum cross wind component for streaming tail parachute.	20 knots.

In the event of the gust strength being revised approximately or in overriding operational circumstances a maximum of 350 knots I.A.S. is permissible from handling considerations. As for Mk.1 0.90 I.M.N. should not normally be exceeded.

All other current Vulcan Mk.1 limitations are applicable.

It is requested that the first Service aircraft converted to Mk.1A fit be made available to this establishment for the outstanding brief tests mentioned within this letter.

Conway development continues

Stripped down XA902 on 19th May, 1958.

Vulcan XA902 first flew 13th April, 1957 and delivered to No.230 O.C.U. at Waddington on 9th May, 1957. It was badly damaged in a landing accident on 28th February, 1958 whilst serving with No.83 Squadron.

With the loss of VX770, Rolls-Royce needed to continue the development of the Conway jet engine and XA902 was chosen for this purpose. The aircraft had returned to Woodford by road for repair and fitted with Rolls-Royce R.Co11 engines, all the required modifications were also carried out at Woodford, which included a complete new nose section from Chadderton. It was delivered to Rolls-Royce Hucknall airfield on 17th July, 1959.

Rolls-Royce had made a strong bid to put the Conway into the B.Mk.2 Vulcan, it was argued to achieve commonality with the Victor B2 and to widen its sale to airlines.

The aircraft went for tropical trials of the Conway and on completion of endurance trials the new Rolls-Royce Spey engine was located in the outboard engine positions. On completion of the Spey trials the aircraft was dismantled at Hucknall by No.60 Maintenance Unit (MU) and then transported by road to Dishforth during 1963 for subsequent scrapping.

Conway engine installation.

Crash site at Waddington of Vulcan B. Mk1 XA902 on 28th February, 1958.

In-flight refuelling

Another significant development of the B.Mk1A and B.Mk2 was the incorporation of a flight refuelling system. Although proposals for flight refuelling dates back to early studies for the Type 698 it wasn't until 1959 that this facility was tried. Vulcan XH478 was used for testing this system along with Valiant B1 tanker WZ376 during June 1959 and April 1961. Clearance trials for the B.Mk2 Vulcan were later completed on XH538 during the first three months of 1961.

Flight refuelling significantly increased the range of the Vulcan as witnessed by the Vulcan during the Falkland Islands conflict with Argentina when XM606 flew from Ascension Island and dropped a full load of bombs on Port Stanley airfield, flying over 7,778 miles in sixteen hours.

Vulcan XH478 refuelling from Vickers Valiant WZ376 during a test flight on 26th June, 1959.

The last flying Vulcan XH558 seen in its early colour scheme. It first flew from Woodford on 25th May, 1960. The aircraft was on a systems check when the picture was taken. Below the fuselage can be seen the Ram Air Turbine (RAT) which was used to provide emergency electrical power in the event of engine failure, once lowered the RAT could not be retracted

PART FIVE

B.Mk2 DEVELOPMENT

The ultimate Vulcan

The first production B.Mk2 XH533 pictured on 9th September, 1958.

In June 1955 a report looked at a further extension of the phase 2 outer wing. The proposal of the phase development was not tied to any particular engine or the ability to carry a stand-off bomb, as the centre section of the aircraft which contained the bomb bay and engine remained substantially unchanged.

March 1956 brochure

An early brochure issued in March 1956 described the aircraft as a high altitude long range bomber powered by four Olympus B.01.6 jet engines of 16,000 or 16,500 lb each depending on which engines were installed also quoted were four Rolls-Royce Conway's stage 3 at 16,500 lb at sea level static thrust. Cruising altitude was quoted as being 45,000ft - 65,000ft with a cruising speed of 500 knots. Range was with a normal 10,000 lb load or 13,000 lb special store was 5000 to 5,500 n.m. Provision was to made for serial aerial refuelling, either as a tanker or receiver. The gross weight had increased to 190,000lb. A full structural strength testing programme was being undertaken at the time the brochure was printed and calculations showed that the specified weight of 190,000lb would be fully met.

The wing span had increased to 111ft and a new A.C. electrical system fitted. Another major change was made to the flying controls from elevators and ailerons. These were in the form of four elevons spit outboard and inboard on each wing. The term elevon was a combination of elevator & aileron. The rear E.C.M. kit fitted to later B.Mk1A aircraft was not included in the brochure.

An artificial stability system was included in the form of a pitch damper system at altitude in excess of 20,000ft. An auto-mach-trim system was introduced to counteract the tendency towards instability and designed to leave the pilot with impression of an aircraft with positive static stability throughout. The natural stability of the aircraft in yaw was supplemented by the introduction of a yaw damping system to fulfil the stringent requirements of various roles.

Also mentioned was reference to a special store weighing 13,000 lb, no illustration was included in the brochure.

B.Mk2 contract review 1957

Items listed in Ministry contract S.P.6/aircraft/11301/CB.6(a)

(a)   Modified wing completed with control services.

(b)   Strengthened centre section.

(c)   Power flying controls to suit A.C. electrical system.

(d)   Strengthened main undercarriage.

(e)   Revision of de-icing system.

(f)   Revision of radio and radar cooling

(g)   Pressurisation of radio and radar cooling.

(h)   Changes to emergency decompression system to suit increased rate of
        decompression at higher altitude.

(i)   Possible changes to operational equipment (supplied by Ministry of Supply) for
        operation at higher altitude.

(j)   Introduction of revised integrated auto-stabiliser equipment (yaw pitch and auto
        trimmer) superseding Modification No. 240.

(k)   Modified rudder and elevator artificial feel units (cast box type) incorporating
        failure warning.

(l)   Aileron artificial feel units incorporating failure warning.

(m)   Pressurised rudder power units.

(n)   Introduction of firewire resetting detector system for fuel tanks.

Required amendments dated May 1957

Installation of Bol. 106 Engines

Provision for high thrust engines etc.

Introduction of new A.C. fuel pumps for high thrust engines.

Provision of electrical troughs to facilitate retrospective fitment of Mod. 199.

Introduction of Auto-Pilot Mk.10a.

Smiths Military Flight Instrument System

Flight refuelling receiver version fixed fitting to cater for 1,000 G.P.M

Shortened nose undercarriage.

Introduction of T.4 bomb site and associated equipment.

The following modifications were to be included in all Mark 2 aircraft.

Mod

143   **Centre section wing** - Modification of front spar and No.2 tank for carriage of
        new store.

198   **Fuselage** - centre section - to modify rear end of bomb bay for carriage of
        new store.

199   **Armament** - to introduce wiring and equipment for carriage of new stores.

234   **Electrical** - Introduction of A.C. electric's system.

266   **Radio** - To revise mounting for amplifier Mk.1V.

276   **Primary Structure** - To introduce cadmium plating of high strength steel parts
        manufactured to close tolerance.

358   **Bomb Bay** - To modify crutch pick-ups to provide interchangeability for
        the carriage of 10,000 lb. M.C. Store.

New flying controls layout

Flying controls

A major change was to the flying control surfaces, from elevators and ailerons to elevons. The elevon control surfaces were operated independently by there own jacks and controlled from its own power unit, which was actuated by the common pilot's control on the input side. Failure of a power unit or jack will cause the corresponding section of the control surface to trail in the neutral position. The other three sections remain unaffected so that control of the aircraft at three-quarters of the full normal rate is then obtainable.

Conventional push-pull rods connected the control grips and rudder pedals to the power units. Artificial feel is provided to give a variation of stick force with control movement from the trimmed position. In order to give pleasant control forces and harmonisation over the speed range, the stick force rates are related to the response of the aircraft. An automatic stabilisation system was also incorporated as stated.

Air brakes

Six efficient air brakes were situated in the centre section wing and extend above and below the aerofoil. They were actuated simultaneously by a centrally mounted actuator with duplicated electric motors controlled by a three-position lever in the cockpit. In the two extended positions the air brakes were used for three main purposes. These were to achieve high rates of descent without exceeding the speed limitations, to effect rapid deceleration from high air speeds and to give additional drag on the approach and landing.

Braking parachute

One 24-foot diameter ribbon parachute was installed on the starboard side of the tail fuselage below the rudder. It is provided primarily for use in emergency landings such as a return to base soon after take-off. The position of the parachute installation changed when the new rear fuselage E.C.M. was a fitted.

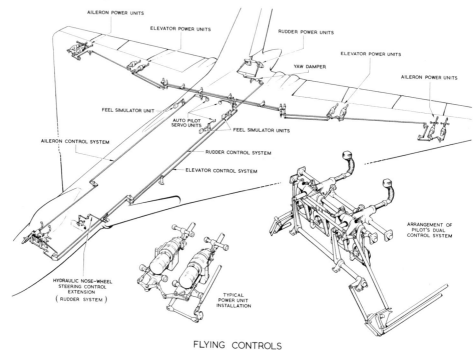

FLYING CONTROLS

New electrical system

The electrical power was supplied by four 40 KVA, 200 volt, 3 phase, 400 cycles A.C. engine driven alternators arranged to supply either independently or in parallel via a synchronising ring mains system. Reserve power was supplied by the Ram Air Turbine (R.A.T.) at high altitude and then by the auxiliary power unit below 30,000 ft.

115 volt, 400 cycles A.C. supplies is provided by means of various transformers from the 200 volt supplies, and 115 volt, 1600 cycles, A.C. supplies by means of three B.T.H. frequency changers also from the 200 volt system.

D.C. power is provided at 28 volts through two 7.5 KW transformer rectifier units and a single 28 volt battery provides sufficient power for crash and emergency services.

All 200 volt A.C. services use 3 phase wiring from a star connected supply, the neutral being brought out for use with MERZ PRICE protection. All 28 volt D.C. services use single pole wiring, the negative return being taken through the airframe. An extensive voltage regulation and alternator protection system is provided and all services are protected by fuses and in some cases, by circuit breakers.

The location of the main items of electrical equipment is shown below. Two international ground supply plugs are installed on the port side of the fuselage, one for 200 volts A.C. and the other for 28 volts D.C.

In the event of the unlikely failure of all four alternators, the primary concern would be the power operated flying controls. Sufficient power to maintain control for a limited period would be available from the R.A.T. at high altitude and then the auxiliary power unit.

Power supplies are used for the following services

200-volt, 3 phase	Flying controls, fuel pumps and their controls, 400 cycle A.C. air brakes, radar, emergency hydraulic power (Alternators) pack and instruments.
115-volt, 400 cycle	Radar, controls for cabin atmosphere, bomb bay A.C. heating, anti-icing; and lighting and instruments.
115-volt, 1600 cycle	Radar
A. C. 28-volt D.C.	Instruments, warning lights, radio, bomb gear, lighting and controls for alternators, secondary power supplies and electro-hydraulic equipment.
28-volt D.C.(Batteries)	Vital service i.e. crash and fire and starting (Batteries) for the auxiliary power unit.

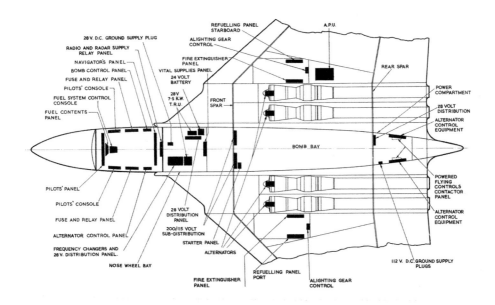

Additional safety features

An early issue that concerned the electric's was the running of the carbon pile voltage regulators which required twenty minutes warming time before the alternator voltage could be set to 115 ± 5 phase to neutral to allow correct load sharing when paralleled. Subsequently these were replaced by Silicon Controlled Rectifier (S.C.A.) static regulators which were set up during manufacture to the correct voltage and eliminated the need for pre-flight adjustment.

In the event of failure of the aircraft alternators a Ram Air Turbine (R.A.T.) which comprised a mechanically governed, air driven turbine assembly coupled to a 22 kVA alternator was fitted to the Vulcan. The unit was mounted on a platform and lowered into the airstream, once lowered the R.A.T. could not be retracted back into the fuselage. Development work on the R.A.T. was carried out on XH560.

Ram Air Turbine (R.A.T.)

A safety feature for the Auxiliary Power Unit (A.P.U.) was that the RAT permitted airborne starting of the Rover gas turbine.

Airborne Auxiliary Power Unit

The airborne auxiliary power unit (A.P.U.) comprised a Rover gas turbine engine driving a 40 kVA a.c. generator through a train of gears. A supply of compressed air could also be bled off. The engine was a single-sided centrifugal compressor driven by a single stage axial turbine mounted on a common shaft and supported on two bearings.

Limits on a typical flight performance were 23 kW for a period not exceeding four minutes, 0 to 5,000 ft with undercarriage down, 13kW for periods up to 30 minutes, 0 to 10,000 ft at 130 -415 E.A.S. and 17 kW for periods up to 30 minutes, 10,000 to 30,000 ft at 185-415 Kt or Mach 0.95 (whichever is less).

Changes to Radar and Radio equipment

The new E.C.M. that was fitted to the B.Mk1A Vulcan was not covered in the initial B.Mk2 brochure.

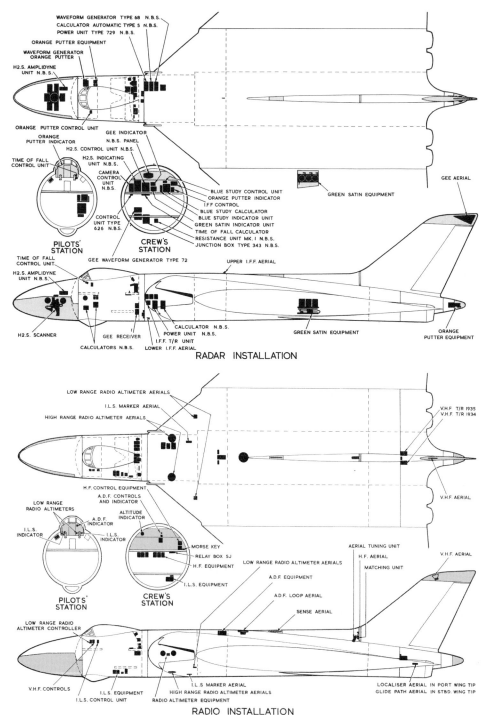

RADAR INSTALLATION

RADIO INSTALLATION

Radar and radio

The radar and radio equipment was more or less similar to B.Mk1 Vulcan's which included bombing, navigational and landing aids, tail warning equipment and an I.F.F. installation.

The additional aid to bombing, known as Blue Study, was provided by equipment which controlled the aircraft automatically on a defined track.

Tail warning radar which indicated the range and direction of fighters approaching from the rear was installed as a complete unit in the tail fairing of the fuselage. The equipment, known as Orange Putter, was controlled from the signaller's station and indicators were provided for the signaller and the pilots.

A Marconi AD 7092 D Radio Compass was installed with a master indicator and controls at the master navigator's station. Repeaters were fitted to both pilots' panels. The receiver was mounted above No.2 tank bay and the loop and its drive mechanism in the roof of the bomb bay. A sense aerial was built into the forward end of the dorsal fin and immediately aft of the radio compass.

Fuel system

The number of wing fuel tanks and capacities remained the same as B.Mk1, include was the option of bomb bay fuel tanks as illustrated below. The fourteen bag-type fuel tanks were contained in magnesium-allow compartments. The control of the fuel supply was arranged so that the balance of the aircraft was maintained between the desired limits.

The aircraft could also be equipped either as a receiver or tanker using the well-known probe and drogue system. Total fuel weight was quoted for a 10,000 lb bomb load was 4,358 lb and with the special 13,000lb store as 4,512 lb.

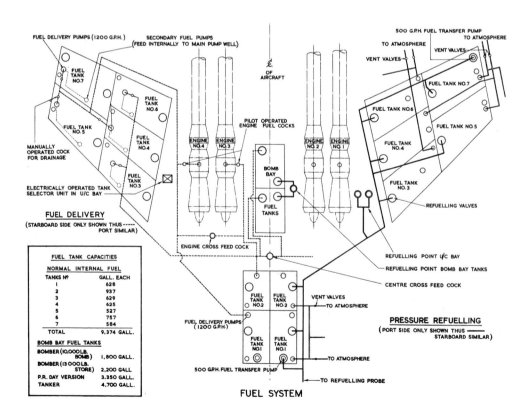

FUEL TANK CAPACITIES	
NORMAL INTERNAL FUEL	
TANKS Nº	GALL. EACH
1	628
2	937
3	629
4	625
5	527
6	757
7	584
TOTAL	9,374 GALL.
BOMB BAY FUEL TANKS	
BOMBER (10,000LB. BOMB)	1,800 GALL.
BOMBER (13 000LB. STORE)	2,200 GALL
P.R. DAY VERSION	3,350 GALL.
TANKER	4,700 GALL.

FUEL SYSTEM

Leading particulars

General Dimensions

Length overall	97 ft. 1 in.
Span overall	111 ft.
Height	26 ft. 6 in.

Mainplane data

Chord at centre line	63.40 ft.
Chord at tip	10.00 ft.
Chord mean	35.71 ft.
Aerofoil section at wing joint N.A.C.A. 0010.	
Thickness chord ratio	10 per cent.
Aerofoil section at wing tip RAE.101 modified.	
Thickness chord ratio	5 per cent.
Incidence	5 degrees.
Dihedral	0 degrees.
Aspect ratio	3.11.
Sweepback	
(leading edge at wing joint)	49 deg. 54 min.

Fin and rudder data

Sweepback (leading edge)	49 deg. 30 min.
Thickness chord ratio	10 per cent.

Wing loadings (in square feet)

Gross	3964
Elevons - inner	241.78
Elevons - outer	109.73
(Aft of hinge line)	

Fin and rudder data

Sweepback (leading edge)	49 deg 30 min.
Thickness chord ratio	10 per cent.

Areas (in square feet)

Fin and rudder	325
Fin (nett)	160
Rudder (Aft of hinge line)	63.4.

Hydraulic system

Working pressure	3,600 lb/sq.in.
Off load pressure	4,000 lb./sq.in.
Reservoir capacity	2 1/4 gall.
System capacity	12 gall.

Pneumatic system

Charging pressure	2000 lb./sq.in.
Total capacity (2 cylinders)	1,666 litres

Internal arrangement - March 1956

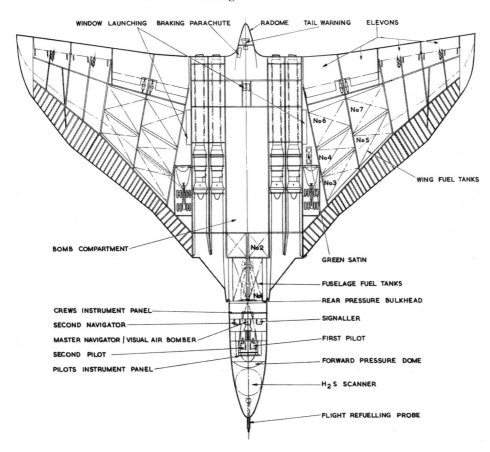

Phase 2C wing dimensions

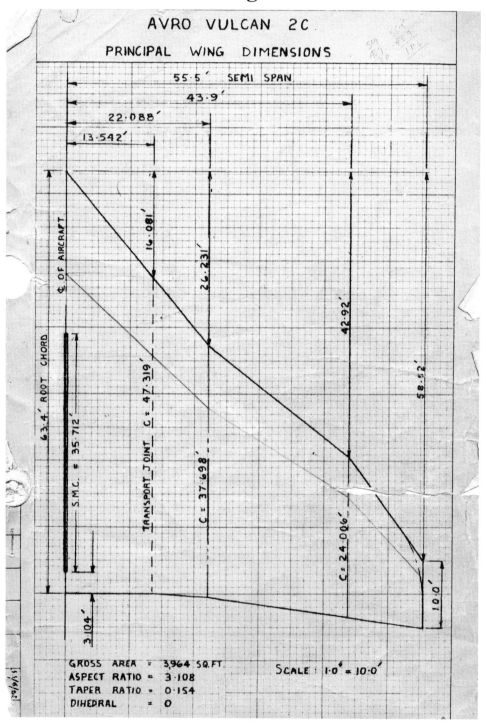

This data sheet Aero/698.2C/101 was produced on the 29th September, 1955 and shows the principle wing dimensions for the Phase 2C wing.

Phase 2C planform comparison

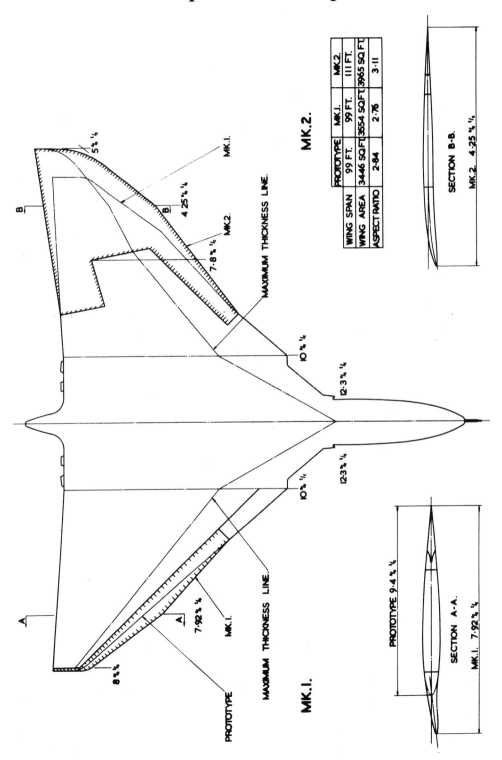

	PROTOTYPE	MK.I.	MK.2.
WING SPAN	99 FT.	99 FT.	111 FT.
WING AREA	3446 SQ.FT.	3554 SQ.FT.	3965 SQ.FT.
ASPECT RATIO	2·84	2·76	3·11

B.Mk2 summary

As stated earlier the aerodynamic testing of the Vulcan B.Mk.1 had indicated that if full advantage was to be taken of the Olympus engine power potential, then further changes to the outer wing would be required.

During the first half of 1955, sufficient full scale data were available to enable a submission to be made to the Ministry of Supply in August/September, 1955, of a wing planform design change to make full use of the anticipated development of the Olympus B.01.6 engine.

Design started on the B.Mk2 towards the end of 1955 under the guidance of Roy Ewans. A prototype contract was placed in March, 1956, followed in April 1956 by a production contract for Vulcan B. Mk.2 aircraft.

The wing design changes for the B. Mk.2 relative to the production Mk.1 and original prototype wing planforms is shown on the previous page. New outer wings for the Mk.2 were made and fitted to the existing second prototype Vulcan VX777. This aircraft in its modified form had its first flight on the 31st August, 1957, followed by the first production aircraft in August 1958.

The major design changes introduced in the Vulcan B.Mk.2 were as follows:
a.   More powerful engines Olympus B.Ol.6.
b.   New outer wing and leading edge.
c.   Elevators and ailerons of the Mk.1 changed to elevons.
d.   New and enlarged rear fuselage to accommodate additional equipment.
e.   A.C. electrical system.
f.   Rover auxiliary power unit,
g.   Strengthened main and nose undercarriage.
h.   Larger air intake for future Olympus, e.g. B.0l.21 approximately 20,000 lb. sea level static thrust.

Both the second prototype in its Mk.2 configuration and the first production aircraft were used for the handling and performance trials. As indicated earlier, some B.Mk1 aircraft were used for system developments for the production B.Mk.2 aircraft. These systems covered engine installations, (Bristol Olympus B.01.6) and the A.C. electrical system.

The second production aircraft was used to carry out the official A. & A.E.E. trials during the early part of 1960.

The initial C.A. Release for the Vulcan B.Mk.2 was issued by the Ministry of Supply in May 1960. The delivery of the first Mk.2 (XH558) aircraft took place the following month - June 1960.

POST C.A. RELEASE

As took place with the B.Mk.1 aircraft, some early B.Mk2 production aircraft were used to clear the Vulcan B.Mk.2 weapon systems, autopilot, flight system, radio and radar, armament, etc.

Further developments of the B.Mk.2 took place on later production aircraft, covering electronic equipment, the Blue Steel stand-off weapon and the introduction of the Olympus B.01.21 engine.

A major development was the proposed introduction of the United States airborne ballistic missile 'SKYBOLT'. An intensive development programme was carried out in close collaboration with the Douglas Aircraft Corporation up to the time (December 1962) when this weapon was abandoned as a result of Government policy decisions.

B.Mk2 flight development programme

	1957	1958	1959	1960
1st Proto. Mk.2 VX777		Handling & Development		
Vulcan Mk.1 XA893		A.C. Electrical System		
Vulcan Mk.1 XA899		Mk.10A Auto pilot & Military Flight System		
Vulcan Mk.1 XA891		BOL. 06 Engine Development		
Vulcan Mk.2 XH533		Handling & Performance		
Vulcan Mk.2 XH534		A&AEE Release trials		
Vulcan Mk.2 XH535		Final Conf.		
Vulcan Mk.2 XH536		Radio & Radar		
Vulcan Mk.2 XH537			Armament	
Vulcan Mk.2 XH538			Blue Steel	
Vulcan Mk.2 XH557			Enlarged Air Intake Bomb Bay Fuel Increase Gross Weight	
Vulcan Mk.1 XA895		R.C.M. Development		
Vulcan Mk.2 XH558				R.C.M. (Service Trials)

Ground picture of the first production B.Mk2 XH533 pictured on 30th August, 1958 the day of its first official flight. The aircraft was used for handling, performance and automatic landing trials.

Paving the way

Vulcan XH536 at the S.B.A.C. Show at Farnborough in 1959.

Avro had the backing of the larger Hawker Siddeley Group of Company's as the logo shows.

Aerodynamic prototype for the B.Mk2 VX777 takes off from Woodford.

The Vulcan has been a star performer at many air shows throughout the U.K.

Vulcan's participated in many bombing, navigation and reconnaissance competitions in the U.S.A., seen here are early B.Mk1 aircraft XA898 and XA891. Although the weather and terrain conditions were different to those experienced in Europe they provided valuable experience in operational tactics.

VIPs fly in the Vulcan

During the early years of the Vulcan various V.I.Ps were invited to experience the capabilities of the aircraft.

Most notable of these was when Prime Minister Sir Anthony Eden flew XA890 on a 35 minute flight with Roly Falk as Captain and passenger Sir Roy Dobson. They flew from Farnborough over the South coast to Blackbushe airfield on 6th September, 1955.

During his visit to R.A.F. Wyton on 24th June, 1958 the Duke of Edinburgh flew XA900 with W/C Frank Dodd (C.O. No.230 O.C.U.). A simulated bomb attack on the R.A.F. station at Andover ensued, involving a maximum-rate turn away from the target area and a fast let-down to Farnborough.

The Duke of Edinburgh at R.A.F Wyton.

Aerodynamic prototype B.Mk2 (XX777) pictured on 15th November, 1957.

First production B.Mk2 (XH533) used for flight development photographed on 5th March, 1959.

This competition was held at Pinecastle Air Force Base in Florida, between 30th October and 5th November, 1957. Participating were two Vickers Valiant's, 66 Boeing B-47 Stratojets, B-36s and B-52 Stratofortresses.

B.Mk2 flight assessment - 1959

A report on pilot and engineering assessment on B.Mk2 was produced by Avro Chief Test Pilot Jimmy Harrison and C. F. Bethwaite, Chief Flight Development Engineer in 1959. The report summarised as briefly as possible the stage of development reached at the time of submitting the Vulcan B.Mk2 for A.& A.E.E. preview trials. The first aircraft had completed approximately 40 hours flying before preview but much of the development of the features which distinguish the B.Mk2 from the B.Mkl aircraft has been carried out separately, using development aircraft VX777, XA893, XA891 and XA899 aircraft as flying test beds.

No attempt was made in the report to trace the various development troubles which had occurred on these test beds. Attention was focussed rather on the overall standard of the B.Mk2 in its present form. It was generally considered that the flying qualities of the Vulcan B.Mk2 fulfilled the design expectations and even at the preview stage there appear to be only minor problems still to be investigated before full C(A) release trials. The general reliability of the aircraft can be judged from the fact that the 30 hours up to the first minor inspection were completed in 29 days.

The general position was briefly summarised as follows:-

a) The change of wing aerodynamics has completely fulfilled the original predictions with regard to high Mach number buffet so that the increased thrust of the Olympus 200 series engines can be utilised as altitude performance without prejudice to the manoeuvrability of the aircraft.

b) The altitude performance was naturally superior to the B.Mk1 and it is interesting to record that the change of wing aerodynamics alone yields a dividend of 2,000 ft. on the cruise ceiling of the aircraft. The additional engine thrust gives a further 4,000 ft. so that the target height of the B.Mk2 should be some 6,000 ft in excess of the B.Mk1 figure at comparable weights. The possible inclusion of higher thrust engines would increase this still further.

c) The handling qualities of the B.Mk2 are improved in several respects over those of the B.Mkl. In particular, both visibility and control on the approach is superior and the aircraft has a high degree of manoeuvrability at cruising conditions.

d) The high Mach number characteristics of the basic aircraft are similar to those of the B.Mk1 and the static instability and loss of damping in pitch which occur well above cruising Mach number are corrected by artificial stabilisation, similar to the B.Mkl equipment but of improved design. This equipment has functioned extremely well so far.

e) The A.C. electrical system has so far given very little trouble and this is almost certainly due to the thorough test programmes carried out in flight on B.Mkl aircraft and also on ground rigs.

Improvements can still be made in certain features, however, the time between A. & A.E.E. preview and C(A) release target should be adequate to carry out any further development necessary.

CONCLUSIONS

There are still one or two development aspects which have to be finalised before the Vulcan B.Mk2 is in a stage for submission for full C(A) release trials.

The major uncertainties at the present time are concerned with the possible effects of the modified shape of the rear fuselage to accommodate the R.C.M. It is generally felt that these effects will be small but, nevertheless, there may be unexpected changes in handling characteristics. These will be assessed in the very near future when XH534 is flown.

Similarly, the aircraft had not yet been loaded to the maximum all up weight which will apply to the entry of the aircraft into service and this can only be achieved after the inclusion of a number of structural modifications which have become necessary as the results in progress on the structural specimen. The present programme schedules the introduction of these modifications into XH534.

Other engineering improvements noted were the ability to support essential electrical loads from wind milling engines to avoid the necessity for placing complete reliance upon the R.A.T. should total flame out occur. Simple and rapid engine starting, even without ground supplies, should make easy world-wide operation and high state of readiness. At best cruising Mach number for height and range the aircraft is not dependant on artificial longitudinal stability. Success of the new wing in delaying the onset of buffet so that when cruising at the same weight but at much higher altitude than the B.Mk1 the buffet threshold is encountered at about 1.4 g compared with 1.15 g in the latest B.Mk1 with Olympus 104 engines. The docile take-off, approach and landing conditions, which should result in far lower break-off heights than the B.Mk1 which probably has the highest break-off height than of any large aircraft in service.

Criticisms that might be of concern to the A & A.E.E. were high Mach number behaviour was unsatisfactory above .95 I.M.N. Buffet and trim change due to high drag airbrakes at high Mach number. Excessive throttle friction. Interference on intercom especially with I.L.S. Forward view in conditions of rain or external misting was no better than that of the B.Mk1.

Mach trimmer installation

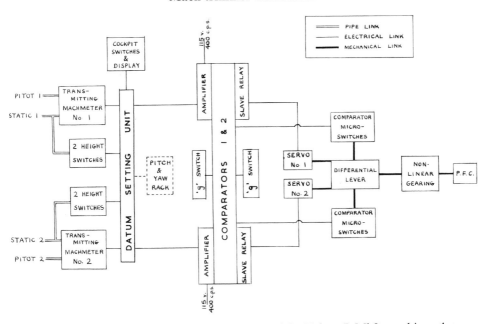

With higher weight and improved performance of the Vulcan B.Mk2 to achieve the same effective degree of stick, free stability as the B.Mk1, the total authority of the Mach trimmer in terms of movement of the trailing edge controls had to be increased. The system was altered to improve both the reliability and protection against malfunctioning and this was largely achieved by duplication of all components.

B.Mk2 production

An order was placed for 37 B.Mk1 aircraft in September 1954; there were two amendments to this order. *Amendment (1), April 1956, was for thirty B.Mk1 and seven B.Mk2.* Amendment (2), June 1957, was for twenty B.Mk1 and seventeen B.Mk2.

A contract for eight B.Mk1 aircraft placed on 31st March, 1955 was amended to eight B.Mk2 aircraft on 1st June, 1956 and a contract for twenty four B.Mk1 placed on 26th February, 1956 was amended on 1st June to B.Mk2. A final contract was issued for forty B.Mk2 placed on 22nd January, 1958. Total number built including prototypes was 136.

Vulcan B.Mk2 production in full swing.

B.Mk2 contracts

B. Mk2	17 aircraft	XH533-XH563	Sets 1-25
B. Mk2	8 aircraft	XJ780-XJ825	Sets 26-49
B. Mk2	24 aircraft	XL317-XL446	Sets 50-67
B. Mk2	40 aircraft	XM596-XM657	Sets 68-89
Batch numbers			Production Set No.
B. Mk2 Batch 5	25 aircraft	XH533-XJ825	Sets 46-70
B. Mk2 Batch 6	24 aircraft	XL317-XL446	Sets 71-94
B. Mk2 Batch 7	18 aircraft	XM569-XM603	Sets 95-112
		XM596	Set 60 FTS
B. Mk2 Batch 8	22 aircraft	XM604-XM657	Sets 113-134

The last aircraft to be delivered was XM657 set number 89 which made its first flight on 21st December 1964 and delivered 14th January 1965.

Significant milestones

Vulcan Mk.2 proposed.	August 1955
Wing leading edge modification designed.	September 1955
Leading edge modification fitted (VX777).	October 1955
Vulcan Mk.2 prototype contract.	March 1956
First flight of Vulcan Mk.2 (VX777).	August 1957
Vulcan Mk.2 E.C.M. proposed.	May 1958
First flight of production Vulcan Mk.2 (XH533).	August 1958
Vulcan Mk.2 C.A. release.	May 1960
Vulcan Mk.2 to squadron (XH558).	July 1960
Vulcan Mk.2 with E.C.M. fitted.	November 1960
First production Mk.2 Vulcan modified for Blue Steel (XL317).	June 1961
First production Mk.2A with Olympus 301 engines (XJ784).	August 1961
First Mk.2 converted to carry Skybolt.	September 1961

All British - principal suppliers

The manufacture of the Vulcan required a number of UK companies to supply materials and equipment, shown below are some of the principal suppliers:-

T. I. Aluminium, Ltd.; Automotive Products Co., Ltd.; Avica Equipment, Ltd.: Bell's Asbestos and Engineering, Ltd.; Belling and Lee, Ltd.; Birmetals, Ltd.; Birmingham Aluminium Castings Co., Ltd.; Thomas Bolton and Sons, Ltd.; Thomas Boom and Co. Ltd.; James Booth and Co. Ltd.; Boulton Paul Aircraft, Ltd.; British Aluminium Co., Ltd.; British Electric Resistance Co., Ltd.; British Insulated Callender's Cables, Ltd.; British Thomson-Houston Co., Ltd.; Brown Bayley Steels, Ltd.; Cellon, Ltd.; Deritend Drop Forgings Ltd.: Diamond "H'S Switches, Ltd.; Dowty Equipment, Ltd.; Dunlop Rubber Co. Ltd.; Dzus Fasteners (Europe), Ltd.: English Steel Rolling Mills Corp. Ltd. Ferranti, Ltd.; Flight Refuelling, Ltd.; Fireproof Tanks, Ltd.; Firth-Vickers Stainless Steels, Ltd.; Thos. Firth and John Brown,Ltd.; S. Fox and Co. Ltd.; Hellerman, Ltd.; High Duty Alloys, Ltd.; Hymatic Engineering Co. Ltd.; General Electric Co. Ltd.; Sir George Godfrey and Partners, Ltd.; Graviner Mfg. Co., Ltd.; Marconi's Wireless Telegraph Co. Ltd.; Marston Excelsior, Ltd.; Martin Raker Aircraft, Co. Ltd.; Miller Aviation, Ltd.; Normalair, Ltd.; Northern Aluminium Co. Ltd. Palmer Aero Products, Ltd.; Plessey Co. Ltd.; Pulsometer Engineering Co. Ltd.; Rotax, Ltd.; Rubery Owen and Co. Ltd.; Sangamo Weston, Ltd.; Self Priming Pumps and Engineering Co. Ltd.; Smiths Aircraft Instruments, Ltd.; Simmonds Aerocessories, Ltd.; Standard Telephones and Cables, Ltd.; J. Stone and Co. Ltd.; Teddington Aircraft Controls, Ltd.; Teleflex Products, Ltd.; Herbert Terry and Sons, Ltd.; Triplex Safety Glass Co. Ltd.; Tungum and Co. Ltd.; and Vickers-Armstrongs, Ltd.

First production B.Mk2 (XH533) pictured on 5th March, 1959. It first flew on 30th August, 1958.

Fire at Chadderton

Fire damage to Vulcan centre sections at Chadderton Bay One in October 1959, production resumed after a six weeks delay. Unfortunately a majority of company historic records and photographs were destroyed in the fire. Most of the Company's photographic negatives were actually spoiled by water and owing to the Company's insurance claim had to be destroyed without being restored.

Ultimate power

The final engines used on the Vulcan were the Olympus 201 and 301 versions. The Olympus 301 led to the Vulcan being re-designated B.Mk2A.

The Olympus 200 started life under the designation B.01 6 which produced 16,000 lb of thrust. It first ran at Patchway in September 1954, later a developed version, the B.01 7 produced 17,000 lb of thrust. In May 1958 B.01 7 had completed its test programme and was fitted to XA891 in spring 1958 for further work at both Filton and Woodford.

The first Olympus 200 engine flew in the first production Vulcan B.Mk2 (XH533) on 19th August, 1958. In 1959 the second B.Mk2 (XH534) was equipped with Olympus 201 engines of 17,000 lb thrust and used for A. &A.A.E. trials

When the series 201 entered service it was to encounter problems of engine surging mainly with the inboard engine at medium to high altitude, this led to attempts by Avro to improve the airflow at the intake. The aircraft used for these trials was XH560 which had returned to Woodford on 23rd December, 1960 and was later allotted for Skybolt development on 29th May, 1961. The surge problem was finally solved by cut back of the LP turbine stators by 2% and that combined with a revised fuel system schedule resulted in surge free handling.

With the requirement for more thrust a new Olympus was designed to give an increase in thrust of 20,000 lb. These changes were made so that a 201 could easily be converted to the new standard and bore the type number B.01.21. the new engine first ran at Patchway in January 1959. With the increase in thrust Avro designed intakes to accept the larger capacity of the new engine. By this time Bristol's had merged with Armstrong Siddeley Engines in 1959 and became known as Bristol Siddeley Engines Limited (BSEL).

Vulcan XH557 had been allotted to BSEL for the new engine installation. So that the larger B.01 21A could replace the 201 Olympus engines on XH557 structural alterations had to be made to the airframe, XH557 flew for the first time with the new engine on 19th May, 1961 and was then delivered to Woodford for handling assessment trials. Later 301 engines were used for handling, calibration and engine performance. The Olympus 301 was not a trouble free engine, as with the 201 the engine it was to encounter surge problems on the inboard engine, this led to a raising of the idle speed by 10% to help solve the problem, but engine surging was to plague the 301 version of the Olympus throughout its career. Avro had fitted intake vortex generators to XJ784 in an attempt to improve inboard engine handling, a slight improvement was observed but insignificant to justify Service use. At high altitude oil loss was also experienced with the rear turbine bearing, various alterations were tried before a final solution was found. Avro converted XJ784 to accept four Olympus 301 engines and the aircraft went to the A. &A.A.E. in April 1962 for initial C(A) release trials. Following a limited clearance the 301 finally entered service with RAF in June 1963.

Another problem experienced by the Vulcan especially in its daytime role was the smoke trail which could be seen from some distance. A series of Service trials were held in 1971 and 1972, this involved changing of the core angle of the fuel spray. The first trial took place on XH558 and the smoke trail was effectively reduced but with engine handling problems. A second trial on XL392 found that insignificant smoke reduction had occurred for the modification to be accepted for Service use. A final trial on Olympus 202 engines achieved a compromise between handling and smoke emission and this version was accepted for Service use, all 201/202 in service were modified. In August 1975, XM648 with modified burners on two 301 engines, was used to help eliminate the smoke trail problem, but this was not without handling problems and this version was not proceeded with due to the expense and limited life of the Vulcan in service.

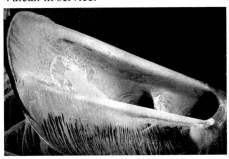 

Engine surge problems were to plague the Vulcan, due in part to the common air intake and disturbance to air on the inboard engine. For the Olympus 301 engine XJ784 was used for Vortex generator test. The vortex generators were placed inboard the air intake, a slight improvement was noticed. Here it can be seen, above (left), during airflow test with the boundary layer extended without vortex generators. The larger intake on XH554, shown above (right), was designed for the more powerful Olympus engines. Also shown is the boundary splitter used to ensure the entry of undisturbed high speed air to help increase the maximum flow rate of air into the engine.

One of the noticeable airframe differences between Olympus series 200 and 300 series engines was the tail pipe shroud of the 200 series which was longer and narrower and more tapered compared with the Olympus 301 series engine.

Olympus 301 series engine

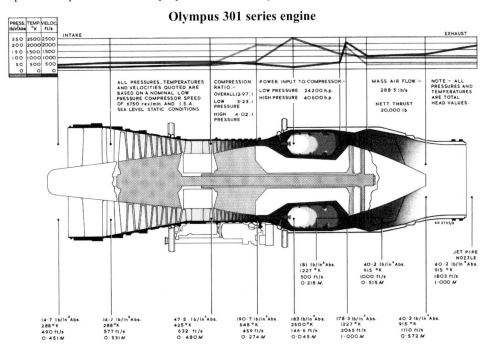

Engine running - associated controls - 1963

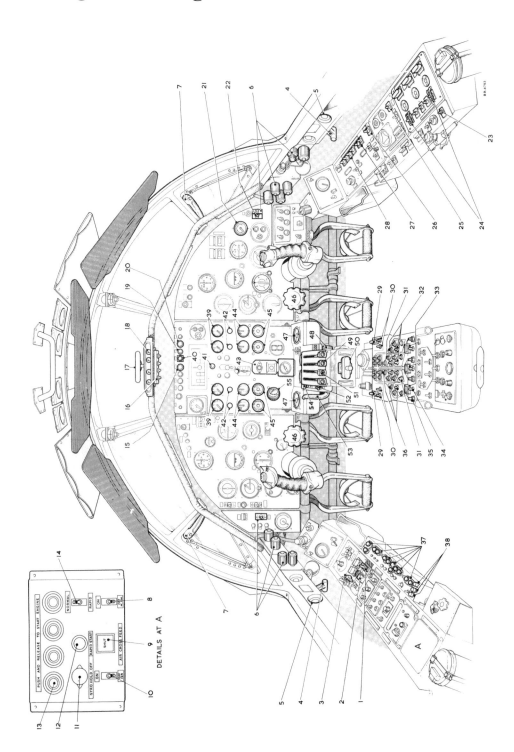

Key to cockpit layout

1 EMERGENCY DECOMPRESSION SWITCH
2 ABANDON AIRCRAFT SWITCH
3 BOMB DOOR CONTROL NORMAL SELECTOR SWITCH
4 CANOPY RELEASE LEVERS
5 VISUAL CANOPY LOCK
6 CABIN ILLUMINATION SWITCHES
7 DIRECT VISION WINDOW LOCK
8 ENGINE MASTER SWITCH
9 AIR CROSS FEED INDICATOR
10 IGNITION SWITCH
11 GYRO HOLD-OFF BUTTON
12 MASS RAPID START BUTTON
13 ENGINE STARTER BUTTONS AND WARNING LAMPS
4 STARTING AIR SELECTOR SWITCH
15 GENERATOR FAILURE WARNING LAMP
16 L.P. FUEL COCK SWITCHES
17 RAM AIR TURBINE RELEASE TOGGLE
18 FIRE WARNING LAMPS AND EXTINGUISHER BUTTONS
19 COCKPIT CANOPY WARNING INDICATOR
20 MAIN ENTRANCE DOOR WARNING INDICATOR
21 FUEL FLOWMETER
22 FUEL FLOW RESET SWITCH
23 AIR VENTILATION SUIT (A.V.S) SWITCH
24 ANTI-ICING SWITCHES
25 FUEL TANK PRESSURIZATION SWITCH
26 A.A.P.P. BLEED VALVE SWITCH

27 CABIN AIR SWITCHES
28 ENGINE AIR SWITCHES
29 CG. TRANSFER SWITCHES
30 AUTO-MANUAL TANKS GROUP SWITCHES
31 FUEL TANK CONTENTS PUSH-SWITCHES
32 FUEL TANK (STARBOARD) PUMP SWITCHES
33 FUEL TANK CROSS FEED INDICATORS
34 FUEL TANK CROSS FEED SWITCHES
35 RATE OF FLOW PUSH-SWITCHES
36 FUEL TANK (PORT) PUMP SWITCHES
37 POWERED FLYING CONTROLS INDICATORS AND STOP BUTTONS
38 POWERED FLYING CONTROLS START BUTONS
39 JET PIPE TEMPERATURE GAUGES
40 BOMB DOOR WARNING INDICATOR
41 ENGINE CONTROL INDICATOR
42 FUEL LOW PRESSURE WARNING INDICATORS
43 ALIGHTING GEAR CONTROL INDICATORS AND SWITCHES
44 ENGINE SPEED TACHOMETER INDICATORS
45 ENGINE OIL PRESSURE GAUGES
46 RUDDER PEDAL ADJUSTER
47 FUEL TANK CONTENTS GAUGES (GROUP OR TANK WHEN BUTTONS ARE PRESSED)
48 THROTTLE CONTROL DAMPER
49 THROTTLE CONTROLS
50 AIR BRAKE SWITCHES
51 RELIGHT BUTTON
52 J.P.T. LIMITER SWITCH

Engine development

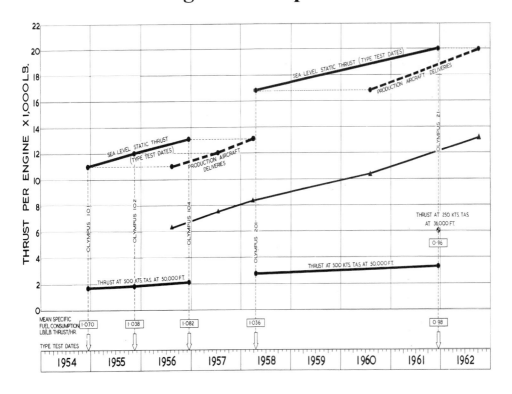

B.Mk2 development with Blue Steel

In November 1956 a brochure was produced on the further development of the B.Mk2 Vulcan which outlined a series of developments.

The brochure outlined a series of developments under the designation of Phase 5 which could be incorporated in a future Mk. 3 Vulcan shown later in this book under conceptual projects.

The largest engines at that time proposed by either Rolls-Royce or Bristol's could be installed in later B.Mk.2 aircraft which would have enlarged intakes to accommodate the greater mass flows involved.

Introduction

In addition to the proposals for the outer wing changes laid down in the Vulcan Phase 2C (Brochure I.P.B.62) a number of internal changes had been made to the aircraft. The most important of these was provision for the installation of the AVRO Blue Steel Weapon, together with Radio Counter Measures Equipment and extra fuel tanks in the bomb bay, the installation of more powerful engines - initially the Rolls Royce Conway 11 at 16,500 lb. S.L.S.T. or the Bristol Olympus 6 at 16,000 lb. S.L.S.T. with the possibility of later development to the Conway 31 or Olympus 21 Stage 3 ratings.

Wind tunnel tests made in the high speed tunnel at the R.A.E. confirmed the aerodynamic characteristics predicted for the Mk.2 Vulcan and it was now possible to contemplate further aerodynamic refinements to make it possible to cruise at higher lift coefficients and consequently to use engines of 19-20,000 lb. S.L.S.T., namely the Bristol Olympus 21 stage 3 and the Rolls-Royce Conway 31), with a consequent valuable increase in altitude.

Design studies of the installation of these engines had, therefore, been made. In this connection it should be remembered that the carriage of Blue Steel externally increases the drag of the aircraft and the cruising lift coefficient is therefore reduced for the same engine power. Since at the time of writing no decision had been made between Olympus 6 and the Conway 11, Vulcan Mk.2 components now on the production line were being built with fittings to take either engine.

Blue Steel as shown in the 1956 development brochure on the B.Mk2

Engine bay sizes

The Bristol Olympus B.Ol.21 and Rolls-Royce Conway 31 engines could be accommodated within the rib spacing of the present Vulcan. The installation of both engines called for careful positioning of the engine accessories and whilst the Conway was a slightly bulkier engine than the Olympus this was offset by the need for fire-proofing in the case of the Olympus. This fire-proofing is not required by the cooler by-pass engine. The size of the present engine access doors was satisfactory, although detailed alterations to the doors to give increased clearances were required.

Enlarged engine air intakes

In order to achieve maximum efficiency from these engines which have a much greater air mass flow even than those which were foreseen for the Vulcan, it has been found necessary to increase the size of the air intakes. The larger intakes had been accommodated without any major alterations to other components of the aircraft. The upper wing surface and top intake lips remained unaltered but the lower wing surface forward of the front spar was revised in order to achieve the greater intake cross sectional area, whilst retaining a bottom lip of similar shape to the present intake. These shapes of lips have been retained because their behaviour was known to be satisfactory throughout the speed range of the aircraft and no development difficulties were, therefore, anticipated with the larger intakes. The existing airbrake legs which straddle the intakes remain unaltered and clear the larger ducts. The enlarged air intake will not be incorporated in the first few B.Mk.2 aircraft, which will therefore only be suitable for the Conway 11 at 16,500 lb. S.L.S.T. or the Olympus series up to 17,500 lb.

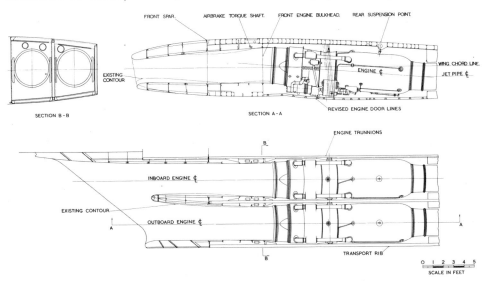

Jet pipe installations

The maximum diameter of the jet pipe that could be fitted to the Vulcan was dictated by the rear spar banjo rings, which had an internal diameter of 32 in. The jet pipe diameter them present was 29.6 in. and this diameter was suitable for the Conway 31 and Olympus 21 engine. The exhaust diameter of the Conway 31 was 30.8 in. and 31 in. for the Olympus 21. A detachable conical piece of jet pipe would be installed immediately after the engine in order to produce the required reduction from engine exhaust to jet pipe diameter.

Integration of bomb bay equipment

In order to develop the concept of a weapon system for the Vulcan, the arrangement of the various stores together with other equipment located in the bomb bay has been co-ordinated in order to achieve maximum interchange ability, compatible with efficiency.

The three main items to be carried are:

(a) The Store i.e. Blue Danube, Blue Steel, Yellow Sun or Red Beard, etc.

(b) R.C.M. installation, including the glycol cooling system.

(c) Extra long range internal fuel tanks located in the bomb bay.

With the exception of Blue Steel all the other stores mentioned above are stowed internally within the bomb bay. It has been found possible to design the R.C.M. installation in such a manner that it is similar for all stores, but to achieve maximum range the extra fuel tanks for Blue Steel are different from those required for the Blue Danube and Yellow Sun installations.

Blue Danube installation with R.C.M. and bomb bay fuel

The extra long range bomb bay tanks were to have a total capacity of 1,310 imp. gallons nett, contained in 6 tanks, located along each side of the bomb bay and adjacent to the store. It was also proposed to achieve this increase in fuel capacity would require a revision of the

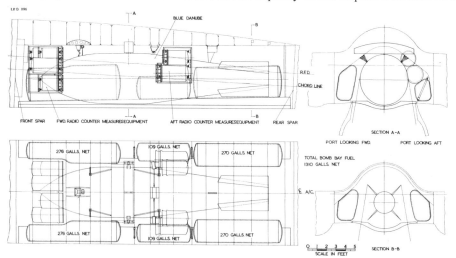

BLUE DANUBE INSTALLATION WITH R.C.M. AND EXTRA FUEL TANKS

bomb door mechanism, a single externally opening door would replace the existing double internally folding doors and the volume previously "swept" by the opening of these doors has been utilised to carry fuel. The R.C.M. equipment was to be suspended in two crates from the roof of the bomb bay at the forward and aft ends of the compartment.

Blue Steel installation with R.C.M. and bomb bay fuel

The installation of the Blue Steel store is not totally enclosed within the bomb bay, but is half-submerged. This has necessitated the replacing of the present bomb doors by a fixed fairing, extending in the fore and aft direction from the front to rear spar and in the lateral direction across the bomb bay. This fairing is dished to accommodate the upper surface of the Blue Steel missile. The bottom boom of the front spar has been cranked to pass over the top of the nose of the missile. Minor modifications have been required to the aircraft structure forward of the front spar and small changes made to the fuel tanks in that region.

Inside the bomb bay the R.C.M, installation is similar to that used with the Blue Danube or Yellow Sun stores, but considerably more space is available for fuel and consequently two tanks of larger capacity have been designed to carry some 2,450 gallons. All B.Mk.2 aircraft will have the modifications necessary to carry Blue Steel.

Shortened nose wheel

As was believed that the requirements for the equipment and payload to be carried by the Blue Steel missile may be increased, some lengthening of the missile body may become necessary. To meet this it is proposed to shorten the nose undercarriage of the aircraft so that it clears the missile upon retraction. The nose undercarriage leg has been reduced in length by 12. 6 in., this in turn reduces the ground angle of the aircraft by 2° giving a ground incidence of 3°43'. This reduction in ground angle does not materially affect the nose wheel raising speed of the aircraft since the change of the control surfaces from elevators and ailerons to elevons on the B.Mk.2 aircraft makes adequate pitching power available

If for any reason a further increase in the missile length becomes necessary, then it is possible to telescope the leg prior to its retraction and so provide further clearance. The lengthening of the missile does not in any other way effect the installation, but the nose of the missile is now below the bottom skin line of the aircraft The shortening of the nose undercarriage is combined with the introduction of a strengthened nose wheel leg to meet the increased braking torque on the B.Mk.2 undercarriage.

Proposed changes to allow for new store

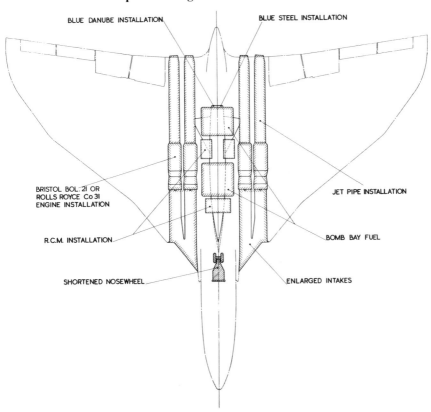

BLUE DANUBE INSTALLATION

BLUE STEEL INSTALLATION

BRISTOL BOL. 21 OR ROLLS ROYCE Co 31 ENGINE INSTALLATION

JET PIPE INSTALLATION

R.C.M. INSTALLATION

BOMB BAY FUEL

SHORTENED NOSEWHEEL

ENLARGED INTAKES

A further implication of the shortened nose undercarriage is that the height of the fin is increased by some 13 in. to 27 ft. 2.5 in., due to the rotation of the aircraft about the main wheels. This was not thought to be an embarrassment, as all the hangars that will house the Vulcan are expected to have door clearances of at least 30 ft. The Blue Steel missile would normally loaded from the rear of the aircraft and consequently as the clearance between the rear spar and the ground is increased by shortening the nose undercarriage, loading of the missile is facilitated.

Aircraft drag

The drag of the Vulcan B.Mk.2 was based directly on the comprehensive drag measurements made by A.V. Roe and A.& A.E.E. on the present series of Vulcan B.Mk.1 aircraft.

Confirmation of these results had also been obtained from Bomber Command after a series of long flights made under strictly controlled cruise conditions. Preliminary confirmation of the basic B.Mk.2 aircraft drag had been obtained from the tests being made at in the R.A.E. high speed wind tunnel. These tests also confirmed that the compressibility drag rise is delayed to a considerably higher Mach number than on the B.Mk.1 aircraft, probably due to the thinner outer wing. The results have been modified for the new wing planform of the B.Mk.2 aircraft and for the carriage of the Blue Steel missile. The additional drag due to Blue Steel was based on the High Speed tunnel tests reported in RAE/T.N./Aero/2365.

Blue Steel installation November 1956

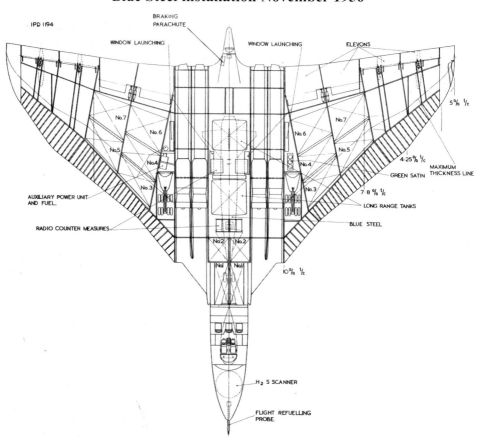

Installation of Blue Steel in Vulcan B.Mk1 (XA903)

MINISTRY OF SUPPLY.

CERTIFICATION OF DESIGN.

Aircraft Type...... **VULCAN B, MK. 1** ...XA. 903..... Constructor's No...... **698**......

Contract No. **6/ACFT/12662/CB. 6A**

I/We the designer(s) of the above aircraft hereby report and certify that:—

(i) With the exceptions stated at (v) overleaf the design of the above aircraft complies with M. of S. Aircraft Specification No.**See note** together with amendments up to and including No......**overleaf**.

(ii) The calculations made during the course of the design have been checked in a manner acceptable to the Director General of Technical Development (Air) and every reasonable precaution has been taken to ensure accuracy.

(iii) The recommendations of A.P. 970, Volume 2, where applicable, have been considered.

(iv) The design data, calculations, reports on tests, and drawings furnished by me/us to the Director General of Technical Development (Air) are a true and accurate record of the design of this aircraft.

[P.T.O.

MoS form dated 10th October, 1960.

Vulcan XA903 was converted to carry out trials with a research and development missile. The missile was carried by a centre hoist structure with relevant bomb bay arch structure reinforcements. Forward and aft crutching pads steadied the Missile. The forward crutching structure was attached to the front spar and the rear crutching structure to the bomb arch. Both front spar and bomb arch had been reinforced to carry the extra loads imposed. Pre-crutching of the Missile took place at the rear crutching assembly.

The bomb doors were modified to enable the Missile to fit underneath the aircraft, they were braced and secured in the closed position, but they could be opened when the aircraft was on the ground to facilitate servicing in the bomb bay.

A warm air, refrigeration and a hydraulic system had been added to the aircraft to cater for the Missile requirements.

The release unit for the Missile was a number 3 Mk.3 E-M release unit, a secondary release was also incorporated. The release unit had provision for a locking pin, this was fitted in order to avoid in-advertent operation of the release bit allowing for the removal of the locking pin during flight to provide means of emergency jettison of the Missile.

The crew of six members consisted of two pilots, three observers facing aft viewing a large panel of telemetering equipment and one observer who sits on an occasional seat facing forward viewing a small panel. This person had a rearward facing crash seat on starboard side for normal use.

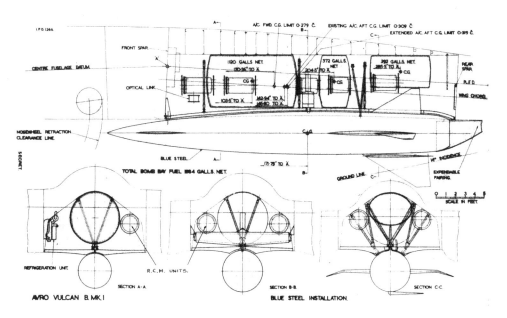

Drawing from the February 1957 brochure on the carriage of Blue Steel.

Blue Steel comparison with B.Mk1

A study was produced for the carriage of Blue Steel stand off missile for B.Mk1 Vulcan aircraft in February 1957. It answers a question why the B.Mk1 never operationally carried the Blue Steel missile. Shown below are extracts from that report.

Introduction

This brochure is submitted in reply to a request made in a letter from the Resident Technical Officer (Ref. V/03/1/3214.7) dated 19th November, 1956.

At a meeting held at Messrs. A.V. Roe & Co. Ltd. Chadderton factory on the 29th January 1957 to discuss Blue Steel installations on both B.Mk.1 and B.Mk.2 aircraft, the firm demonstrated that it would be possible to carry the store on the B.Mk.1 aircraft. However, as the lower boom of the centre section front spar was not cranked on these aircraft, it was not possible to submerge the missile as much as on the B.Mk.2 aircraft and this had an adverse effect upon the aircraft's performance.

The all-up-weight of the aircraft with Blue Steel installed and bomb-bay fuel tanks was 190,163 lb. To achieve this weight together with an extension of the aft c.g. limit would require some flight development.

Wind tunnel tests showed that the lower position of the Blue Steel missile on the B.Mk.1 aircraft would not affect the emergency escape of the rear crew members, at speeds up to 250 kts. E.A.S.

The position of the missile was identical with that adopted for the development installation being designed by Messrs Helliwells under subcontract to A. V. Roe & Co. Ltd., (Weapons Research Division). This design was not originally intended to be of a standard required for production aircraft and the design of the installation would therefore require further production design.

The maximum weight at which a Vulcan B.Mk.1 had flown was 167,000 lb. and a flight development programme would be required to increase the all-up-weight to 190,000 lb. This was required for roles other than the carriage of Blue Steel and it was recommended that an aircraft should be allocated for these tests.

Comparison with Vulcan B. Mk.2

The B.Mk.2 Vulcan had a better Blue Steel installation than was possible on the B.Mk.1 due to the cranked front spar. Furthermore the larger engines envisaged were more capable of absorbing the increased weight and drag of the missile. The range penalties were therefore not as great.

Blue Steel missile confiuation for B.Mk.1

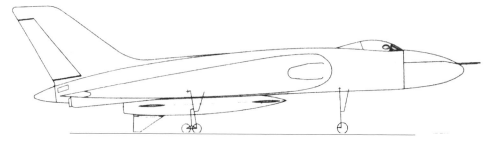

0   5   10   15
SCALE IN FEET

Blue Steel development

General view of early test model missile 7th January, 1957.

As stated earlier in the book, as far back as 1954 the Ministry of Supply (MoS) were aware that Guided Weapons (GW) defence would pose a threat to 'V' bombers flying over or within about 50 miles of the target by 1960. A note from the MoS stated it would require a flying bomb which would have its maximum use between 1960 and 1965. It was recognised due to the speed range of Mach 2+ that the production of the many vehicles would be required for firing trials would lengthen the development time.

In 1954, Avro employed R. H. (Hugh) Francis who came from the R.A.E. Armament Development Division at Farnborough. Mr Francis along with his colleagues from the R.A.E. had worked on various flying bomb and missile designs and was a leading authority in this area. This had led to the establishment of a Weapons Research Division at Woodford in 1954 and to a development contract being awarded to Avro in March 1956 for a stand-off missile to meet (OR 1132) missile requirement for the 'V' bomber force. The warhead finally chosen was the nuclear fission device known as Red Snow.

As mentioned earlier, scale models were used for in the development of Blue Steel with Vickers Valiant aircraft. These models were carried in the Valiant's bomb bay. Further test were completed on B. Mk1 Vulcan XA903 using full scale missiles. XH534 and XH539 aircraft were used to develop the B.Mk2 for use with Blue Steel. The first B.Mk2 production aircraft carrying Blue Steel modifications was XL317.

The Type 102/103 series were powered by the de Havilland Double Spectre rocket engine. The Double Spectre ran on high-test peroxide and kerosene and had two superimposed chambers. The final production Type 100 Series was powered by the Armstrong Siddeley, later Bristol Siddeley, Stentor. It was a two-chamber rocket engine. One chamber was used for initial boost and then a smaller cruise chamber was used for most of the flight.

Type 103 version of Blue Steel missile used the de Havilland Double Spectre rocket engine.

Avro sub-contracted work to the Gloster Aircraft Company which was part of the Hawker Siddeley Group. They completed a number of design and structural tests on the missile, along with constructing W102, W103 variants at their Hucclecote factory, in their former experimental No.3 hangar. The Aviation Division of Elliott Brothers (London) Ltd formed in 1953, based at Borehamwood, designed the guidance system which was the most advanced type at that time and one of the world's first inertial navigation systems. It was a mixed inertial and Doppler system that gradually corrected the gyro drifts as it approached the launch point. The flight rules computer (FRC) and autopilot were both developed by Avro. Problems were encountered with the early giro system and cooling of the missile and a great deal of time was spent in rectifying these problems. Blue Steel had to fly up to Mach 2+, so the airframe was to be of stainless steel rather than aluminium; this gave Avro new challenges in the production of the missile.

Missile testing

The development of Blue Steel raised a number of problems in the field of aerodynamics, cooling, propulsion and automatic control. Tests were first carried out with free flight models at the Royal Aircraft Establishment missile range at Aberporth in Wales. The models were made of cast alloy and contained instruments and miniature telemetry systems, which automatically transmitted the instrument readings by radio throughout the flight. These models were not powered, launching being carried out by large booster rockets. The results showed close agreement with predicted figures. The trials involved twenty three firings spread over three years, valuable data was obtained to assist technicians in their calculations of performance, autopilot design, aileron and fin size which could effect the full-size missile. The next step was to fly larger models and the British and Australian authorities agreed to use facilities in Australia. The Woomera Range was jointly controlled by the Australian Weapons Research Establishment and the Royal Australian Air Force.

The Blue Steel trials team arrived in Australia in July 1957, with missile testing starting in August 1957. The first model tested (S1) was a 2/5th scale missile which was dropped in August 1957 from Vickers Valiant WZ370. The first powered scale model (S2) was fired from a Vickers Valiant in February 1958. More scale model flights (rounds S3 - S15) were tested throughout 1958 and 1959 using the Vickers Valiant.

In 1960, No.4 Joint Services Trials Unit (No.4 J.S.T.U), which was formed at Woodford on 1st September, 1956 arrived in Australia and started testing full scale versions of Blue Steel using Vulcan's and Victor's as test vehicles. Round 001 was launched un-motorised on 1st November, 1960. Between 1960 and October 1964 over fifty launches were completed which included high and low level trajectory. The main element of the trials unit returned to the U.K. in November 1964.

Further tests were conducted in the U.K. by (No.18 J.S.T.U.) based at Scampton using Blue Steel aircraft allotted to No.617 Squadron the first service unit to operate the missile.

Missile test site at Boscombe Down 17th June, 1959. Shown is Blue Steel with the Armstrong Siddeley Stentor rocket motor under test.

W100 missile at Boscombe Down 25th October, 1960.

This picture of a test missile in a Valiant bomb bay was taken on 12th January, 1957.

Wiring of 19/15 telemetry tank 13th June, 1958.

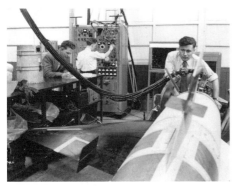

Telemetry checks on 19/15 missile 13th June, 1958. The missile was powered by a Jackdaw solid rocket motor developed by the Rocket Propulsion Establishment (R.P.E.) at Westcott in Buckinghamshire. It had two exhausts from a single chamber. The missile was designed to be air launched from a Vickers Valiant.

Early 19/15 model having its final checks on 12th January, 1958.

Doppler aerial check on 102 missile 13th August, 1958.

A section of monitoring console installed in the parent aircraft.

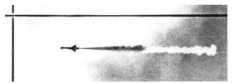

Early test firing at Woomera.

Design features

Full scale missile powered by the de Havilland Double Spectre rocket engine, at Woodford on 13th August, 1959.

Directional control of the missile was on the 'twist and steer' principle, in which each turn is begun by rolling with the ailerons and then maintained by increasing lift on the foreplanes. For the first part of the mission, the course was monitored continuously and the position determined by radar and astro-tracking equipment in the parent aircraft. At the moment the navigator flicked a switch and the computer inside the missile was told the exact position from which it was starting, its speed and the direction it was heading. The missile fell freely and after a few seconds delay the rocket motor fired and the missile accelerated and began its climb. The inertial navigator in the missile then took over and computed every change of velocity and direction from ultra-sensitive acceleration measurements made within the missile, with reference to the position at which it left the carrier. Once launched no signals from Blue Steel were required from outside and so it could not be jammed.

A further development of Blue Steel to meet a requirement to be launched at low level was met by a simple alteration to the missile and proved capable of flying at 1000 ft. The original missile was designed to cruise at 70,000 - 80,000 ft.

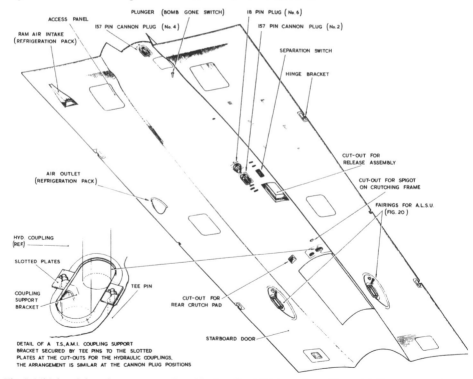

The B.Mk2 bomb bay doors were replaced by two fixed fairings shaped to match the upper contours of the missile, a retractable cut out catered for the missiles upper fin. Connecters were provided for store release, hydraulic supply, hot air, electrical fusing, butt joints and bomb gone indicator plunger.

This picture shows "Mod 200" bomb bay door fairings for the Blue Steel missile, in the background is XH537 used for Skybolt missile development.

Test firing from XA903 shows the missile accelerating away.

Rear view of Blue Steel taken at Woodford in 1960. Note the missile is powered by the Armstrong Siddeley Stentor rocket engine.

Vulcan B.Mk2 XH539 seen here pictured on 15th August, 1961 was fitted with considerable instrumentation and had all the essential equipment to meet the O.R.1132 requirement. It first flew on 10th May, 1961 and performed the first live firing of Blue Steel for No.4 J.S.T.U at Woomera after arriving at Edinburgh airfield in Australia on 12th December, 1961.

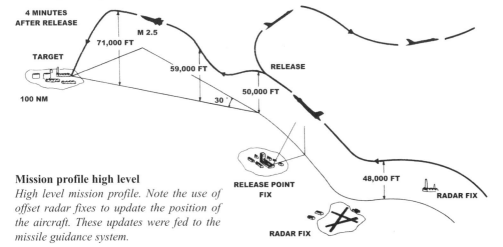

Mission profile high level

High level mission profile. Note the use of offset radar fixes to update the position of the aircraft. These updates were fed to the missile guidance system.

Early missile underneath B.Mk1 Vulcan. Note the missile is not recessed into the fuselage.

Blue Steel round 37 at Woodford on B.Mk2 Vulcan XH539, pictured at Woodford 7th August, 1961. The missile is now recessed into the fuselage.

Blue Steel W100A missile on trials at Woodford with a heating blanket taken 28th May, 1962.

The above picture shows XH675 Victor Mk2 with a Blue Steel missile taken on 24 August, 1961. The Victor XL161 was used as the test aircraft for Blue Steel. It went from Woodford to Australia and was based at Edinburgh airfield. On 17th August, 1962 it was involved in a flying accident when it went into a flat spin. Avro test pilot Johnny Baker employed the brake parachute and successfully recovered from the spin. The Blue Steel missile was then dropped into the sea.

Vulcan B.Mk1 XA903 first flew on 10th May, 1957 and was allotted for Blue Steel development on 27th January, 1958. In November 1960 it went to Australia for Blue Steel trials work, before returning to Woodford for Airborne Auxiliary Power Pack (A.A.P.P.) trials in 1962. In 1963, it went to Bristol Siddeley for conversion as an engine test bed for the Olympus 593 which was part of the Concorde development programme. In 1971 the aircraft went to Marshalls of Cambridge for conversion to the Rolls-Royce RB199 which was to be used by the Tornado multi-role combat aircraft. In 1984 it was scrapped with the nose going to the Wales Air Museum. The nose then went into private ownership when Colin Meers acquired it in 1993.

Vulcan B.Mk1 XA903 at Woodford November 1960.

Production

A recoverable version of Blue Steel (W104) was proposed but not proceeded with as it could have delayed the development of the missile. The last test missile was a W105 which was built of stainless steel and fully functional apart from not having a warhead with this being replaced by test equipment. Over fifty operational Blue Steel W105 missiles were delivered to the Royal Air Force along with W103 training rounds. Sixteen W100A launch capable pre-production rounds were also made available as part of the trials programme along with eight B.Mk2 aircraft under the control of H.Q. Bomber Command.

Blue Steel under construction at Woodford.

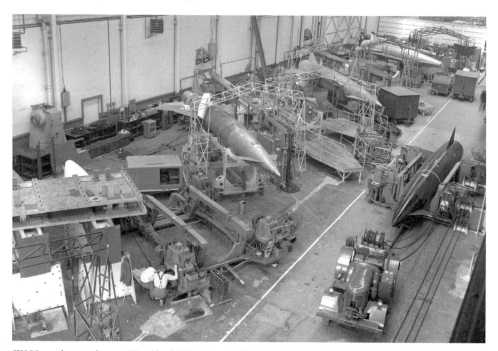

W100 production line at Woodford 12th May, 1960.

Blue Steel production in the large secure compound at Chadderton 13th August, 1959. Passes had to be shown before anyone could enter this fenced top secret area.

Blue Steel at Woodford in 1959.

Weapons Research Division (W.R.D.)

The Woodford Weapons Research Division was not only involved in designing missiles but also produced the components. At the 1957 S.B.A.C. Show, for example, it demonstrated equipment that included an autopilot suitable for the control of a missile, an aerial field pattern recorder which indicated the radiation pattern of a guided missile aerial and a minute-wavelength transmitter.

The W.R.D. exhibit for an "aerial field pattern recorder", was indicated on a cathode tube the radiation pattern of a guided missile aerial. In the exhibit itself a minute-wavelength transmitter directed a narrow radio beam on to a rotating model of a missile containing a miniature receiver. The received signal was then fed to a cathode tube and its pattern was revealed. By adjusting the position of the aerial in the missile the desired pattern could be obtained. Completing an interesting trio of exhibits from W.R.D. was the demonstration of a magnetic amplifier for driving moving parts of missile control surfaces.

With the formation of Hawker Siddeley Dynamics Ltd in 1963 all missile work was to be centralised and Blue Steel came under the Hawker Siddeley banner. The Avro Weapons Research Division left Woodford in 1965 to go to the nearby Stanley Green, Business Park at Handforth Dean, Wilmslow, Cheshire and remained there until 1971.

Blue Steel development aircraft at Woodford dispersal 14th May, 1962.

Seventh production version of the B.Mk2 with Blue Steel missile pictured 15th August, 1961. XH539 and XL317 were used to develop the Blue Steel missile and associated equipment for Service use.

Further Blue Steel missile developments

The greatest criticism of the Blue Steel was its range, this led Avro to experiment further to improve the W100 missile. This involved a version with a smaller warhead, more compact guidance system and two rocket booster rockets. This allowed more room for fuel and would have increased the range to 400 miles.

Further versions included the Mk.1B which used high speed fuel, the Mk.1C with external boosters, Mk.1D a long range Blue Steel powered by improved Stentor rocket motor and two solid rocket boosters with external fuel tanks, the Mk.1E using highly toxic hydrozine fuel and the Mk.1S with external mounted fuel tanks.

An operating requirement (O.R.1149) was issued in May 1956 for a 1000 mile missile with the last 100 miles flown at 100 ft. Avro proposed the W112 which was to be powered by four ram jets designed to meet this requirement. This proved too ambitious for the time and a less demanding operating requirement (O.R.1159) was issued in May 1958. This was met by the W114; this was a modified version of Blue Steel W100 and is often referred to as Blue Steel Mk.II. The new design carried on the upper surface of the body two booster rockets, designed to provide the propulsion of the missile after it was released from the aircraft at about M = 0.90. These provided the acceleration until the four Bristol Siddeley BRJ.824 ram jets on the wing tips became effective at M = 2.0. The boosters were then discarded. A nose plane effected longitudinal stability, and lateral stability was provided by means of a single fin placed on the lower surface of the model.

A 1/28-scale model was tested in the 3ft by 3ft Supersonic Wind Tunnel at the Royal Aircraft Establishment Bedford, Thurleigh between August and September 1959. Tests were carried out with various combinations and at Mach numbers between M = 0.8 and 2.0. These experiments proved the integrity of the design.

The W114 had a planned increased in range of 1000 miles or shorter and a speed of Mach 3.8 - 4. The internal guidance system was to be replaced by rear mounted Doppler radar. This was a demanding specification and many difficulties were encountered with guiding the missile accurately over the required specified distance. After spending some £825.000 the project was cancelled in December 1959.

Shown here is a mock up of a further development of Blue Steel. It was a low altitude only version with the rocket motor replaced by a 4000 lb thrust Viper turbojet fed by a ventral intake. It would have had speed of at Mach 0.9. and a range of 600 n.m. at 500 ft.

Progress on the W114 missile 28th August, 1960.

One twenty-eighth scale W100 conversion 28th July, 1959.

W114 missile boost unit at the instant of jettison.

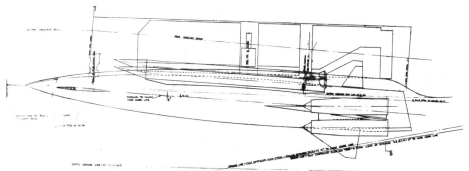

This I.P.D . drawing dated 5th December, 1958 shows the installation of the W114 missile.

Carriage and release of Blue Steel

The A.&.A.E.E. at Boscombe Down produced a report which described the successful trials on the Carriage and Release of Blue Steel. The period of the trial was from November 1961 to January 1962.

A type 100A Blue Steel missile fitted with instrumented pod was used for the majority of carriage trials. The High Test Peroxide and Kerosene tanks in the missile were filled with either sand or a water/glycol mixture to ballast the missile to its correct weight and Centre of Gravity. A Type 102A dummy weighted alloy Blue Steel missile was used for the remaining carriage trials and release trial. Resulting from this single release a limited clearance was recommended.

Subject to incorporation of certain modifications detailed in the report it was recommended that the Vulcan B.Mk2 aircraft modified to the Blue Steel role was suitable for Service use for the carriage and release of Blue Steel with the following limitations:-

Carriage

To the maximum height and speed and manoeuvre limitations of the aircraft.

Release

At 0.84 I.M.N. in straight and level flight ±5°at 50,000 ft ± 5,000 ft.

The primary means of withdrawing the in-flight safety lock was by means of an electronic actuator controlled by a switch mounted at the captain's position in the aircraft. To release the missile a pneumatic release was operated via an electronic operated solenoid valve, controlled by a switch on the navigator's panel, a magnetic indicator in the cockpit showing missile release.

There was concern on the release of the missile to fulfil the requirement that no one man shall be able to release the store, the flap covering the secondary in-flight safety lock handle is locked by a Yale lock. The key to this lock was to be held by the captain of the aircraft. It was recommended to strength the lock so that it could not be forced open. The re-position of the secondary in flight safety lock was also recommended.

The release of the Type 102A dummy weighted missile was photographed by cine-cameras mounted in the wings, nose and underside of Vulcan B.Mk2 XH534 (the aircraft used for the drop). Additionally, a further cine record was made using a hand held cine camera operated from a chase Javelin aircraft. During the test a type 102A dummy weighted alloy missile was released at 48,000ft and 0.84 I.M.N. in straight and level flight and filmed by a chase Javelin.

Rear Fairing

All trials were carried out without the jettison fairing which was produced and fitted to certain aircraft at the aft end of the missile. No reason could be seen which would justify the fitting of the particular jettisonable fairing. If it should be fitted it was recommended that an alternative means of jettisoning should be provided.

Conclusions

The functioning of the missile was subject to separate trials to be carried out in Australia.

No Electromagnetic compatibility tests had yet been carried out and these recommendations were conditional on E.C.M. and similar apparatus not being used until such time at it has proved that the electrical release and in-flight safety lock systems will not be affected by such use. The release recommendation was based on one release only and be further expanded by the Australian trials. Eleven flights were completed using Blue Steel round 042 and Blue Steel Type 102A.

The Captain was responsible for the fin gap doors, both normal and emergency, plus the release lock and the stowage for the safety lock key.

R.A.F. Scampton wing

The famous 'Dambusters' of Lancaster bomber fame, No. 617 Squadron, was re-formed at Scampton in May 1958 to fly Vulcan's, joined by No.83 Squadron in October 1960. In 1969 No.230 OCU training unit arrived. Another Vulcan squadron was added to the station complement when No. 27 was re-formed in 1971, joined later by No.35 Squadron.

The first B. Mk2 to be delivered to Scampton with a Blue Steel capable missile was XL317 in June 1962. It was given emergency operational capability in August 1962, two months before the Cuban missile crisis in October 1962. It was not until February 1963 that the missile was fully released for service. By the end of 1964, Nos.83 and 27 Squadrons were equipped with Blue Steel sharing weapons with Wittering's Wing Nos.139 and 100 Squadrons Victor B2 aircraft. Blue Steel was officially retired on 31st December, 1970 when the United Kingdom's strategic nuclear capacity passed to the Royal Navy's submarine fleet.

A line up of Blue Steel missiles at their operational base at R.A.F. Scampton. The first Squadron, No.617, became operational at R.A.F. Scampton in early 1963.

Operational HS Blue Steel shows its associated equipment.

Vulcan B.Mk2 XL321 of No 617 Squadron with Blue Steel missile pictured on 18th July, 1962. The Squadrons insignia was anti flash roundel "pink."

Service trials began in 1961 with the trials unit No.4 J.S.T.U. based at Scampton being responsible for reporting all defects or unsatisfactory features on the missile and ground support equipment to Air Staff and Ministry of Aviation (M.o.A). This was to allow the M.o.A. to recommend clearance of the weapon system for release to the Service. The warhead capsule required little servicing by R.A.F. personnel, the main servicing of this component being the responsibility of Atomic Weapons Research Establishment (A.W.R.E.). Several company representatives were based at Scampton during the trials and advised only to improve liaison between the service and industry.

Pictured in February, 1963 is XL445 of No.27 Squadron which was based at Scampton.

XL446 in camouflage scheme pictured in October, 1964. First flown on 16th November, 1962 and went to No.27 Squadron at Scampton on 31st November. Note the two flat plate antennas between the engine nacelles which were fitted to Blue Steel aircraft.

Thirty five production B.Mk2 aircraft were modified at Woodford to carry Blue Steel along with three trials aircraft B.Mk1 XA903, B.Mk2 XH538 and XH539. The production aircraft were fitted with Olympus 201 series engines of 17,000lb thrust and completed between June 1961 and November 1962. These aircraft were:- XL317, XL318, XL319, XL320, XL321, XL359, XL360, XL361, XL384, XL385, XL386, XL387, XL388, XL389, XL390, XL391, XL392, XL425, XL426, XL427, XL443, XL444, XL445, XL446, XM569, XM570, XM571, XM572, XM573, XM574, XM575, XM576, XM594, XM595, XM597.

Alterations included a crank to the front bomb-bay spar, cut out at the rear spar and new bomb-bay fairings. Modification kits were produced for fitment at R.A.F. bases so that the aircraft could be converted to either conventional bombing or Blue Steel role.

XL320 first flew 9th November, 1961 and delivered to No.617 squadron 4th December, 1961. On 30th September, 1965 it became part of the Scampton Wing and later went to No.230 O.C.U. on 29th March, 1972. It was sold for scrap on 31st August, 1981. It is seen here pictured in all white anti flash scheme in 1963.

Seen here pictured in its low level role is XL320 in its camouflage scheme on 16th December, 1966 .

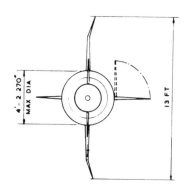

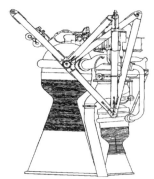

Dual Chamber Armstrong Siddeley Rocket motor. One chamber was used for initial boost, then the smaller cruise chamber was used for most of the flight.
It was fuelled by hydrogen peroxide and kerosene propellant.

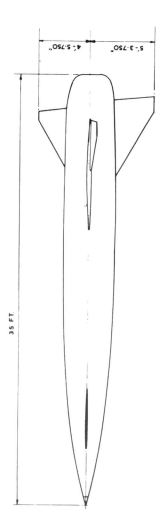

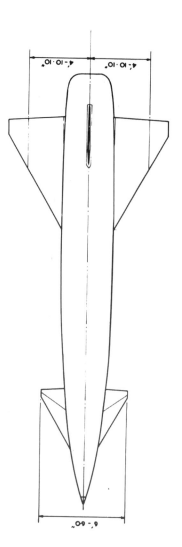

AVRO BLUE STEEL   AIR–TO–GROUND GUIDED MISSILE

Blue Steel cockpit (final conference)

First pilots position and side panels. The use of the unconventional fighter style single stick control column offered the advantage of saving space within the confines of the cockpit.
It was confirmed at the Blue Steel Final Conference on 19/21st December, 1960 that the full pressure suit was not being introduced into the B.Mk2 aircraft.

Second pilot's position and side panels.

Pilot's front panels. Unique to the Vulcan was the control surface indicator shown in the rectangular case above. It was an added safety feature and represented the tail view of the aircraft.

Set operator and navigator's plotters position. At the time the Vulcan used the GEE navigation system which synchronized pulses transmitted from the UK which allowed the Navigator to calculate the aircraft's position from the time delay between pulses. It was later replaced in the mid 60's by the military Tactical Air Navigation system (TACAN) and the American, Long Range Navigator (LORAN) system, both of these systems relied on ground antenna transmitter stations.

Air Electronics Officers (A.E.O.) position. The A.E.O. was in charge of all electrical systems and counter measures equipment. By the time Blue Steel aircraft had entered service a comprehensive counter measures suite was fitted.

Set operators front panel. Shown is the CRT screen. Above the screen is a camera used for recording the mission and ballistic computing. A joy stick was used to move the picture around, it was also connected to the autopilot so that the Nav. Radar operator could steer the aircraft. The Blue Steel inertial guidance system was integrated with the navigation equipment on the Vulcan and the Nav. Radar operator would periodically feed in H_2S fixes to the missile.

Counter measures

It was first proposed in May 1958 to fit a new Electronic Counter Measures (E.C.M.) suite to the Vulcan. This was retrospectively fitted to B.Mk1A aircraft, with the second production aircraft XH534 being the first B.Mk2 to be fitted with this equipment.

B.Mk1A & B.Mk2 electronic counter measures equipment.

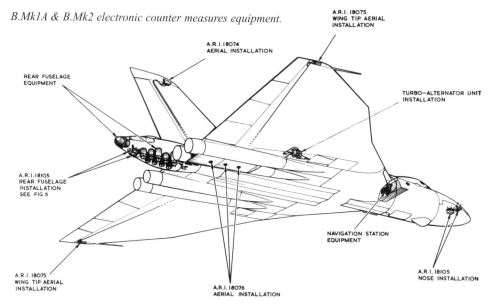

General view of E.C.M. canister heat exchangers on test rig frame 10th April, 1963.

Arrangement of E.C.M. test rig in its final form 10th April, 1963.

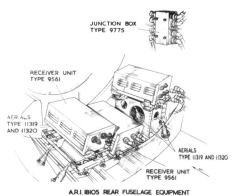

A.R.I. 18105 REAR FUSELAGE EQUIPMENT

Blue Saga rear fuselage warning receiver 7th July, 1960.

ARI 18105
Blue Saga radar warning receiver

ARI 18074
Green Palm - voice communications jammer.

ARI 18075
Blue Diver - (airborne radio installation) low band VHF jammer replaced Green Palm.

ARI 18076
Red Shrimp - airborne high band jammer.

The above pictures show XH534 with the R.C.M. tail unit to best advantage on 7th July, 1959.

Making final adjustments to the large R.C.M. fairing at Woodford on 7th July, 1959.

Douglas Skybolt adventure

Early Douglas Skybolt dummy missile installation note the different warhead design.

Skybolt dummy missile on XH537 pictured at Woodford 21st September, 1961.

The USAF began accepting bids for development of large ballistic missiles that could be launched from strategic bombers at high altitude in early 1959. Douglas Aircraft received the prime contract in May and in turn subcontracted to Northrop for the guidance system, Aerojet for the propulsion system and General Electric for the re-entry vehicle. The system was initially known as WS-138A and was given the official name GAM-87 Skybolt in 1960. In May 1960 the British Government agreed to purchase 144 Skybolt missiles. By agreement, British funding for research and development was limited to that required to modify the aircraft to take the missile with Avro being selected as the UK main contractor. The first three B.Mk2 Vulcan's allocated to be fitted out to carry the Skybolt missile were XH537, XH538 and XL391. The missile was powered by an Aerojet General two-stage solid-fuelled rocket. It weighed 11,000 lb and had a length 39.63 feet and a maximum diameter of 36 inches. It had a range of 1,150 miles with a flight ceiling of 300 miles and a speed of 9,500 miles per hour.

The Vulcan's port and starboard wing were fitted with a hard point so that a pylon could be fitted to carry the missile. This pylon was strength tested at Whitworth-Gloster Aircraft Co. In the bomb bay in the vicinity of the rear spar a Douglas instrumented crate was used for the research and development role.

The pylon and missile was similar to the Blue Jay/Gloster Javelin configuration. Extensive flight tests measuring the Blue Jay aerodynamic loads and comprehensive calculations on the flow field beneath the Javelin wing provided considerable ground work for a reliable estimate of the aerodynamic loads on the Skybolt missile.

By 1961, several test missiles were ready for testing from USAF B-52 bombers, with drop-tests starting in January. In England compatibility trials with mock-ups started on the Vulcan. Powered tests started in the USA in April 1962, but the test series went badly, with the first five trials ending in a combination of dissimilar failures.

Back at Avro a report issued on 6th March, 1962 stated that problems were encountered with flow visualisation test around the Star Tracker window due to large cross flow found to exist over the nose of the missile which did not exist on the B52 installation. This would have a serious effect on the missiles navigation and involved extra man hours by Avro photographic personnel which were not anticipated. This complication led to some 350 missiles drops compared with an anticipated thirty.

The first fully successful flight in the U.S.A. occurred on 19th December, 1962, but by this time the American Government had lost confidence in the project which led to its cancellation. Avro received notice of the cancellation of contract KD/B/01/CB.6(a) for 40 Vulcan Mk2 Skybolt aircraft along with contract KD/B/0118/CB.6(a) for Research and Development (R&D) work in early January 1963.

Take-off from Woodford in 1961. This was to test the Vulcan's ability to fly with a single Skybolt missile.

Rear view of XH537 taken 17th October, 1962.

Aerodynamic trials were carried out by XH537 with two dummy Skybolts. On 9th December, 1961 XH538 began dummy drop tests over the West Freugh range in Scotland.

XH537 carrying Skybolt missiles 17th October, 1962 note the new warhead.

In January 1961 a No.83 Squadron Vulcan went to the Douglas plant at Santa Monica, California, for electrical compatibility tests. The following year the R.A.F. sent 200 personnel to Elgin Air Force Base in Florida to act as the British Joint Trials Force for advanced testing of Skybolt with a Vulcan B Mk2.

The Nortronics Division of Northrop provided the miniaturised stellar-monitored inertial navigation system consisting of an astro-inertial system and star tracker tied together by a ballistic missile computer.

First flight of XH537 pictured on 29th September, 1961.

Deterrent role change

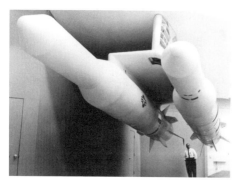

Skybolt missiles under Boeing B52 wing mock up 14th April, 1961.

Gilbert Whitehead at Woodford in November 1961 discussing aspects of the Skybolt Missile with Air Vice-Marshal Sir Keith Cross.

In November 1962 the Americans announced they were cancelling the Skybolt programme. A new replacement plan was hammered out that led to the Nassau Agreement, in December 1962 and to the United Kingdom purchasing the Polaris Submarine launched ballistic missile system (S.L.B.M.), equipped with British warheads. The UK would thus retain its independent deterrent force, although its control passed from the R.A.F. largely to the Royal Navy. The R.A.F. kept its tactical nuclear capability.

Installation of Skybolt missile

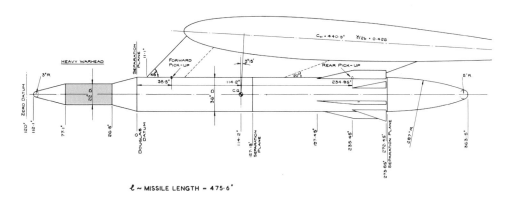

The shaded area of this drawing of the Skybolt missile shows it with a heavy warhead, a light warhead version had a length of 40 inches and a diameter of 20 inches. The heavy warhead had a length of 50.6 inches and diameter of 22 inches.

The control fin had a length of 37 inches by 18.5 inches in depth. The strakes had a length of 75 inches by 28.5 inches in depth. The maximum diameter to the extremity of the fins was 73 inches.

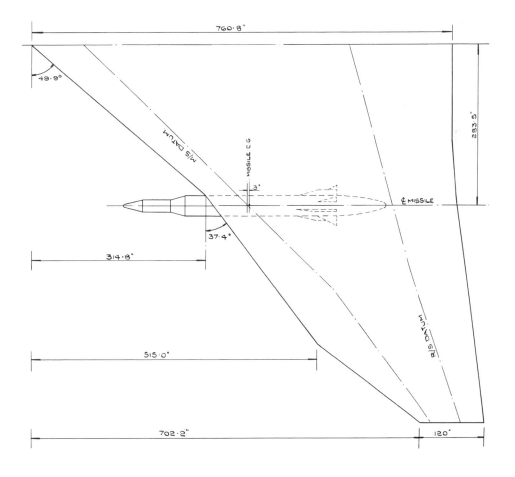

Vulcan in the Headlines

Shown below is an article printed in the 1961 October issue of Avro news on the Vulcan's exploits to that date.

Almost thirty-one years after the first historic flight to Australia made by Ross and Keith Smith in four weeks two days, an Avro Vulcan bomber took off from Scampton, Linconshire, and headed for the same destination, "down under". It touched down at Richmond, Sydney, exactly 20 hrs. 3 mins. after take-off.

This epic flight took place on June 21st this year. Squadron Leader M. G. Beavis piloted the 617 "Dambuster" squadron's Vulcan 11,500 miles to Australia at an average speed of 574 m.p.h., refuelling in the air from a Valiant jet tanker over Cyprus, Pakistan and Singapore. This was the Vulcan's longest non-stop flight and the first non-stop journey to be made by any aircraft to Australia. Yet this is only one of the recent successes which proved the Vulcan's superiority in speed, mobility and power.

Two months earlier, on 10th April, a Vulcan from the same Dambuster squadron made a return journey from Scampton to Karachi, Pakistan. The Vulcan completed a total of 8,500 miles in 17 $\frac{1}{2}$ hours, averaging 500 m.p.h. and again refuelling during flight.

Once more it was Squadron Leader Beavis and his crew who made this journey and who, later, scored a triple success by winning the individual award for bombing and navigation in Bomber Command's annual competition. This has been a yearly award since 1956 (although R.A.F. squadrons have completed for a bombing trophy since 1927), and has been won twice previously in1957 and 1959 by a Vulcan aircraft squadron.

Following the Vulcan's successful return journey flight to Karachi, exercises involving Vulcan's of No. 83 squadron were arranged for 11th May with the aim of testing Britain's retaliatory power in the event of a nuclear attack. The "mock war", named Exercise Mayflight, proved Bomber Command's readiness for any emergency. The speed at which take-off was accomplished, following the practice warnings of 30, 10, 5 and 3 minutes, was remarkable. The first of the aircraft was airborne in less than two minutes and the last was off the runway within 3 minutes, ready to join aircraft from Fighter Command for Exercise Matador. In this complementary exercise different U.K. targets were attacked. To add to the difficulty of the test, R.A.F., American, Canadian and French aircraft stationed in Europe joined in "attack" against the British force.

The Vulcan's power as a deterrent will be appreciably increased when it is equipped with the Avro Blue Steel air-to-ground missile. As many readers will know, this is a stand-off weapon which is launched from the carrier aircraft at a considerable distance from the target, to which it is guided by an automatic navigation system.

Meanwhile, a Vulcan aircraft has flown to Los Angeles for tests to check compatibility between the aircraft and the Skybolt missiles. The Douglas Skybolt is an air-launched ballistic missile which is scheduled to arm the B-52s of the USAF Strategic Air Command in 1964 and should be in service with Vulcan's of Bomber Command about twelve months later.

Along more peaceful lines a Vulcan aircraft also flew to Africa where it took part in a flypast over Freetown, Sierra Leone, during the independence celebrations in April. It flew from its temporary base at Dakar 500 miles to Freetown and returned to its base without landing.

Other Vulcan achievements which were, perhaps, not as startling as the Australian record have included demonstration flights in the Pensacola flying display in June, which commemorated the golden anniversary of naval aviation in America, and an impressive exhibition at the Paris international air show in May where the Vulcan B.Mk2 appeared.

To conclude this survey of the Vulcan's outstanding performance on an amazing note - during the mock H-bombing competition in April, where the targets were identified by radar, a single corner of a section of a paper mill at Hemel Hempstead was "obliterated" from a height of eight miles! Shown below is the visit to America of Vulcan XH535 for Skybolt compatibility trials.

 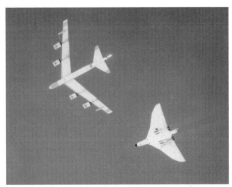

Boeing B-52 in formation with XH535 note the difference in wing length.

High above the Mojave Desert, near California, Avro Vulcan XH535 flies in formation with an American B-52 bomber. Piloted by Tony Blackman and 'Ossie' Hawkins. the Vulcan was in America to take part in tests for Skybolt installation. Like the Avro Vulcan the B-52 was also to carry the Skybolt air-to-surface missile.

Development programme 1957 - 1962

It is worth noting that in 1959 it was announced that Avro was to enter the civil market with the Avro 748 turbo-prop feeder airliner. This was due to the slow down in military work and the lack of new military projects, this combined with military defence cuts led to Vulcan being the only viable long range nuclear bomber available to Royal Air Force in the mid 1970's.

For the Vulcan to be a reliable weapons system it was continuously updated to meet the different roles that it was assigned and kept the innovative Avro initial projects department team busy for over two decades.

As can be seen from the chart below most of the major developments had been completed by 1962/63 with the introduction into service of the B.Mk2.

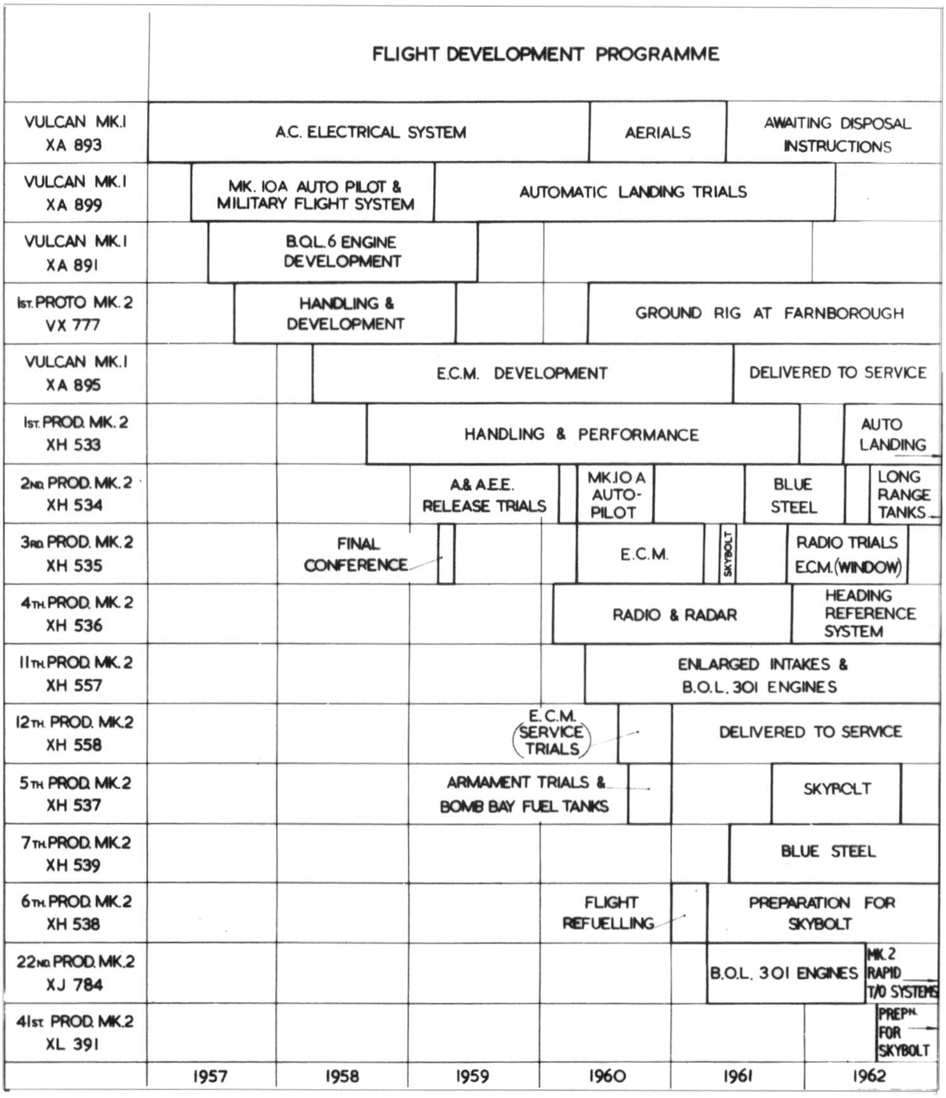

FLIGHT DEVELOPMENT PROGRAMME						
	1957	1958	1959	1960	1961	1962
VULCAN MK.I XA 893	A.C. ELECTRICAL SYSTEM			AERIALS	AWAITING DISPOSAL INSTRUCTIONS	
VULCAN MK.I XA 899	MK. IOA AUTO PILOT & MILITARY FLIGHT SYSTEM	AUTOMATIC LANDING TRIALS				
VULCAN MK.I XA 891	B.OL.6 ENGINE DEVELOPMENT					
Ist. PROTO MK. 2 VX 777	HANDLING & DEVELOPMENT	GROUND RIG AT FARNBOROUGH				
VULCAN MK.I XA 895	E.C.M. DEVELOPMENT			DELIVERED TO SERVICE		
Ist. PROD. MK. 2 XH 533	HANDLING & PERFORMANCE				AUTO LANDING	
2ND. PROD. MK. 2 XH 534	A& A.E.E. RELEASE TRIALS	MK.IO A AUTO-PILOT		BLUE STEEL	LONG RANGE TANKS	
3RD. PROD. MK. 2 XH 535	FINAL CONFERENCE	E.C.M.	SKYBOLT	RADIO TRIALS E.C.M.(WINDOW)		
4TH. PROD. MK. 2 XH 536	RADIO & RADAR		HEADING REFERENCE SYSTEM			
IITH. PROD. MK. 2 XH 557	ENLARGED INTAKES & B.O.L.301 ENGINES					
12TH. PROD. MK.2 XH 558	E.C.M. (SERVICE TRIALS)	DELIVERED TO SERVICE				
5TH. PROD. MK.2 XH 537	ARMAMENT TRIALS & BOMB BAY FUEL TANKS	SKYBOLT				
7TH. PROD. MK.2 XH 539	BLUE STEEL					
6TH. PROD. MK.2 XH 538	FLIGHT REFUELLING	PREPARATION FOR SKYBOLT				
22ND. PROD. MK.2 XJ 784	B.O.L. 301 ENGINES	MK.2 RAPID T/O SYSTEMS				
41st. PROD. MK.2 XL 391	PREPN FOR SKYBOLT					

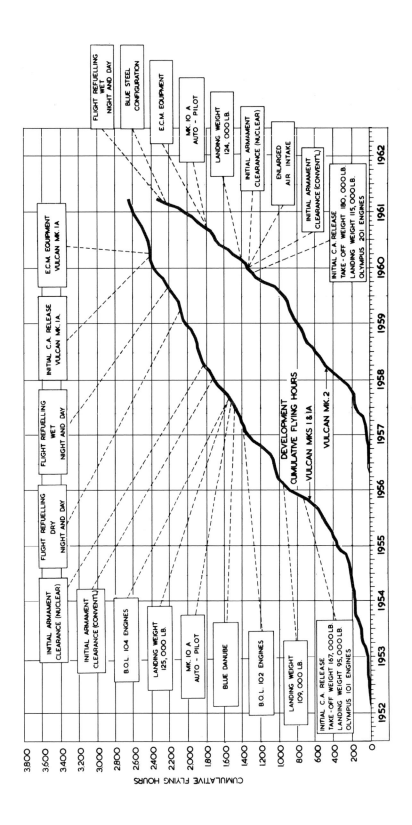

Alert readiness & rapid take-off proposals

A design study was issued in January 1961 on alert readiness and rapid take-off requirements for the Vulcan pre - 1963 B.Mk1/1A & Mk2 and post - 1963 for the Vulcan B.Mk2 aircraft. Shown below are the requirements from that report.

1. Statement of Policy and Requirement

The Air Staff require that where the above aircraft are deployed on "30s day Alert Readiness" the rapid take-off capability shall be such as to meet the following warning time scale.

(a)   Up to 1963 - 15 minutes reducing to 3 minutes.

(b)   Post 1963   - 30 seconds from inert to first aircraft rolling.

These requirements are such as to dictate the need to achieve engine starting etc:- in the minimum possible time, and to ensure that connections to the aircraft from the various items of ground equipment necessary to ensure crew comfort, store conditioning, electrical supplies etc., are kept to the absolute minimum and are capable of quick disconnection with the minimum of ground crew attendance.

2. Operational Conditions.

It is necessary to consider the above against the variations introduced by changes in climatic conditions, type of weapon carried, availability of capable ground equipment etc., and certain fundamental assumptions are made as follows :-

(a) That the crew are in the aircraft with entrance door closed.

(b) The climatic environment ranges from -26°C to +40°C.

(c) That the use of automatic pull off, self sealing, spring flap covered type quick
    disconnects, using restraining cables anchored to the O.R.P. is favoured.

(d) That Vulcan B.Mk.1 & 1A aircraft are confined to operation with free falling stores only.

(e) That Vulcan Mk. 2 aircraft may operate with either free falling stores, Blue Steel, or
    Skybolt in that date order.

(f) That no ground conditioning of radar, N.B.S., or E.C.M., equipment is required.

(g) That no aircraft refuelling is necessary.

(h) That each aircraft would be on immediate readiness for four hours followed by a
    period of "stand-down" for changing crews, replenishment and servicing of ground
    equipment, etc:-

It is appreciated that during the initial pre-1963 period ad hoc arrangements will be necessary pending the phasing in of modifications and taking into account types of ground.

Engine starting *post 1963 period B.Mk.2 Vulcan aircraft only.*
At this stage the Rotax L.P. Air Starter on the Olympus engines will have been replaced with the Rotax Combuster Starter to ensure that the engines can be started simultaneously in 15 seconds. It is envisaged also that a master "Scramble" button will be fitted, the operation of which will start:- (a) The four engines. (b) The Powered Flying Controls (PFCs) from the electrical ground supply.

It is considered that subsequent to initiation of the start the 2nd Pilot will select the pitot head heaters ON, together and one booster pump in each group.

The alternators which were already selected ON during the "Alert" will now come on automatically and take over their own loads as each engine reaches the flight idling speed, thus leaving no load on the ground supply trolley when all alternators are on line.

It was proposed that the Blue Steel Mk2 missile would be covered with a pre-conditioned air to an envelope shroud round the store beneath the aircraft. The shroud was to be secured quick release attachments.

MK II BLUE STEEL or FREE FALLING STORE
take off in 30 secs
using existing conditioning and electrical trolleys

AVS supply angled behind fairing

Blue Steel air connections

intercomm & telescramble

cabin air supply
angled behind fairing

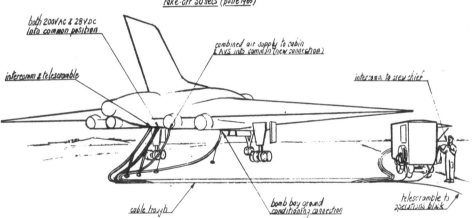

MK II FREE FALLING STORE
with single multipurpose ground trolley.
take-off 30 secs (paste 1963)

both 200VAC & 28VDC
into common position

combined air supply to cabin
& AVS into common (new connection)

intercomm & telescramble

intercom to crew chief

cable trough

bomb bay ground
conditioning connection

telescramble to
operations block

Quick Reaction Alert (Q.R.A.)

Along with the adoption of Quick Reaction Alert (Q.R.A.) the Vulcan would fly to dispersal bases around the United Kingdom to avoid being destroyed at their main bases.

Quick Reaction Alert was inaugurated in February 1962 with Blue Steel squadrons forming the spearhead of Bomber Command's Quick Reaction Alert Force and was to do so for over five years. The original procedure was to keep one aircraft from each squadron maintained in an armed condition. Staging points were constructed at the end of the runways, with aircraft parked on short strips to aid rapid take-off.

During a Quick Reaction Alert the ground crew would scramble from their nearby caravan, where they had been living, to their designated Vulcan, the crew chief would then check the pre-flighted aircraft simultaneously starting of all four engines by compressed air from the nearby Palouste, this was accomplished by pressing the rapid start button. The aircrew would then arrive and taxi the aircraft to the end of the runway and await instructions. It was not unknown for a Q.R.A. exercise to be trialled at 0300 hrs on a Sunday. Four Vulcan's could be scrambled within 90 seconds of starting to roll. During normal times ground crews would live in their caravans for two weeks once a year as part of their Q.R.A. practice.

Rocket assisted take-off trials

To help overcome the problems of performance of a jet engine in hot and high conditions it was proposed to fit a rocket assisted take-off RATOG system. This was to allow the Vulcan to maintain the aircrafts operational weight from short runways and tropical conditions. In May 1959 Vulcan B.Mk1 was allotted to test this system.

A study produced by the Avro Engineering Research Division and carried out by the Rocket Division of the de Havilland Engine Company in January 1961 reported to determine the effects of Spectre rocket assisted take-off. A specimen rig was used which consisted of a Vulcan Mk.1 rear fuselage section from the rear spar aft and from rib 62.5 port to and including the inboard starboard elevator mounted on a steel dummy rear spar. Twenty five tests were completed with a running time of approximately one minute. The report contained information on reflected vibration, noise and efflux on adjacent aircraft structure and operation efficiency of the DC and AC electrical system. The A.T.O. system had been looked at for some time in various design reports from the 1950's to improve the take-off performance of aircraft. But with the change in operational requirement and improved performance of the Olympus engine it was not required. On 14th July, 1960 Victor XA930 successfully took-off from Hatfield assisted by two Spectre rocket pods between the engines intakes, this layout would have been a similar to that used by the Vulcan.

Resultant test completed by the deHavilland Engine Company on a speciman Vulcan rear fuselage and wing section.

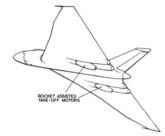

Spectre rocket assisted installation. The two units were to be jettisoned after take-off.

Change of role

When Francis "Gary" Powers flying a Lockheed U2 as a covert surveillance aircraft was brought down near Degtyarsk, Ural Region, of the Soviet Union, by SA-2 Guideline (S-75 Dvina) missiles on 1st may 1960, it became apparent that any high flying aeroplane would be vulnerable to any surface to air missiles defences. Intelligence reports indicated that this would extend to the "V" force and a requirement was issued to revert to the less vulnerable low level role which would delay detection by radar.

With the Valiant being phased out in 1964 due to metal fatigue and the Victor not being suitable for the low level role it was left to the Vulcan to fulfil this role with its inherent stronger structure capable of withstanding the buffeting experienced at low level.

Low level training began with B.Mk1A aircraft in April 1963 and became operational in June 1963. Vulcan B.Mk2 Squadrons began training at the beginning of 1964 and declared operational in May that year.

It was recognised that the resulting fatigue life would be effected by this role and a production B.Mk2 (XM596) was taken of the production line for structural test which led to strengthening modifications to allow the Vulcan to have a longer fatigue life of 12,000 hrs in the low level role. These structural modifications were completed at Bitteswell under a future remediable programme.

Production B. Mk2 Vulcan XM596 was taken off the production line to be a structural test specimen to determine the fatigue life of the Vulcan in its new low level role. Pictured here on 8th May, 1959.

Camouflage

The first B. Mk2 Vulcan to have the new low level camouflage scheme was XM645. It was to have a dark green and medium sea grey upper surface and white anti-flash underside. The aircraft were usually given a glossy Polyurethane finish. Particular attention was paid to giving the white underside a smooth finish, all rivets were made flush fitting and any gaps filled in. In the early 70s some aircraft were given a light aircraft grey lower surface and the black radome began to disappear along with a general toning down.

When the Vulcan was manoeuvring at low level it was found that the white anti-flash underside was clearly visible, so the Vulcan adopted an overall matt "satin" camouflage scheme to make it less visible at low level. Two aircraft in 1977 were given a disruptive desert camouflage of sand and stone on the undersurface for the 'Red Flag' exercise in the United States.

Pictured at low level XM649 on 16th June, 1964. It made its first flight from Woodford on 28th April, 1964 and was based at R.A.F. Waddington with Nos. 9, 12 and 35 Squadrons.

A decade of service

In June 1969 the first of the Blue Steel missiles were withdrawn which brought about the squadrons operating Blue Steel being disbanded starting with No.83 Squadron on 19th July 1969. Towards the end of 1969 there were only five squadrons left in the United Kingdom operating the Vulcan, Nos. 27 and 617 at Scampton and Nos. 44, 50 and 101 Squadrons at Waddington continued in the tactical service of the Supreme Allied Commander Europe (SACEUR). The Cottesmore Wing of Nos.9 and 35 Squadrons moved to Akrotiri in Cyprus to provide back-up for NATO's Southern Flank and to provide support for CENTO originally known as The Middle East Treaty Organisation or METO if required. The last Vulcan Blue Steel sortie was with No.617 Squadron on 21st December, 1970.

Five man crew ready to board the Vulcan.

Guard dogs were used to provide security on air bases operating the Vulcan.

Vulcan exercise at Scampton 11th May, 1961.

PART SIX

CONCEPTUAL PROJECTS

Paper projects

Avro had an initial projects department which was responsible for the design and further development of aircraft projects, most of the work remained secret and never went further than paper ideas but some projects like the Avro Vulcan did meet the light of day. I have included some of these paper projects as they give an idea of the thinking at that time. Because the government could not go to the expense of competitive prototypes most of these projects went no further than the drawing board and at best mock-up stage.

If a project got beyond some scribbled notes, a drawing may have been created. These were allocated an initial project drawing number (I.P.D). and sometimes several different I.P.D. numbers were produced and number of these have survived.

Shown below is a drawing produced by initial project department issued on 29th September 1953, for an air launched Avro Type 720 rocket powered interceptor which was to be carried by the Vulcan. The 720 was built to meet requirement OR.301   F.137D specification which was issued to A. V. Roe & Co. Ltd for a rocket powered interceptor in competition with Saunders Roe P.177. The drawing below shows the dual powered version powered by a Spectre rocket and Viper jet engine. A mock-up and prototype of the Type 720 interceptor were built by Avro, the prototype was attributed serial number XD696, however the project was cancelled by the Ministry in 1956 due to cost limitations and the prototype was broken up. Also shown is a missile version of the 720.

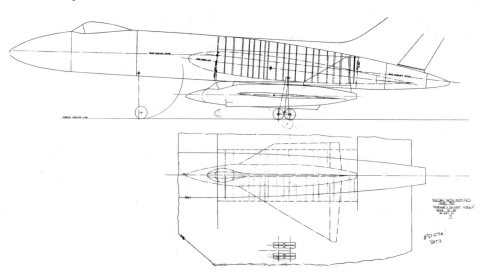

I.P.D. 514 shows the Vulcan with modified Type 720 duel powered interceptor.

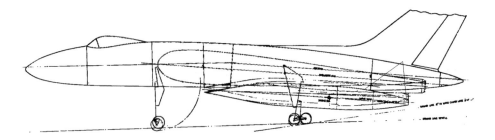

This I.P.D. drawing shows the Type 720 missile. A shortened version was also proposed.

Vertical take-off

In February 1954 an interesting project was proposed by Avro for a vertical take-off aircraft based on the Type 707B. At that time vertical take-off had been carried some distance by the "Flying Bedstead" built by Rolls-Royce at Hucknall. The Ministry of Supply issued specification No. E.R.143T to cover the next logical step of a jet lift research aircraft. The major part of the experiment was to be the development for the control during take-off, landing and the transition from hovering to normal flight and vice-versa.

It was to be powered by six Rolls-Royce R.B.108 engines which were being developed for a high thrust to weight ratio specifically for this application.

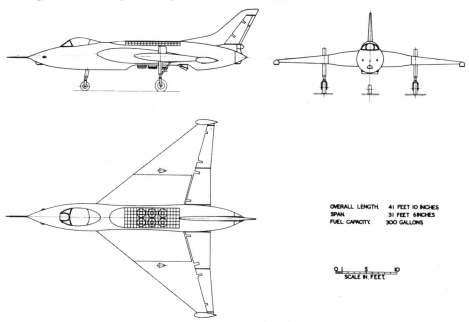

OVERALL LENGTH	41 FEET 10 INCHES
SPAN	31 FEET 6 INCHES
FUEL CAPACITY	300 GALLONS

SCALE IN FEET

Proposed Phase 2B development

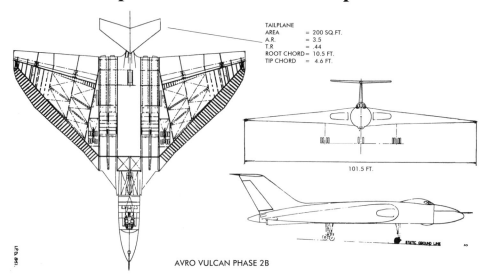

TAILPLANE
AREA　　　　　= 200 SQ.FT.
A.R.　　　　　= 3.5
T.R　　　　　 = .44
ROOT CHORD = 10.5 FT.
TIP CHORD　 = 4.6 FT.

101.5 FT.

AVRO VULCAN PHASE 2B

This was the proposed Phase 2B development of Phase 2A but not officially submitted.

Glider bomb

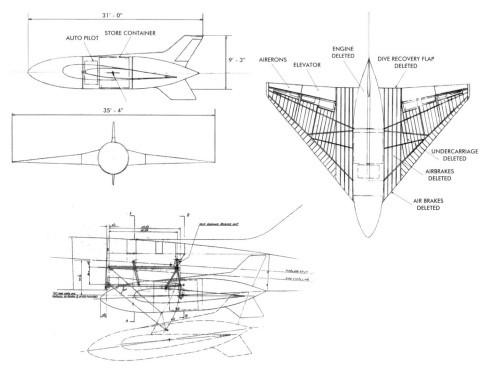

**GENERAL ARRANGEMENT OF AVRO 707 GLIDER BOMB
AND RELEASE UNIT**

A project looked at by the Initial Projects Department in 1954 was a glider bomb based on the Type 707 aircraft, to be released by the Avro Vulcan.

Winged bomb

In May 1955 the Royal Aircraft Establishment at Farnborough produced a report on test completed at the High Speed Wind tunnel of a winged bomb mounted under the fuselage of the Vulcan. The bomb was tested in two configurations one was partially recessed into the underside of the aircraft fuselage with the option of mounting clear of the fuselage.

Extract from R.A.E. report

In general, the conventional method of bomb stowage within an aircraft fuselage is impossible with a large winged bomb, since the wing span of the bomb is much greater than the width of any practicable bomb bay. The bomb must therefore be carried externally, the most obvious method being to mount it on a short strut under the fuselage. A possible aerodynamic refinement of this mounting at the cost of some structural complexity is to eliminate the strut and recess the lower surface of the aircraft fuselage to take the upper part of the bomb body.

In the case of an aircraft having a moderately high aspect ratio wing, mounted in either the mid or shoulder position, it can be assumed that the interference effects between the wing of the aircraft and the wing of the bomb, are small. For a delta winged bomber, such as the Avro Vulcan, or an aircraft having a wing set low on the fuselage, the proximity of the bomb to the aircraft wing invalidates such an assumption. Hence, tests had to be made in the R.A.E. 10ft x 7ft High Speed Tunnel to determine the effects of a representative strut-mounted, and semi-recessed winged bomb on the aerodynamic characteristics of a 1/30th scale model of the Avro Vulcan, and to compare the relative merits of the two mounting positions. The aircraft model was sling-supported and had an internal six-component strain gauge balance. For these tests, the balance was used to measure only lift, drag and pitching moment. Two winged bombs were constructed in Tufnol resin to represent the alternative mounting positions. For the bomb in the recessed position, the upper surface of the bomb body was shaped to suit the contour of the under surface of the Vulcan fuselage. The other bomb was attached to a short steel strut for mounting under the aircraft fuselage

It was concluded that both versions had no marked effect on the lift of the aircraft and that the partially recessed bomb had little effect on drag divergence.

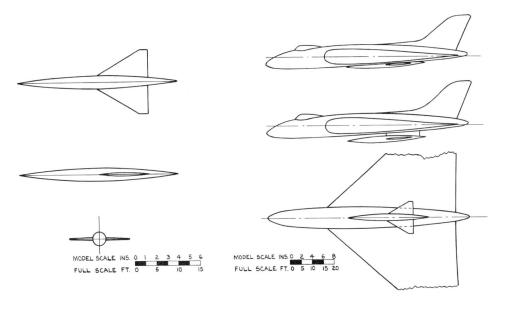

MODEL SCALE INS. 0 1 2 3 4 5 6
FULL SCALE FT. 0   5   10   15

MODEL SCALE INS. 0 2 4 6 8
FULL SCALE FT. 0 5 10 15 20

Missile delivery schemes

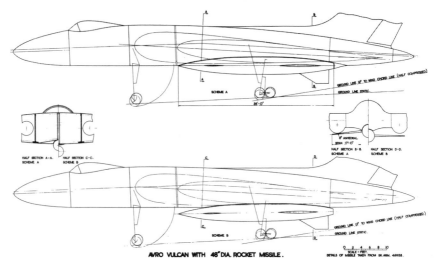

AVRO VULCAN WITH 48" DIA. ROCKET MISSILE.

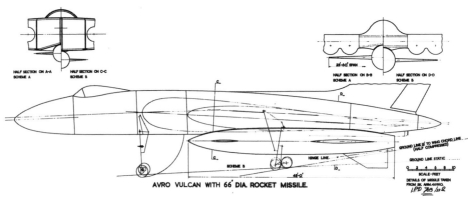

AVRO VULCAN WITH 66" DIA. ROCKET MISSILE.

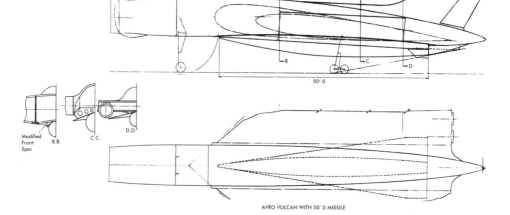

AVRO VULCAN WITH 50'.0 MISSILE

This I.P.D.1044 drawing shows a 50'.0 missile issued on 2nd March, 1956.

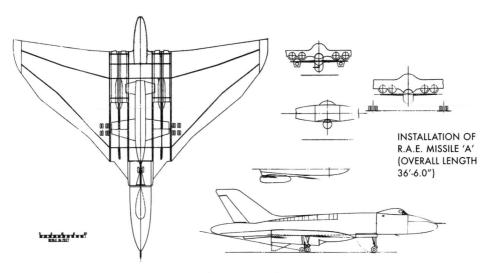

INSTALLATION OF
R.A.E. MISSILE 'A'
(OVERALL LENGTH
36'-6.0")

INSTALLATION OF RAE MISSILE 'A' (OVERALL LENGTH 36'-6.0")

The above drawing dated 16th July, 1957 shows the Vulcan with a R.A.E. Missile (A) designed to meet O.R.1149 issued in May 1956. It was to be powered by a Olympus 21R jet engine. It was one of the first missiles proposals designed to meet this requirement. Shown below are three missiles designed by Avro to be carried by the Vulcan to meet O.R.1149 and covered ranges of up to 1800 nautical miles. The W.107 was powered by the Gyron Junior turbojet and the W.109 was to be rocket powered.

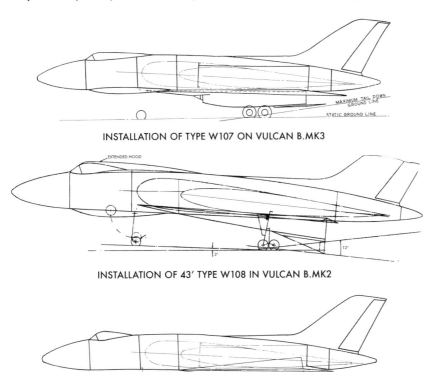

INSTALLATION OF TYPE W107 ON VULCAN B.MK3

INSTALLATION OF 43' TYPE W108 IN VULCAN B.MK2

INSTALLATION OF TYPE W109 ON VULCAN B.MK2

Type 734

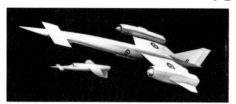

Pictured is the Type 730 with the Type 734 drone in escort.

The Avro Type 734 of October 1956 was a radio controlled proposed decoy counter measures aircraft powered by one Armstrong Siddeley P176 engine. It was designed to be launched from the Avro Vulcan to assist the Type 730 reach their target. The Vulcan had sufficient range to accompany the Type 730 and provide counter measures lacking in the 730.

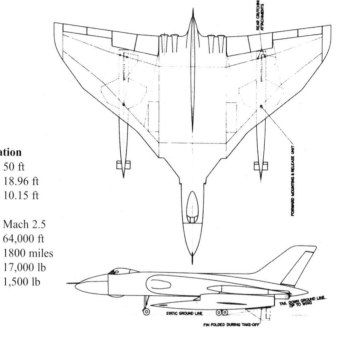

Type 734 Specification

Length	50 ft
Span	18.96 ft
Height	10.15 ft
Speed	Mach 2.5
Altitude	64,000 ft
Range still air	1800 miles
Weight	17,000 lb
Counter measures	1,500 lb

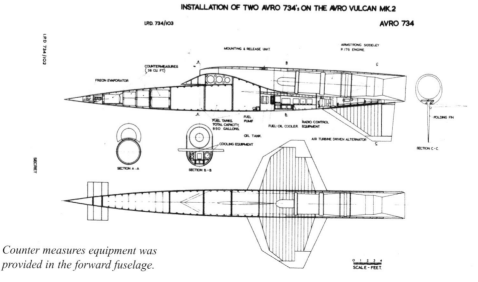

INSTALLATION OF TWO AVRO 734's ON THE AVRO VULCAN MK.2

Counter measures equipment was provided in the forward fuselage.

Phase 5

The Vulcan phase 5 proposals issued in November 1956 were basically a collection of modifications that was offered for further development of the Vulcan to an eventual Mk.3 standard. The report is reproduced below and covered the installation of a missile to Operating Requirement O.R.1149, the provision of ejector seats for the rear crew members, a new main undercarriage to meet a higher all-up-weight, additional fuel capacity and an alternative Radio Counter Measures (R.C.M.) installation. It was not proposed to embark upon any major aerodynamic modifications until the B.Mk.2 aircraft flight performance was known.

This montage shows Avro W.107 installation as shown in the 1956 development brochure on the proposed B.Mk3 Vulcan.

Installation of ejection seats for rear crew members

The need for ejection seats for the rear crew members has been thought to be desirable for some time, but the specification, did not make this requirement. However, with the development of seats which provide means of successful escape even when the aircraft is very near to the ground, the fitting of ejection seats for the rear crew members becomes attractive. Though such an installation carries weight and structural penalties, it is felt that ejection seats should be fitted to all Vulcan aircraft as a retrospective modification.

Details of seat installation

In order to eject the rear crew members it is necessary to manoeuvre the ejector seats prior to their ejection, so that they clear the backs of the pilots' seats and the edge member of the cockpit rail. In the case of the centre crew member, the seat is rotated aft through some 80°. The two outer rear crew members are also rotated inboard by some 14°. With the seats in this position it is now possible to eject all members of the crew independently of each other, that is, no one member is dependent upon the ejection of another to make good his escape. A time delay mechanism will be required in order to ensure that there will be suitable interval between two seats leaving the aircraft should their occupants have selected together.

The motions of the seats prior to ejection would be interconnected with the single action by the crew member of pulling the blind over his face. As it is not possible to invert the ejection guns so that the piston rod leaves with the seat and the cylinder is left in the aircraft it is essential that the extended telescopic piston rods of the pilots' seats should be rotated clear of the paths of other crew members. It is considered that this can be achieved by an automatic device which will be tripped by the base of the seat as it leaves the ejection rail. The action of the first crew member in pulling down his blind automatically initiates the forced release of the canopy. The present canopy release by the pilots in the event of ditching is, of course, retained.

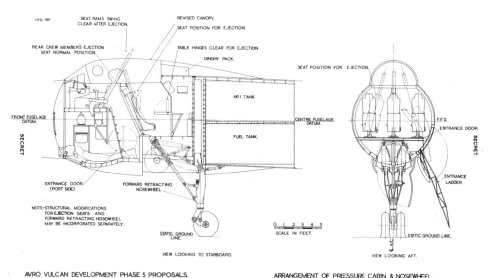

AVRO VULCAN DEVELOPMENT PHASE 5 PROPOSALS.   ARRANGEMENT OF PRESSURE CABIN & NOSEWHEEL.

Modifications to structure of pressure cabin

It has been found possible to introduce a structural member in the middle of the enlarged aperture immediately aft of the pilot's seat, and this tie will considerably reduce the weight penalty involved. Further subsidiary modifications to strengthen the crew members floor to react the ejection loads are necessary and the navigator's table will have to be hinged so that it will fold clear of the knee line. It would be desirable to introduce these structural modifications at the same time as the forward retracting nose wheel was introduced, but there is no conflict between these two alterations,

New Canopy

The increased aperture in the pressure cabin entails a redesigned canopy, which will be extended in order to cater for the revised dinghy stowage, The detachable piece of the canopy will be larger than the present one, requiring a larger explosive charge to jettison it; tests will be required to determine its behaviour upon release. The canopy shape will be improved aerodynamically, postponing the onset of buffeting and reducing drag.

Revised Dinghy Stowage

It is necessary to re-position the dinghy stowage further aft on the top of the fuselage, in order that it shall clear the knee ejection line of the rear crew members. At the present time the dinghy release handle is attached directly to the dinghy container and is readily accessible to the pilots when standing on the pilot's floor. It will be necessary to fit a remote control or alternatively, if acceptable, the handle would be reached by standing on the rear crew member seats.

Repositioning of miscellaneous equipment

A number of minor items in the pressure cabin would have to be repositioned, for example, the A.C. electrical equipment for the flight instruments which is now situated below the starboard rear seat and also the sextant location,

Carriage of missile to O.R. 1149
Carriage of Avro Weapons Research Department W.107 Missile

In order to mount the W.107 missile it will be necessary to retract the nose wheel forward in order to install the missile. The overall length of the present missile is 54.7 feet with a body length of 44 feet. It has been found possible to install the missile and still retain an adequate ground angle of some 12° provided that the fin of the missile is folded; this angle is considered sufficient for normal landings and take-offs. The c.g. of the missile is compatible with respect to the aircraft c.g. and with the change in trim upon release of the missile. The missile fuselage is mated with the underside of the aircraft, with the main planes of the missile immediately below the engine jet pipe tunnels. A revised bomb bay fairing is required to suit the upper surface of the missile and this replaces the existing bomb doors. Consequently the bomb bay is virtually left free for the installation of the R.C.M. equipment, missile launching equipment and extra long range internal fuel tanks. There are two of these tanks with a total capacity of 2460 gallons. In order to ensure the correct functioning of the missile prior to launching it is essential that the turbo-jet engine should be running, consequently some revision to the aft fuselage of the aircraft to replace the existing light alloy structure by a stiffened titanium structure is required. This makes it possible to utilise the power from the engine to increase the target altitude of the aircraft. It is of interest to note that the cranked front spar lower boom is not now required, but will be retained for carriage of the Blue Steel.

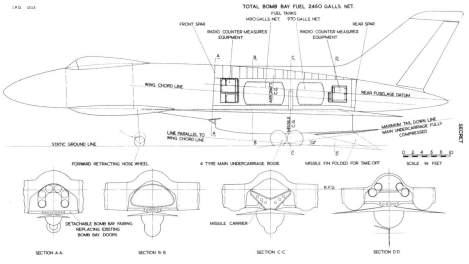

AVRO VULCAN DEVELOPMENT PHASE 5 PROPOSALS   INSTALLATION OF AVRO W.107 MISSILE TO O.R. 1149

Carriage of R.A.E. Missile A.T.V.4

This R.A.E. missile can be installed in a similar manner to the W.107 missile, again the missile fits under the belly of the aircraft with the wings of missile projecting below the inboard jet pipe tunnels. However, due to the configuration of the missile, the cranking of the front spar lower boom as on the Mk, 2 aircraft will still be required together with some considerable modification to the forward fuselage lower surface in order that it can be indented to house the missile.

This missile is also powered by turbo-jet engines and consequently a large base drag has to be overcome when the missile engines are not running. The fins of the missile require folding in order to give adequate clearance.

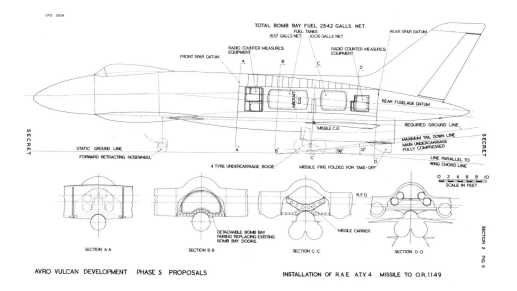

AVRO VULCAN DEVELOPMENT PHASE 5 PROPOSALS   INSTALLATION OF R.A.E. A.T.V.4 MISSILE TO O.R.1149

Forward Retracting Nose wheel.

With the installation of the large W.107 and A.T.V.4 missiles, it is essential in order to provide adequate ground clearance and compatible c.g. positions between the aircraft and the missile that the nose wheel of the Vulcan should be made to retract forward. The aircraft ground incidence has been reduced by 2° to 3° 43' and the leg is made to telescope during retraction.

The result of the forward retraction of the nose wheel is to introduce into the pressure cabin an un-pressurised compartment to house the retracted leg. The aft pressure bulkhead is still a complete circle and the mounting point for the undercarriage leg is in a similar position to the present. However, the drag struts now no longer pick up the vertical members on the aft pressure bulkhead, but are located immediately below the rear crew members' floor. The un-pressurised nose wheel bay is, therefore, bounded on the top surface by the rear crew members' floor and at the sides by two vertical walls introduced between the rear crew members' floor and the fuselage. The existing bomb aimer's blister has been modified and extended aft to fair-in the retracted nose wheel. However, the bomb aimer's window and position have not altered. This modification will naturally require new strength and fatigue tests to be made on the pressure cabin.

It will be appreciated that the forward retraction of the nose wheel means that the wheel now sweeps through what was the main entrance door and consequently an alternative arrangement is necessary. Entrance to the cabin is now by means of a door on the port side of the aircraft located between the pilots and rear crew members and at a position of some 550 from the vertical. An extendable ladder is provided and carried in the aircraft. It is inherent in this scheme that the rear crew seats are replaced by ejection seats as the entrance door is now no longer intended as a means of emergency escape in the air.

New Main Undercarriage

With the increase of all-up weight to values of 225,000 lb. it has become necessary to redesign the main undercarriage. In order to withstand these increased loads and at the same time reduce the Load Classification Number (L.C.N.) values the main present undercarriage bogie of four wheels and eight tyres has been replaced by a four wheel four tyre configuration, the four tyres being of 40 in. diameter as against the present diameter of 27 in, This undercarriage unit is housed within the present main undercarriage bay depicts the variation of L.C.N. and tyre pressures against all-up weight for the present undercarriage and the proposed four tyre configuration. It will be seen that there is a large reduction in both tyre pressure and L.C.N. at all all-up weights.

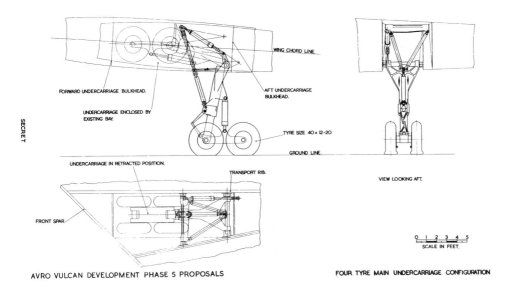

AVRO VULCAN DEVELOPMENT PHASE 5 PROPOSALS   FOUR TYRE MAIN UNDERCARRIAGE CONFIGURATION

Mounting of Radio Counter Measures (R.C.M.) equipment in the rear fuselage

Although the forward movement of the aircraft c. g. that is caused by the above installations of additional equipment in the Vulcan is acceptable, it is desirable to install some large units aft of the c.g. The installation of the whole R.C.M. equipment in an enlarged tail unit of the aircraft would provide such an aft moment. The modified rear fuselage lines give an aerodynamic improvement by the application of "area-rule" principles. The main electrical bay is practically unaffected, but the drag parachute and its release have been repositioned. The existing fin and rudder are retained. The rudder power units are housed in a similar fashion as at present, but some detail modifications of the control runs are required. The A.1.20 Radar unit is installed in the tail. The remaining volume is occupied by the R.C.M.

equipment and its cooling gear. This installation thus produces a desired rearward movement of the c.g. and provides an improvement upon the bomb bay R.C.M. installation in as much as it does not interfere with the maintenance of existing equipment in the aircraft. Since the R.C.M. equipment is still under development any reasonable increase or alteration in size could be accommodated without influencing other installations.

Access doors are provided in order that daily inspections and adjustments can be carried out with the units installed in the aircraft. If it is required to remove any unit this is easily accomplished by means of a cable and winch which lowers the unit down guide rails on to a trolley. A feature of this installation is that any unit can be removed without interference with any other unit. Dependent on the number of aircraft that are required to have R.C.M. this modification could be applied retrospectively to Mk.1 or Mk.2 aircraft; it provides a much more satisfactory R.C.M. installation than the present proposals for a bomb bay installation, and makes more space available for bomb bay fuel.

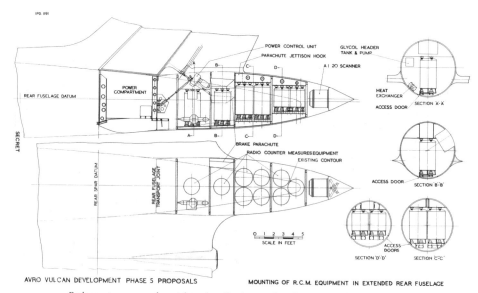

Early counter measures layout, later the tail unit was enlarged to accommodate the equipment.

Outer Wing Integral Tanks

In order to increase the range of the aircraft it is proposed to add extra internal fuel tanks. A 700 gallon integral tank could be built into each outer wing outboard of the existing tanks. It was essential that this tank be of an integral type, in order that the volume can be efficiently used because the wing at these sections is only 6% thick and consequently a bag type tank with an inner skin inside the stringers would lose a large proportion of the volume. The structural modifications required to introduce this tank include the modification of the ribs at either end of the tank, modified outer front spar booms and the deletion of holes in the spar webs. These holes provide escape paths for the de-icing air. Consequently an alternative escape path has been provided via a louvre fitted to the lower surface of the wing at the tip.

The position of the landing light requires alteration as it is at present in the region of the tank. The balance of the fuel is maintained by introduction of the new fuselage tank together with extra fuel in the bomb bay forward of the centre of gravity.

Outer Wing Integral Tanks

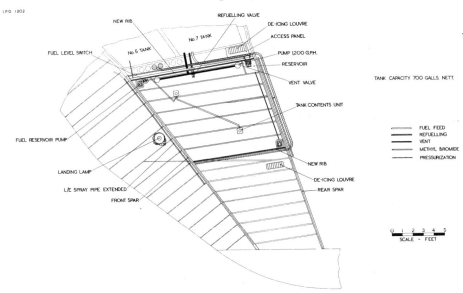

Proposed Vulcan B.Mk3 Phase 5 modifications

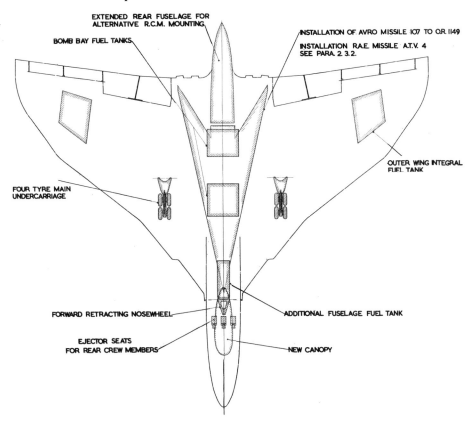

Type 698/5 Phase 6

Brochure I.P.B.104 was produced in 1960 by Avro to meet a requirement to remain airborne for a longer duration. Shown below are extracts from that first report.

The requirement

A requirement had been stated for a weapons system which had sufficient endurance to enable it to remain airborne in a time of emergency in an area remote from risk of enemy attack. The total requirement, including sufficient range to enable it to proceed to and from the chosen targets is stated as an endurance of 13 to 14 hours. The specified armament was four Douglas Sky Bolt missiles.

By having the deterrent force continually airborne it would be virtually indestructible by the enemy and comparison with other systems shows that the long endurance aircraft provides the maximum deterrent for given expenditure.

The typical endurance of a Vulcan B.Mk.2, with its present fuel capacity (the modification introducing long range fuel tanks in the bomb-bay not having been authorised), and with Olympus 200 engines is 7 hours, with an internal weapon load. To raise this to the 13 to 14 hours required, with in addition the weight and drag of the four missiles is obviously a formidable undertaking. The design proposals made in the brochure, which are for convenience designated Phase 6, comprise an increase in internal fuel capacity to more than double by fitting a large outer wing with partly integral and partly bag fuel tankage, an increase in the lift drag ratio by the greater span of this new outer wing, the fitment of developed Olympus engines with improved specific fuel consumption, together with the possible fitment of aft fans giving further improvement in specific fuel consumption and greater thrust at take-off. The increase in the weight of the missiles carried and the very substantial increase in fuel capacity increase the all-up weight of the proposed aircraft to about 350,000 lb. and this in turn necessitates an entirely new undercarriage. Larger wheels and tyres are fitted in order to keep the runway loading moderate and to give increased braking capacity.

2. Design Description

The Vulcan Phase 6 proposals are basically a collection of modifications designed to be applied retrospectively to the Vulcan Mk. 2. Two alternative arrangements are considered depending on the type of engine modification used. These are the aircraft fitted with Bristol Siddeley Olympus 21 or 21/2 engines with reheat, and the aircraft fitted with the same engines driving aft fan units. These modifications are listed below.

Wing

A new wing is fitted outboard of the transport joint to give an increase in wing area and span, and incorporates an integral fuel tank outboard and bag tanks inboard.

The original outer wing aft of the front spar, modified to form an integral tank, is incorporated in the wing.

The existing outer elevons are retained.

New inner elevons are fitted, but the original power units are retained.

Four Douglas Sky Bolt (G. A. M. 87A - Delta 2/11) missiles are mounted from pylons on the lower surface of the wings.

Fuselage

A dorsal fuel tank is fitted behind the canopy.

A new bomb bay fuel tank is fitted. This can be removed, if necessary, to allow free falling stores to be carried.

The existing E.C.M. rear fairing is retained.

Local stiffening of the centre section is necessary to provide sufficient structural strength and stability during ground manoeuvring at maximum weight.

Fin

The fin height is increased by 3 ft. to provide adequate lateral stability.

Power Plant

Two alternative types of power plant are considered, four Olympus 21 or 21/2 engines with re-heat or the same engines driving aft fans.

In each case the existing air intakes and engine bay installation are retained.

The re-heat units are fitted behind the wing rear spar.

The aft fans are mounted from the rear spar and have air intakes above and below the wing surface.

The four alternative power plant arrangements considered for the Vulcan Phase 6 aircraft and outlined below, are all developed versions of the Olympus engine and are proposed in conjunction with Bristol Siddeley Engines Limited.

Aircraft fitted with Olympus 21 or 21/2 engines with re-heat

With this power plant installation, the four Olympus 21 engines in the Mk. 2 Vulcan are either retained without alteration, or are converted, during a complete overhaul, to Olympus 21/2 engines, with a performance equal to the Olympus 22 engine. This involves replacing the turbine of the Olympus 21 with the larger turbine of the Olympus 22, which is under development for the T.S.R.2 aircraft. No design changes are necessary to either engine mounting, accessories or air intakes in fitting the uprated engine.

The re-heat units are installed in the jet pipes aft of the rear spar. To reduce the penalty in cruise fuel consumption to a minimum, the jet pipe diameter is increased from 29 inches to 35 inches at the re-heat unit for the Olympus 21 engine, and to 32.7 inches for the Olympus 21/2 engine.

Undercarriage

A new main undercarriage with a four tyre bogie is fitted to meet the higher all-up weight. A stronger nose wheel unit is fitted.

Aircraft fitted with Olympus 21 or 21/2 engines and aft fans

The power plant installation for this arrangement consists of four Olympus 21 or 21/2 engines, each driving a 5 ft. - 8 inches diameter propulsion fan. The installation of the Olympus engines is identical to the Mk. 2 Vulcan.

The propulsion fans are mounted in the trailing edge of the wing, one behind each engine and are driven by a single stage turbine installed in the hub, which is supplied by the exhaust efflux from the main engine. Each fan has a self-contained lubrication and cooling system.

The air intake for the fan is divided between the upper and lower surface of the wing trailing edge. Wind tunnel tests are planned to determine the optimum intake geometry.

Phase 6 - 10th January 1962

This report consists of a collection of current data for the Phase 6 Vulcan. It replaced the previous data published in Brochure I.P.D 104, and is in line with the information presented at the Air Ministry on 19th December, 1961.

The aircraft is powered by four powered by four Olympus B.S.01.23-2 engines fitted with a simplified reheat system and variable convergent nozzles. Two, Four or Six "Skybolt" missiles can be carried and at the maximum all-up-weight of 356,000 lb., and with a fuel reserve of one hour, the endurance is 12.2, 10 and 7.4 hours respectively.

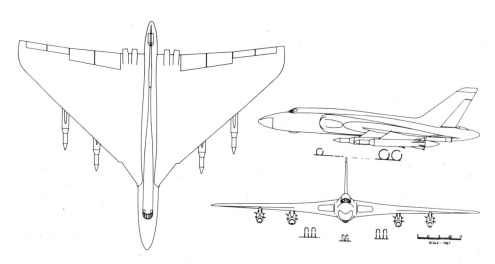

General arrangement with Bristol Siddeley B.01 21/2 engines. Note the faired fuselage, which had two additional 385 gallon dorsal fuel tanks.

Aerodynamic design

The wing area, aspect ratio and span have been fixed by the performance requirements. The planform is optimised for performance rather than span wise loading as was the case on the Mk. 2 Vulcan, as buffet is less critical on the long endurance aircraft where the maximum cruising Mach number is 0. 8 and the maximum Mach number can be limited to about 0. 85 to 0. 87. As large a tip chord as possible has, however, been used to avoid excessive loading at the tip. The exact amount of wing sweep is fixed by the need to keep the centre of gravity of the aircraft without fuel or missiles within the range determined from the aerodynamic centre position of the wing. When aft fans are installed, the aircraft centre of gravity moves back 14 inches and slightly more sweep is necessary to maintain balance. The missiles are located on the wing so that their centres of gravity are symmetrically placed on either side of the aircraft centre of gravity. The fuel tanks are arranged so that the fuel centre of gravity lies within the c. g. range.

Proposals

Costs were submitted for Vulcan Phase 6 aircraft in the following categories:

(1) Existing Mk.2 aircraft with B.01 21 engines converted to Phase 6 aircraft and the engines modified to B.01 21/2 standard, including re-heat.

(2) Existing Mk.2 aircraft with B.01 21 engines, converted to Phase 6 aircraft and fitted with fans.

(3) Existing Mk.2 aircraft with B.01 21 engines converted to Phase 6 aircraft and the engines modified to a B.01 21/2 standard, and fitted with fans.

(4) Supply of new Phase 6 Vulcan aircraft fitted with B.01 21/2 engines and re-heat.

(5) Supply of new Phase 6 Vulcan aircraft fitted with B.01 21/2 engines and fans
Estimates were given for 25 and 50 aircraft in the conversion categories and 25 in the new categories.

Phase six engine development

In November 1961 Bristols proposed using the Olympus 23 engine (originally the 21/2). This comprised a 301 compressor section with 22R turbine section. Partial reheat would have been embodied with the engine as put forward as a conversion of the 301. A single nozzle was proposed to give 25,000lb thrust at take-off (with reheat) with 17,000lb cruise.

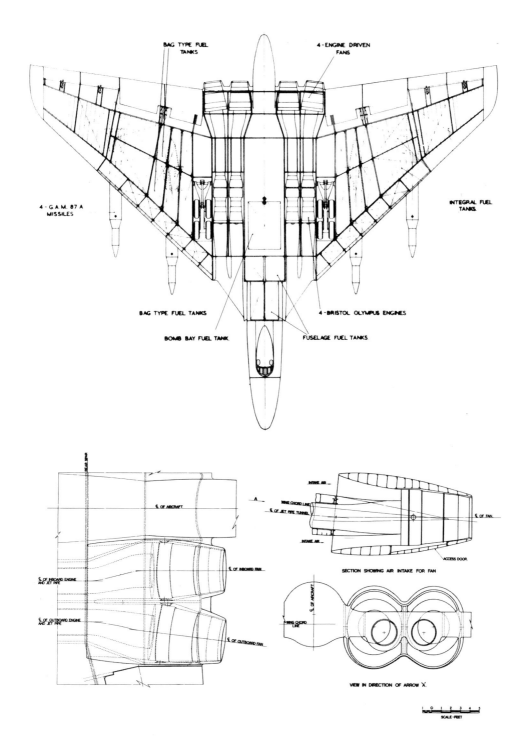

The drawing above shows aft engine driven fans units which along with developed Olympus engine would provide an improvement in specific fuel consumption and greater thrust at take-off.

Phase 6 revised crew layout

The design proposals for the Vulcan Phase 6 aircraft outlined in the Avro Brochure I.P.B.104 retained the same crew layout and pressure cabin as the Mk. 2 Vulcan. The facilities provided by this arrangement were rather limited and may not be considered suitable for an endurance of 13 to 14 hours.

The addendum to I.P.B.104 presented an alternative arrangement in which more space was available for the crew. In addition, provision was made for a supernumerary crew member and ejection seats were provided at all stations.

The pressure cabin was extended by inserting a 10 ft. 9 in. portion of fuselage immediately forward of the rear pressure bulkhead. The arrangement of the nose and the forward portion of the cabin including the pilots and bomb aimer's station were identical to the Mk. 2 Vulcan. Four forward facing crew stations were located in pairs on the starboard side of the cabin and a gangway was provided on the port aide. A toilet was installed immediately behind the pilot's floor and two rest bunks were mounted on the rear pressure bulkhead. The entrance door was located on the port side and may also be used as a parachute exit.

The increase in fuselage length results in a forward movement of the centre of gravity. This necessitates a change in the planform of the proposed new outer wing in order to maintain balance. The opportunity had been taken to improve the high Mach No. characteristics of the aircraft by reverting to a kinked planform as used on the Vulcan Mk. 2. The existing outer wing was retained as in the previous proposal.

The introduction of ejection seat hatches in the top of the fuselage precludes the use of the Dorsal mounted fuel tanks, these were therefore deleted and replaced by a larger capacity bomb bay fuel tank. The total fuel capacity remained unchanged.

The basic operational weight was increased by 3,840 lb. and with the same total fuel carried the maximum take-off weight is 348,500 lb. As a result of this weight increase, the endurance was reduced by 12 minutes. The take-off distance at maximum take-off weight was unaltered.

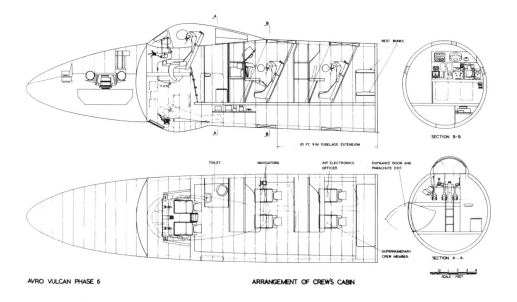

AVRO VULCAN PHASE 6   ARRANGEMENT OF CREW'S CABIN

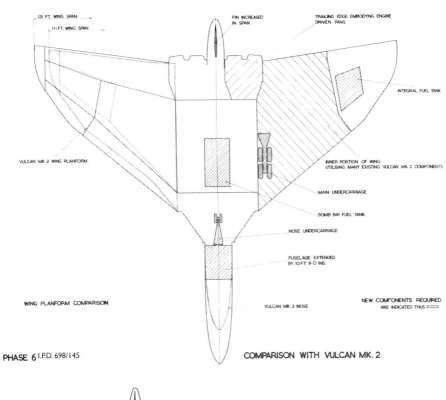

121 FT. WING SPAN

111 FT. WING SPAN

FIN INCREASED
IN SPAN

TRAILING EDGE EMBODYING ENGINE
DRIVEN FANS

INTEGRAL FUEL TANK

VULCAN MK. 2 WING PLANFORM

INNER PORTION OF WING
UTILISING MANY EXISTING VULCAN MK. 2 COMPONENTS

MAIN UNDERCARRIAGE

BOMB BAY FUEL TANK

NOSE UNDERCARRIAGE

FUSELAGE EXTENDED
BY 10 FT. 9·0 INS.

WING PLANFORM COMPARISON

VULCAN MK. 2 NOSE

NEW COMPONENTS REQUIRED
ARE INDICATED THUS ▭

PHASE 6 I.P.D. 698/145

COMPARISON WITH VULCAN MK. 2

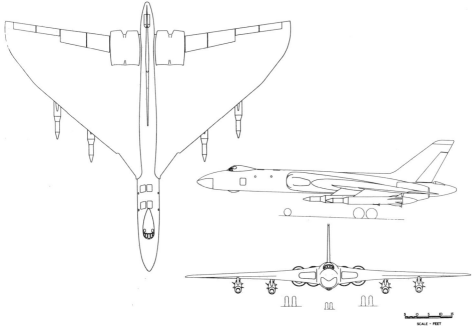

SCALE - FEET

AVRO VULCAN PHASE 6 I.P.D. 698/143

GENERAL ARRANGEMENT
BRISTOL SIDDELEY B.O1.21/2 ENGINES WITH AFT FANS

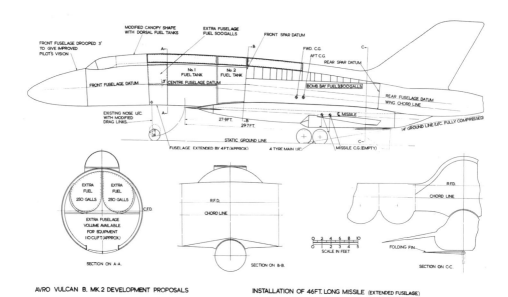

This I.P.D 1376 drawing shows a drooped nose version to help improve the pilot's vision.

Phase 7

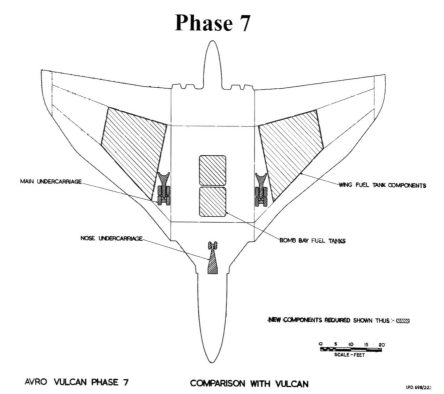

Further to the Phase 6 version of the Vulcan was Phase 7. This drawing dated May 1961 shows a comparison with the Vulcan B.Mk2. It was to give the aircraft more range and endurance. One scheme stated that it was to be powered by the Rolls-Royce RB117; a fan powered version was also looked at.

Vertical take-off Vulcan

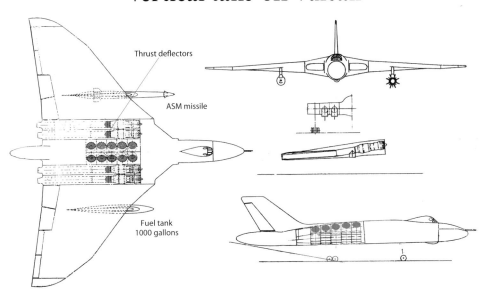

This IPD/126 drawing dated 26th April, 1960 shows a proposed vertical take-off Vulcan powered by ten Bristol Siddeley BE59 engines 14,000 lb thrust each and four Olympus engines giving a total thrust of 72,000 lb. Vertical thrust available using both the Olympus (vectored thrust) and BE 59 engines was 212.000 lb. All up weight was 188,400 lbs using 6,600 lbs of fuel for five minutes hover giving a cruise range of 3000 n.m.

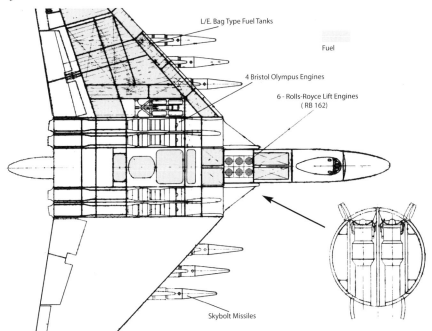

This IPD/260 drawing shows a proposed Phase 6 development to help the take-off performance of the Vulcan. It was to be powered by six Rolls-Royce (RB162) lift engines and four Olympus engines. Another project looked at by Avro was the Type 769 a V.T.O.L weapons system for the Vulcan dated June 1959.

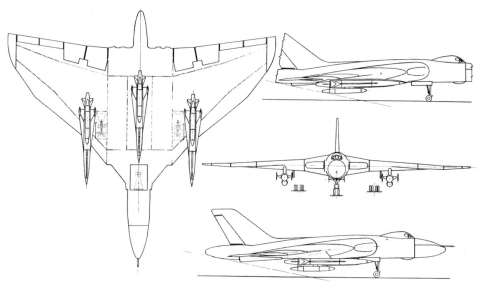

INSTALLATION OF 3 MISSILES ON VULCAN MK.II.

This 3 View G.A. shows B.Mk2 Vulcan with the Avro W140 missile which Avro designed to meet Operating Requirement OR.1182 issued on 10th January, 1961. The W140 missile was capable of Mach 3 at 70,000 ft and Mach 1.5 at sea level. It was powered by a single Rolls-Royce RB.153 turbojet at 6,850 lb dry thrust and 11,645 with reheat. As with the Blue Steel missile, range was a major concern which was originally 580 n.m. this was later improved to 950 n.m. The requirement also stated that it was to be terrain following at low level for the last 100 miles.

Gnat aircraft schemes

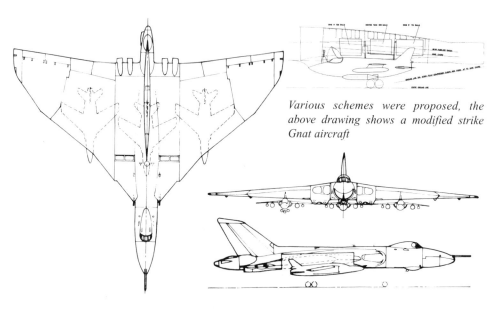

Various schemes were proposed, the above drawing shows a modified strike Gnat aircraft

This unusual project was for three piloted Folland / HS Gnats light weight fighters armed with nuclear warheads and long range fuel tanks to be carried under a Vulcan. They would have used the pylons for Skybolt missile.

Red Drover

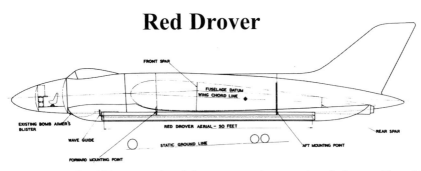

In 1954, requirement O.R.330 was produced for a reconnaissance aircraft that could avoid air defences. The Type 730 was designed to meet this requirement using "Red Drover" X band sideway looking radar, but the project was cancelled in 1957 after an extensive research program. Shown above is a proposal for the Vulcan using the same "Red Drover" radar system.

Supersonic venture

This IPD 698/321 (sheet 1) scheme dated 30th January, 1963 for a supersonic Vulcan. It had a wing span of 695 ft and a wing area of 2640 sq. ft.

One of the schemes looked at for the Avro 730 carrying a stand-off missile.

AVRO 730 SUPERSONIC BOMBER

Avro had looked at a various number of designs for a supersonic bomber. One these was the Type 730 which was originally for a Mach 2.5 reconnaissance aircraft flying at 60,000 ft with a maximum range of 5000 n.m. built to O.R.330/Spec B.156T issued in 1954. This O.R. was later amended in October 1955 to RB156D to incorporate a bombing capability and various schemes were looked at to meet this requirement.

The Company received a contract to build a prototype Type 730 in 1955 but this was cancelled in the Governments 1957 defence white paper.

During this time Avro also looked at developing a supersonic version of the Vulcan capable of carrying a stand-off missile. These designs were known as the Type 732.

Type 732 - alternative schemes

Continuing the theme for the development of a supersonic bomber a series of designs were produced under Type 732 designation of July 1956. It was to be based on the Vulcan and powered by four turbojet engines.

I.P.D. 1120 issue:-1 dated August 1956.

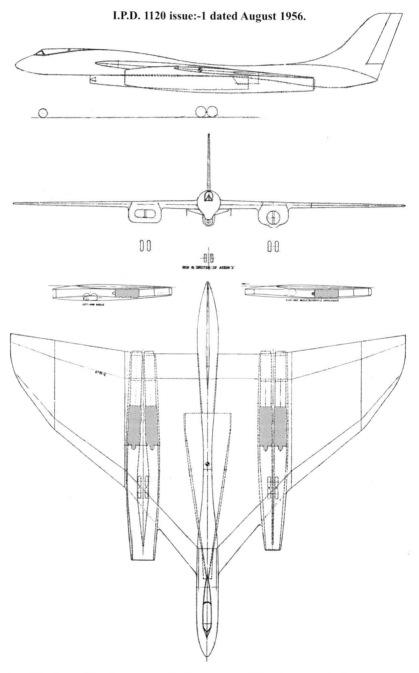

Three view GA shows 4% wing supersonic development. The right nacelle depicts an alternative arrangement.

I.P.D. scheme E

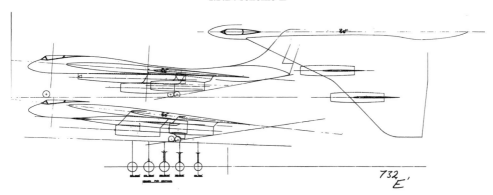

These designs show the engine in a pod nacelle much favoured by the Americans which allowed for a more slender wing thus creating less drag when compared with the engine buried in the wing root. This layout also has the advantage that the wing provides each engine with air undisturbed by the fuselage or wing as experienced by the Vulcan. Interestingly the Americans later buried engines in the wing on the B-2 stealth aircraft to give a minimal radar cross section (RCS) and sacrificed aerodynamic performance.

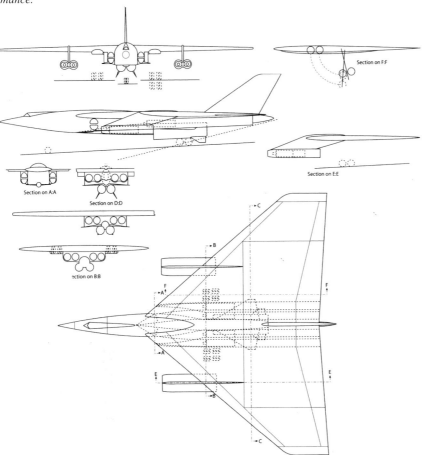

I.P.D. 1125 issue:-1 dated July 1956.

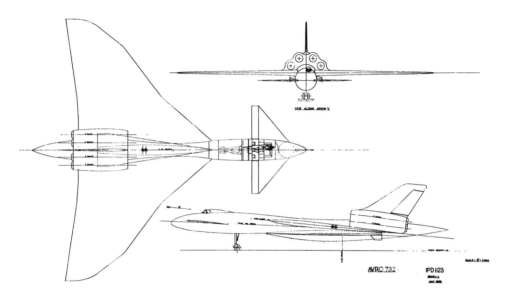

I.P.D. 1122 issue:-1 dated August 1956.

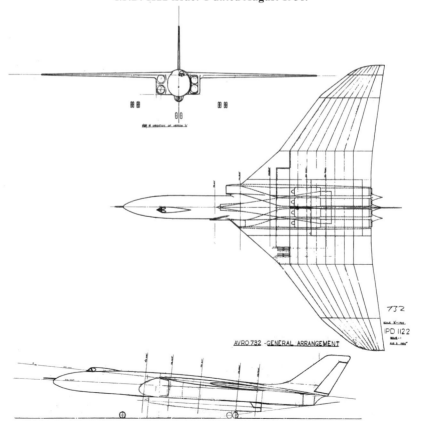

Missile developments

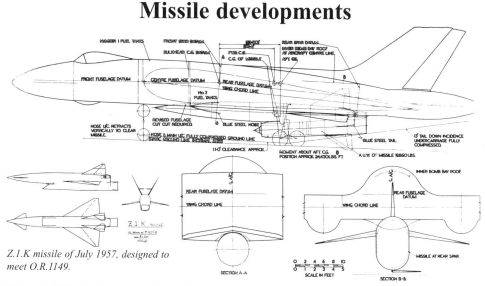

Z.1.K missile of July 1957, designed to meet O.R.1149.

Vulcan B.Mk2 development with installation of developed Blue Steel missile. A series of new missile designs were looked at by Avro known as the Z series. The W110 was powered by a de Havilland Gyron Junior supersonic turbojet and two Armstrong Siddeley Gamma rocket engines.

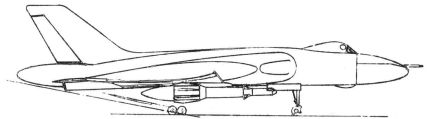

Early drawing showing Skybolt "Able-1" installation. The drawing (I.P.D.698/111) showed that it would have carried two A.S.M. missiles or one missile replaced by a fuel tank on it's pylon.

Type 759 scheme

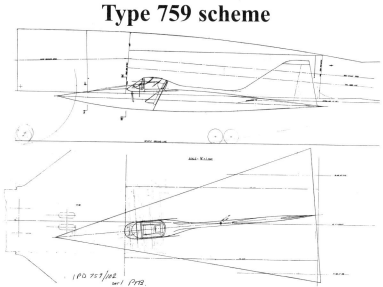

Narrow-delta piloted research glider of October 1958 was to be launched from the Vulcan.

Sea Dart missile system

One of the last projects investigated by Avro for the Vulcan was for an air to air launched Sea Dart missile system for the purpose of intercepting and destroying hostile aircraft such as the Mig-25 before they could reach their target.

The Vulcan's large airframe was able to accommodate the large radar required for the Sea Dart to intercept a target flying at 70,000 ft at Mach 2.5 - 3. It would maintain a combat air patrol (CAP) some 200 miles from base flying at 40,000 ft. over the critical area of a combat zone, or air defence area.

By this time the I.P.D. projects numbering system stopped in December 1958, for example the drawing shown below was given the number I.P.D.698/464. The Initial Projects Department moved from Chadderton to Woodford in May 1965.

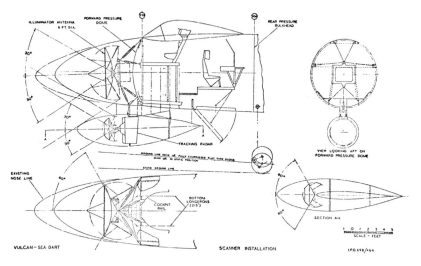

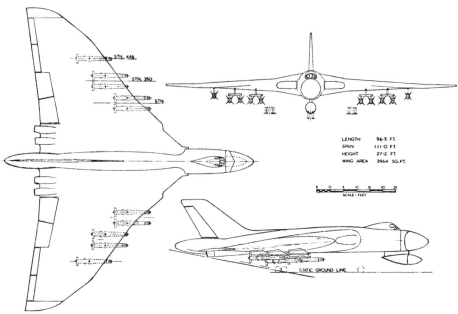

Martel and Phoenix missile systems

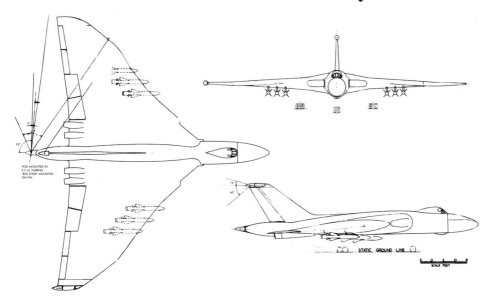

This drawing (I.P.D.698/385 sheet 1) dated November 1968 shows six Hawker Siddeley/Matra Martel missiles mounted on the wings and possible positions for systems equipment. This drawing shows the data link pod mounted in the E.C.M. fairing with the 'Red Steer' radar mounted on the fin. A later drawing dated December 1968 had the data link pod mounted on a pylon outboard the wing. The Anglo French missile was used as an anti-ship, TV guided missile controlled by a data link from the launch aircraft. A anti-radar (AS.37) version was also available. Both versions were used by the Blackburn Bucaneer. During the Falklands conflict flight trials were completed by the Vulcan using the anti-radar version.

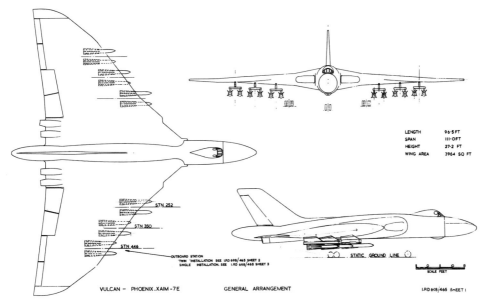

The Phoenix / XAIM-7E missile shown here was a long range air to air missile manufactured by Hughes Aircraft and Raytheon. It was capable of multi-launch against more than one target. This I.P.D.698/465 drawing shows the Vulcan carrying twelve Phoenix missiles.

Type 722 - Civil transport project

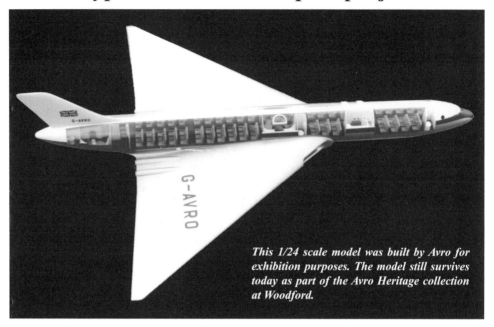

This 1/24 scale model was built by Avro for exhibition purposes. The model still survives today as part of the Avro Heritage collection at Woodford.

In December 1952 Avro looked at an airliner based on the Vulcan. It was given the Type number 722 and was known as the Avro Atlantic.

The basic version was designed to carry 94 passengers from London to New York in under seven hours at a cruising speed of 600 m.p.h. a luxury version was also looked at to carry 76 passengers and a tourist version carried 113 passengers. Extra passengers could be carried if a bar was not fitted.

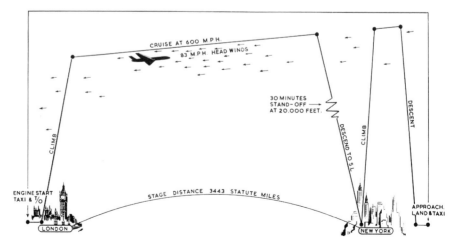

Avro Atlantic General Data

Details taken from sales brochure issued in June 1953.

Span	121 ft.
Length	145 ft.
Fuselage diameter	12.5 ft.

Weights

Gross take-off weight	Approx. 200,000 lb.
Payload (dependent on route and stage distance)	20,000 to 45,000 lb.

Performance

Cruising speed	exceeds 600 m.p.h.
Cruising altitude	exceeds 40,000 ft.

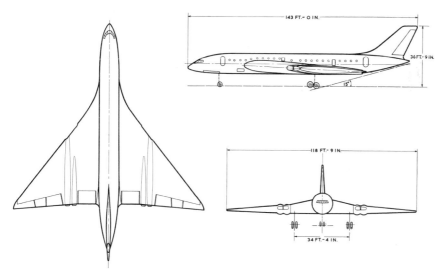

Wing layout as shown in the September 1953 brochure produced for the S.B.A.C Show. The wing was blended to the fuselage with the engines outside the transport joint. The seating layout below shows the basic version with rearward-facing seats, with and without bar. In the end there was not sufficient interest in the machine to persuade the Ministry of Supply to finance a prototype. There was no question of Avro building a prototype as a private venture.

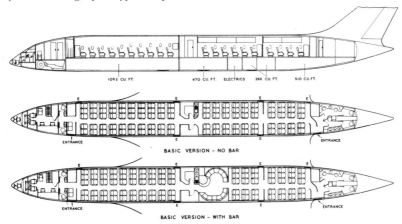

Wind tunnel model - 1954

Various schemes were looked at to develop a transport aircraft using the Vulcan design as a basis. This picture of a wind tunnel model using the kink wing planform was requested by Mr Roy Ewans 31st December, 1954.

Type 718 - Military transport project

The Type 718 was a military transport aircraft based on the Avro Vulcan powered by four Olympus turbojets. Once again Avro adopted the rearward seating arrangement which, at that time, was being considered as an additional safety feature.

It was to meet a requirement communicated by the Director of Military Aircraft Research and Development at the Ministry of Supply in June 1951. It was designed to carry eighty fully equipped troops over 4,280 n.m. at 576 mph at 47,000ft. Powered by four Olympus OL3 engines giving 12,150lb of thrust. Different seating layouts could be adopted, these included a 110 or 80-90 seat version for shorter ranges and a casualty evacuation version was also considered.

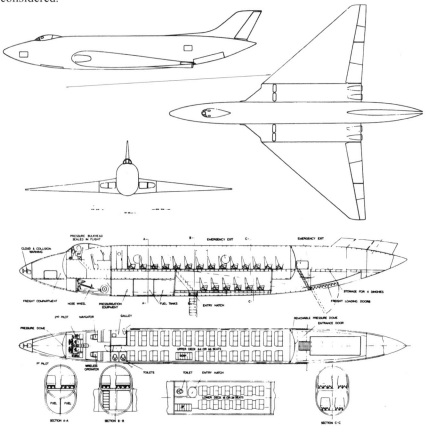

Different roles - 1962

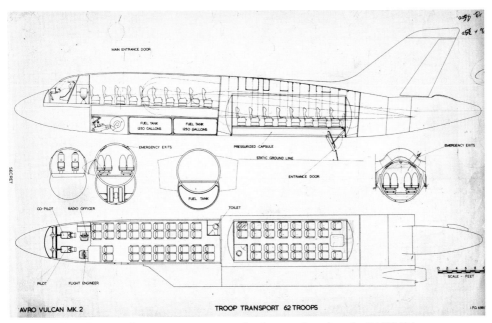

This I.P.D./698 drawing shows a troop transport development based on the B.Mk2 Vulcan.

IPD 698/294 dated 15th August, 1962 shows that a rear fan was considered for the B.Mk2 Maritime Reconnaissance (MR) Vulcan.

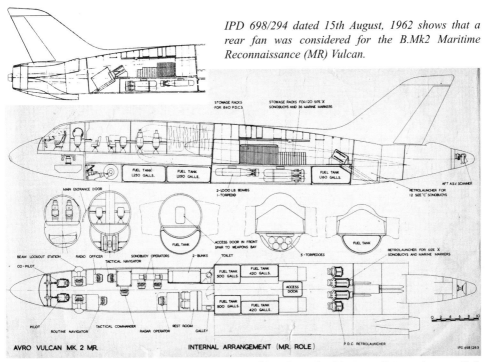

This I.P.D. /698/285 drawing shows a Vulcan B.Mk2 MR in the Maritime Reconnaissance Role (M.R.R.) issued mid 1962 as a replacement for the Avro Shackleton. Avro later designed the Type 801 dated June 1964. Under the banner of Hawker Siddeley Aviation (HSA) the HS 801 Nimrod as it was known was based on the de Havilland Comet civil airliner. It made its first flight in May 1967.

Air launched missile proposals

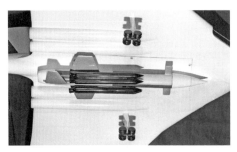

This photograph dated 22nd January, 1958 shows a model of the proposed high-altitude aerodynamic research vehicle in position for air-launching from a Vulcan.

Mr. J. E. Allen, head of the aerodynamics, projects and assessment department of the A. V. Roe weapons research division gave a lecture before the Manchester branch of the Royal Aeronautical Society on 22nd January, 1958. In the lecture he described that Avro were looking at an air launched four-stage flight corridor research vehicle. Three stages were to be propelled by solid and liquid rockets respectively. Four adaptations were considered; a satellite and manned version and two variants carrying a different payload of 40 lb and 300 lb.

Large air launched missile proposals

The Vulcan's capability to carry a large missile led to various schemes being studied. Amongst these was the BAC Filton's Grand Slam II; two missiles were to be carried under the wing using the Skybolt pylon locations, the smaller air launched BAC Blue Water missile was also considered. An air launched version of the Polaris missile was also deliberated carried semi-recessed in the fuselage.

Vulcan launched satellite interceptor (Z116)

The launch of artificial satellite Sputnik 1 on 4th October, 1957, detected in the U.K. by the Jodrell Bank Observatory in Cheshire, caused much concern within American and U.K. Government circles and started a Space Race within the Cold War.

A memorandum issued on 10th July, 1962 by the Avro's WRD special projects group described the payload capabilities of two types of vehicles based on Blue Steel for intercepting and destroying a satellite: (1) Z116-Vulcan launched, modified Blue Steel (Z.109) with hypothetical 2nd stage. (2) Ground launched - 1st stage Thor; 2nd stage, Z.109; hypothetical 3rd stage. It was assumed that the Vulcan would be guided into the orbit plane of the satellite before launch of the interceptor. The memo went on to support the feasibility of such projects in more detail.

Eurospace technical study group

Due to its ability to carry large missiles the Hawker Siddeley Vulcan was proposed to be a missile launcher by a technical study group of French based organisation Eurospace in 1965. The group looked at placing a payload of 200-650 lb into Earth orbit, orbital heights of 300 n.m. were also considered. One of the many missile combinations analysed was a Blue Steel development for a satellite launcher shown opposite. Another version to be considered to be launched from a Vulcan was the large French Diamant ballistic missile satellite launcher.

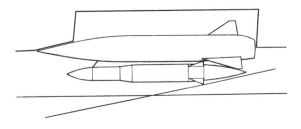

Satellite launcher developed from Blue Steel shown below a Vulcan. The second and third stages beneath the missile would use solid propellants.

Tel: 061.439.5050. Extn 207

MINISTRY OF AVIATION SUPPLY

Resident Technical Officer (Aircraft) at
Hawker Siddeley Aviation Ltd.,
Woodford,
Stockport, Cheshire.

LH 16D

Hawker Siddeley Aviation Ltd.,
Woodford,
Stockport,
Cheshire.

Your reference

Our reference
VUL/01/10/212

Date
29th March, 1971

PART SEVEN

TYPES FOR ALL TASKS

Dear Sir, Minutes of a meeting at R.R.E. to discuss
H2S mods. in Vulcan aircraft

Please find attached a copy of RRE minutes
RAR/64/017 dated 17th February, 1971.

There would appear to be little we can do until
RRE and MAS confirm their requirements.

Yours faithfully,

F. FALLON
for J.W. BLINKHORN, R.T.O(A)

Enc.

Low level development

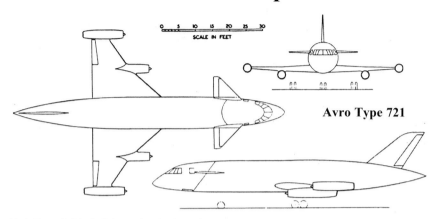

Avro Type 721

The R.A.F and Air Ministry looked at the idea of a low level strategic bomber to avoid enemy radar in 1952 and the MoS issued specification B126T to meet this requirement. The specification called for an aircraft that could deliver a 10,000 lb. nuclear bomb at an operational radius of 1500 miles at a speed of Mach 0.85 with at least 80% of the mission flown at a height of 500 ft. One of the earliest attempts to meet this specification was submitted by Avro in December 1952 and given the Type number 721 shown above. It was to have a range of 5,500 miles and a take-off weight of 124,000 lb. Unlike the Vulcan it had a very high wing loading to satisfy its low level role. The specification was later abandoned due to the technology not being available at the time to ensure accurate navigation, terrain following and low level performance. In 1955, further studies were looked at which led to the British Aircraft Corporation (BAC) TSR2 Tactical Strike Reconnaissance aircraft.

As mentioned earlier in the book tests were performed on a B.Mk2 airframe to check that the structure fulfilled the requirements of SP.970 Volume leaflet 200/4 and to establish the limit of serviceability of the aircraft under loads arising Flight Case 'C' of the flight envelope, 90.5% of the test load was applied to the specimen without a major failure.

Terrain Following Radar (TFR)

In 1964, the Air Staff issued requirement A.S.R.380 for the Vulcan in the low level role, reverting back to free fall nuclear loads. Before terrain following radar was introduced Vulcan crews practised low level flying using maps and the H2S radar. To help improve this capability to fly at low level A.R.I.5959 introduced by Mod 2057 the General Dynamics terrain following radar. Trials were carried out on Vulcan B.Mk2 XM606 from June 1965 and were cleared for service in 1966.

The system utilised an elevation monopulse, 'on-bore sight' non-scanning, technique to detect changes of terrain height immediately ahead of the aircraft flight path. The system operated in conjunction with the F.M. Mk.7B radio altimeter, the M.F.S. equipment and various aircraft sensors, indicating and control units to produce pitch command signals which assisted pilot manual control during low level flight. The Airborne Radio Installation (A.R.I.) measured the slant range to terrain ahead of the aircraft, receiving inputs from other aircraft sensors and computed pitch control signals for display at the pilot's head-up indicators. The displayed control signals assisted manual control of the aircraft in the pitch plane to give a resultant flight path which followed the rise and fall of the terrain at the pre-selected altitude adjustable between 200 and 1000 ft. The installation provided safe low level terrain following over land, water and man made obstacles within specified limits.

The radar section of the installation measured 'range to terrain' (R) along the fixed depression angle of the radar beam, while the F.M. Mk.7B radio altimeter accurately measured height above terrain (H). This information, range (R) and height (H), was compared in the T.F.R. computer with a reference range (r) and a reference height (h). The reference range (r) was pre-programmed into the computer to suit the flying characteristics of the aircraft and the reference height (h) was selected at a height selector switch on the T.F.R. control unit.

When the measured values of (H) or (R) deviated from the references (h) and (r), as a result of changes in terrain, a corresponding pitch-up or pitch-down signal was generated and displayed at the pilot's head-up display (HEAD-UP indicator) or head-down display (M.F.S. director horizon). The pilot was thus able to alter the altitude of the aircraft in the pitch plane to null the climb or dive indication and thereby cause the aircraft to follow the rise and fall of the terrain. This technique is illustrated below.

T.F.R. mode of operation

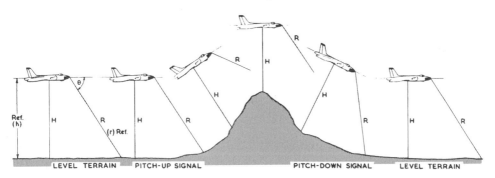

The T.F.R. comprised an 8 in. diameter, 36 in. long pod immediately below the flight refuelling probe. Post Mod 2395 the length of the pod was increased by 7.6 in. to accommodate a filter unit. The forward end of the pod which projects into the airstream housed a microwave aerial sub-assembly, while the rear end of the pod was enclosed by the aircraft nose contained the associated transmitter-receiver, signal processing, computing and power pack sub assemblies.

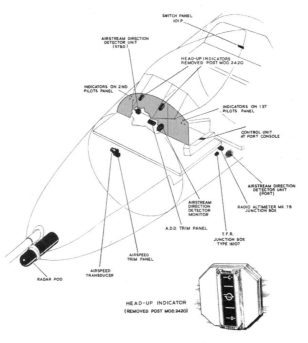

Strategic Reconnaissance (S.R.) role

On 23rd February, 1971 Avro formally applied to the Ministry of Aviation Supply for contract cover for a feasibility study for the Vulcan B.Mk2 in the S.R. role. The study proposed that the Avro Vulcan should replace Victors in the Strategic Reconnaissance Role to contract K6A/128/V. This required improved H_2S NBC radar with data handling, long range navigation aid, air monitoring facility and improved photographic facilities. An earlier contract for Air Monitoring system dated 5th March, 1970 stated that the pod would use Skybolt pick-ups for the pod forward suspension. The eight aircraft originally nominated for the S.R. role embraced this particular Skybolt modification. Long range navigation was satisfied by the incorporation of the Loran 'C' ADL 21 equipment, comprising of an aerial, amplifier, C.R.T. indicator and read-out unit. Kelvin Hughes was to be responsible for the data handling and proposed radar display which used the existing Naval Radar, Type 1006. It was presumed that the bombing facility would not be required and the N.B.S. would be retained other than for the double off-set bombing unit, the armament panel 9p and the time delay unit of the low level visual release system.

Nine B.Mk2 aircraft were converted to the Maritime Radar Reconnaissance (M.R.R.) role XH534, XH537, XH558, XH560, XH563, XJ780, XJ782, XJ523 and XJ525. They were delivered between 1973 and early 1977 to No.27 Squadron which had just reformed at R.A.F. Waddington. They were given a high gloss protective paint finish to protect against sea spray effects. The Terrain Following Radar (T.F.R.) was deleted but aircraft were given the LORAN navigation aid. Five aircraft were further modified for Air Sampling Role taking over from the Handley Page Victor S.R.2 of No.543 Squadron. They retained the gloss finish with light grey underside when B.Mk2 Vulcan's were given a matt all-surface camouflage.

Air monitoring

The air monitoring system was used for the detection and collection of radio-active particles from the upper atmosphere. The system combined four separate functions:
(1) Radiation detection.
(2) Collection and density monitoring.
(3) Sample collection of radio-active particles.
(4) Cabin air sampling.

Two pods were fitted with sampling pods using the de Havilland Sea Vixen drop tanks which used the mounting points that would have carried the Skybolt missile. The drawings shown below are from AP 101B-1902-1C dated April 1976.

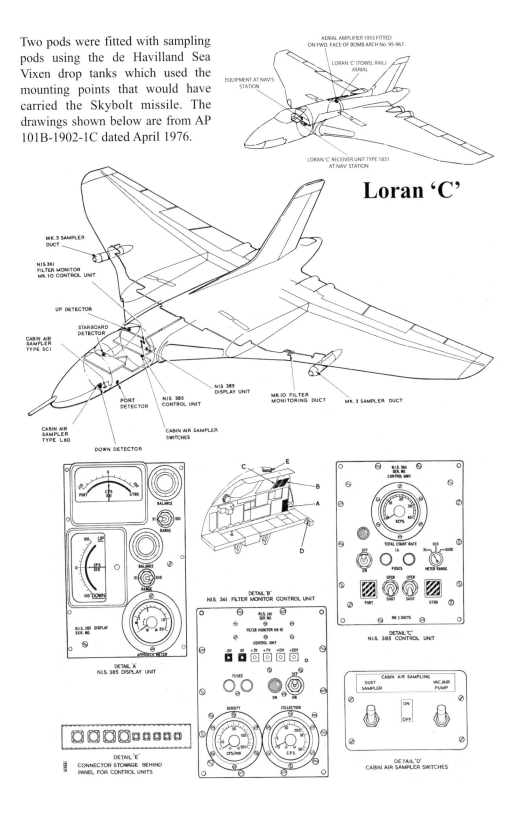

AERIAL AMPLIFIER 1953 FITTED ON FWD. FACE OF BOMB ARCH No. 95-967.

LORAN 'C' (TOWEL RAIL) AERIAL

EQUIPMENT AT NAV'S STATION

LORAN 'C' RECEIVER UNIT TYPE 1831 AT NAV' STATION

Loran 'C'

MK.3 SAMPLER DUCT

NIS 361 FILTER MONITOR MK.10 CONTROL UNIT

UP DETECTOR

STARBOARD DETECTOR

CABIN AIR SAMPLER TYPE SC1

PORT DETECTOR

NIS 385 CONTROL UNIT

NIS 385 DISPLAY UNIT

MK.10 FILTER MONITORING DUCT

MK.3 SAMPLER DUCT

CABIN AIR SAMPLER TYPE L60

CABIN AIR SAMPLER SWITCHES

DOWN DETECTOR

PORT   CPS   STBD
X10

BALANCE

X1   X10
RANGE

UP
100   CPS   0   X10   100
DOWN

BALANCE

X1   X10
RANGE

APPROACH METER

N.I.S. 385 DISPLAY SER. NO.

DETAIL 'A'
N.I.S. 385 DISPLAY UNIT

DETAIL 'E'
CONNECTOR STOWAGE BEHIND PANEL FOR CONTROL UNITS

C   E   B   A   D

DETAIL 'B'
N.I.S. 361 FILTER MONITOR CONTROL UNIT

N.I.S. 361 SER. NO.
FILTER MONITOR MK 10
CONTROL UNIT

-15V   0V   +3V   +7V   +15V   +20V

FUSES   OFF   ON   ON

DENSITY   COLLECTION
CPS/MIN   C.P.S.

N.I.S. 385 SER. NO. CONTROL UNIT

KCPS

TOTAL COUNT RATE   X10
OFF   1A   X1   X100
ON   FUSES   METER RANGE

OPEN   OPEN
PORT   SHUT   SHUT   STBD

MK 3 DUCTS

DETAIL 'C'
N.I.S. 385 CONTROL UNIT

CABIN AIR SAMPLING
DUST   VAC./AIR
SAMPLER   PUMP

ON   OFF

DETAIL 'D'
CABIN AIR SAMPLER SWITCHES

The Concorde connection

Not only was the Vulcan powered by the Olympus which was developed for use on Concorde and tested on XA903 shown opposite, it was also used along with the Type 707 aircraft in the development of materials, aerodynamics and flying systems for the Concorde programme.

Because of the large delta wing low flying characteristics and being more representative of the inertia weight of Concorde, Vulcan B.Mk1 XA890, still with its straight wing, was operated by the Aerodynamics Research Flight at R.A.E. Bedford to prove the use of the Concorde "Ogee" slender wing plan-form to overcome the problems of low speed handling on take-off with engine failure. The specialists developed the Take-Off Director (T.O.D.) system which was extensively tested on XA890 to help overcome these problems, it was also used to show commercial pilots how the system worked.

The aircraft had arrived at R.A.E. Bedford in January 1964 after completing radio, radar and armament trials and flew some 100 hours evaluating the T.O.D. system. The aircraft was taken off charge on 12th September, 1969.

Engine test development

Since the design of the jet engine a number of Avro aircraft were involved in their development. The Lancaster prototype BT308 shown below was the first aircraft to test the Metrovick F2/1, the first axial flow engine developed in the U.K. which first flew in June 1943. The Vulcan continued this tradition of developing new engine designs on Avro aircraft.

The first prototype VX770 seen here landing at the Rolls-Royce Hucknall facility was powered by four Rolls-Royce Conway R.Co7 engines and with the tragic loss of this prototype, Vulcan XA902 was converted to carry the Rolls-Royce Conway engines flying from the Rolls-Royce Flight Test Establishment at Hucknall. In 1968, it became the first aircraft to fly the Rolls-Royce Spey low-bypass turbofan engine when two of the engines were installed in place of the Conway's with little external difference in the appearance of the aircraft.

XA894 first flew on 9th January, 1957 and was used for de-icing system clearance, auto-pilot development and later official trials of the auto-pilot and Navigation Bombing System (N.B.S.) at Boscombe Down. After these trials it was allocated to Bristol Siddeley Engines Ltd., Filton for development of the Olympus B.01 22R which was to be used for the B.A.C. TSR-2 low level supersonic reconnaissance and tactical strike aircraft .

After arrival at Filton on 18th July, 1960 it was converted to carry the 22R engine in a bifurcated pod under the fuselage, it made it's first flight with this engine on 23rd February, 1962. Unfortunately XA894 was destroyed by fire on 3rd December, 1962 when the under-slung engine shed a low pressure turbine disc which entered the bomb bay fuel tanks; it had nearly completed eight hours flying time with the Olympus 22R by the time of the accident.

B. Mk1 Vulcan XA903 first flew on 10th May, 1957 and used for Blue Steel development trials. In late 1962 it was re-allotted for auxiliary power unit (APU) development. On 3rd January, 1964 it went to Bristol Siddeley Engines Ltd., at Filton for conversion to Olympus 593 flying test bed. This engine was a further development of the Olympus 22R and was being worked up for the Concorde programme. It made its first flight on 9th September, 1966 and by 1971 had completed over 400 hours flying hours with the 593 engine.

On 4th August, 1971 XA903 arrived at Marshalls of Cambridge for conversion of the pod to allow fitment of the Rolls-Royce RB.199 engine. This engine was being developed for the Multi-Role Tornado which would eventually provide the R.A.F with the bombing and reconnaissance roles provided by the Vulcan. It was delivered to Rolls-Royce in February 1972 and made its first flight with the RB.199 on 19th April, 1973. In 1976 it was used for ground firing trials of a Mauser 27mm cannon made from the RB.199 pod. before it completed its trials in1971. On 22nd February, 1979 it arrived at the R.A.E. at Farnborough for ground training before it was struck off charge on 19th July, 1979. The nose was acquired by Wartime Museum at Wellesbourne Mountford airfield near Statford on Avon.

Auto landing system development

Tony Blackman OBE. MA, FRAeS, FRIN, pictured in his office 28th September, 1956. Blackman joined Avro as a test pilot in August 1956 and previously worked at Boscombe Down 'B' Squadron which was responsible for the evaluation of bomber aircraft. It was here that Blackman was involved in some of the earliest handling assessments of the Vulcan.

He was employed by Sir Roy Dobson to assist Roly Falk and Jimmy Harrison in the development of the Vulcan for Service use. This led to him being extensively involved in the development of an automatic landing system.

Initially blind landing trials were carried out at Martlesham Heath by the Blind Landing Experimental Unit (BLEU). The unit was formed after experimental work at T.R.E. Defford in 1945. It later moved to Bedford where they tested the auto throttle system on the Avro Type 707A required for this method of landing.

At the time Vulcan B.Mk1 XA899 was developing the Smiths Military Flight System (MFS) which was a military development of the system used by commercial airlines. The MFS used remote sensing from several instruments to provide heading and altitude information, radio beam displacement and comprehensive director displays on two instruments, called the director horizon and the beam compass. These tests were not without their problems, but the system was eventually made to work and fitted to Service Vulcan's. Along with the MFS system XA899 was flight testing the auto throttle system which Tony Blackman first trialled in October 1957. It became apparent that BLEU incredibly had failed to realise that an auto throttle needs a pitch rate term as well as speed error from datum. They made Avro's waste time evaluating different pitot systems before reluctantly allowing Smiths to introduce pitch rate giro's along with a new pilot interface. This system was successfully flown 11th April, 1958.

After XH533 had completed its initial B.Mk2 clearance trials at Boscombe Down in June 1959 it returned to Woodford for fitment of a complete automatic landing system whilst XH536 continued with the MFS trials now called MFS 1B. BLEU's design of the automatic system required the use of a 'leader cable' installation for lateral guidance on to the runway in addition to the standard ILS localiser offset from the runway centre lines by 3°. The aircraft would hold the localiser down to 300ft above the runway and then the leader cable receiver would turn and line up the aircraft with the runway. These trials were made at Bedford where the leader cable was fitted. The first automatic landing with XH533 was made on 31st August, 1961 and over 60 flights were required to get the necessary standard of performance under all wind conditions. The lateral accuracy was better than required and unfortunately the cost of the leader cable ground installation probably spelt the death knell of the programme since only a localiser is needed for making auto landings.

The official clearance trials for the Mk10B Autopilot, Military Flight System MFS Mk.1B and auto landing system began in May 1963 on XH533 and were tested at Boscombe Down and Bedford. The last flight of XH533 using this feature was on 27th June, 1967 with over ninety successful automatic landings being made at Bedford. Vulcan XL319 based at Scampton was the only operational aircraft to use this system before the requirement for this type of automatic landing system for the Vulcan and Victor was cancelled in 1967.

The first fully certificated automatic landing system on the DH Trident airliner confirmed that a leader cable was unnecessary for automatic systems.

PART EIGHT

FINAL CHAPTER

Celebration of twenty five years in service

To celebrate twenty five years in service with the Royal Air Force an exhibition and display was held at R.A.F Scampton on 25th July, 1981. These pictures were taken at that event by Avro photographer Geoff Newton who was Paul Cullerne's deputy at that time.

The flying display included a four-aircraft scramble after which the Vulcans separated with three aircraft of the Scampton Wing making a number of formation flypasts before finally pealing off for a stream landing. Another aircraft from 617 (Dam Buster) Squadron treated the crowd to a fine solo flying display with some spirited manoeuvres. Norman Barber, Managing Director of the then Manchester Division of British Aerospace presented the R.A.F with a fine action painting of the Vulcan. John Gray and Harry Holmes from the Public Relations department also represented the Company.

50 day wonder - 1982

At the start of the Falklands war Woodford and Chadderton factories of British Aerospace were heavily involved in providing refuelling capabilities for the Nimrod to support missions to the Falklands. Not long after the need arose to make Nimrods capable of taking on fuel in flight, the Royal Air Force also required more tanker aircraft to supplement the hard pressed Victor force operating intensively in support of the Falkland Island operations. The idea of using Vulcan's was discussed at Woodford on 30th April, 1982 and the feasibility was established during the May Day week-end break. Go ahead was given on Tuesday 4th May, 1982 and fifty days later on Wednesday 23rd June the initial C(A) release to service was given and the first Vulcan Tanker XH561 was delivered to the RAF at Waddington.

At first it was thought that it might take only three weeks to first flight but the decision to mount a Hose Drum Unit (HDU) in the former ECM bay of the Vulcan meant the removal of much support structure and a consequently large amount of detail stiffening of the remainder. The Hose Drum Unit had to be split in order to fit it into the aircraft, but the choice of position allowed a third cylindrical tank to be put in the bomb bay to increase the disposable fuel load. The aircraft fuel system was modified to enable bomb bay tanks to be topped up in flight, the bomb bay heating air supply was adapted to drive the HDU fuel pump and condition the HDU bay, also electrical supplies were run for HDU and associated equipment.

The whole job involved design groups in both Nimrod and Development Design Centres supported especially by Structures and Mechanical Systems and Avionics. Detail manufacture was undertaken at both Woodford and Chadderton with help from British Aerospace Warton Division and Flight Refuelling Ltd helped with redesign of the HDU to make it fit in the Vulcan.

Royal Air Force assistance

A fairing to cover the HDU was the only outward sign of the Vulcan's change in role and this was built in No.3 Work Centre at Chadderton. The strip and modification to the airframes was handled by No.3 Work Centre at Woodford. Especially welcome to the Manchester team was the first class assistance from RAF Vulcan Crew Chiefs backed by W/O Dan Barker of the Nimrod Liaison Office.

Throughout the design, manufacture and assembly, a tremendous effort was maintained. When it came to Flight Testing it was disappointing not to have the hose trailed during first flight on Friday 18th June. However, it was the turn of the Flight Departments with A&AEE Boscombe Down plus RAF Vulcan crew members to put some hours in and the culmination of five day development effort was the passing of fuel to Victor tanker and Vulcan bomber aircraft after "dry" contact with a Nimrod from Woodford all on the same flight.

Night illumination tests were completed later. Coming, as it did, straight after the effort on Nimrods, this considerable task might fairly be called a 50-day wonder. The "impossible" task on Nimrod was done immediately and the Vulcan "miracle" took a little longer.

The additional fuel load in the Vulcan K.2 was carried in three standard Vulcan long-range tanks, which were fitted in the bomb bay. This gave a total fuel capacity of 100,000 lb. Six Vulcan's were then commissioned into service with 50 Squadron from 1982 to 1984. The Squadron's principal role was the provision of Air-to-Air refuelling (AAR) for the Air Defence of the UK, but also carried out Maritime Radar Reconnaissance (MRR) and the Air Sampling Role.

Vulcan's XH558 and XH560 embodying Mod 2390 Parts A&B Air Monitoring pods and Mod 2600 Tanker conversion (Mk.17 H.D.U.) were not permitted to use combined operations in the tanker dispensing and air monitoring mode. For both wet and dry contact dispensing operations, the air monitoring pods were removed before flight.

Six Vulcan B.Mk2 aircraft were converted to the tanker role they were, XH561, XJ825, XM571, XL445 and B.Mk2 (M.R.R.) XH560 and XH558 the latter aircraft remains the only fyling Vulcan. The aircraft remained in service with No.50 Squadron until the unit disbanded on 31st March, 1984 it was the last squadron to fly the Vulcan. They were replaced by the Vickers VC10 which had been converted to the air-to-air refuelling role.

Close up of hose drum unit (H.D.U.) on XH558 at Woodford 21st September, 1982 XH558 also retained its M.R.R. capability.

Avro test pilots Harry Nelson and Al McDicken deliver Vulcan K2 tanker to No.50 Squadron based at Waddington on 21st September, 1982.

XH560 refuelling Lighting interceptor.

Refuelling Tornado 22nd November, 1982.

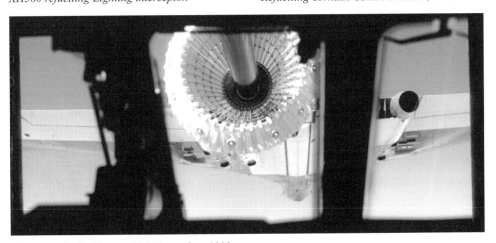

Close up of refuelling on 14th September, 1982.

The Unforeseen Challenge

Weapons and system trials continued throughout the life of the Vulcan with a variety of options looked at including the dropping of laser guided bombs.

The Falklands conflict

During the Falklands campaign in 1982 the Vulcan was successfully equipped with the American A.G.M.-45A Shrike anti-radar missile, with two carried under each wing. Shrikes missiles managed to hit two targets during the conflict. Flight trials were also tried with the Anglo-French Martel anti-radiation missile (A.R.M.) which was already carried in stock by the R.A.F. for the Blackburn Buccaneer low-level strike aircraft along with the Westinghouse AN/ALQ-101(V) E.C.M. pod which provided additional Electronic Counter Measures. These were fitted to improvised pylons on the Vulcan's wings using the Skybolt hard points. To navigate across the huge ocean, the Delco Carousel inertial navigation system (I.N.S.) was borrowed from the Vickers Super VC10 airliner, with two installed in each Vulcan.

In 1981, the run down of the Vulcan force had began with the disbanding of No.230 O.C.U. on 30th June, 1981 at R.A.F. Waddington. One of the first Squadron's to lose its Vulcan's was No.617 Squadron, when it finished operating the Vulcan on 31st December, 1981. It later converted to the Panavia Tornado GR1 in January 1983.

Six Vulcan's were originally chosen for operation "Black Buck" from the last remaining Vulcan squadrons based at R.A.F. Waddington. The aircraft nominated were to be B.Mk2A aircraft which were fitted with 301 engines as it was assumed that they would all be equipped with the Skybolt hard points, it was found that XM654 had no hard points so only five were made available, these were XL391, XM597, XM598, XM607 and XM612. These aircraft had to be converted to the full conventional bombing role and due to lack of use the refuelling probes had to be reactivated. Intensive crew training ensued with practice dropping of a full bomb load of twenty one 1000 lb bombs, flight refuelling and crew procedures.

It was found that problems were encountered with fuel spillage when flight refuelling and various modifications were made by the R.A.F. to help solve this problem, gutters, deflector plates and vortex generators were fitted forward of the wind screen without success. The problem was eventually solved by Flight Refuelling Limited. The aircraft were also given a non standard dark aircraft grey undersurface camouflage.

Black Buck Missions

Of the seven 'Operation Black Buck' missions organised five were actually flown from the Ascension Island in the South Atlantic Ocean. They flew some 7,800 nautical miles with a total flying time of 16 hours. Supported by Victor K2 tankers the Vulcan was refuelled seven times on the outward journey and once on the return journey. A Nimrod aircraft provided navigation and communications backup.

The first mission is perhaps the most famous, known as "Black Buck 1" XM607 captained by Flight Lieutenant Martin Withers aided by his crew dropped a stick of twenty one 1000 lb bombs on Stanley airfield damaging the airport tower and scoring a single direct hit in the centre of the runway. The last "Black Buck" mission was also flown by XM607 against radar installations using a full load of 1000 lb HE and anti-personnel air-burst bombs.

It is interesting to note that Argentina had considered purchasing the Vulcan on its retirement for the Fuerza Aerea Argentina which were still operating the Canberra bomber. A majority of the aircraft and equipment used by Argentina was supplied by the United States, France, Italy and the United Kingdom before the conflict began. Most of the equipment was already obsolete but still effective as weapons systems. After over two decades of service the Vulcan had not only proved a useful deterrent but in its swan song it was still capable of providing the Royal Air Force with a capability beyond it's years.

During the Falklands conflict six Vulcan's were converted to the airborne refuelling role. They were operated by No.50 Squadron in support of the U.K. air defence operations. Additional fuel was carried in three large tanks fitted in the bomb bay giving a total fuel capacity of 100,000 lb. Shown is XM571 trailing refuelling drogue on 13th July, 1982. To aid refuelling red semi-fluorescent stripes were provided on a white satin finish undersurface.

End of era

The second prototype Vulcan VX777 seen here at Farnborough where it was scrapped after serving as a valuable development aircraft. It survived a heavy landing at Farnborough in 1954 and was later converted as a aerodynamic prototype for both the Phase 2 and Phase 2C wing planform. It was struck off charge on 18th October, 1962.

Vulcan farewell at Woodford

On Tuesday 27th March, 1984 at 4pm a lone Vulcan of No.50 Squadron, performed a low fly-past and two touch and goes at Woodford. It then flew back to its base at Waddington in Lincolnshire and returned 30 minutes later with three more Vulcan's.

    The final flypast was made by the four Vulcan's XL426 and XM597 and two K2 tankers XL445 and XM571. Vulcan B.Mk2 XM597 was the aircraft which had diverted to Rio de Janeiro during the Falklands campaign, short of fuel after its refuelling probe was damaged during air-to-air refuelling on its way back to Ascension Island.

Flypast by four Vulcan's from R.A.F. Waddington at Woodford 27th March, 1984.

Conclusion of the RAF Vulcan display flight

On 23rd March, 1993 XH558 made a farewell flypast to the work force at Woodford before going to Bruntingthorpe for a final display to the public after being retired by the Royal Air Force Vulcan Display Flight.

Sixteen years later XH558 returned to Woodford on 27th September, 2009 to celebrate its return to the air. It is seen here on approach to Manchester Airport where it performed a touch and go after flying over Woodford's own Vulcan XM603.

XH558 makes a low pass with the bomb doors open displaying its farewell message.

The Cold War Icon - XH558

Perhaps the most famous and last Vulcan to fly is XH558; it was the first Vulcan B.Mk2 to be delivered to the Royal Air Force. It first flew on 25th May, 1960 and delivered to No.230 O.C.U. on 8th July, 1960. In its time with the Royal Air Force it was operated not only as a nuclear and conventional bomber but in its latter days it was used in the M.R.R. and Tanker roles by No.50 Squadron based at R.A.F. Waddington.

In 1984 with the disbandment of No.50 Squadron it became part of the Station Flight at Waddington along with XL426. It was found that it had more flying hours left before its next major service than any available Vulcan and due to public demand it was decided to keep XH558 for display flying. It reverted back the B.Mk2 configuration and used by the Vulcan Display Flight and began displaying to the public at Air shows in 1986. On the 20th September, 1992 it made its last flight and was delivered to Bruntingthorpe on 23rd March, 1993. The Walton brother's owners of Bruntingthorpe airfield had purchased XH558 and bought enough spares to support the objective of getting the Vulcan to fly again.

Public demand was so great that with the help of Heritage funding and donations and the support of BAE Systems, Chadderton and Woodford sites, Marshall Aerospace and the Vulcan to the Sky Trust under the guidance of Dr Robert Pleming, XH558 was able to take to the air again.

With over £7 million spent, Vulcan XH558 took to the air again on Thursday 18th October, 2007 fourteen years after its last flight, in the capable hands of Al McDicken and Dave Thomas both ex Vulcan display pilots. It was granted her Permit to fly on 3rd July, 2008 and returned to the Air Show circuit, two days later it starred at the RAF Waddington Airshow, her former home; it is now part of the Cold War story.

This air to air picture shows XH558 resplendent in its all white original anti-flash white colour scheme.

Evening flight - XH558 takes-off from Woodford 17th September, 1982. Note the sampling pods under the wing along with hose drum refuelling unit.

XH558 pictured at Woodford 14th October, 1982.

Outside support

In this final chapter it is worth mentioning the work of the Repair and Servicing Department C.W.P. (Contractors and Servicing Working Party) based at Bracebridge Heath. The departments function, when it was first formed in 1941, was to support Avro built aircraft in the field. The department's personnel were permanently out working in the U.K. and overseas.

In 1943, Bracebridge Heath had its own design office, manned by a small team led by Gilbert Whitehead, who became Divisional Technical Director for the Manchester Division before retiring in 1979, to back up the main design office at Woodford on repair drawings and modification work of Manchester built aircraft in service with the Royal Air Force. The department was later expanded and included the support of civilian aircraft.

In April 1982, it was announced that Bracebridge Heath was to close in light of reductions in MoD expenditure.

This Vulcan from R.A. F. Finningly made a wheels-up "pancake" landing during a midnight training flight in 1965. After removal from the runway the C.W.P. workers repaired the aircraft to fly with the Squadron again.

Royal Air Force St. Athan

On 6th September, 1978 a major milestone was reached when personnel at St. Athan celebrated the completion of the 500th major servicing of a "V" aircraft - Vulcan XM573. The occasion represented, in fact, a double milestone for the handing-over of the Vulcan to the crew from No.230 O.C.U. for delivery to R.A.F. Waddington, coincided with the 40th Anniversary of the inauguration of St. Athan as an R.A.F. base.

Last Vulcan Major Service

On 21st May, 1981 R.A.F. St Athan bid farewell to the last Vulcan bomber XL426 to have a major service. Major servicing on the Vulcan began at St. Athan in 1962 - then it was the B.Mk1. A total of thirty one Mk1 types were majored during the next four years before the B.Mk2 appeared at the base in 1966. XL426 was the 267th B.Mk2 to have a major service.

For those who like statistics 27,500 man-hours were expended on one major service. So the total "cost" at St. Athan was approximately eight million man-hours over a nineteen year period. Turnaround time started at forty six days but increased to fifty six as the aircraft grew older. One major service involved eighty five highly skilled personnel. Major servicing was carried out every 1,280 flying hours.

During the ceremony XL426 was handed back to group Captain V. L. Warrington, Officer Commanding R.A.F. Scampton, where the aircraft was based, by the Air Officer Commanding Maintenance Units Headquarters, Support Command, Air Vice-Marshal D.W. Richardson and Air Commodore Geof Tyler, Station Commander at St. Athan.

XL426 later went to 50 Squadron at R.A.F. Waddington in 1982 and later became part of the Station Flight in 1984 for the Vulcan Display Flight. In 1986 it was sold to Mr R. Jacobson and delivered to Southend airport on 19th December, 1986.

This picture taken by Dave Draycot shows the last flying Vulcan XH558 at the 2009 Royal International Air Tattoo at Fairford, Gloucestershire. It is seen here with a Boeing B-52H Stratofortress still operated by the United States Air Force.

The B-52 first flew on 5th April, 1952, with the final version the B-52H first flight being on 6th March, 1961. The B52H had a wing span of 185 ft and a length of 157 ft 7 inches and was powered by eight TF-33 turbofan engines of 17,000 lb. thrust. It had a range of some 10,000 miles, with a ceiling of more than 50,000 ft, at 650 mph, gross weight was 488,000 lb. Production reached 744 aircraft manufactured by the Boeing Seattle, Washington, and Wichita, Kansas, plants between 1952 and 1962.

Paul Cullerne aviation photographer

The majority of pictures in this book were taken by Avro photographer Paul Cullerne, throughout his career his pictures have graced many a publication. He retired from the then British Aerospace as Chief Photographer for the Manchester Division in 1983. This was an end of an era as far as famous aviation photographers were concerned, for Paul was the last active member of the "old school" which included such famous names as Charles E. Brown, Cyril Peckham, Russell Adams, etc., all of whom made a name for themselves in the post war years. Paul joined Avro in January 1946 after completing war service with the R.A.F. and photographed every aircraft to come out of the Avro stable during his time at Manchester.

Paul in his working environment 20th March, 1962.

The rear turret of a Bomber Command Bombing School Avro Lincoln provided the ideal platform for this fine photograph.

Paul's classic pictures

This picture shows the first prototype Vulcan VX770 taken by Paul in August, 1953.

An iconic picture of the two prototype Vulcan's accompanied by the four Avro 707s was taken on the 14th September, 1953 from an Avro Lincoln, during a flight along the South Coast between Portsmouth and Southampton.

Paul Cullerne used a camera of his own design and mostly shot using 5x4 film. Much of his work was sadly lost in the devastating fire at Chadderton in October 1959. The photographic department was originally based at Chadderton but later moved to Woodford in 1983 after Paul had retired. The department was fully equipped to produce Black and White and colour prints. He was kept busy during the 70s and 80s taking pictures of the 748 airliner for the marketing department promotional items.

This famous picture shows XA891 flying over Mersey Estuary.

The S.B.A.C. Show at Farnborough was a perfect opportunity to take pictures of the latest aircraft from leading manufactures. This picture shows XA891 landing at the Show in 1957.

XJ783 pictured on 1st August, 1961.

A welcoming site to many an air crew was Lincoln Cathedral which meant that they were close to returning to base. This famous picture taken by Paul Cullerne shows XM575 on 10th August, 1982. Of all Paul's pictures this must be one of the most reproduced.

Photographed on the same sortie XM575 of No.44 (Rhodesia) Squadron was based at R.A.F. Waddington on 10th August, 1982. It was flown by Flt Lt Martin Withers who flew the first "Black Buck" mission in the Falklands campaign.

One of Paul's later air to air pictures of the Vulcan was of XM603 which made its last landing at Woodford during 1982 and was used as a mock-up for the Vulcan B.Mk2K Tanker aircraft and also donated it's refuelling probe for the first Nimrod converted for flight refuelling during the Falklands conflict. It remained at Woodford as an exhibit managed by retired members who formed the 603 Club, many of whom have now sadly passed away.

It was flown to Woodford by Sir Charles Masefield with the crew including retired Ted Hartley and Bob Pogson. The aircraft was also used as a donor aircraft providing parts for XH558 to help assist this aircraft back into the air.

Pictured with XM603 on its last flight (Sir) Charles Masefield who later became General Manager of the Manchester Division and left Bob Pogson and right Ted Hartley both survivors of the Vulcan XA891 crash in 1959.

Call sign Avro One

Avro One was the assigned to the Chief Test Pilot at Manchester.

Avro/Manchester Chief Test Pilots

A.V. Roe	1908-1910
C. H. Pixton	1911
Lieut W. Parke R.N.	1912
F. P. Raynham	1913-1916
Capt H. A. Hammersley	1919-1921
H.J.L. Hinkler	1921-1927
Capt H.A. Brown	1928-1945
S. A. Thorn	1945-1947
J. H. Orrell	1947-1955
R. J. Falk	1955-1958
J. G. Harrison	1959-1970
C. B. G. Masefield	1978-1981
J. A. Robinson	1981-1987
P. Henley	1987-1993
A.A. McDicken	1993-1998
J.E. Davies	1998
J. W. A. Bolton	1998-2000
A. A. McDicken	2000-2003
J. Turner (based at Warton)	

Serial numbers and first flight dates

Aircraft	First Flight	Aircraft	First Flight
1952		XH478 B.Mk1/A	14th July
VX770 1st Prototype	30th August	XH479 B.Mk1/A	1st March
		XH480 B.Mk1/A	21st March
1953		XH481 B.Mk1/A	8th April
VX777 2nd Prototype	3rd September	XH482 B.Mk1/A	16th April
1954		XH483 B.Mk1/A	1st May
-	- -	XH497 B.Mk1/A	15th May
1955		XH498 B.Mk1	6th June
XA889 B.Mk1	4th February	XH499 B.Mk1/A	23rd June
XA890 B.Mk1	24th August	XH500 B.Mk1/A	12th July
XA891 B.Mk1	22nd Sept	**XH533 B.Mk2**	30th August
XA892 B.Mk1	23rd November	XH501 B.Mk1/A	21st August
		XH502 B.Mk1/A	4th October
1956		XH503 B.Mk1/A	31st October
XA893 B.Mk1	16th January	XH504 B.Mk1/A	30th November
XA895 B.Mk1	12th August	XH505 B.Mk1/A	8th December
XA897 B.Mk1	10th July		
XA898 B.Mk1	26th November	**1959**	
		XH506 B.Mk1/A	20th January
1957		XH532 B.Mk1/A	25th March
XA894 B.Mk1	9th January	**XH536 B.Mk2**	3rd May
XA896 B.Mk1	30th January	**XH534 B.Mk2/A *(R)**	18th June
XA899 B.Mk1	16th February		
XA900 B.Mk1	7th March	**1960**	
XA901 B.Mk1	19th March	**XH557 B.Mk2/A *(R)**	2nd April
XA902 B.Mk1	13th April	**XH535 B.Mk2**	7th May
XA903 B.Mk1	10th May	**XH558 B.Mk2**	25th May
XA904 B.Mk1/A	31st May	**XH559 B.Mk2**	29th June
XA905 B.Mk1	26th June	**XH537 B.Mk2/A *(R)**	4th August
XA906 B.Mk1/A	19th July	**XH560 B.Mk2**	30th August
XA907 B.Mk1/A	21st August	**XH561 B.Mk2**	17th September
XA908 B.Mk1	28th August	**XH562 B.Mk2**	21st October
XA909 B.Mk1/A	20th September	**XH563 B.Mk2**	1st November
XA910 B.Mk1/A	22nd October	**XJ780 B.Mk2**	28th November
XA911 B.Mk1/A	31st October	**1961**	
XA912 B.Mk1/A	13th November	**XH538 B.Mk2/A *(R)**	4th January
XA913 B.Mk1/A	26th November	**XJ781 B.Mk2**	10th January
XH475 B.Mk1/A	19th December	**XJ782 B.Mk2**	16th January
1958		**XJ783 B.Mk2**	3rd February
XH476 B.Mk1/A	8th January	**XH554 B.Mk2**	18th February
XH477 B.Mk1/A	29th January	**XJ784 B.Mk2/A *(R)**	9th March

Aircraft	First Flight	Aircraft	First Flight
XJ823 B.Mk2	30th March	**XM576 B.Mk2A**	16th May
XJ824 B.Mk2	24th April	**XM594 B.Mk2A**	4th June
XH539 B.Mk2	10th May	**XM595 B.Mk2A**	4th July
XH555 B.Mk2	9th June	*XM596 B.Mk2*	*F.T.S.*
XL317 B.Mk2	24th June	**XM597 B.Mk2A**	12th July
XJ825 B.Mk2	7th July	**XM598 B.Mk2A**	15th August
XL318 B.Mk2	11th August	**XM599 B.Mk2A**	30th August
XH556 B.Mk2	31st August	**XM600 B.Mk2A**	6th September
XL319 B.Mk2	1st October	**XM601 B.Mk2A**	21st October
XL320 B.Mk2	9th November	**XM602 B.Mk2A**	28th October
XL321 B.Mk2	6th December	**XM603 B.Mk2A**	15th November
		XM604 B.Mk2A	15th November
1962		**XM605 B.Mk2A**	22nd Nov
XL359 B.Mk2	10th January	**XM606 B.Mk2A**	28th November
XL360 B.Mk2	31st January	**XM607 B.Mk2A**	29th November
XL361 B.Mk2	21st February	**XM608 B.Mk2A**	24th December
XL384 B.Mk2/A *(R)	16th March		
XL385 B.Mk2/A *(R)	30th March	**1964**	
XL386 B.Mk2/A *(R)	2nd May	**XM609 B.Mk2A**	2nd January
XL387 B.Mk2/A *(R)	16th May	**XM610 B.Mk2A**	22nd January
XL388 B.Mk2/A *(R)	25th May	**XM611 B.Mk2A**	23rd January
XL389 B.Mk2/A *(R)	13th June	**XM612 B.Mk2A**	13th February
XL390 B.Mk2/A *(R)	3rd July	**XM645 B.Mk2A**	25th February
XL392 B.Mk2/A *(R)	19th July	**XM646 B.Mk2A**	16th March
XL425 B.Mk2/A *(R)	6th August	**XM647 B.Mk2A**	2nd April
XL426 B.Mk2/A *(R)	13th August	**XM648 B.Mk2A**	17th April
XL427 B.Mk2/A *(R)	14th September	**XM649 B.Mk2A**	28th April
XL443 B.Mk2/A *(R)	18th September	**XM650 B.Mk2A**	12th May
XL444 B.Mk2/A *(R)	12th October	**XM651 B.Mk2A**	1st June
XL445 B.Mk2/A *(R)	30th October	**XM652 B.Mk2A**	16th July
XL446 B.Mk2/A *(R)	16th November	**XM653 B.Mk2A**	14th August
XM569 B.Mk2/A *(R)	11th December	**XM654 B.Mk2A**	2nd October
		XM655 B.Mk2A	2nd November
1963		**XM656 B.Mk2A**	25th November
XM570 B.Mk2/A *(R)	31st January	**XM657 B.Mk2A**	21st December
XM571 B.Mk2/A *(R)	31st January		
XM572 B.Mk2/A *(R)	9th February		
XM573 B.Mk2/A *(R)	27th February		
XM574 B.Mk2A	28th March		
XM575 B.Mk2A	19th April		
XL391 B.Mk2/A *(R)	14th May		

Note

B.Mk2A aircraft designation was for aircraft fitted with Olympus 301 engines.

Twenty six aircraft were retro-fitted with Olympus 301 engines. See key *(R).

Chadderton and Woodford facilities

Above - Chadderton factory and Avro Headquarters pictured in June 1958. The power station supplied heat and electricity to the factory.

Pictured left - Woodford flight sheds.

Woodford new assembly, pictured in June 1958, when the Vulcan programme was in full production.

PART NINE

SPECIFICATIONS
B.Mk2

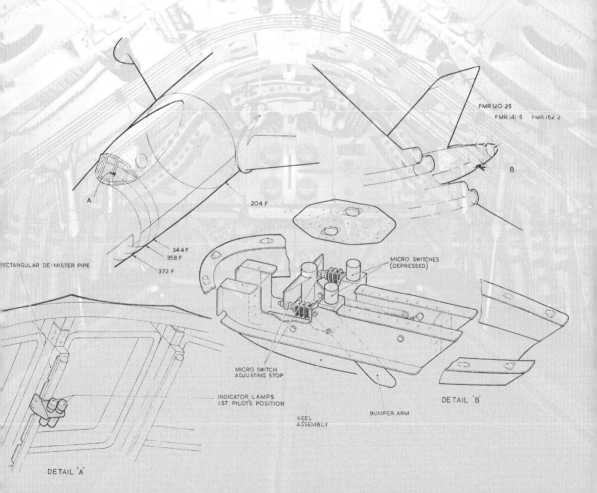

FMR 120·25

FMR 141·5   FMR 162·2

B

A

204 F

344 F
358 F

372 F

RECTANGULAR DE-MISTER PIPE

MICRO SWITCHES
(DEPRESSED)

MICRO SWITCH
ADJUSTING STOP

INDICATOR LAMPS
1 ST PILOT'S POSITION

KEEL
ASSEMBLY

BUMPER ARM

DETAIL 'B'

DETAIL 'A'

B.Mk2 Vulcan
General Arrangement - 1960

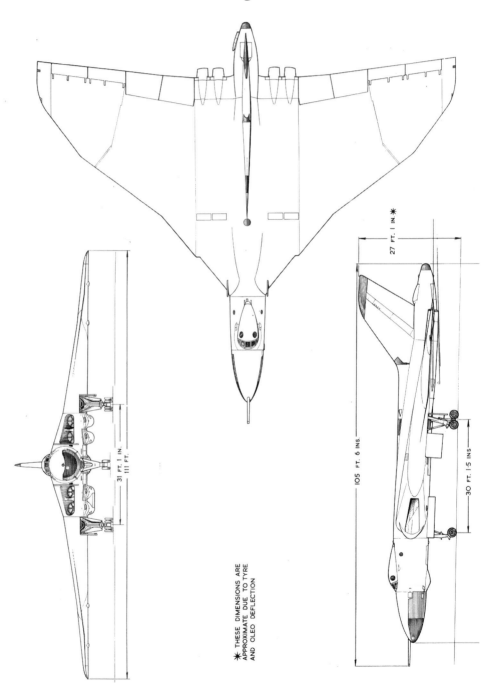

27 FT. I IN. *

105 FT. 6 INS.

30 FT. I·5 INS

31 FT. I IN.

111 FT.

* THESE DIMENSIONS ARE
APPROXIMATE DUE TO TYRE
AND OLEO DEFLECTION

Weights and dimensions B.Mk2

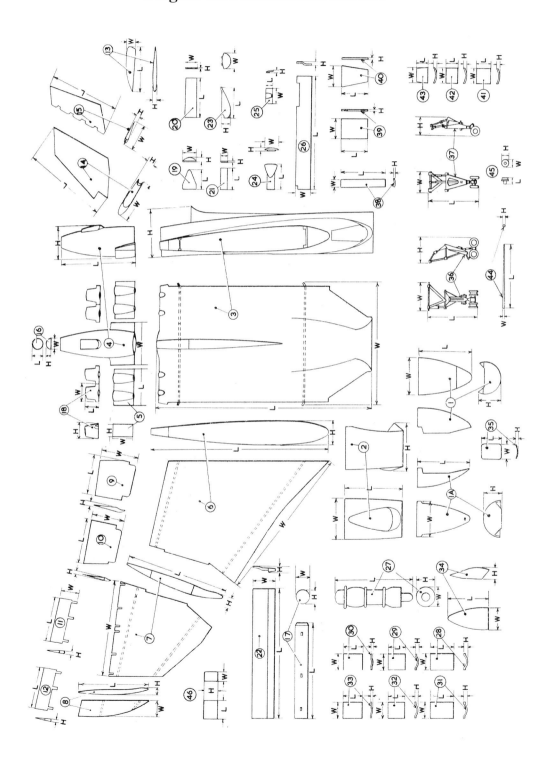

Weights and dimensions B.Mk2 continued

ITEM	COMPONENT		LENGTH (ft.)	WIDTH (ft.)
1	NOSE (lower portion, composite)		13.5	8.75
1	NOSE (upper portion, metal)		13.5	8.7
2	FRONT FUSELAGE		16.75	9.2
3	CENTRE SECTION		52.85	28.85
4	REAR FUSELAGE		18.5	10.6
5	REAR FUSELAGE FAIRING		8.25	5.0
6	WING INNER (Starboard)		50.0	35.5
6a	WING INNER (Port)		50.0	35.5
7	WING OUTER (Port and starboard)		24.5	20.5
8	WING TIP (Port and starboard)		14.8	3.75
9	ELEVON INNER (Inboard, port and starboard)		9.75	10.6
10	ELEVON INNER (Outboard, port and starboard)		10.25	8.75
11	ELEVON OUTER (Inboard, port and starboard)		9.75	4.25
12	ELEVON OUTER (Outboard, port and starboard)		9.75	4.25
13	FIN CAP		11.33	2.25
14	FIN		21.0	10.0
15	RUDDER		19.25	6.0
16	TAIL RADOME		2.47	24.7
17	JET PIPE		22.98	2.63
18	JET PIPE CAP		3.25	4.25
19	FAIRING (counterpoise plate, each)		4.0	3.58
20	COUNTERPOISE PLATE, FRONT (each)		7.6	3.08
20a	COUNTERPOISE PLATE, REAR (each)		5.75	3.25
21	SPLITTER PLATE FRONT (each)		3.87	1.75
21a	SPLITTER PLATE REAR (each)		5.75	2.54
22	BOMB BAY DOORS (each)		29.25	5.2
23	EXPENDABLE FAIRING		7.5	3.75
24	BOMB BAY FAIRING, REAR		6.33	3.25
25	BOMB BAY FAIRING, FRONT		6.0	7.0
26	130MB BAY FAIRING, PORT		29.0	4.75
26a	BOMB BAY FAIRING, STARBOARD		29.0	5.75
27	ENGINE (Olympus 20101) (including oil and starter)		13.68	3.75
28	ENGINE DOOR, FORWARD	Inboard, port and stbd.	5.29	4.08
29	ENGINE DOOR, CENTRE	Inboard, port and stbd.	4.85	4.04
30	ENGINE DOOR, REAR	Inboard, port and stbd.	5.83	4.79
31	ENGINE DOOR, FORWARD	Outboard, port and stbd.	5.29	4.08
32	ENGINE DOOR, CENTRE	Outboard, port and stbd.	4.83	4.08
33	ENGINE DOOR, REAR	Outboard, port and stbd.	5.83	4.79
34	CANOPY		10.5	4.66
35	MAIN ENTRANCE DOOR		5.0	2.75
36	MAIN WHEEL UNIT (each)		12.75	5.0
37	NOSE WHEEL UNIT		13.5	3.5
38	NOSE WHEEL DOOR (each)		10.75	1.75
39	MAIN WHEEL DOOR		6.5	4.75
40	MAIN WHEEL FAIRING		5.25	4.0
41	REAR FUSELAGE ACCESS DOOR (front)		4.27	4.04
42	REAR FUSELAGE ACCESS DOOR (centre)		3.29	4.08
43	REAR FUSELAGE ACCESS DOOR (rear)		3.25	4.0
44	REFUELLING PROBE		9.7	0.5
45	RAM AIR TURBINE		1.3	1.16
46	AIRBORNE AUXILIARY POWER PLANT		4.5	2.0

ITEM	COMPONENT		HEIGHT (ft.)	STRUCTURE tare weight (lb.)
1	NOSE (lower portion, composite)		5.5	290
1	NOSE (upper portion, metal)		4.25	230
2	FRONT FUSELAGE		10.25	2,081
3	CENTRE SECTION		12.0	17,979
4	REAR FUSELAGE		6.33	962
5	REAR FUSELAGE FAIRING		3.33	258
6	WING INNER (Starboard)		5.0	6,457
6a	WING INNER (Port)		5.0	6,446
7	WING OUTER (Port and starboard)		2.5	1,708
8	WING TIP (Port and starboard)		0.79	107
9	ELEVON INNER (Inboard, port and starboard)		1.66	326
10	ELEVON INNER (Outboard, port and starboard)		1.5	323
11	ELEVON OUTER (Inboard, port and starboard)		1.6	210
12	ELEVON OUTER (Outboard, port and starboard)		1.6	203
13	FIN CAP		1.41	80
14	FIN		1.87	919
15	RUDDER		1.0	305
16	TAIL RADOME		1.54	14
17	JET PIPE		2.63	492
18	JET PIPE CAP		2.87	97
19	FAIRING (counterpoise plate, each)		0.5	17
20	COUNTERPOISE PLATE, FRONT (each)		0.08	39
20a	COUNTERPOISE PLATE, REAR (each)		0.08	31
21	SPLITTER PLATE FRONT (each)		0.16	10
21a	SPLITTER PLATE REAR (each)		0.16	23
22	BOMB BAY DOORS (each)		0.66	713
23	EXPENDABLE FAIRING		1.0	60
24	BOMB BAYFAIRING, REAR		1.0	23
25	BOMB BAY FAIRING, FRONT		0.75	4.8
26	BOMB BAY FAIRING, PORT		1.5	444
26a	BOMB BAY FAIRING, STARBOARD		1.6	520
27	ENGINE (Olympus 20101) (including oil and starter)		4.35	4,761
28	ENGINE DOOR,FORWARD	Inboard, port and stbd.	0.5	54
29	ENGINE DOOR, CENTRE	Inboard, port and stbd.	1.33	80
30	ENGINE DOOR, REAR	Inboard, port and stbd.	1.25	68
31	ENGINE DOOR, FORWARD	Outboard, port and stbd.	0.5	52
32	ENGINE DOOR, CENTRE	Outboard, port and stbd.	1.33	82
33	ENGINE DOOR, REAR	Outboard, port and stbd.	1.25	73
34	CANOPY		1.4	284
35	MAIN ENTRANCE DOOR		1.0	100
36	MAIN WHEEL UNIT (each)		6.0	2,485
37	NOSE WHEEL UNIT		3.08	990
38	NOSE WHEEL DOOR (each)		0.33	48
39	MAIN WHEEL DOOR		0.75	164
40	MAIN WHEEL FAIRING		0.41	32
41	REAR FUSELAGE ACCESS DOOR (front)		0.79	27
42	REAR FUSELAGE ACCESS DOOR (centre)		0.79	23
43	REAR FUSELAGE ACCESS DOOR (rear)		0.87	22
44	REFUELLING PROBE		0.5	38
45	RAM AIR TURBINE		1.25	94
46	AIRBORNE AUXILIARY POWER PLANT		3.16	420

Vulcan B.Mk1 and B.Mk2 comparison

Vulcan B.Mk1 (Sraight wing) July 1954 brochure

Normal gross weight:	165,500 lb.
Normal cruising speed:	500 knots
Cruising altitude:	45,000 - 55,000 ft.
Bomb capacity: normal:	10,000 -30,000 lb.
Bomb capacity: overload:	58,000 lb.
Range (10,000 lb bomb)	4,000 lb - nautical miles
Range (58,000 lb bomb)	1,200 nautical miles
Range (photo-reconnaissance)	5,600 - 7,200 nautical miles
Engines x4	Olympus B.01.101 or B.01.6

General Dimensions

Length overall	97 ft. 1 in.
Span overall	99 ft.
Height (dimension approximate due to tyre and oleo deflection)	26 ft. 6 in.
Wheel base	29 ft. 2 in.

Wing

Aspect ratio	2.84
Swepback (leading edge)	49 deg. 54 min.
Gross wing area	3446 sq. ft.
Chord at tip	6.84 ft.
Chord (mean)	34.81 ft.
Thickness chord ratio	8 per cent
Incidence	5 deg.
Aerofoil section at wingtip	Squire "B"

B.Mk1 (kink wing)
General Dimensions

Length overall	97 ft. 1 in.
Span overall	99 ft.
Height (dimension approximate due to tyre and oleo deflection)	26 ft. 6 in.
Wheel base	29 ft. 2 in.

B.Mk1A
General Dimensions

Length overall (from nose) 99 ft. 11 in	(from refuelling probe)	105 ft. 6in.
Span overall	99 ft. 5 in.	
Height (dimension approximate due to tyre and oleo deflection)	26 ft. 6 in.	
Wheel base	29 ft. 2 in.	

Wing

Aspect ratio	2.76
Gross wing area	3554 sq. ft.

Vulcan B.Mk2 - March 1956 brochure

Normal gross weight:	190,000 lb.
Normal cruising speed:	500 knots
Cruising altitude:	45,000 - 65,000 ft.
Bomb capacity: normal:	10,000 -30,000 lb.
Range (10,000 lb bomb or 13,000 lb. special store)	5,000 - 5,500 n.m.
Range (photo-reconnaissance)	5,850 - 6,110 n.m.

General Dimensions

Length overall (without E.C.M. fairing)	97 ft. 1 in.
Span overall	111 ft.
Height	26 ft. 6 in.
Wheel base	29 ft. 2 in.

Wing

Aspect ratio	3.11
Sweepback (leading edge at wing joint)	49 deg. 54 min.
Gross wing area	3964 sq. ft.
Chord at tip	10.00 ft.
Chord (mean)	34.71 ft.
Thickness chord ratio	10 per cent
Incidence	5 deg.
Dihedral	0 deg.
Aerofoil section at root	N.A.C.A. 0010
Aerofoil section at wingtip	RAE.101 modified.
Power Units x 4	*Olympus B.01.6*

Fin

Fin sweepback, leading edge	49 deg. 30 min.
Fin sweepback trailing edge	25 deg. 30 min.

Vulcan B.Mk2 - 1968

General Dimension

Length overall (from nose) 99 ft. 11 in	(from refuelling probe)	105 ft. 6in.
Span overall		111 ft.
Height (dimension approximate due to tyre and oleo deflection)		27 ft. 1in.

Wing

Aerofoil section	RAE.104, 5% modified.
Chord (mean)	35.712 ft.
Chord (root)	63.4 ft
Power Units x 4	*Olympus 201, 202 or 301.*

Weights

Prior to production set 41 maximum permissible A.U.W.	180,000lb.
Maximum permissible A.U.W. with plus Mod. No.1302, 1309, 1321 and 1334.	190,000 lb.
Maximum permissible A.U.W. with plus Mod. No.1456, 1587, and 1627.	195,000 lb.
Maximum permissible A.U.W. (overload case).	210,000 lb.
Maximum permissible Landing Weight (overload case).	210,000 lb.
Maximum Normal Landing Weight.	195,000 lb.

Systems summary - December 1960

HYDRAULIC SYSTEM

This was electrically controlled and operated the alighting gear, bomb doors, wheel brakes and nose-wheel steering. A reserve pressure supply for the brakes was retained by two accumulators charged from the main hydraulic system. An electro-hydraulic power pack was available for the emergency operation of the bomb doors and to recharge the brake system when the hydraulic pumps are not operating. When certain special stores were carried an independent electrically driven hydraulic power pack is fitted in the bomb bay.

COMPRESSED AIR SYSTEM

A compressed air system was installed to lower the alighting gear in an emergency. A further compressed air system was provided to open or close the main entrance door and also to initiate jettisoning of the canopy.

AIR CONDITIONING SYSTEM

The air conditioning system was installed to maintain the air in the crew's compartment at reasonable temperatures and pressures. Air from the engine compressors was used for pressurisation and heating, the flow of air being automatically maintained by flow controllers. Air conditioning equipment in the nose wheel bay controls the temperatures of the air entering the cabin and the pressure in the cabin is maintained by pressure controllers which regulate the amount of air allowed to pass to atmosphere through discharge valves. Provision was also made for cabin ventilation during un-pressurised flight. A further air conditioning system, supplied with engine compressor air, was fitted in the bomb bay when certain special stores were carried.

DE-ICING SYSTEM

Thermal de-icing provided protection against ice accretion on wing, fin and engine air intake leading edges; hot air for the systems was bled off the engine compressors and mixed with cold air to give a controlled temperature for distribution. A further system, utilising de-icing fluid, was provided for the pilots' and air bomber's windscreens.

FUEL

Fuel was carried in fourteen bag-type tanks contained in magnesium-alloy compartments, four tanks in the fuselage and five in each outer wing. Each tank was equipped with contents gauge transmitters, electrically-operated fuel pumps, a maximum fuel level cut-off switch and refuelling valves. In addition, No.1 and No.7 tanks each had a transfer pump which could be used to balance the fuel load should the aircraft become nose or tail heavy. The tanks were arranged in groups so that each engine was normally fed by a particular group of tanks. Cross-feed cocks were provided so that in emergency any engine may receive fuel from any tank or group of tanks. All tanks were pressurised to prevent vaporisation and consequent loss of fuel at altitude, air from the engine compressors being used for this purpose. To protect the tanks from internal fires or explosions, a Graviner Explosion Protection system was fitted. A pressure refuelling system was provided, in which the distribution of fuel load amongst all the tanks is automatically controlled to ensure correct aircraft loading.

FIRE PROTECTION

The fire protection system consisted of two separate methyl-bromide installations, one for the engines and the other for the fuel tank bays. Hand-operated water glycol extinguishers were disposed at convenient positions in the crew's compartment.

AIRBORNE EQUIPMENT

Additional airborne equipment was mounted in the rear fuselage. Temperature control of the E.C.M. canisters was affected by water/glycol and vapour cycle heat control systems, whilst the tail warning unit, which formed the fuselage rear cone, was provided with pneumatic and cooling systems. Three doors on the underside of the rear fuselage give access to this equipment. Counterpoise plates of honeycomb construction were mounted below the starboard centre engine rib, between the jet pipe curvatures.

Electrical power was supplied by four 40 kVA, 200 volt, 3 phase, 400 c/s. a.c. engine-driven alternators, arranged to supply independent load or in parallel via a synchronising ring main system. Reserve power was supplied from the auxiliary airborne power plant or the ram air turbine at 200 volt, 3 phase, 400 c/s, a.c. Power at 115 volt, 3 phase, 400 c/s, a.c. was provided, through various transformers, from the 200 volt system and from the same source by means of two frequency changers, a supply at 115 volt, single phase, 1600 c/s, a.c. was also available. D.C. power was provided at 28 volts through two 7.5 kVA transformer rectifier units and a single 24 volt battery provides sufficient power for crash and emergency services. A ground supply plug was provided on the port side aft fuselage for the 200 volt a.c. system and two 28 volt plugs were provided, adjacent to the nose wheel bay for ground servicing supply. In the unlikely event of the failure of all four alternators, sufficient power to maintain control would be available from the auxiliary power units.

CREW ACCOMMODATION

The Vulcan was equipped to carry five crew members although a sixth seat was provided with oxygen probe telecommunications / lead and static line. A ventilated suit system was provided for the five crew members, the air for which is tapped from the main cabin pressurisation system. Modification 1696 introduced swivel seats for the rear crew members. The navigator/radar and the A.E.O. were provided with swivel seats and the navigator/plotter had a modified static seat. Each seat embodied an assisted cushion and carried an Mk.46 parachute incorporating demand emergency oxygen set. All three seats could slide fore and aft on rails.

SPECIAL INSTRUMENT

To enable the crew to scan areas to the rear, above and below the aircraft a Kelvin Hughes rear viewing periscope was installed at the navigator's station.

WIRELESS

Wireless equipment consisted of general purpose H.F. (under control of the air electronics officer), U.H.F., I.L.S. and twin V.H.F. installations (controlled by the navigator). A low range radio altimeter provided indication for, and was controlled by, the first pilot. A high range radar altimeter provided indication for, and was controlled by, the navigator / air bomber. Radar installations, consisted of Gee, Green Satin, Tail Warning, I.F.F., N.B.S. and E.C.M. were fitted. Intercommunication between crew members was provided by a separate system, with switching facilities for introducing radio signals and conference inter-com. Five aerials were fitted externally to the fuselage, consisting of two U.H.F., two I.F.F. and one V.H.F. The H.F. transmitter-receiver was fed with signals from a resonant slot in the aircraft fin. The I.L.S. installation had three aerials, two being tuned notches (one in each wing tip) and the third a tuned metal strip contained in a box fitted below No.2 starboard tank bay. The A.D.F. utilised a loop aerial contained in a shallow dish which was fitted in the bomb bay roof, and the radio and radar altimeter installations use recessed reflector type aerials. The H_2S installation employed a rotating scanner in the nose.

Guidance systems

NAVIGATION AND BOMBING SYSTEM - 1971

The Vulcan was fitted with Mk.1A Navigation Bombing System (N.B.S. 1A), Auto Pilot Mk.10, Military Flight System (M.F.S.), True Airspeed Unit (T.A.S.U.) and Heading Reference System (H.R.S.) Mk.2. The equipment did not contain any inertial sensing devises.

The Airborne Radar Installation (A.R.I.) utilised the Doppler techniques to compute along and across heading velocity data, determining ground speed, drift angle and distance gone for display. This data was also routed to the aircraft Heading Reference System (H.R.S.). The Green Satin Doppler radar navigation aid had been used since the early days of the Vulcan and was later updated to the more reliable Green Satin Mk.2.

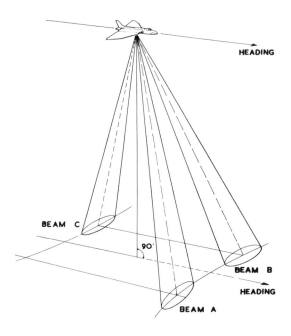

Airborne Doppler system - A.R.I 5972. Heading information was displayed at the Nav/plotters position.

By 1970 Green Satin had been replaced by A.R.I.5972 introduced by Mod.2256 this comprised a 'J' band lightweight navigational radar aid which could operate under all flight conditions to determine accurate navigational data. The A.R.I. was a compact installation comprising a transmitter-receiver and aerial unit and a control indicator. The installation operated between attitudes of 15 to 60,000 ft in all weather conditions and in limited pitch and roll configurations over land or sea. Use of the Doppler technique eliminated inaccuracies resulting from rough terrain. A built in facility permitted manual correction of errors arising from increased refraction and scatter encountered over calm water.

The Navigation and Bombing System Mk.1A was used in medium and long range aircraft beyond the range of ground aids. The system was primary used for accurate radar blind bombing but incorporated facilities for rapid fixing, wind finding and homing thus relieving the navigator of many of the calculations involved in D.R. navigation. The complete system comprised two distinct sub-systems.

(A) H2S Mk.9A (primary radar), was developed and produced by Electrical and Musical Instruments (E.M.I).

(B) Navigation and Bombing Computer (N.B.C.) Mk.2 was produced by Associated Electrical Industries Ltd (A.E.I).

H2S Scanner

The antenna was used for both transmission and reception of signals; it rotated through 360° at a rate which varied with each scale. The rate was 32 r.p.m. on 1/8 and 1/4 million, 16 r.p.m. on 1/2 million and 8 rpm on 1 million. The scanner could be made to sweep a selected sector instead of rotating through 360°, the size and bearing of the sector being set by the operator.

The scanner could also be tilted downwards to give a clearer picture at shorter ranges. The scanner assembly was stabilised in pitch and roll by an earth-tied giro controlled servo system, so that within certain limits, the display was not affected by aircraft attitude.

A secondary radar system provided automatic identification as a friendly when the aircraft was properly challenged by a suitably equipped ground or airborne radar. A coded reply, independent of the mode of interrogation, was provided as an emergency signal and indicated that the aircraft was in distress.

A further system A.R.I. 5924 was introduced that radiated interrogation pulses and received a reply and identification pulses from the A.R.I. 5922 fitted in tanker aircraft. The information was displayed continuously on a cathode ray tube screen of an indicator unit. The trace provided range, heading and identification information at distances up to a maximum of 100 nautical miles and a minimum of 400 yards.

Dead Reckoning (DR) Navigation computing

The navigation and bombing computer could be split into the following systems. (a) D.R. navigation computing. (b) Steering and range computing. (c) Ballistic computing. (d) Height computing.

The navigation computer had the following inputs:-

(a) Heading from the M.F.S. (b) True airspeed from T.A.S.U. (C) Wind velocity from wind monitor unit or hand set. From this information it calculated the track, ground speed and integrated ground movement, North South and East West. Track, ground speed and true airspeed were displayed at the navigator's panel.

TACAN

TACAN replaced GEE Mk.3 radio navigation aid and was a world wide navigation aid which provided the following information:- Magnetic bearing of the aircraft from a selected beacon, slant range of the aircraft from a selected beacon in nautical miles, a flag alarm circuit which operated in the absence of correct distance signals. It was also used in the air to air role to provided range information between aircraft.

Astro Navigation

Astro navigation was an integral part of the navigation techniques. It was used to monitor the ground position indicator (G.P.I.) when other aids were not available i.e. over large sea areas. It was also used as a standby in the event of failure of N.B.S. and M.F.S. systems. Problems associated with this system were accurate readings in turbulent conditions and daylight readings with only the Sun being available.

Autopilot and Landing System

The Mk.10A/Mk.10B autopilot was provided in the aircraft to relieve the pilot of much of the physical and mental strain to which he is subjected when controlling high speed bombing during long flights. The autopilot also improved the stability of the aircraft under difficult flying conditions.

The system operated on the 'rate-rate' principle and would stabilise and aircraft in each of pitch, roll and yaw axes. In addition to the above functions the autopilot may be used by the pilot to change an aircraft's heading or attitude, maintain a constant altitude or indicated airspeed, turn on to and maintain a pre-selected heading or make fully automatic approaches to an airfield equipped with I.L.S.

During bombing runs the autopilot could also be used to manoeuvre the aircraft in response to signals from the N.B.S. Mk.1A or from a turn controller by the air bomber. Bombing, heading and radio information was passed to the system via the Military Flight System (M.F.S.) with which the autopilot was integrated.

With the deletion of the automatic landing facility on the Mk.10B autopilot, the Mk.10B functioned in the same way as the Mk.10A autopilot.

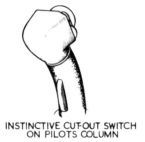

INSTINCTIVE CUT-OUT SWITCH
ON PILOTS COLUMN

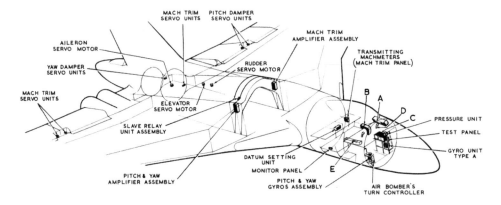

Location of auto controls

Ballistic computing

Ballistic information relevant to the type of bomb carried was contained in a short piece of 35 mm. film. Information from the film was fed into the Calculator Type 3. Mk 1 which was connected to the static line of the starboard pitot-static system. The equipment then operated to calculate the required track to the release point steering signals which were fed to the M.F.S. via the bombing system selector switch and the M.F.S. selector switch. These signals were then displayed on the azimuth directors and could be interlocked with the Mk.10A or 10B autopilot through the Computer Unit (Navigational) of the M.F.S. Signals to open the bomb doors and release the bomb were also provided.

Mounted immediately above the indicating unit type 301 was a camera which photographed the Plan Position Indicator (P.P.1.) at intervals of 8 seconds throughout the bombing run. The film was marked, automatically at the moment of bomb release and would continue to photograph the P.P.1. until completion of the bombing run.

The aircraft could be guided along a pre-determined track for a bombing run, by signals from either the bomb aimer's controller or the N.B.C., operating through the autopilot.

Opening the bomb doors caused extra drag on the aircraft fuselage resulting in a nose-down pitch error. Provision was made in the autopilot and aircraft wiring for compensating signals to be applied to the elevator servo channel and also disconnection of the pitch monitor, which results in elevator movement. This movement corrected the aircraft trim so that steady flight was maintained. Compensation was not applied once the doors were fully open or whilst they were closing.

PITOT STATIC SYSTEM

The pitot-static installation embraced two independent systems, one port and one starboard. The starboard system connected to the N.B.S calculator Type 3, the M.F.S. manometric unit and the bombsight computer.

Pitot head mounting

At the front spar the starboard system connected to the bomb fuse switch and ground test valve. The fatigue meter airspeed switch and V.G. recorder were fed by the starboard system. The port system fed the artificial feel warning switches and the starboard system fed the three artificial feel units. These units were linked to the flying controls rods and their action was controlled by actuators operating in conjunction with transmitter units which were sensitive to airspeed. The pilots instruments on the first pilots panel were supplied by the starboard system, this included the Pressure - A.S.I. and mach meter, Static - A.S.I. mach meter, altimeter and rate of climb indicator. A duplicate set of instruments on the second pilot's panel was supplied by the starboard system.

Pitot-static system

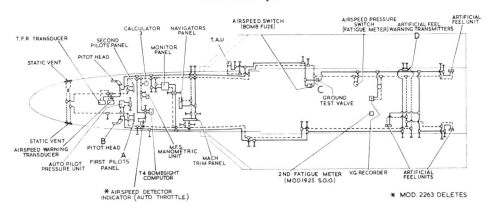

Arrangement of flying instruments

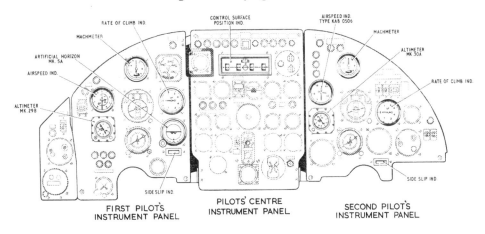

Three airspeed indicators were fitted in the aircraft along with three altimeters, one on each pilot's panel and one each on the plotters panel at the navigator's station.

Dorsal aerial

A multi-channel transmitter-receiver provided radio telephone, carrier wave or data communication within the high frequency band from 2 MHz to 30 MHz. The equipment could transmit or receive on any one of 28,000 selected carrier frequencies spaced at intervals of 1 KHz. The unit was controlled by unit Type M53 located at the port side of the navigators panel. The aerial was of the suppressed type fitted to the lower part of the dorsal fin.

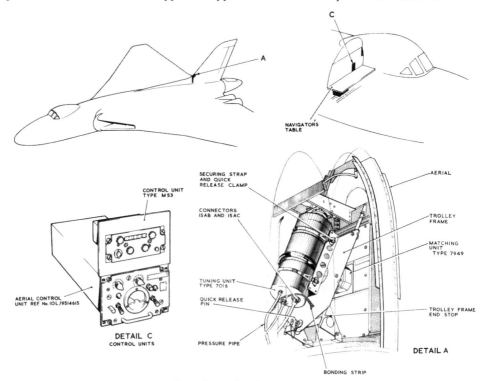

Dorsal aerial and tuning unit

Airborne UHF installation

The A.R.I.18124/2 was an airborne U.H.F. installation designated R/T2, consisting of a multi-channel transmitter and receiver, operating on a crystal controlled frequency range of 225.0 MHz to 399.9 MHz with facilities available to radiate M.C.W. for emergency or direction finding purposes. The A.R.I also incorporated a simulated bombing tone for tactical training on Vulcan aircraft. Two U.H.F. aerials were located, one below the bomb aimer's window and the upper aerial above number one bomb bay and fitted externally on the aircraft. A control unit was fitted on the port console.

Airborne automatic direction

Airborne direction finding equipment provided automatic relative bearing indication from source radio signals. Aerial relative bearing determination was by null signal method, the loop aerial being remotely controlled and aerial reception of modulated or un-modulated radio signals, either by loop or sense aerial. The unit was controlled at the navigator's station.

Other controls consisted of a loop controller and a bearing and tuning indicator. In addition a second bearing and tuning indicator was provided on the second pilot's panel. A change-over switch was provided A.D.F/TACAN/I.L.S. was located on the port console. The sense aerial was an omni directional type and was used initially for the reception of a broadcast station prior to actual direction finding by the loop aerial and associated A.D.F. equipment. This aerial was also used for ARI-23180 on aircraft in the M.R. role.

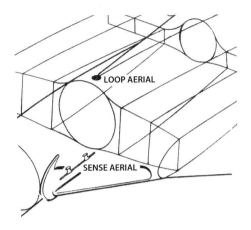

Long Range Navigation (LORAN)

The LORAN ARI-23180 installation was fitted to aircraft in the Maritime Reconnaissance (M.RR.) role. The equipment provided a navigation fix with respect to a chain of ground transmitting stations. The LORAN system uses a pulse technique hyperbolic position fixing aid. Loran group transmitting stations include a master station and two, three or four slave stations. Transmissions propagated from the master station are received at each slave station and any receiver within the service area. Each slave station delays by a precise time interval known as the coding delay and then transmits its own signal.

Instrument Landing System

(I.L.S.) A.R.I. 18011 was an airborne instrument landing system operating in conjunction with ground transmitters. This installation provided the pilot with indications of the aircraft's position relative to the runway touch-down point, when descending to low altitude in bad visibility. The signals were received by the localizer and glide path receiver units and fed via a junction box to the navigator's computer unit. Signals so received were displayed on the beam compass and director horizon instruments, which were also used in conjunction with the Military Flight System (M.F.S.).

Radar Altimeter

The radar altimeter A.R.I 18090 employed a pulse radar technique to measure the height of the aircraft above the terrain immediately beneath the aircraft, through a range of 500 to 50,000ft.

Intercommunications system (i/c)

The comprehensive intercommunication system (A.R.I. 18089) was a service-selecting system which provided three distinct but correlated functions. (1) To provide a channel for distribution of normal and conference i/c. (2) To provide a means of selecting all available air radio installations (A.R.I.'s). (3) To provide a means of mixing two or more receiver services, without one adversely affecting the other.

In addition external i/c facilities were available as an aid to the ground crew during servicing and as a means of alerting the crew for tele-scramble operations. The installation was divided into two systems, viz. normal i/c and conference i/c each having its own amplifier.

Camera installation

A F95 Mk.4 camera was fitted under Mod 2502 to maritime reconnaissance role (M.R.R.) aircraft.

The camera was mounted over the window at the prone bomb aimer's position. A control unit, operated by the navigator/bomber remotely controlled the camera functions. It replaced the F95 Mk.9 camera used for low level bomb scoring.

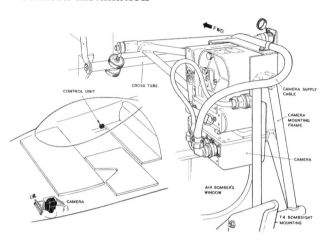

Rear warning radar

By 1972 the Vulcan incorporated Red Steer Mk.2 A.R.I. 5952 X-Band search radar system. The A.R.I. consisted of a tail mounted radar unit, scanner alignment and an indicator azimuth range unit mounted at the navigator's station. The latter unit combined the functions of an indicator and control unit. When airborne the A.R.I. would normally be maintained in a standby condition (not transmitting) for most of the time. This was due to the operation of other E.C.M. equipment. When required the A.R.I. could be switched to transmit in order to find the exact range and bearing of the attacking aircraft.

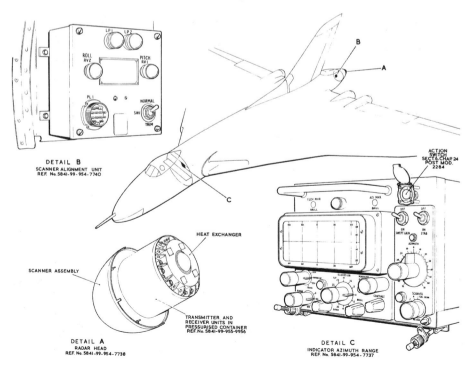

Conversion to Blue Steel role

The conversion of aircraft from the normal bombing role to the Blue Steel role to designated aircraft which had been modified to include special fixed fittings that provided the attachments and connections whereby various removable assemblies could be installed. These removable assemblies were supplied as a change of role kit introduced by Mod 200 and when fitted, converted the aircraft for carriage of the Blue Steel missile.

Conversion of the aircraft consisted primarily of the fitment of replacement control panels in the crew's compartment and the installation of additional equipment in the bomb bay.

This equipment included a carrier beam and crutching frame for suspension of the store, refrigeration and warm air packs, a hydraulic unit and electrical panels, which, in conjunction with the existing aircraft systems provided the necessary services for the store.

Connections between the aircraft mounted equipment and systems and the store were made through umbilical connections mounted on fixed fairing doors. These fairing doors replaced the bomb doors. The hydraulic jacks, levers, piping and the inflatable seals associated with the bomb doors were removed, and sealing angles for the fairing doors were fitted.

The fairings to the front and rear of the bomb bay were also removed and replaced by detachable fairings. Two transportation trolleys were used during conversion; one accommodated the assemblies removed from the aircraft, whilst the other, carried the change of role kit and the handling equipment necessary for its installation. Conversion to the normal bombing role was basically the reverse of the Blue Steel fit.

Vulcan B.Mk2 all up weights of bombing cases

Blue Steel

Operational weight - 5 crew	108,904 lb
Removable bomb gear	1,495 lb
Store	15,700 lb
Rapid blooming window	480 lb
100% Normal Fuel 9,400 gallons @ S.G. 0.77	72,380 lb
Total Take-Off Weight	**199,009 lb**
Landing with store, window & 10,000 lb fuel	136,629 lb
Maximum take-off weight with bay fuel tanks	211,510

7000 lb M.C. Yellow Sun

Operational weight - 5 crew	108,904 lb
Removable bomb gear	295 lb
Store	7,200 lb
Rapid blooming window	480 lb
100% Normal Fuel 9,400 gallons @ S.G. 0.77	72,380 lb
Total Take-Off Weight	**189,259 lb**
Landing with store, window & 10,000 lb fuel	126,879 lb
Maximum take-off weight with bay fuel tanks	198,206 lb

21 x 1000 lb store

Operational weight - 5 crew	108,904 lb
Removable bomb gear	762 lb
Store	21,000 lb
Rapid blooming window	480 lb
100% Normal Fuel 9,400 gallons @ S.G. 0.77	72,380 lb
Total Take-Off Weight	**203,526 lb**
Landing with store, window & 10,000 lb fuel	141,146 lb

Bomb bay fuel tanks

Various combinations were available using the bay fuel tanks.

Bay Fuel System Tanks A and E

Tank A (forward or aft position)	596 lb	718 gallons (S.G. 0.77)
Tank E	654 lb	721 gallons (S.G. 0.77)
Tanks A and E	11,081.0 lb	1,439 gallons (S.G. 0.77)

Cylindrical tanks

Cylindrical Tanks (forward)	7,767 lb	1,008.75 gallons
Cylindrical Tank (aft)	7,767 lb	1,008.75 gallons
Total fuel	15,534 lb	2,017.5 gallons (S.G. 0.77)

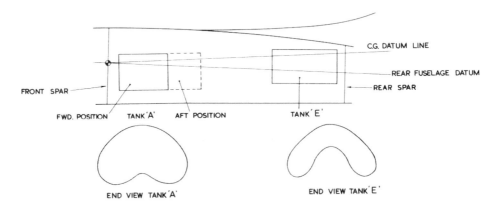

The bomb bay saddle tanks were built to fit round the Blue Steel missile.

Fuel C.G. indicator

This instrument was mainly for use during flight refuelling, to aid the pilot to keep the aircraft in longitudinal trim. It showed any variation in the mean fuel C.G. due to uneven distribution. The gauge was calibrated about the mean C.G. of the fuel and was connected to the tank contents transmitters via a computer box which took into consideration the moment arm of each tank. The limit of each green sector represents 30,000 lb. ft. out of balance moments, giving a total of 60,000 lb. ft. for the aircraft. When fuel is correctly distributed the needles are in the middle of the green sector, i.e., number of out of balance moments zero.

NOTE

This instrument did not give the aircraft C.G. position and did not include the bomb bay fuel system.

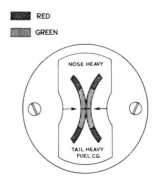

Fuel C.G. indicator

Fuel was carried in fourteen bag-type tanks. Port and starboard tanks 1-7 contained 9,260 gallons AVTAG (Nato Code F-40, USA JP4) - S.G. 0.8 or 9,400 gallons using AVTUR (Nato Code F-34, USA JP8) 40/50 S.G. 0.77 / 0.78. The weight of the fuel depended on the Specific Gravities (S.G.) of the type used.

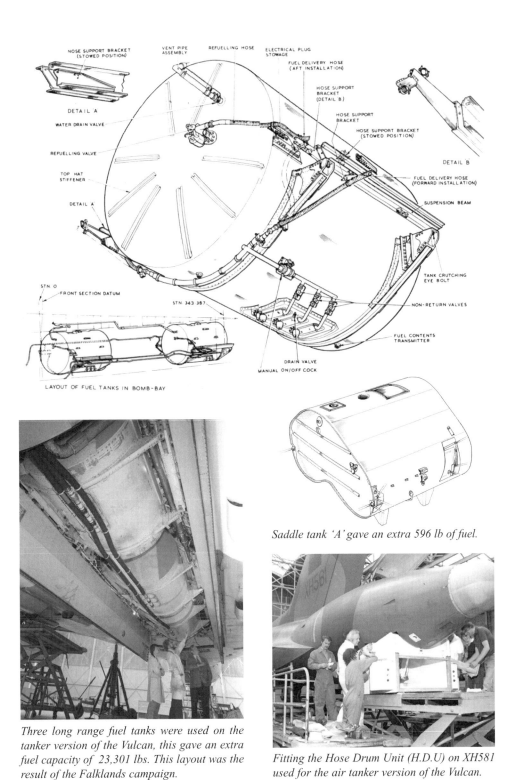

NOSE SUPPORT BRACKET
(STOWED POSITION)

VENT PIPE
ASSEMBLY

REFUELLING HOSE

ELECTRICAL PLUG
STOWAGE

FUEL DELIVERY HOSE
(AFT INSTALLATION)

HOSE SUPPORT
BRACKET
(DETAIL 'B)

HOSE SUPPORT
BRACKET

HOSE SUPPORT BRACKET
(STOWED POSITION)

DETAIL A

WATER DRAIN VALVE

REFUELLING VALVE

TOP HAT
STIFFENER

DETAIL A

DETAIL B

FUEL DELIVERY HOSE
(FORWARD INSTALLATION)

SUSPENSION BEAM

TANK CRUTCHING
EYE BOLT

STN. O

FRONT SECTION DATUM

STN. 343 387

NON-RETURN VALVES

FUEL CONTENTS
TRANSMITTER

DRAIN VALVE

MANUAL ON/OFF COCK

LAYOUT OF FUEL TANKS IN BOMB-BAY

Saddle tank 'A' gave an extra 596 lb of fuel.

Three long range fuel tanks were used on the tanker version of the Vulcan, this gave an extra fuel capacity of 23,301 lbs. This layout was the result of the Falklands campaign.

Fitting the Hose Drum Unit (H.D.U) on XH581 used for the air tanker version of the Vulcan.

Warning and Counter Measures - 1974

A visible change to the top of the fin on the Vulcan was the introduction of A.R.I. 18228/1 radar warning receiver in the mid 1970s.

The E.C.M. equipment fitted to B.Mk1A and B.Mk2 Vulcan's was designed to operate against E.W. /G.C.I. radars, V.H.F. communications and A.I. radar. The installation consisted of three jammers, tail warning radar, radar warning receiver and two window dispensers. The majority of the equipment was housed in the rear section of the fuselage and all control was exercised from the A.E.O.'s station.

Blue Diver (A.R.I. 18075) was used to jam metric ground radars. The installation was designed to transmit randomly keyed pulses of R.F. noise. The noise transmission, derived from a white noise source, was switched on and off automatically at irregular intervals of a few seconds duration. Two transmitters were fitted.

Green Palm (A.R.I 18074) was a V.H.F. jammer, one transmitter was carried which radiated continuously on one frequency or in sequence at random intervals on two or four frequencies. The radiation was on spot frequencies, designed to jam individual channels and was tuneable in the air.

Red Shrimp (A.R.I. 18076) was a high-band jamming system. It had three aerials mounted on two counter-poise plates on the structure between No.3 and No.4 engine jet pipes on the lower surface. There were up to three transmitters and power units in canisters in the rear fuselage. A control unit at the A.E.O. station controlled the three transmitter and power units.

Blue Saga (A.R.I. 18105) allowed the A.E.O to monitor aurally any radar pulses illuminating the aeroplane; it also gave a visible and audible warning when persistently illuminated by a lock-follow radar. To prevent radar equipment in the aeroplane giving spurious indications on Blue Saga, blanking units were used which muted the receiver for each pulse of H2S, Red Steer and Green Satin. Each pair of aerials (one 'S' band and one 'X' band) fed the one receiver located nearby. The receiver outputs were fed to a control indicator.

Red Steer (ARI 5919) was an X band tail warning radar and gave a 90° cone, up to range of about 15-18 miles. The display was un-stabilised and gave a range and bearing relative to the bomber's centre line.

The aerials for the metric jammers were in notches in the wing tips. The V.H.F. jammer used the helmet type aerial in the top of the tail fin. In the aircraft where this was also used for V.H.F. communications, a change-over relay was fitted.

Window The window dispensing equipment consisted of a control unit at the A.E.O.s station and two stripper units. Only one stripper unit could be used at the same time and could dispense continuously at a pre-set rate or in burst of preset duration and interval. Window would be used for general confusion of ground radars or to break and a lock-follow radar.

Shown is (*A.R.I. 18228/1*) fitted to Vulcan's in the mid 1970s by Mod 2304. It was a radar warning receiver (R.W.R.) passive device which did not cause radio interference to other equipment in the aircraft. The A.R.I provided visual and audio warning of illumination by radar operating in the tracking mode. It identified the radar signal and provided directional and frequency band information of the illumination. The equipment replaced the earlier Blue Saga radar warning receiver.

Red Light (A.R.I. 18146) shown below was a barrage jammer operating on the X-band frequencies. It scanned the X-band for threats and locked on to the signal and jammed. The aerials were enclosed by a small radome at the rear fuselage.

A.R.I 18228/1 radar warning receiver which replaced the Blue Saga jammimg installation.

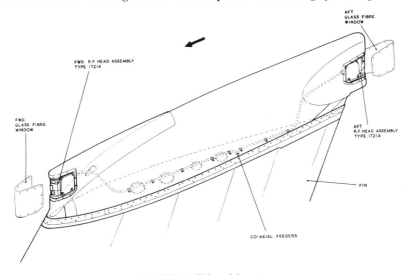

Red Light X-band jammer.

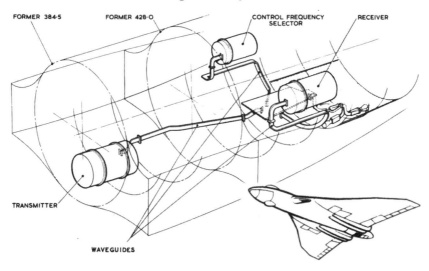

T4 Bombsight and armament instruments

The T4 bombsight was mounted centrally on the aircraft floor at the air bomber's prone position. It was a visual impact bombsight which was designed to commute and indicate continuously (at the instant of bomb release) the point on the ground which will be struck by the bomb. The sight was designed to utilise the accurate ground speed and drift angle supplied by the aircraft's Doppler equipment. When A.R.I.5972 was fitted in lieu of A.R.I. 5951 (Mod 2256), there was no supply of ground speed and drift angle information to the bombsight.

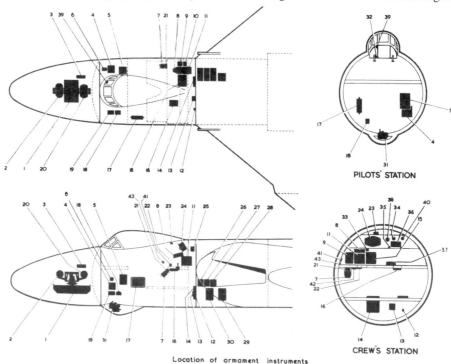

PILOTS' STATION

CREW'S STATION

Location of armament instruments

1.	SCANNER UNIT TYPE 121	22.	CONTROL UNIT, TYPE 626
2.	AMPLIFIER A3703	23.	VARIABLE AIRSPEED UNIT, MK.3
3.	AMPLIDYNE A3XX1	24.	NAVIGATIONAL PANEL, MK.1B
4.	CALCULATOR, TYPE 2, MK.2	25.	WIND UNIT, MK.2
5.	CALCULATOR, TYPE 3, MK.1	26.	POWER UNIT, TYPE 729
6.	GROUND SPEED RESOLVER	27.	CALCULATOR ATUOMATIC 5A
7.	CONTROL UNIT, TYPE 12580A	28.	WAVEFORM GENERATOR, TYPE 68B
8.	CAMERA, TYPE R110 OR R88	29.	CALCULATOR, TYPE 1, MK.1
9.	CONTROL UNIT, TYPE 595	30.	POWER UNIT, MK.2
10.	CONTROL UNIT (CAMERA), TYPE 903	31.	T.4 BOMBSIGHT SIGHTING HEAD
11.	INDICATING UNIT, TYPE 301D		*(inoperative Post Mod .2256 and 2377)*
12.	SUPPRESSOR, TYPE G5	32.	BOMBING INDICATOR, MK.1
13.	RESISTANCE UNIT MK.1	33.	WIND INDICATOR
14.	JUNCTION BOX, TYPE 343	34.	FORWARD THROW INDICATOR
15.	CONTROL UNIT, TYPE 585C	35.	STEERING SIGNAL TEST JB
16.	CONTROL UNIT, TYPE 12558	36.	TRACK CONTROL UNIT
17.	*T.4 BOMBSIGHT COMPUTER	37.	G.P.I., MK.6
18.	*T.4 BOMBSIGHT SIGHTING	38.	COMPASS REPEATER, TYPE B
	HEAD CONTROL PANEL	39.	S.F.O.M. GUNSIGHT TYPE 812 A
19.	*T.4 BOMBSIGHT GYRO	40.	PILOTS' DIRECTIONAL INDICATOR
	CONTROL J	41.	CONTROL UNIT, TYPE 6204
20.	MODULATOR, TYPE 2	42.	JUNCTION BOX, TYPE 6205
21.	BOMBING SELECTOR SWITCH	43.	VOLTMETER
	*Inoperative Post Mod 2256 and 2377.		

Britain's thermonuclear deterrent

In autumn 1941 work on the atomic bomb began in Britain under code-name 'Tube Alloys', working mainly on the problem of separating uranium 235 from natural uranium. A report produced by the Maud Committee in 1941 was sent to the United States where it convinced influential American scientists that an atomic bomb was possible. After the 1943 Quebec Agreement between President Roosevelt and the Prime Minister Winston Churchill, British scientists went to the new laboratory at Los Alamos to assist American atomic bomb work, by now called the 'Manhattan Project'. A plutonium implosion design (Trinity) successfully tested the concept on 16th July, 1945 in the U.S. State of New Mexico, delivering a yield of around 20 kilotons.

In August 1946, the United States passed the 'McMahon Act', stopping wartime collaboration with Britain on nuclear weapons. Nevertheless, the British began the development of their own atomic bomb at Fort Halstead in June 1947; this led to Britain's first operational atomic bomb known as Blue Danube. By November 1953, the Royal Air Force received its first Blue Danube with a modest yield of 10-12 kilotons. The yield had been reduced to supplement stocks of fissile material.

In November 1952, the United States tested the first experimental hydrogen bomb. It used hydrogen fusion to generate neutrons. However, in most applications the bulk of the destructive energy comes from uranium fission. In July 1954, the British Cabinet authorised the production of 'thermonuclear bombs' and in the autumn of 1955 trials of so-called 'megaton' devices got underway. The first was dropped over the Pacific on 15th May, 1957. The yield of this experimental 'hydrogen bomb' was only 300 kilotons. Two other tests failed to reach the one-megaton target and further trials were hurriedly planned. The lack of a viable fission device caused a great deal concern to Service staff. It was not until the "Red Snow" physics package was introduced that the U.K. developed a safe and fully usable true megaton fission weapon.

At the beginning of October 1957, the Soviet Union launched the world's first artificial satellite - something quite unexpected. It was an opportunity for the British Government to approach the United States about renewing collaboration on nuclear weapons. Congress began to amend the 1946 McMahon Act to allow exchanges of information.

Shortly after, the next test of a British hydrogen bomb took place on 8th November 1957. The yield was 1.8 megatons and two more successful series of tests followed.

By 1958, the Royal Air Force 'V' Force was using the dependable American Mk.5 thermonuclear weapon as part of the joint "Project E" programme. The weapon was under the control of the Americans and did not lend itself to Quick Reaction Alert as the weapons were stored away from the dispersal airfields, this programme ended in the U.K. in 1965.

Britain's first operational "high yield" weapons were Violet Club and Yellow Sun which were later replaced by the more flexible and safer Yellow Sun Mk2 which used a 'Red Snow' physics package adapted from an American W-28 warhead design.

In August 1958, the amended McMahon Act became law and an agreement was signed between the United States and Britain on sharing information 'for mutual defence purposes'.

Britain decided to produce a megaton yield American warhead design in 1958 under the code-name 'Red Snow' however, certain aspects of the American design did not meet the British Ordnance Board Requirements and modifications were embodied and trials carried out in Australia. Red Snow was to be used as both a free-fall bomb and as the warhead for the Blue Steel and Skybolt missiles.

Britain's first tactical nuclear weapon Red Beard used the Red Snow physics package and entered service in 1962 before retiring in 1971. Two versions were produced; the Mk.1 and

Mk.2. The Mk.1 was used by high-altitude bombers and the Mk.2 variant was intended for low-level delivery by the toss bombing method referred to as the Low-Altitude-Bombing-System (LABS).

In the early 1960s the development of a small nuclear bomb began - mainly to replace the earlier 'Red Beard' weapon, known as the WE177 it remained with the Royal Air Force and Royal Navy service from 1966 for over three decades. A new implosion system was used in WE177 which was also adopted by American warhead designers and was tested in the first British underground test at Nevada in March 1962.

The Vulcan used Red Beard tactical thermonuclear bomb until replaced by the lighter WE.177A/B in the early 1970s. The WE.177A/B was more flexible that Red Beard and could be used as an lay-down, ballistic, retarded tactical nuclear weapon which could be released at low level; it retired from the Royal Air Force in 1998.

Vulcan Squadrons

No.9 Squadron	Conningsby 1962-1964. Cottesmore 1964-1969. Akrotiri 1969-1975. Waddington 1975-1982.
No.12 Squadron	Conningsby 1962-1964. Cottesmore 1964-1967.
No.27 Squadron	Scampton 1961-1972. 1973-1982.
No.35 Squadron	Cottesmore 1964-1969. Akrotiri 1969-1975. Scampton 1975-1982.
No.44 Squadron	Waddington 1960-1982.
No.50 Squadron	Waddington 1961-1984.
No.83 Squadron	Waddington 1957-1960. Scampton 1960-1969.
No.101 Squadron	Finningley 1957-1961. Waddington 1961-1982.
No.617 Squadron	Scampton 1958-1981.
No.230 O.C.U.	Waddington 1956-1961 Finningley July 1961-1969. Scampton 1969-1981.

Station units adopted an aircraft pooling policy in 1964. Waddington having used aircraft pooling pre-B.Mk2. Individual markings resumed in 1972 with a few exceptions.

For the Model Makers

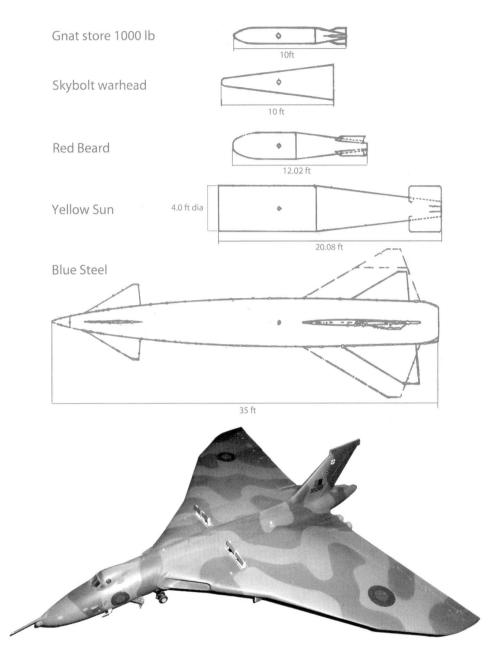

Gnat store 1000 lb — 10ft

Skybolt warhead — 10 ft

Red Beard — 12.02 ft

Yellow Sun — 4.0 ft dia — 20.08 ft

Blue Steel — 35 ft

This model shows the Airfix 1/72 scale model of B.Mk2 Vulcan XH561, this aircraft was one of six aircraft converted to the Tanker role in 1982, it was powered by the Olympus 201 and had tapered engine jet pipes. The Airfix kit normally comes with engine jet pipes for the Olympus 301 series engines used by the B.Mk2A.

Shown overleaf is a plan for a flying model of the Vulcan by Ray Booth Which was printed in Avro News. A detailed plan of the Vulcan B.Mk2 variants is also shown, drawn by J. Henderson an ex-Avro employee who also produced General Arrangement drawings for the Company.

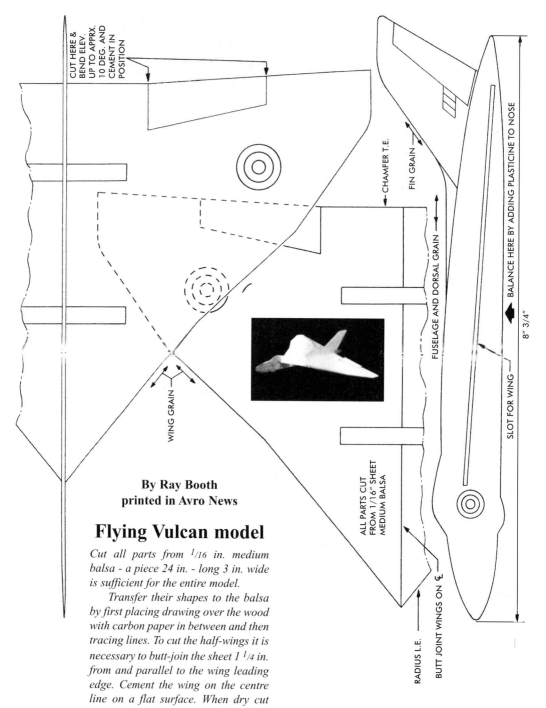

CUT HERE & BEND ELEV. UP TO APPRX. 10 DEG. AND CEMENT IN POSITION

WING GRAIN

CHAMFER T.E.

FIN GRAIN

FUSELAGE AND DORSAL GRAIN

BALANCE HERE BY ADDING PLASTICINE TO NOSE

8" 3/4"

SLOT FOR WING

ALL PARTS CUT FROM 1/16" SHEET MEDIUM BALSA

RADIUS L.E.

BUTT JOINT WINGS ON ₵

**By Ray Booth
printed in Avro News**

Flying Vulcan model

Cut all parts from $^1/16$ in. medium balsa - a piece 24 in. - long 3 in. wide is sufficient for the entire model.

Transfer their shapes to the balsa by first placing drawing over the wood with carbon paper in between and then tracing lines. To cut the half-wings it is necessary to butt-join the sheet 1 $^1/4$ in. from and parallel to the wing leading edge. Cement the wing on the centre line on a flat surface. When dry cut rectangular slots for $^1/4$ in. wide keyed stiffeners - which have the grain lengthwise.

Cement the fin and dorsal in position and allow to dry. Slide completed wing through slot in

fuselage and cement. Then cut control surfaces, bend up to about 10 degrees and fix with cement. Add plasticine neatly to nose until model balances at point shown. Test glide and trim by adding or reducing nose weight and/or bending up or slightly lowering elevators.

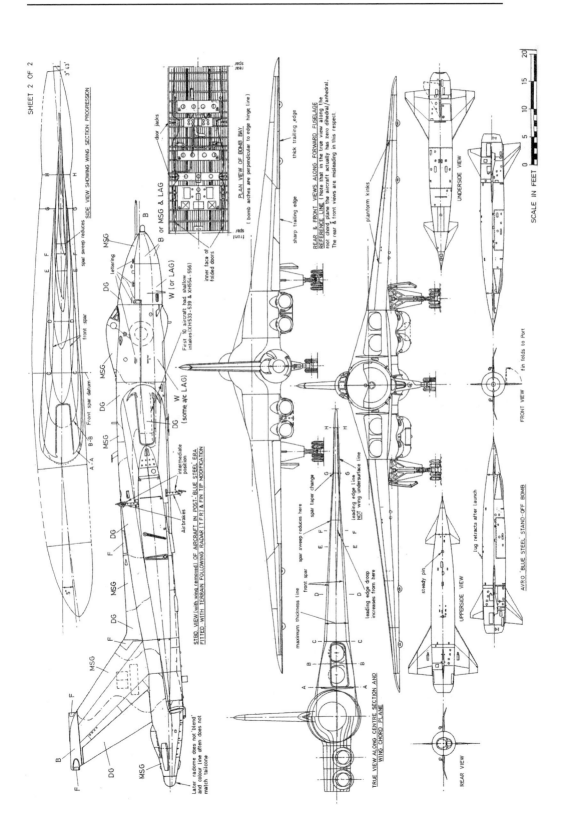

SIDE VIEW SHOWING WING SECTION PROGRESSION

spar sweep reduces

MSG

DG

lettering

W (or LAG)

First 10 aircraft had shallow intakes (XH533-539 & XH554-556)

front spar

Front spar datum

MSG

DG

W (some a/c LAG)

DG

MSG

intermediate position

Airbrakes

STBD. VIEW (with wing removed) OF AIRCRAFT IN POST-'BLUE STEEL' ERA FITTED WITH TERRAIN FOLLOWING RADAR (T.F.R.) & FIN TIP MODIFICATION

F

DG

MSG

F

DG

MSG

F

Later radome does not 'blend' and colour line often does not match tailcone

B

DG

MSG

F

B or MSG & LAG

door jacks

reds rear

front spar

rear spar

inner face of folded doors

PLAN VIEW OF BOMB BAY
(bomb arches are perpendicular to edge hinge line)

thick trailing edge

sharp trailing edge

REAR & FRONT VIEWS ALONG FORWARD FUSELAGE REFERENCE LINE (Note that in the true view along the root chord plane the aircraft actually has zero dihedral/anhedral. The rear & front views are misleading in this respect.

H

H

G

leading edge line
NOT wing undersurface line

planform kinks

spar taper change

G

E

F

E

F

maximum thickness line

front spar

leading edge droop increases from here

D

C

B

A

A

B

C

D

TRUE VIEW ALONG CENTRE SECTION AND WING CHORD PLANE

UNDERSIDE VIEW

steady pin

UPPERSIDE VIEW

lug retracts after launch

AVRO 'BLUE STEEL' STAND-OFF BOMB

fin folds to Port

FRONT VIEW

REAR VIEW

SCALE IN FEET

0   5   10   15   20

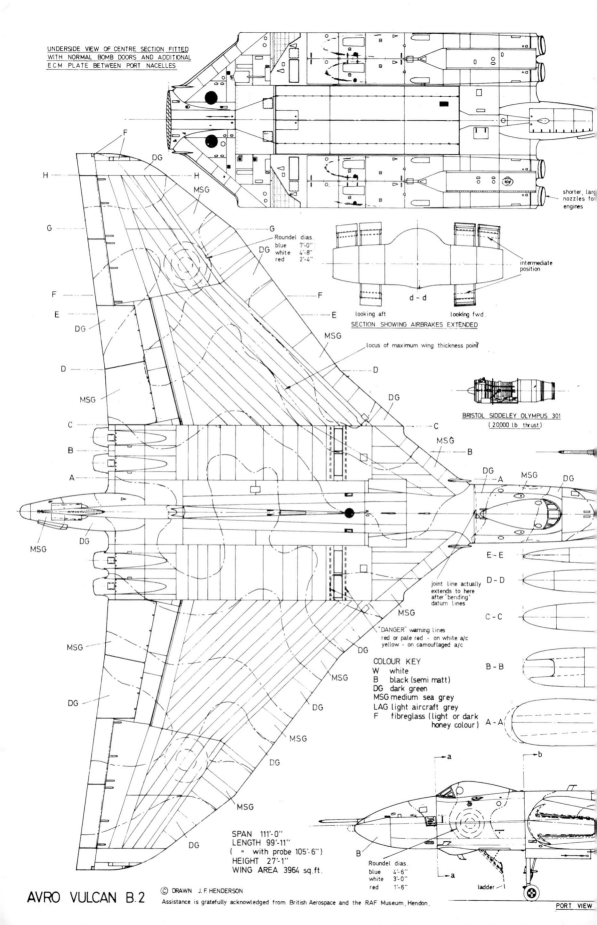

UNDERSIDE VIEW OF CENTRE SECTION FITTED
WITH NORMAL BOMB DOORS AND ADDITIONAL
E.C.M. PLATE BETWEEN PORT NACELLES

shorter, large nozzles for engines

Roundel dias
blue   7'-0"
white   4'-8"
red   2'-4"

intermediate position

d – d

looking aft   looking fwd.
SECTION SHOWING AIRBRAKES EXTENDED

locus of maximum wing thickness point

BRISTOL SIDDELEY OLYMPUS 301
(20000 lb. thrust)

joint line actually
extends to here
after 'bending'
datum lines

'DANGER' warning lines
red or pale red – on white a/c
yellow – on camouflaged a/c

COLOUR KEY
W   white
B   black (semi matt)
DG   dark green
MSG medium sea grey
LAG light aircraft grey
F   fibreglass (light or dark
     honey colour)

E - E
D – D
C - C
B - B
A - A

SPAN   111'-0"
LENGTH 99'-11"
(" with probe 105'-6")
HEIGHT 27'-1"
WING AREA 3964 sq.ft.

Roundel dias.
blue   4'-6"
white   3'-0"
red   1'-6"

ladder

AVRO VULCAN B.2

© DRAWN J. F. HENDERSON
Assistance is gratefully acknowledged from British Aerospace and the RAF Museum, Hendon.

PORT VIEW

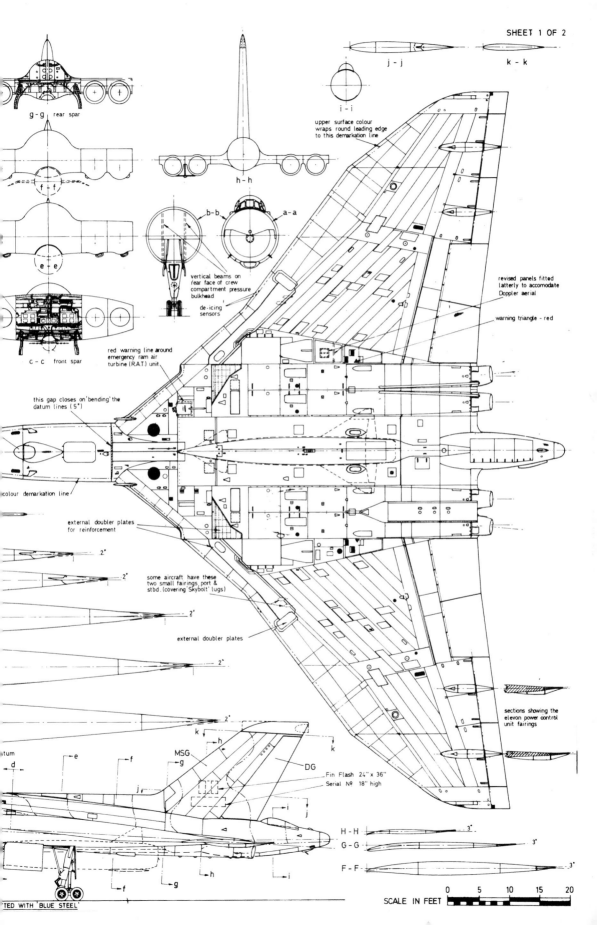

g - g   rear spar

f - f

e - e

C - C   front spar

j - j

k - k

i - i

h - h

b - b   a - a

upper surface colour
wraps round leading edge
to this demarkation line

vertical beams on
rear face of crew
compartment pressure
bulkhead

de-icing
sensors

red warning line around
emergency ram air
turbine (R.A.T.) unit

this gap closes on 'bending' the
datum lines (5°)

colour demarkation line

external doubler plates
for reinforcement

2°

2°

some aircraft have these
two small fairings port &
stbd. (covering 'Skybolt' lugs)

2°

external doubler plates

2°

revised panels fitted
latterly to accomodate
Doppler aerial

warning triangle - red

sections showing the
elevon power control
unit fairings

datum

d

e   f

MSG

g

j

k   h

k

DG

Fin Flash 24" x 36"
Serial Nº 18" high

i   j

f   g   h   i

H - H   3°

G - G   3°

F - F   3°

TED WITH 'BLUE STEEL'

SCALE IN FEET

0   5   10   15   20

486

A method of estimating rapidly the Aerodynamic Centre
and Lift-Curve Slope of Delta Wings.

Page 2

Abbreviations

A&AEE	Aircraft and Armament Experimental Establishment
A.P.	Ministry Air Publication
A.P. 970	Design Requirements for Aeroplanes for the Royal Air Force and Navy
A.R.I.	Airborne Radar Installation
A.U.W.	All up Weight
A.S.R.	Air Staff Requirement
C(A)	Controller of Aircraft equivalent to the Civil Aviation Authority (CAA)
C.G.	Centre of Gravity
CO	Commanding Officer
B.C.D.U.	Bomber Command Development Unit
B.L.E.U	Blind Landing Experimental Unit
E.A.S.	Equivalent Air Speed
FI	Fatigue Index
H.C.	Heavy Casing
I.A.S.	Indicated Airspeed
I.C.A.N.	International Commission for Air Navigation
I.F.F.	Identification Friend or Foe
I.L.S.	Instrument Landing System
I.M.N.	Indicated Mach Number
I.P.B/I.B.D.	Avro - Initial Projects Brochure. I.P.D. Initial Projects Drawing.
I.S.A	International Standard Atmosphere
I.T.P.	Instruction to Proceed
J.S.T.U.	Joint Services Trials Unit
K.W	Kilowatt
K.V.A	Kilowatt/Volt/Amps
L.C.	Light Casing
M.A.P.	Ministry of Aircraft Production
M.C.	Medium Casing
MoD	Ministry of Defence
MoS	Ministry of Supply
M.R.R.	Maritime Radar Reconnaissance
N.B.C.	Navigation Bombing System (N.B.C. + H_2S)
N.P.L.	National Physical Laboratory
O.R.	Operating Requirement
P/D.T.D.(A)	Principle Director of Technical Development (Air)
P.F.C.U.	Powered Flying Control Unit
R.A.A.F.	Royal Australian Air Force
R.A.E	Royal Aircraft Establishment
R.A.T.	Ram Air Turbine
R.A.T.O.	Rocket Assisted Take-Off
R.Ae.S	Royal Aeronautical Society
R.W.R.	Rearward Warning Receiver
S.W.G.	Standard Wire Gauge
S.L.S.T	Sea Level Static Thrust
S.B.A..C.	Society of British Aircraft Constructors
T.A.S.	True Air Speed
t/c	Thickness/chord ratio
T.F.R.	Terrain Following Radar
T.I.	Trial Installation
T.R.E.	Telecommunications Research Establishment
V.D.F.	Vulcan Display Flight

Rainbow Codes

The Rainbow Codes were a series of code names used to disguise the nature of various British military research projects. They were mainly used after the Second World War until 1958, when they were replaced by an alphanumeric code system.

Blue Boar   Blue Boar was a project by Vickers to meet the 1947 requirement OR.1059 for TV guided air-to-surface guided heavy bomb. A proposal to use Blue Boar using the NBC/H2S bombing system was proposed but this went no further than a design study. Cancelled 1954.

Blue Danube   Britain's first operational Nuclear weapon.

Blue Diver   Metric Radar Jammer.

Blue Ranger   Carriage of Blue Steel to18 J.S.T.U. Edinburgh Field, Adelaide.

Blue Saga   R.W.R. for Vulcan (A.R.I. 18105)

Blue Steel Mk.1   W100 to OR.1132 rocket powered missile.

Blue Steel Mk.2   Ramjet powered missile to OR.1159 cancelled 1959.

Blue Study   Automatic blind bombing system for V-bombers.

Indigo Bracket   Centrimetric jamming system using Carcinotron valves to OR3518.

Green Palm   V.H.F. jammer.

Green Satin   Doppler Nav. Radar.

Orange Putter   Vulcan tail warning radar replaced by Red Steer.

Red Beard   Nuclear weapon.

Red Garter   Audio Tail Warning radar replaced by Orange Putter.

Red Shrimp   S-Band radar jammer to ARI.18076 & ARI.18025. Fitted between starboard nacelles, or both sides for Blue Steel.

Red Snow   Nuclear warhead for Yellow Sun Mk.2, Blue Steel & Red Beard.

Red Steer Mk1   Tail Warning radar A.R.I. 5919.

Red Steer Mk2   Tail Warning radar A.R.I. 5952.

Violet Club   Supplemented Blue Danube in 1958. Half-megaton fusion bomb, pending delivery of Yellow Sun Mk1 in 1960.

Yellow Sun Mk.1   7,000lb/1/2mt Nuclear device to ASR.1136.

Yellow Sun Mk.2   7,250lb/1mt Nuclear device to ASR.1136.

ARI 5959   General Dynamics Terrain-Following Radar (T.F.R).

ARI 18228/1   Radar Warning Receiver.

(RF) Radio Frequencies

V.H.F.   (Very high frequency) is the radio frequency range from 30 MHz to 300 MHz.

H.F.   Below V.H.F. are denoted High Frequency.

U.H.F.   The next higher frequencies are known as Ultra High Frequency (U.H.F.).

"S" Band   Short wave 2 to 4 GHz.

"X" Band   Used by radars 8 to 12 GHz.

"J" Band   10 GHz to 20 GHz.

Formulae

AR is the aspect ratio. c is wing chord (ft). $\bar{c}$ is standard mean chord of wing.

C_{Di} is the induced drag coefficient. C_L is the lift coefficient.

D is drag (lbs) D_i is the induced drag.

k is the factor by which the induced drag exceeds that of an elliptical lift distribution, typically 1.05 to 1.15. L is lift (lbs). M is moment (lbs. ft.).

S is the gross wing area: the product of the wing span and the Geometric Mean Chord.

V is velocity (ft/sec). V_e is the equivalent airspeed. V_D is limiting speed in dive.

ϱ is the air density. ϱ_0 is 1.225 kg/m^3, the air density at sea level, ISA conditions.